Space
Academy
(723)

SPACE ACADEMY 123

Published by KOYAMAPress
KOYAMAPress.com
(1st) edition: SEPTEMBER 2018
ISBN: 978-1-927668-63-4
Printed in CANADA

SPACE ACADEMY 123

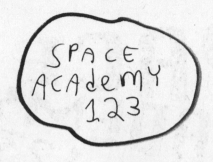

BY MICKEY ZACCHILLI

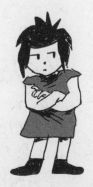

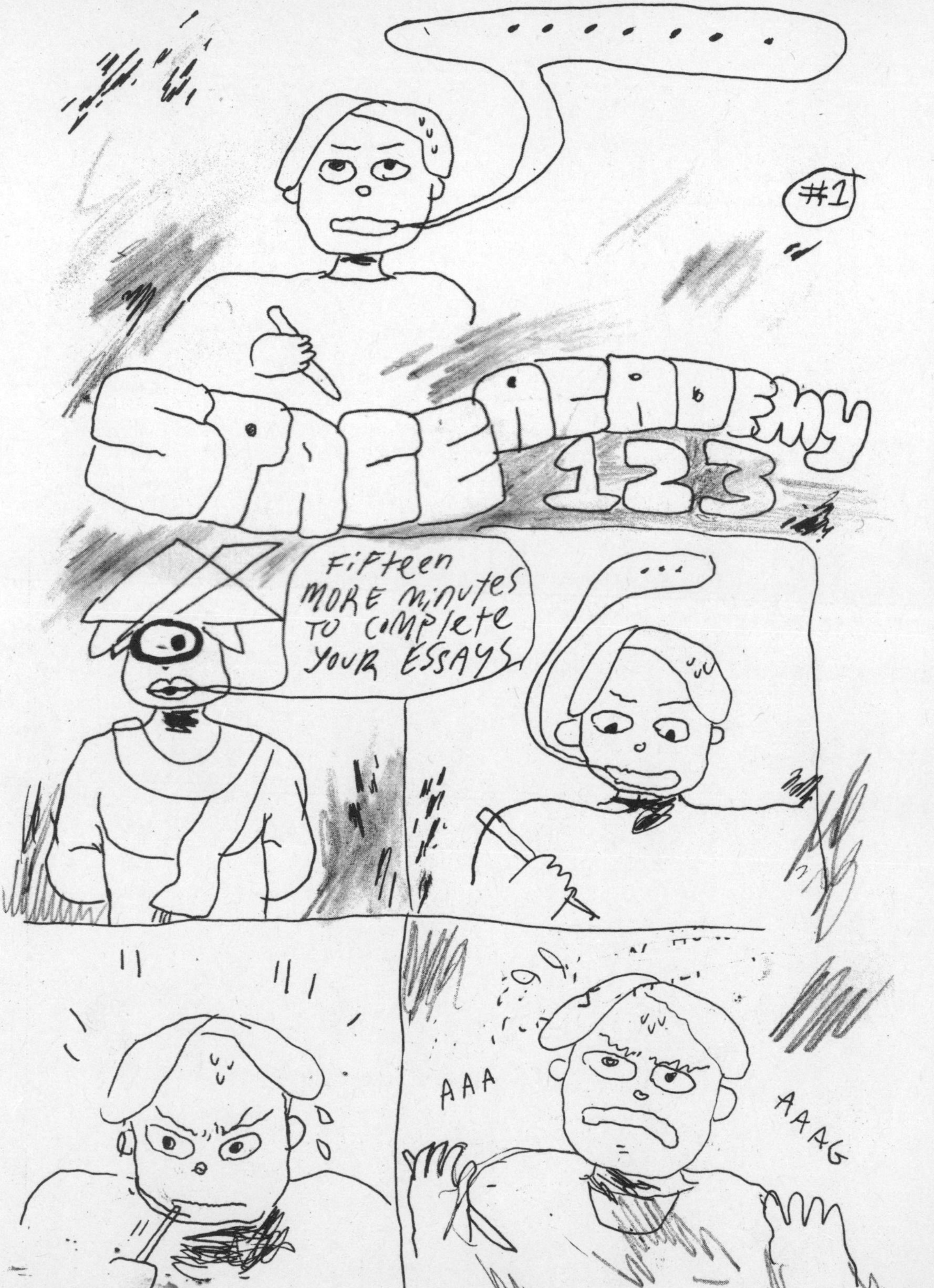
....
#1
SPACE ACADEMY 123
Fifteen more minutes to complete your essays
...
AAA
AAAG

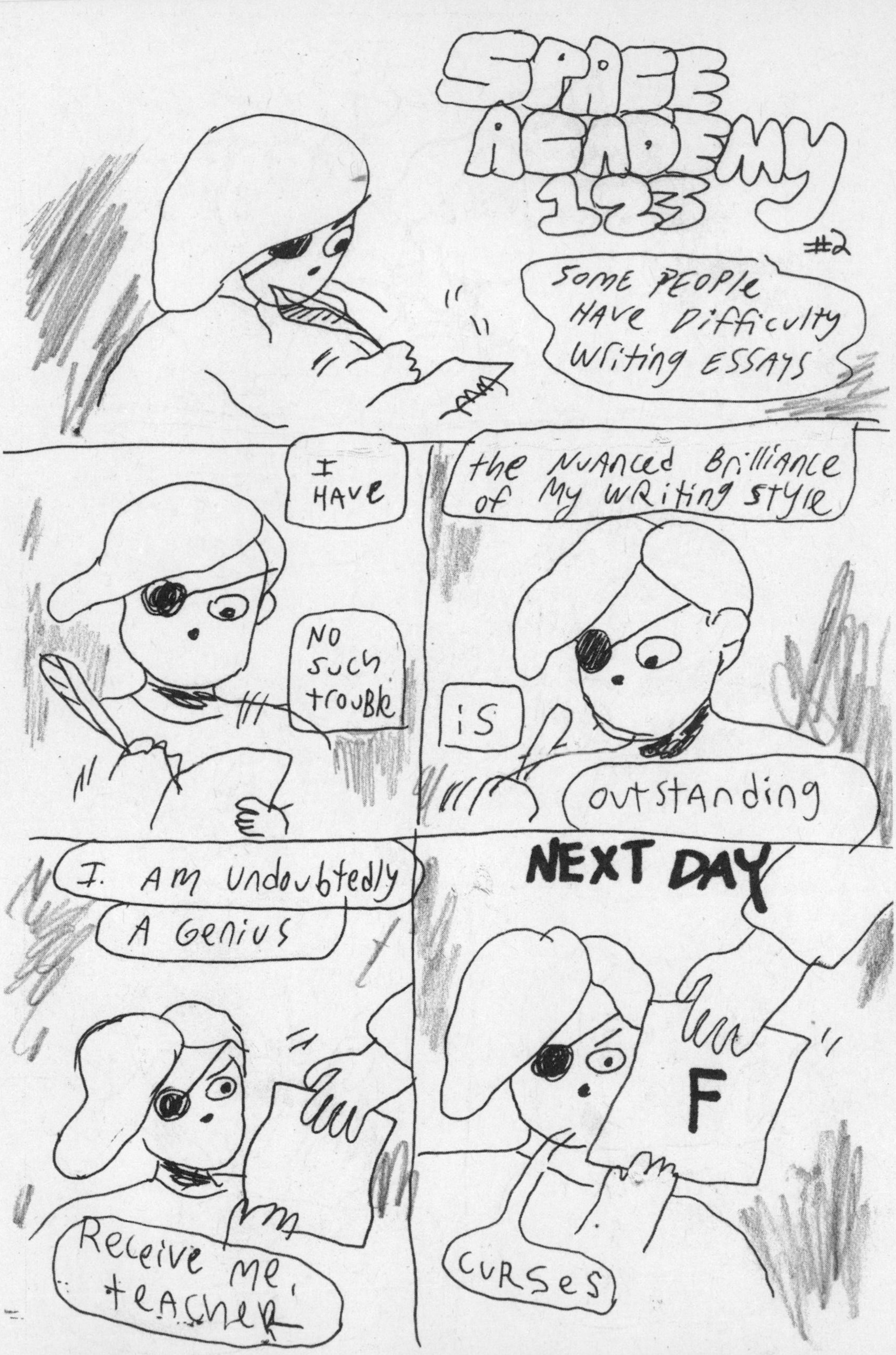
SPACE ACADEMY 123
#2
Some PEOPLE HAVE Difficulty Writing ESSAYS
I HAVE
NO Such trouble
the NUANced Brilliance of My WRiting Style
iS
outstanding
I. AM Undoubtedly A Genius
Receive Me, teacher
NEXT DAY
F
CURSES

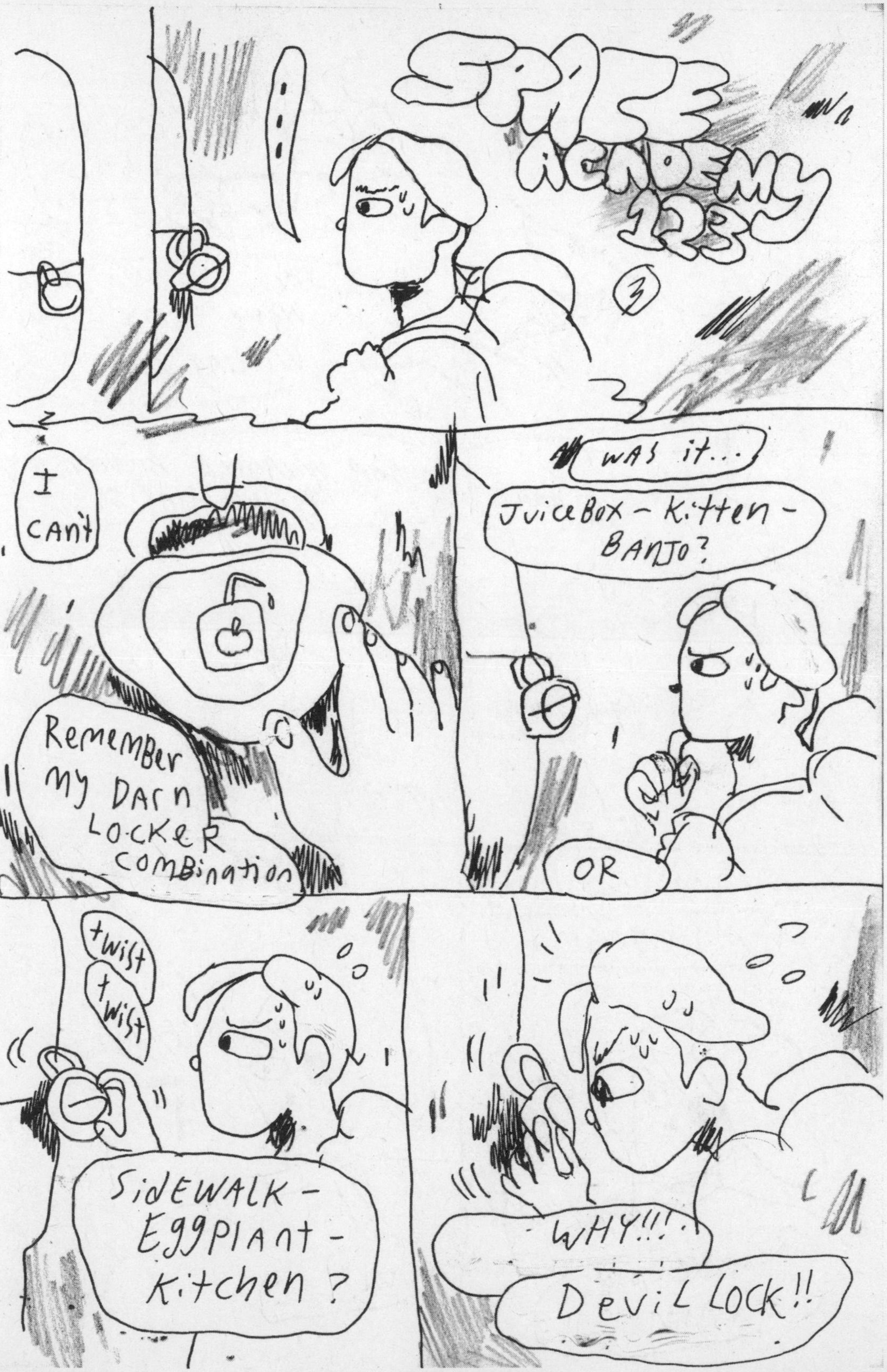
SPACE ACADEMY 123
3
...
I can't
Remember my darn locker combination
was it...
JuiceBox - Kitten - Banjo?
OR
twist
twist
Sidewalk - Eggplant - Kitchen?
WHY!!!
Devil Lock!!

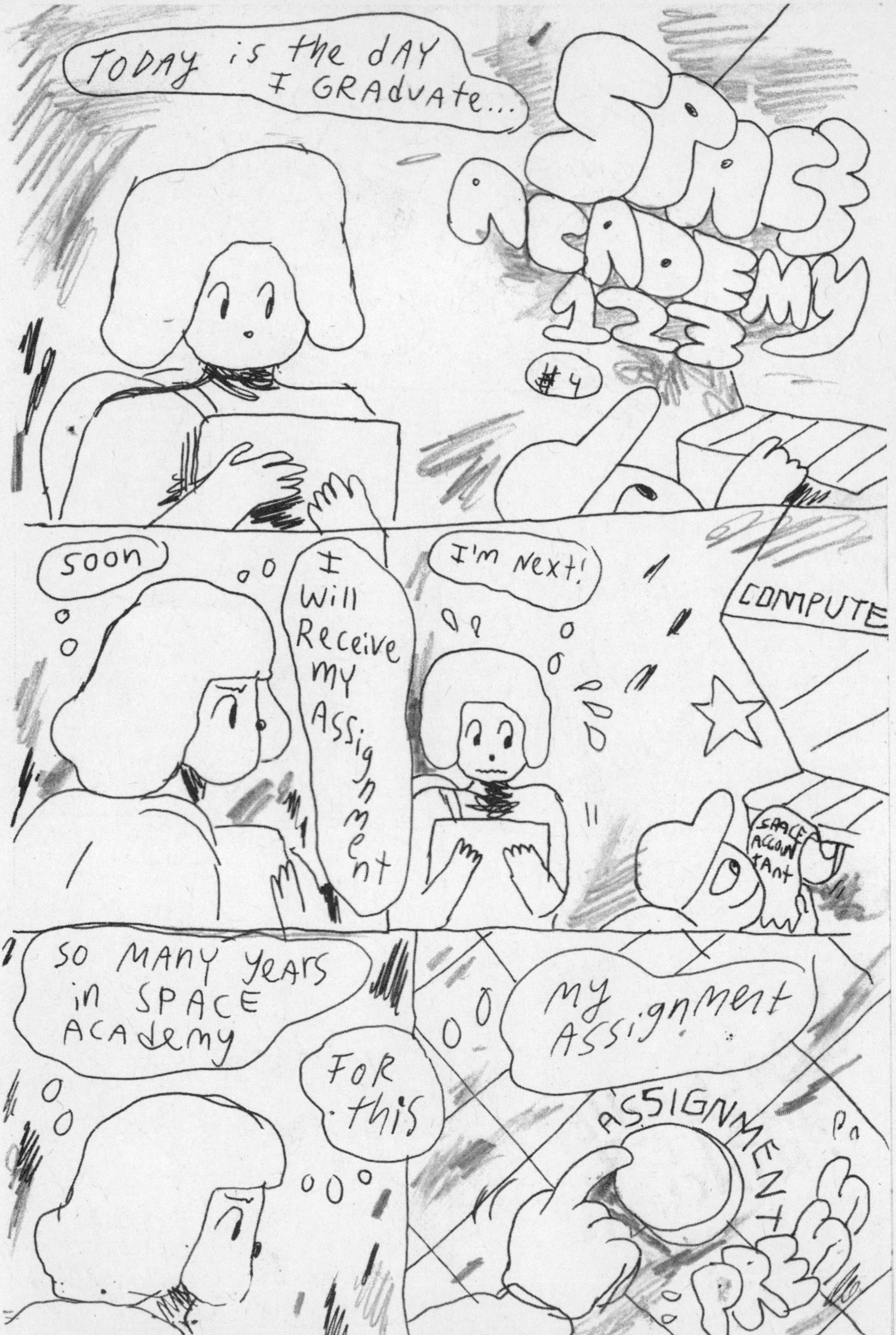

TODAY is the dAY I GRAduate...
SPACE ACADEMY 123
#4
soon
I Will Receive MY ASSignment
I'm Next!
COMPUTE
SPACE ACCOUNTANT
SO MANY Years in SPACE ACAdemy
FOR this
MY ASSignMent
ASSIGNMENT
PRESS

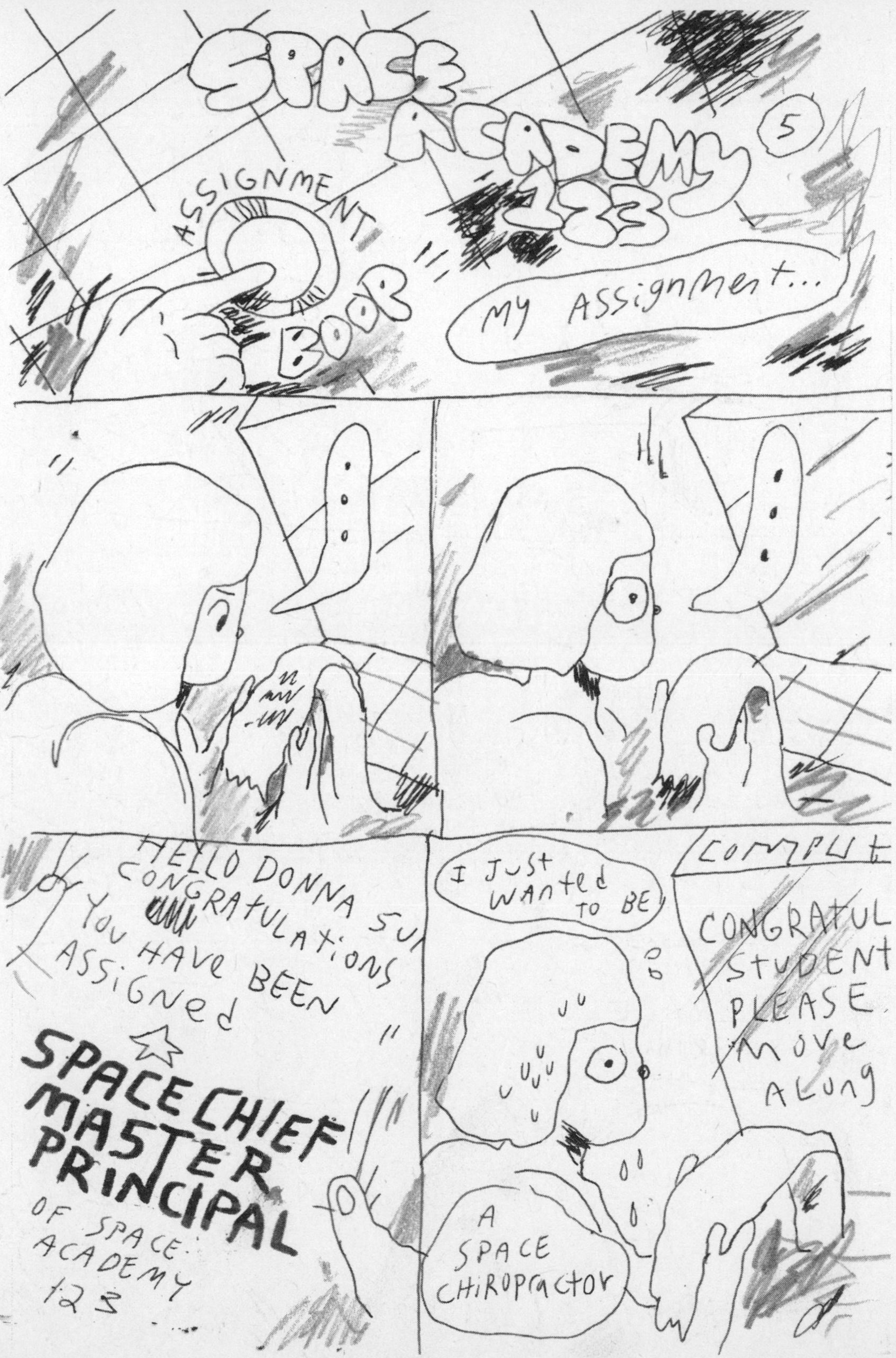

SPACE ACADEMY 123
5
ASSIGNMENT
BOOP
MY ASSIGNMENT...
HELLO DONNA SU
CONGRATULATIONS
YOU HAVE BEEN ASSIGNED
SPACE CHIEF MASTER PRINCIPAL
OF SPACE ACADEMY 123
I JUST WANTED TO BE
A SPACE CHIROPRACTOR
COMPUT
CONGRATUL STUDENT PLEASE MOVE ALONG

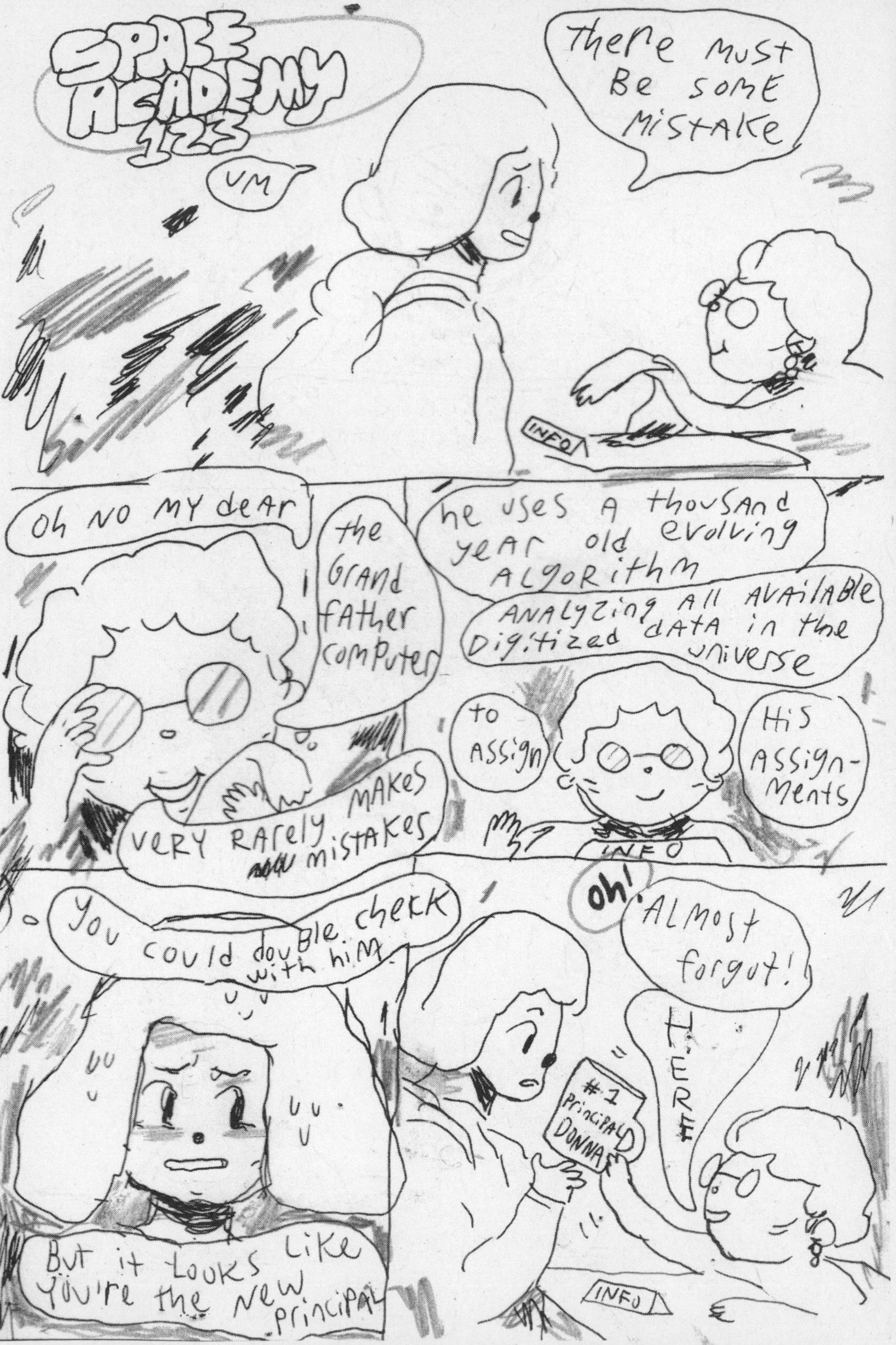
SPACE ACADEMY 123
UM
There must be some mistake
INFO
Oh no my dear
the Grand father computer
very rarely makes mistakes
he uses a thousand year old evolving algorithm
analyzing all available digitized data in the universe
to assign
His assignments
INFO
You could double check with him
But it looks like you're the new principal
Oh!
Almost forgot!
HERE
#1 Principal DONNA
INFO

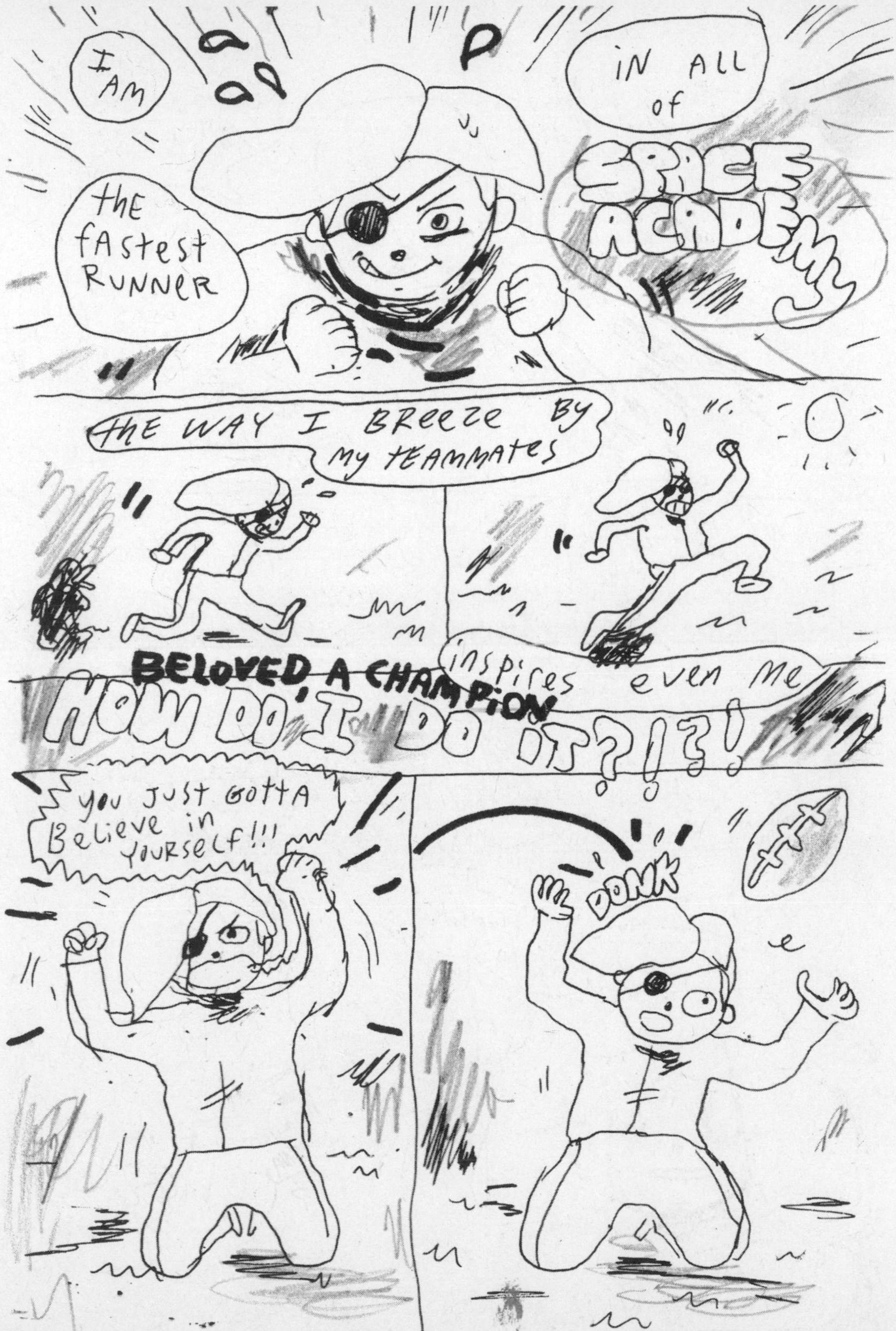
I AM
the fastest RUNNER
in ALL of
SPACE ACADEMY
the WAY I BREEZE by my TEAMMATES
inspires even me
BELOVED, A CHAMPION
HOW DO I DO IT?!?!
you JUST GOTTA Believe in yourself!!!
DONK

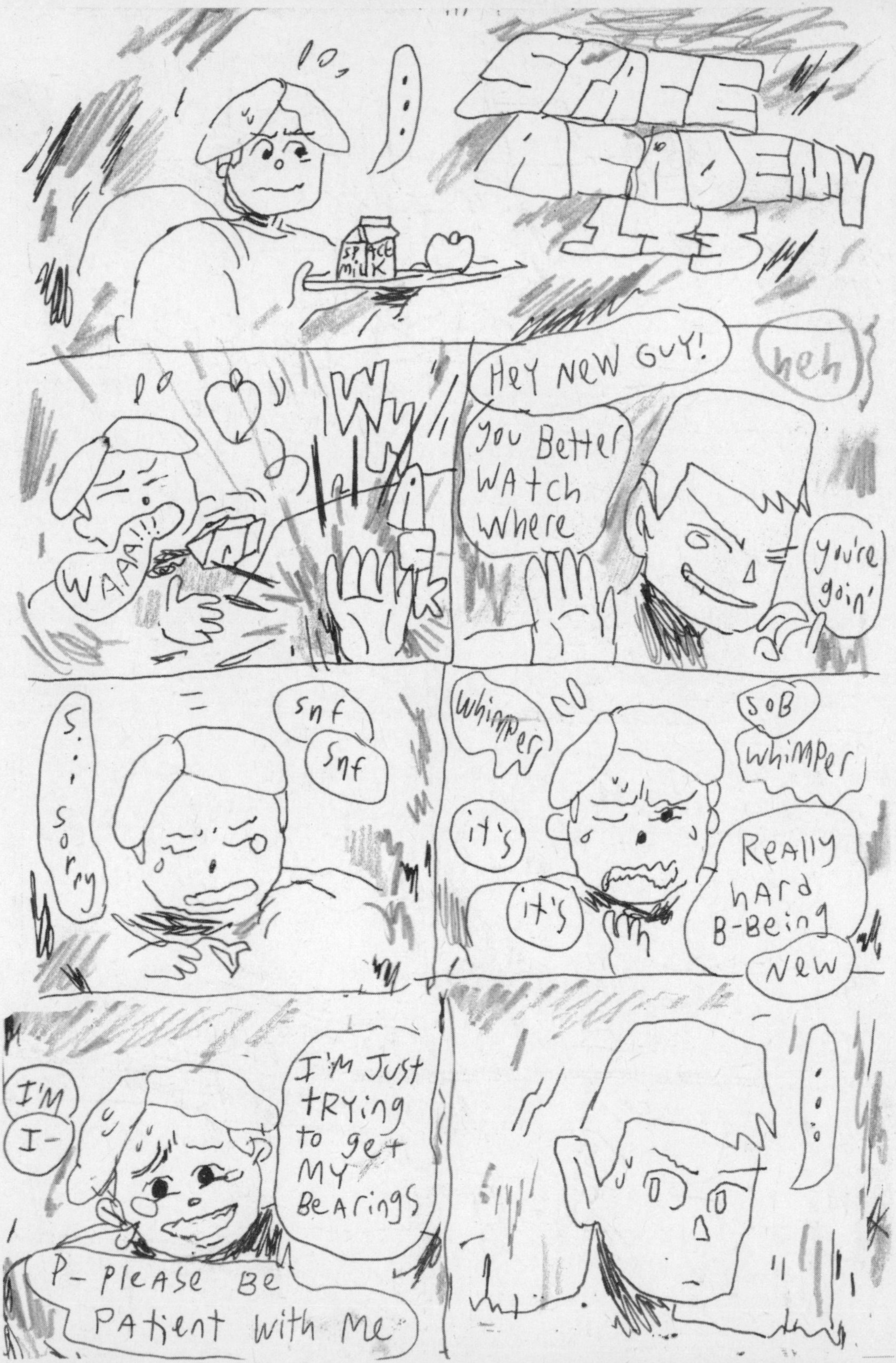

SPACE ACADEMY 1.3
...
SPACE MILK
WAAA!!!
Hey NEW GUY!
heh
You Better WAtch where
you're goin'
s... sorry
snf
snf
whimper
it's
it's
SOB whimper
Really hard B-Being New
I'M I-
I'M Just TRYing to get MY BeARings
P- please Be PAtient with Me
...

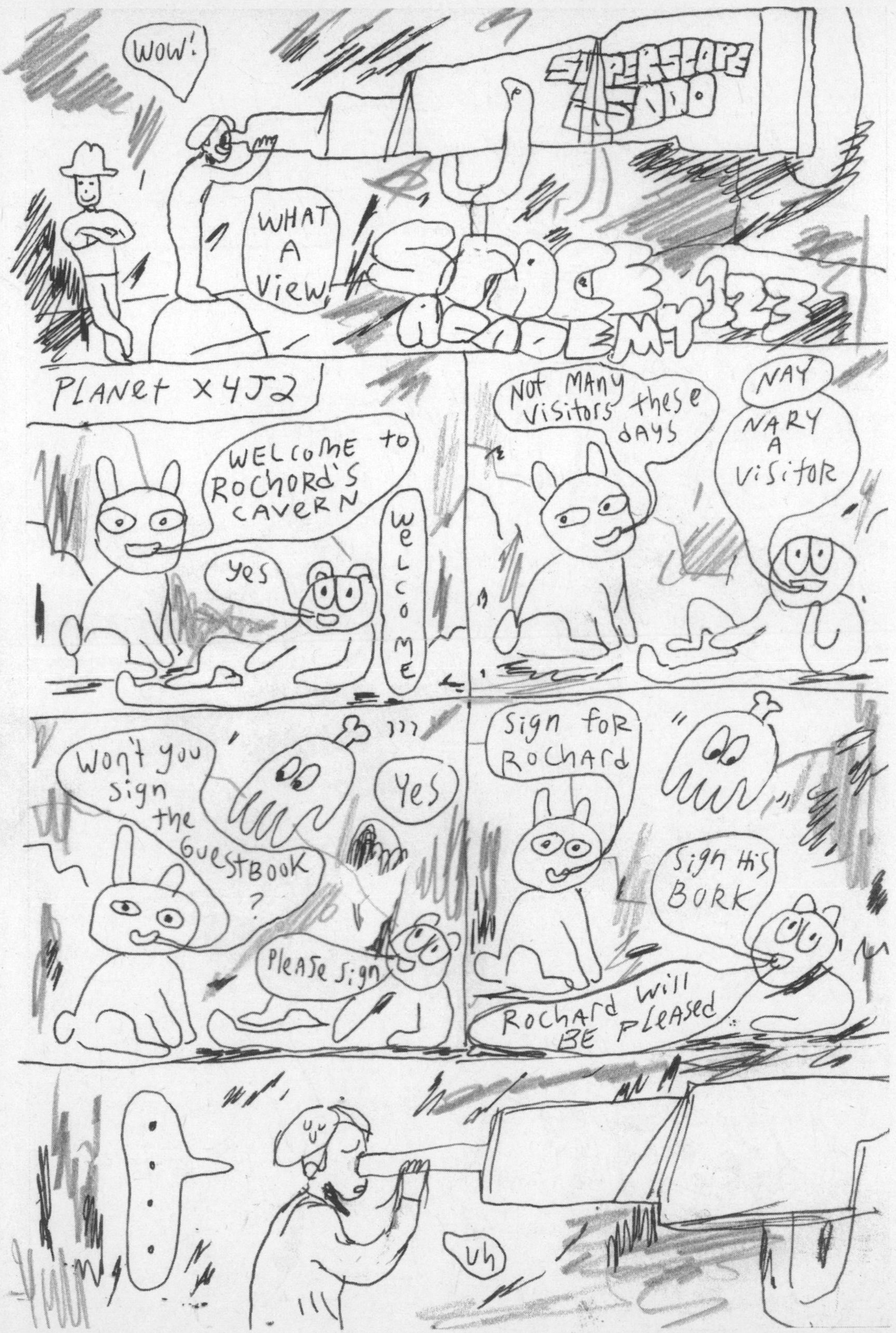
WOW!
SUPERSCOPE 5000
WHAT A VIEW
SPACE ACADEMY 123
PLANET X4J2
WELCOME to ROCHORD'S CAVERN
yes
WELCOME
Not MANY visitors these days
NAY
NARY A VISITOR
Won't you sign the GUESTBOOK?
Yes
Please sign
Sign for Rochard
Sign His BORK
Rochard will BE pleased
Uh

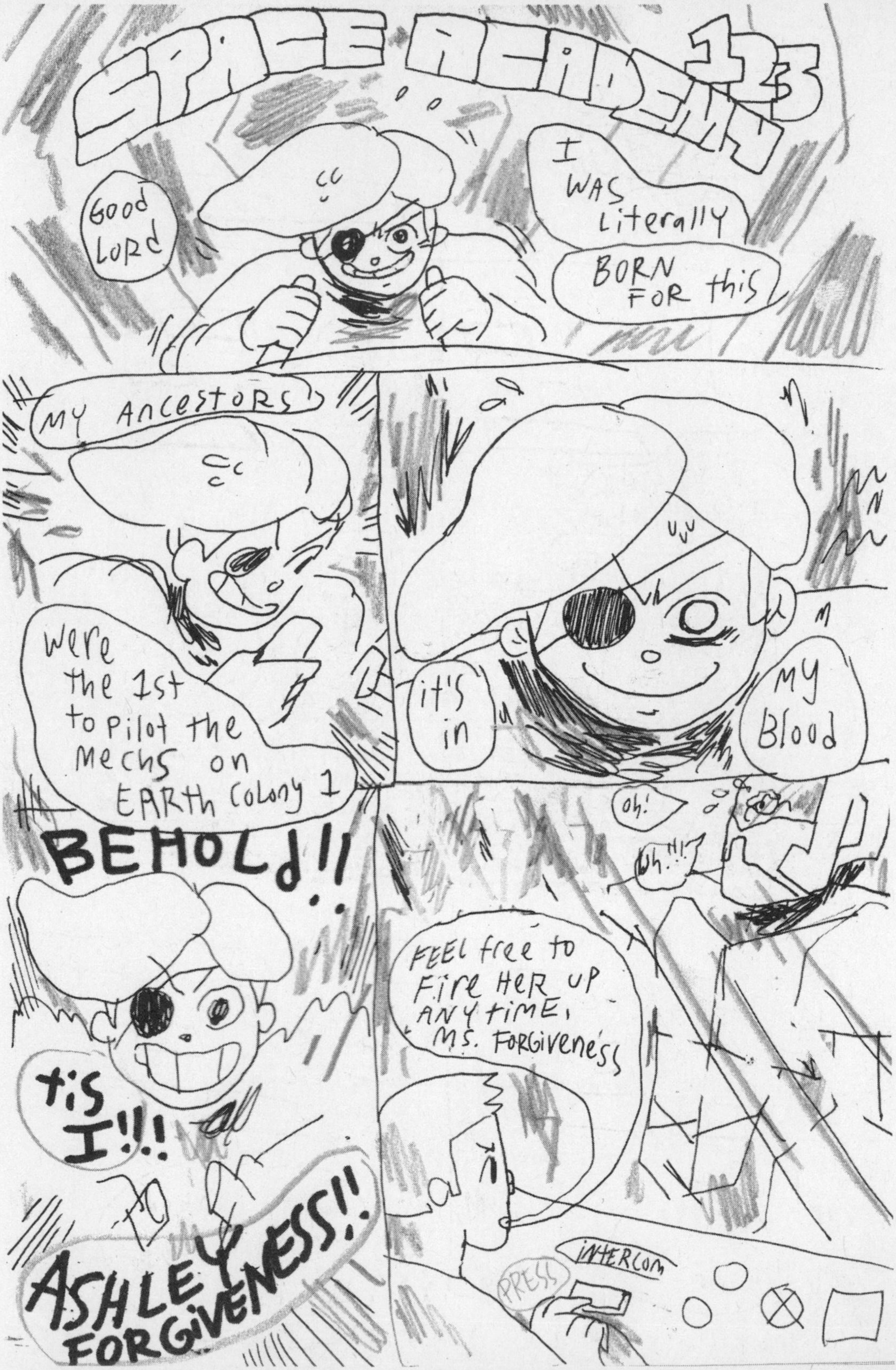
SPACE ACADEMY 123
Good Lord
I WAS Literally BORN FOR this
MY Ancestors
were the 1st to pilot the mechs on EARTH colony 1
it's in
My Blood
BEHOLd!!
tis I!!!
ASHLEY FORGIVENESS!!
oh!
Wh..!!
FEEL free to Fire HER UP ANY time, MS. FORGIVENESS
PRESS
intercom

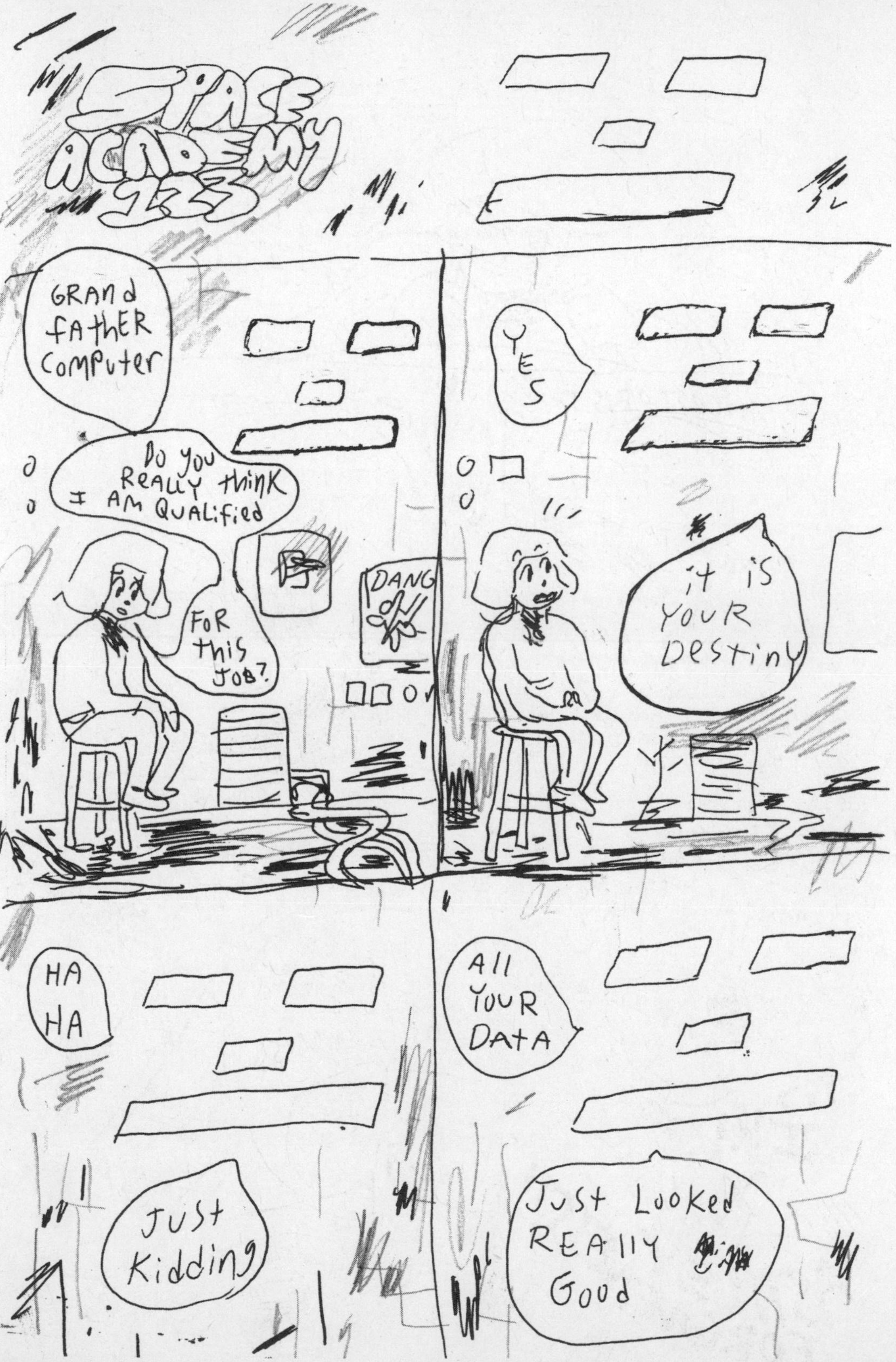
SPACE ACADEMY 123
GRAND fAthER Computer
Do you REALLY think I AM QUALified
FOR this JOB?
DANG
YES
it is YOUR Destiny
HA HA
All YOUR DATA
JUST Kidding
Just Looked REAlly Good

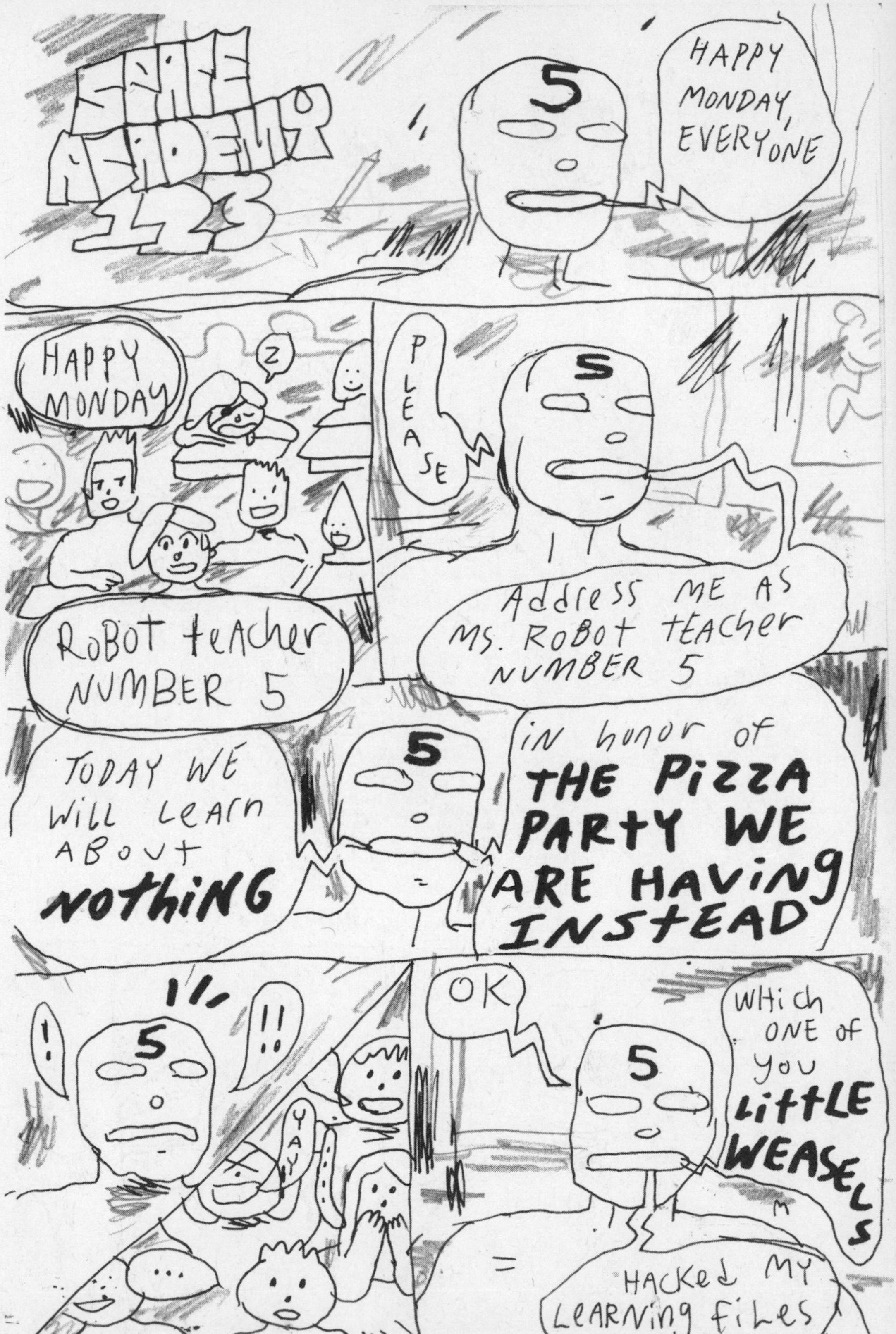
SPACE ACADEMY 123
HAPPY MONDAY, EVERYONE
HAPPY MONDAY
Z
ROBOT TEACHER NUMBER 5
PLEASE
ADDRESS ME AS MS. ROBOT TEACHER NUMBER 5
TODAY WE WILL LEARN ABOUT NOTHING
IN HONOR OF THE PIZZA PARTY WE ARE HAVING INSTEAD
!
!!
YAY
...
OK
WHICH ONE OF YOU LITTLE WEASELS
HACKED MY LEARNING FILES

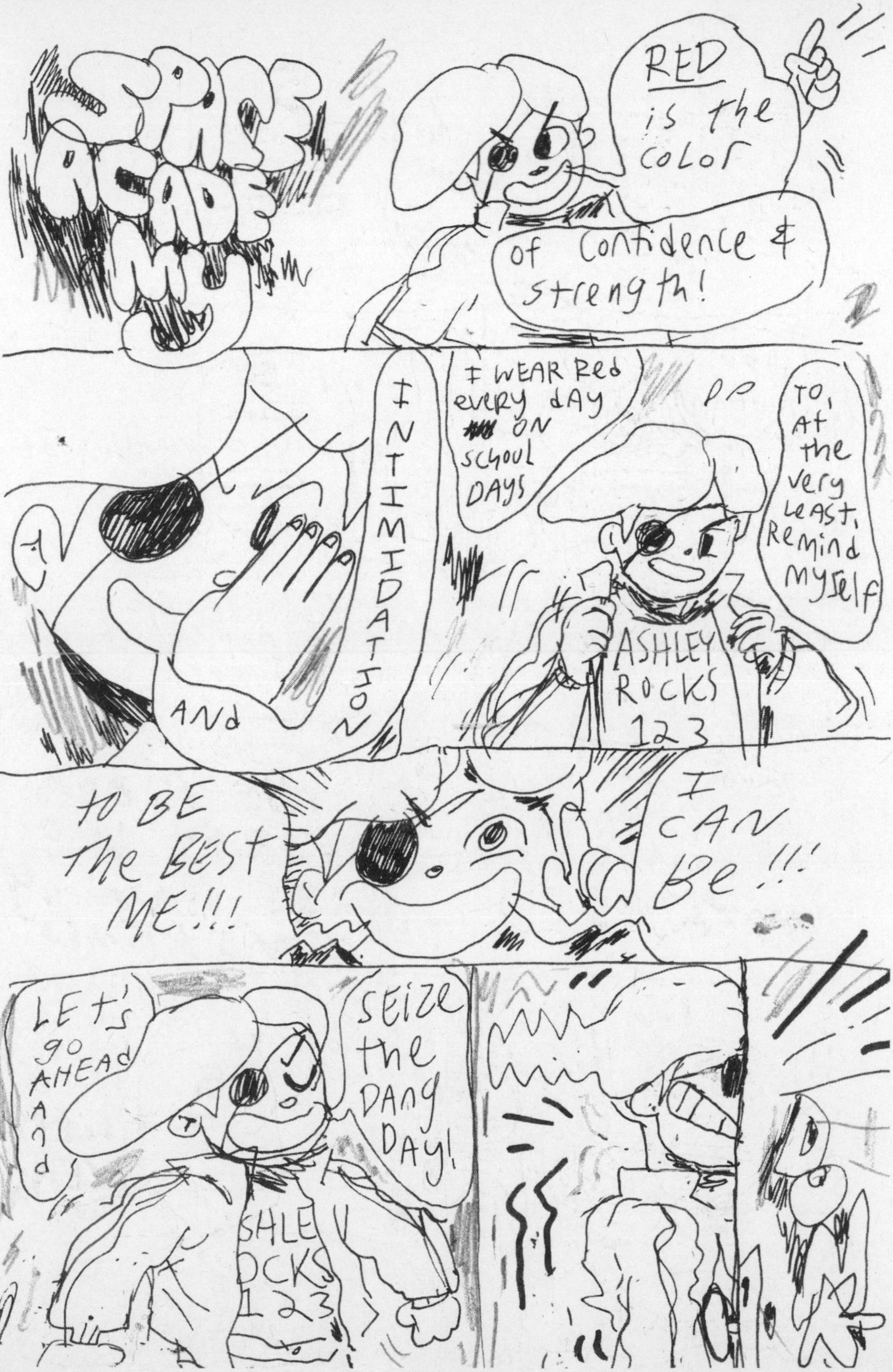
SPACE ACADEMY
RED is the color of confidence & strength!
AND INTIMIDATION
I WEAR Red every day ON SCHOOL DAYS
TO, At the very LEAST, Remind myself
ASHLEY ROCKS 123
to BE the BEST ME!!!
I CAN BE!!!
LET's go AHEAD And
SEIZE the DANG DAY!
SHLE OCKS 123

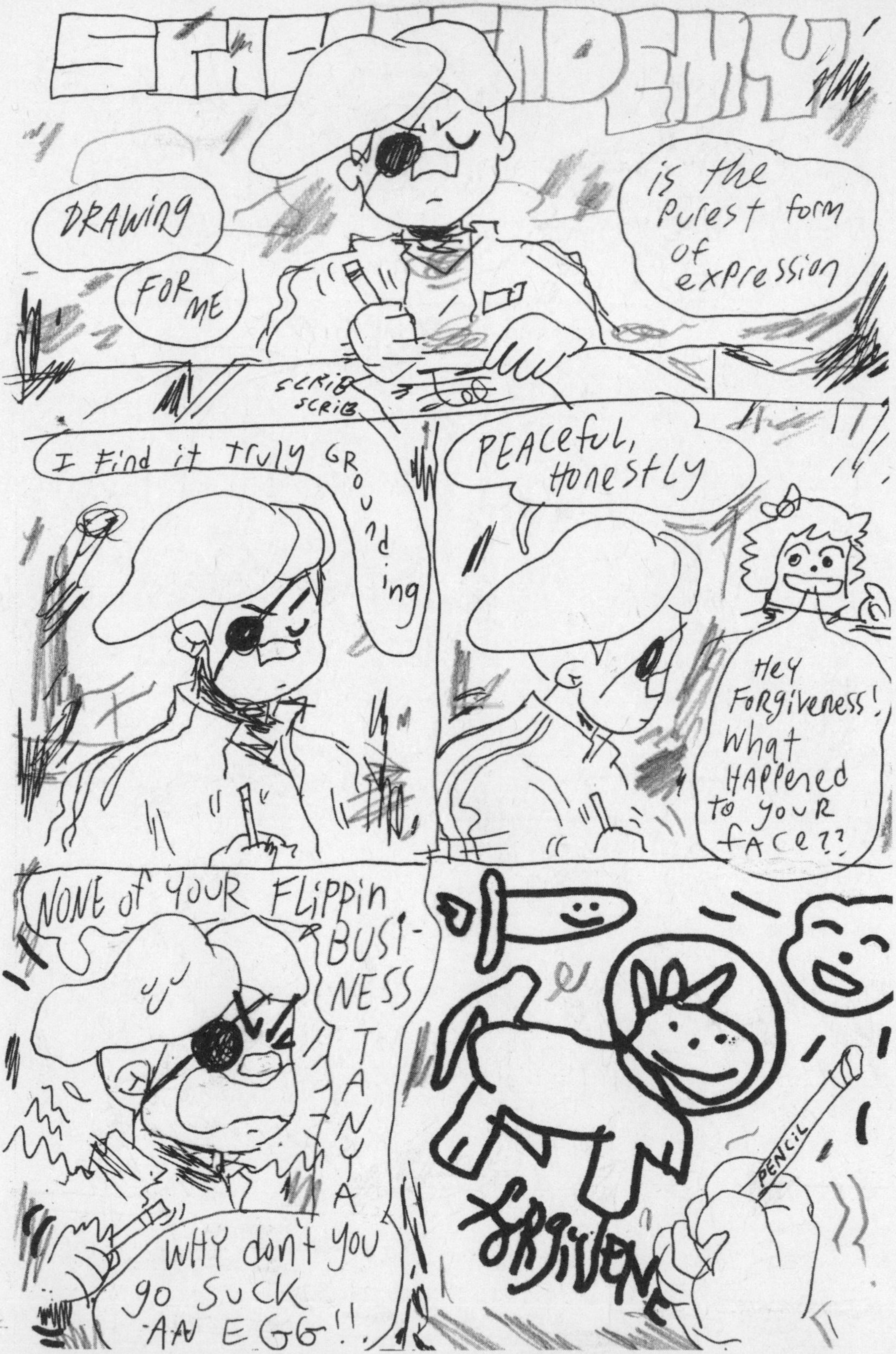
DRAWING
FOR ME
is the Purest form of expression
SCRIB SCRIB
I Find it truly GRounding
PEACEful, Honestly
Hey Forgiveness! What Happened to your face??
NONE of YOUR Flippin BUSI-NESS
TANYA
WHY don't you go SUCK AN EGG!!
PENCIL

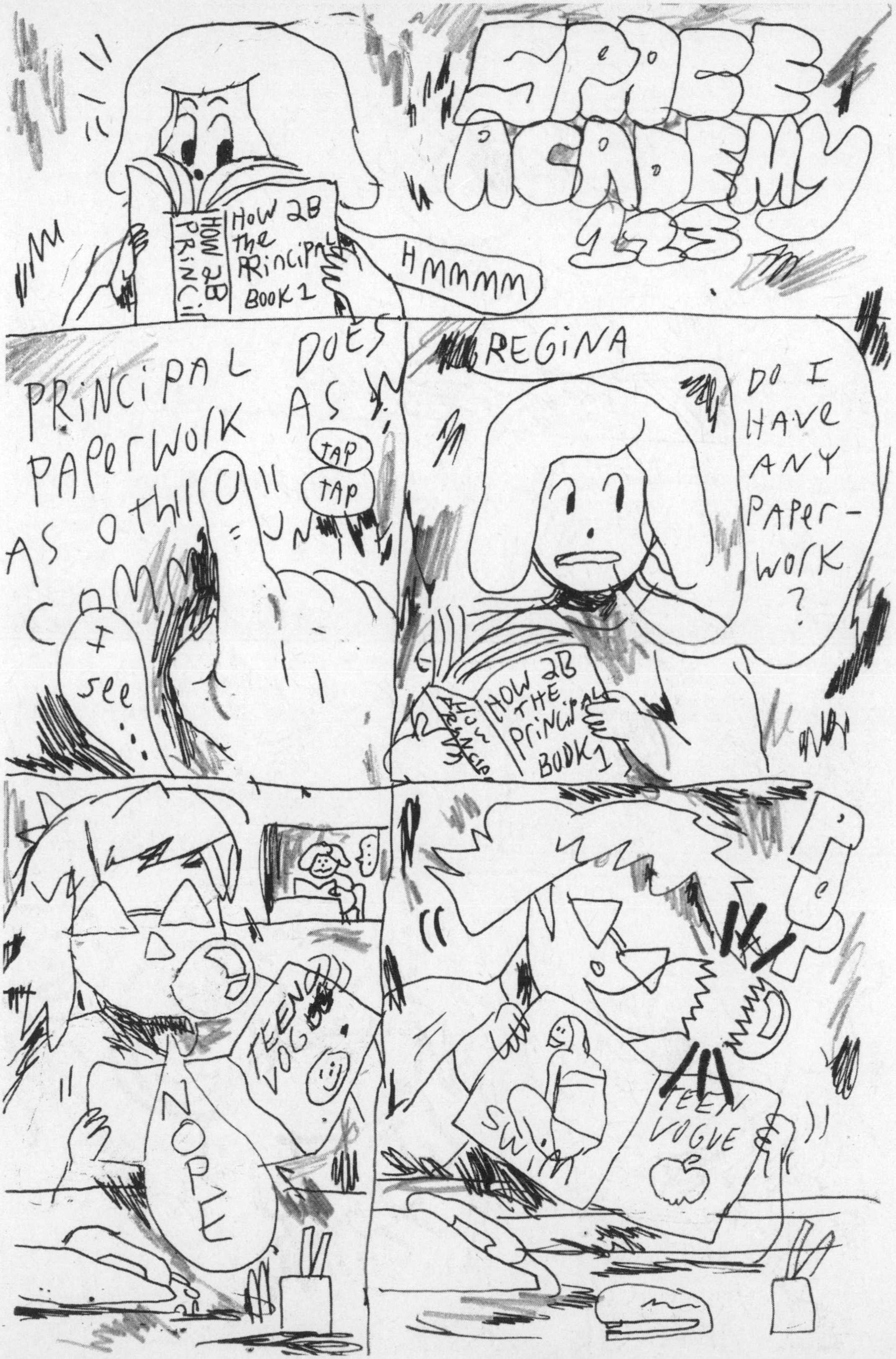

ACADEMY
HOW 2B the PRINCIPAL BOOK 1
HOW 2B PRINCi
HMMMMM
PRINCIPAL DOES PAPERWORK AS
TAP
TAP
I see...
REGINA
DO I HAVE ANY PAPER-WORK ?
HOW 2B THE PRINCIPAL BOOK 1
TEEN VOGUE
NOPE
SWIM
TEEN VOGUE

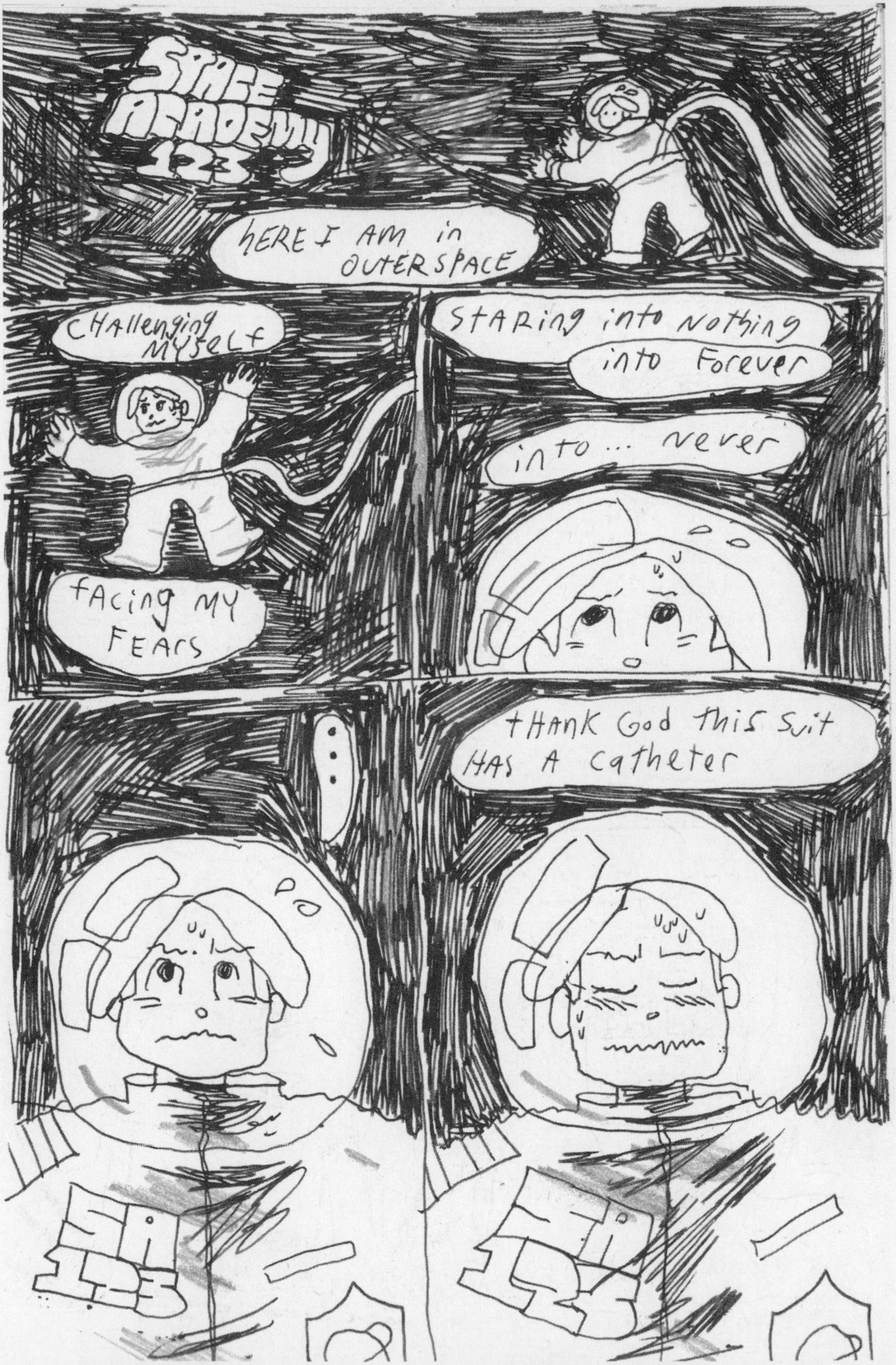
SPACE ACADEMY 123
HERE I AM in OUTER SPACE
CHAllenging MYSELF
facing MY FEARS
STARING into nothing
into Forever
into... never
...
tHANK God this Suit HAS A catheter
SA 123
SA 123

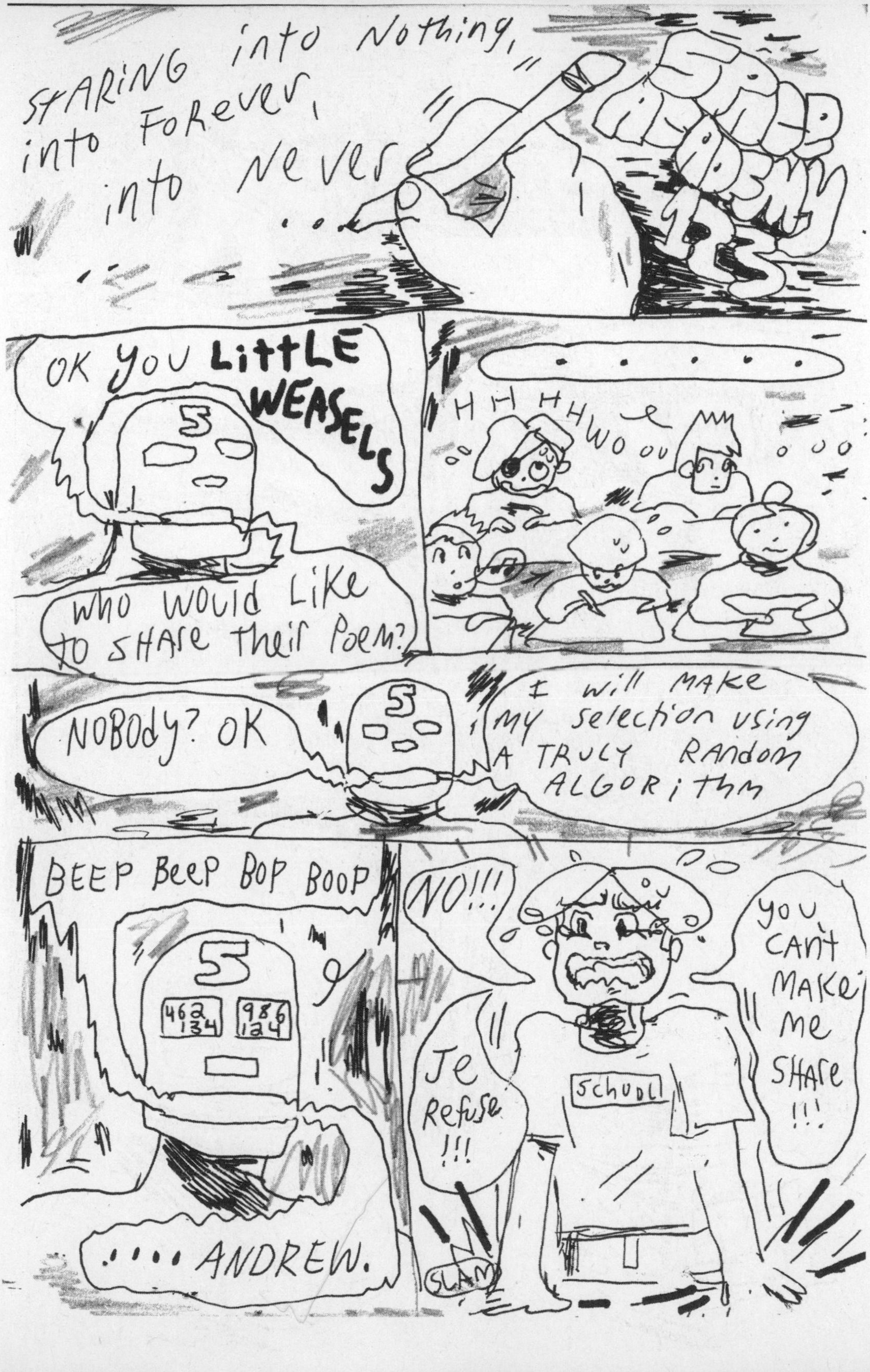
STARING into Nothing, into Forever, into Never ....
OK YOU LittLE WEASELS
who would Like to SHAre their Poem?
. . . . . .
NOBody? OK
I will MAKE my selection using A TRULY Random ALGORithm
BEEP Beep BOP BOOP
462 134
986 124
.... ANDREW.
NO!!!
You CAN't MAKE Me SHAre !!!
Je Refuse !!!
SCHUDL
SLAM

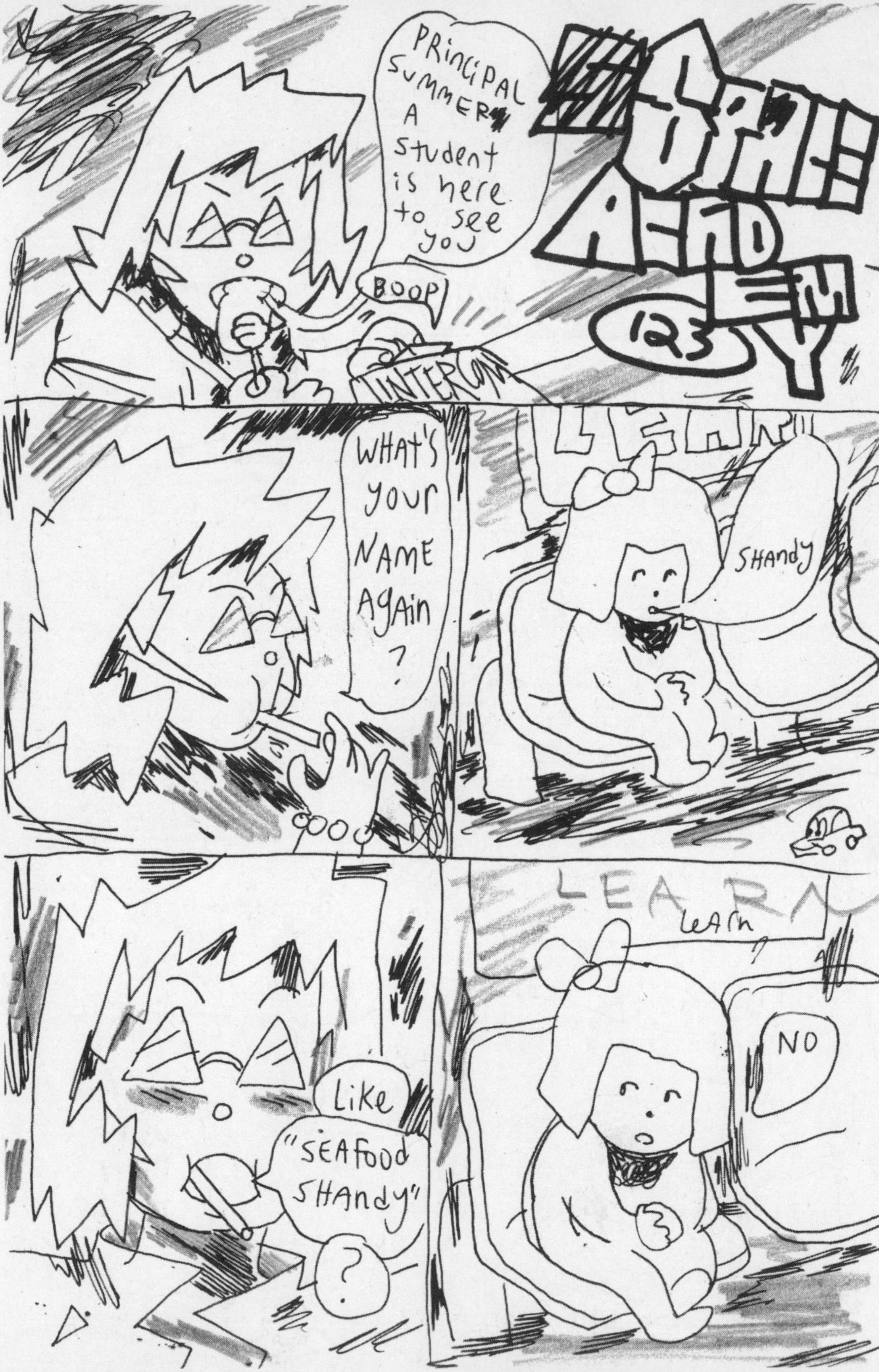

SPACE ACADEMY
123
PRINCIPAL SUMMER A Student is here to see you
BOOP
INTERCOM
WHAT'S your NAME AGAin ?
SHANDY
Like "SEAFood SHAndy" ?
LEARN
Learn
NO

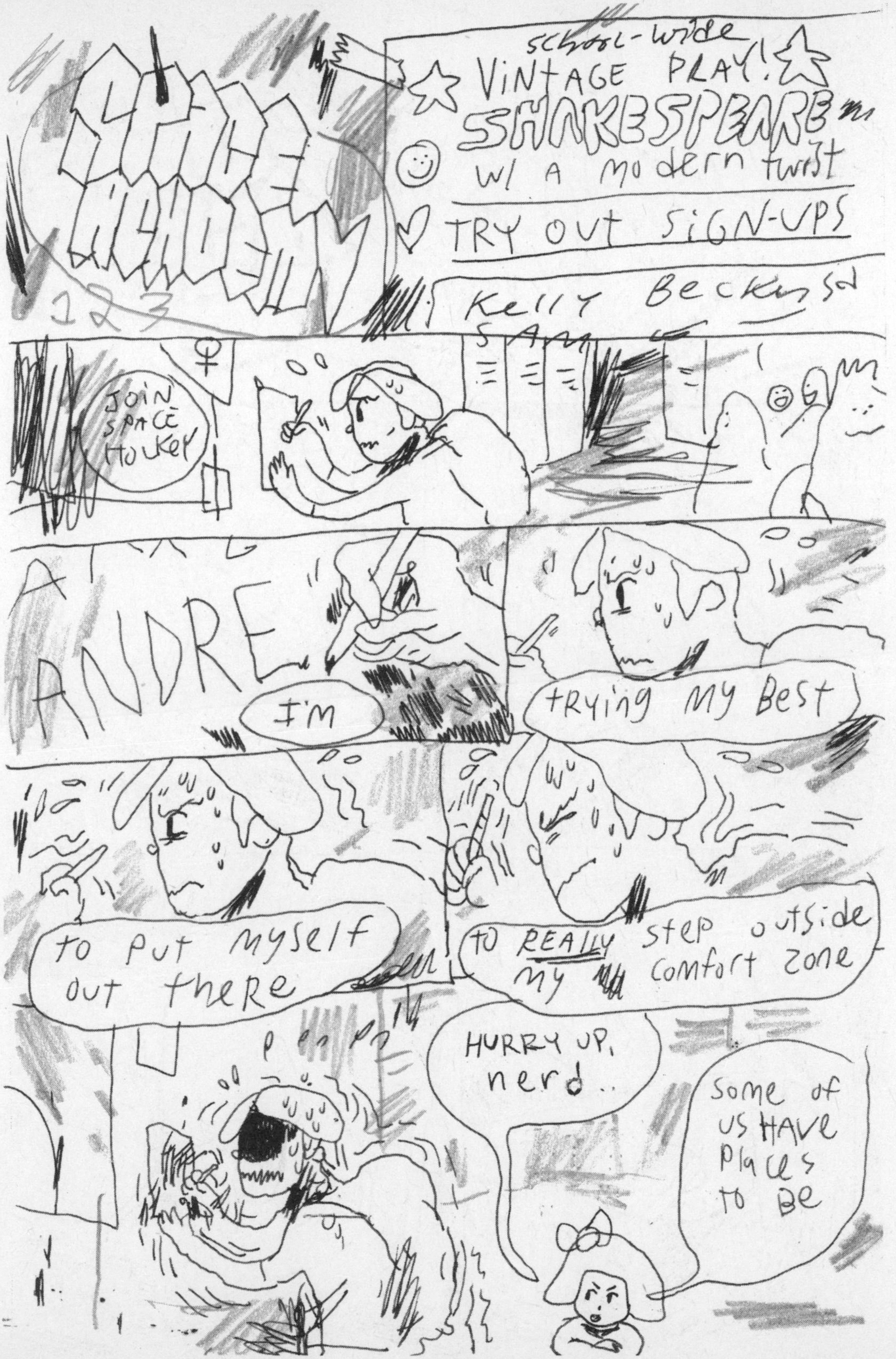
school-wide
VINTAGE PLAY!
SHAKESPEARE
w/ a modern twist
TRY OUT SIGN-UPS
Kelly
SAM
JOIN SPACE HOCKEY
ANDRE
I'm
trying my Best
to put myself out there
to REALLY step outside my comfort zone
HURRY UP, nerd...
Some of us HAVE places to be

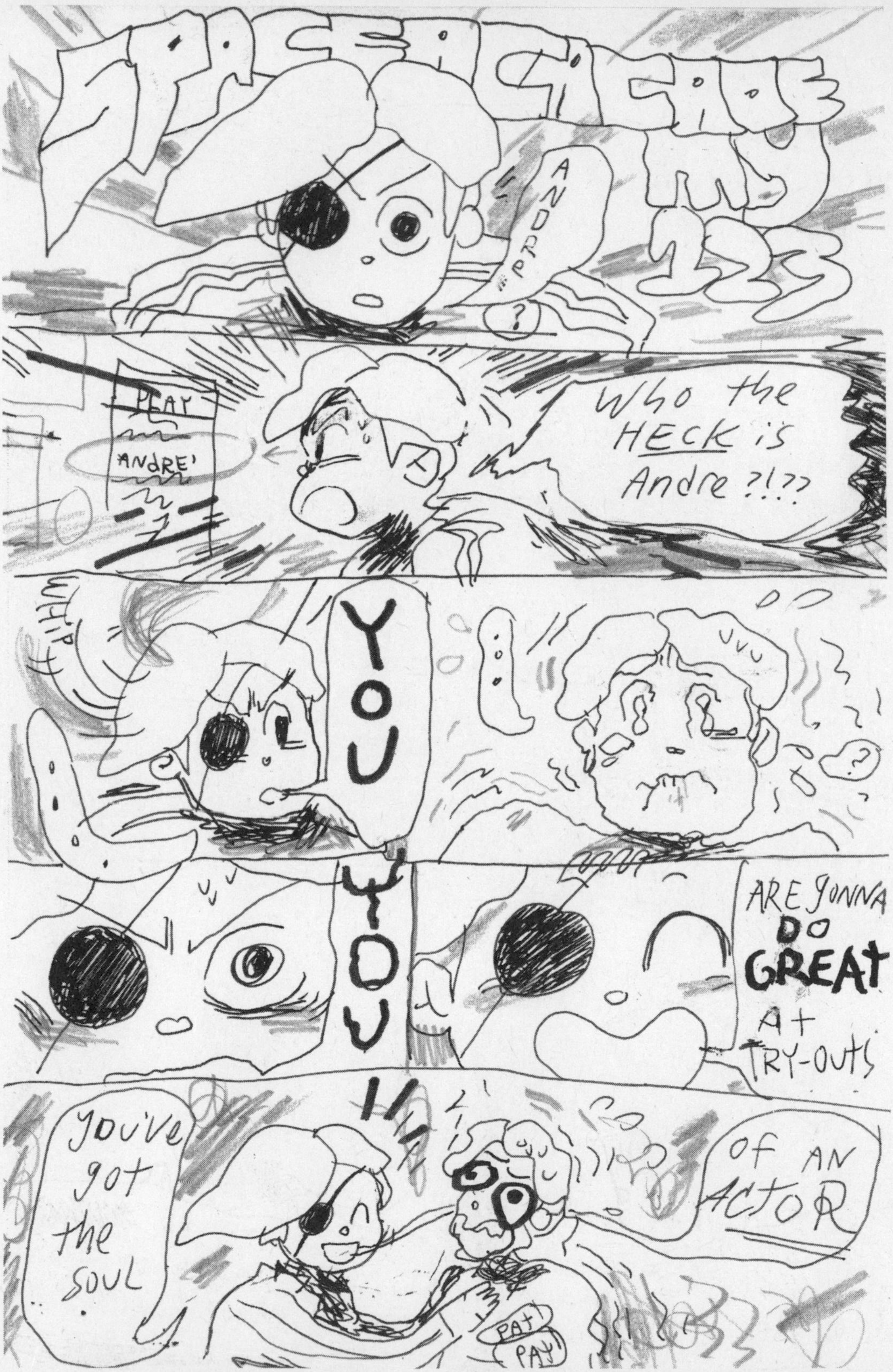
ANDRE ?
PLAY
ANDRE'
Who the HECK is Andre ?!??
WHIP
. . .
?
YOU
YOU
ARE GONNA DO GREAT AT TRY-OUTS
YOU!!
You've got the soul
of AN ACTOR
PAT PAT

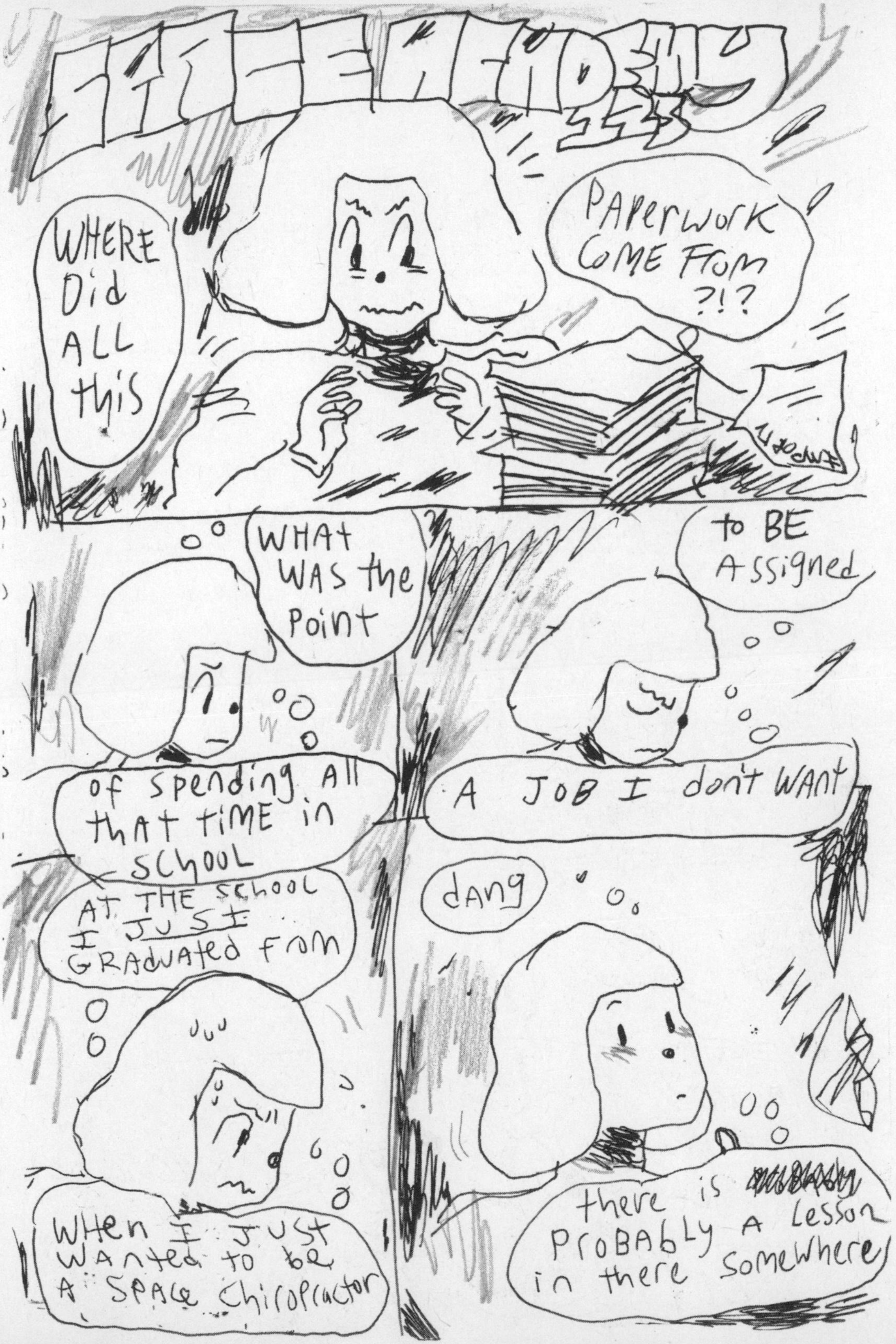
WHERE Did ALL this
PAPERWORK COME FROM ?!?
WHAT WAS the Point
of spending all that time in school
AT THE school I JUST GRADUATED FROM
to BE Assigned
A JOB I don't WANT
dang
WHEN I JUST WANTED to be A SPACE Chiropractor
there is PROBABLY A Lesson in there somewhere

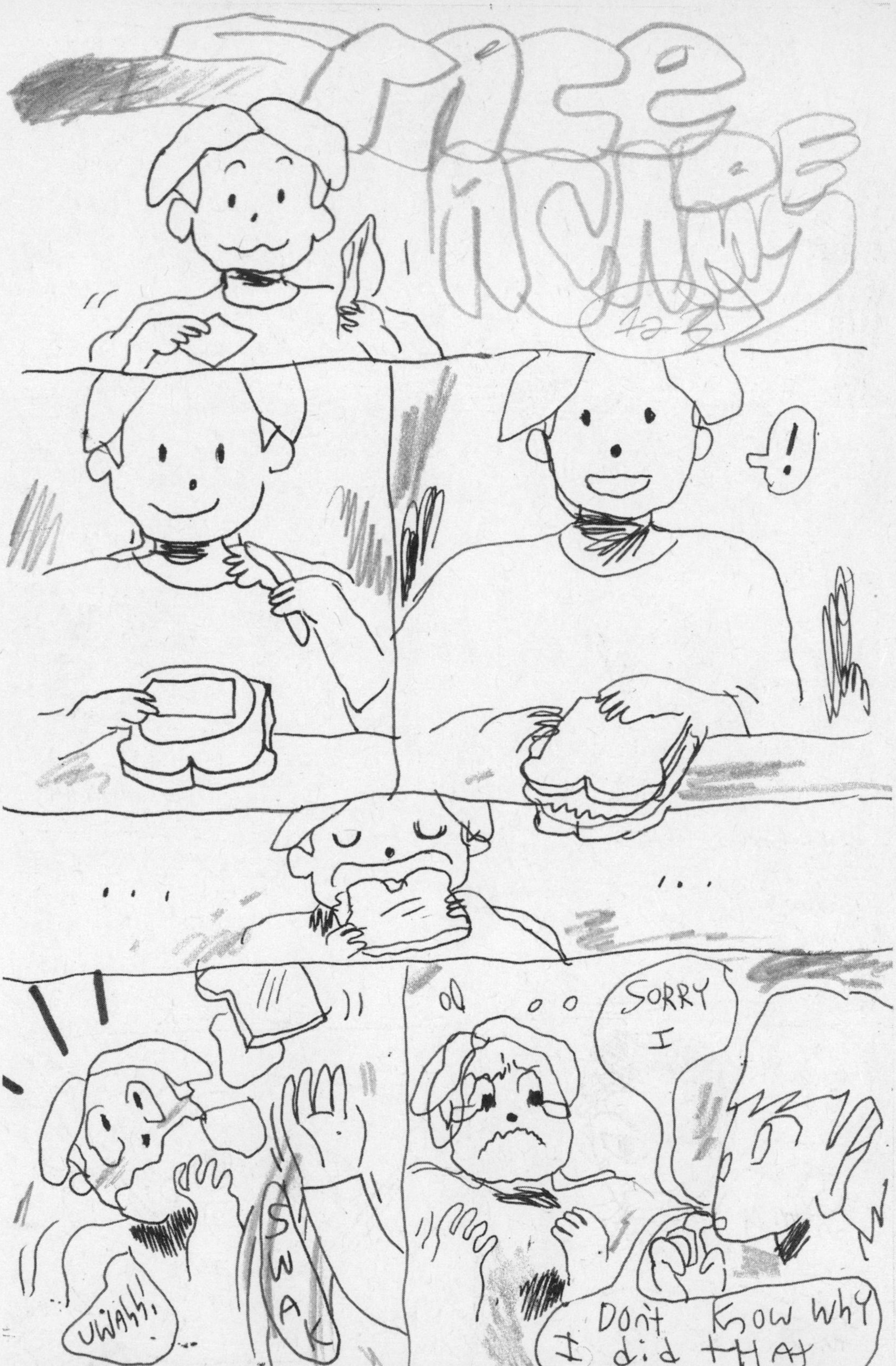
!
...
...
UWAhh!
SWAK
SORRY I
Don't Know why I did tHAt

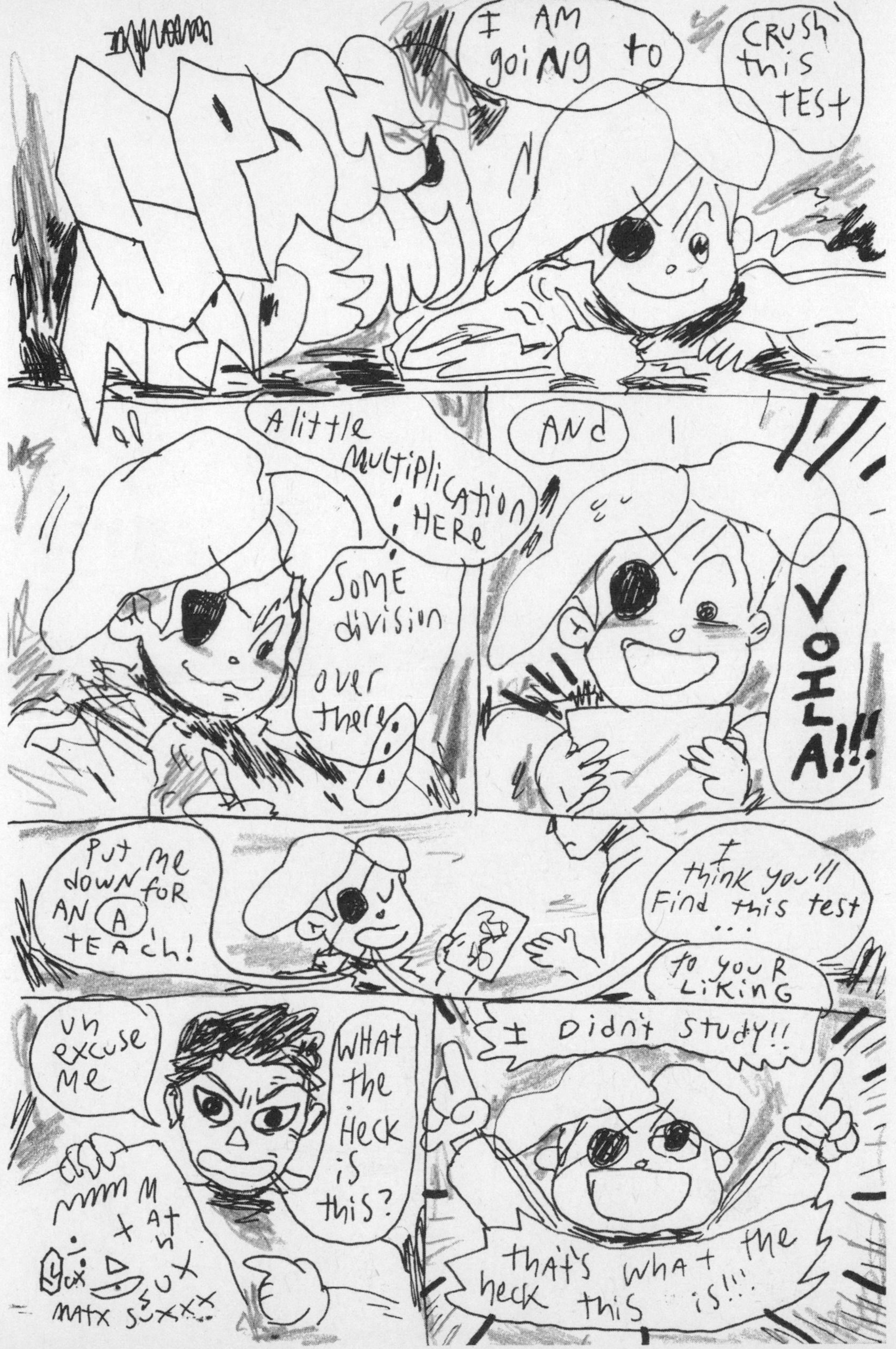
I AM going to
CRUSH this TEST
Alittle MULTIPLICATION HERE
SOME division over there
AND I
VOILA!!!
Put me down FOR AN A TEACH!
I think you'll Find this test ...
to your LIKING
uh excuse me
WHAT the Heck is this?
I Didn't study!!
that's what the heck this is!!!

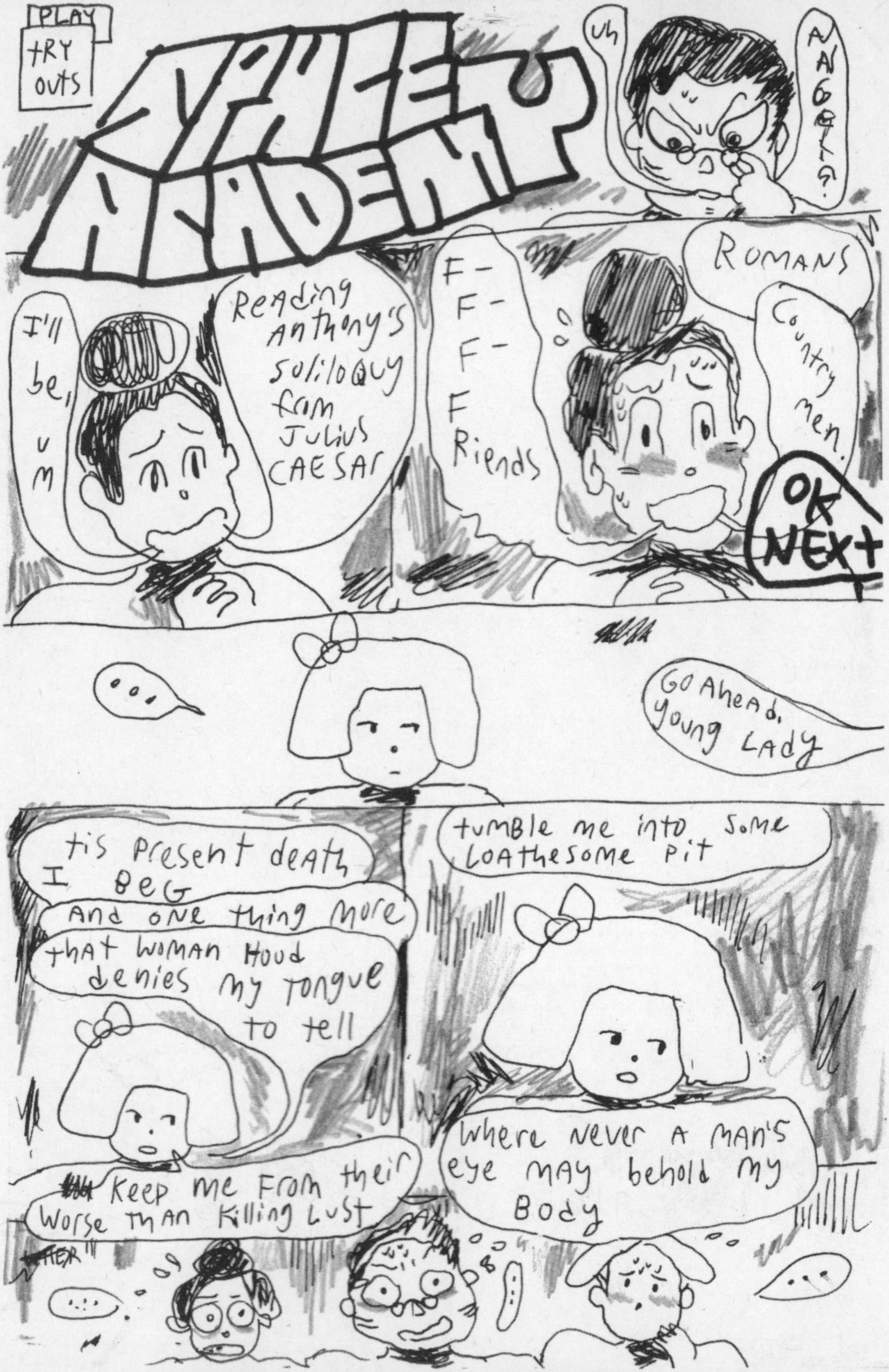
PLAY
TRY OUTS
uh
ANGEL?
I'll be, um
Reading anthony's soliloquy from Julius CAESAR
F- F- F- F Riends
ROMANS
Country men.
OK NEXT
...
Go Ahead, young Lady
tis present death I BEG
And one thing more
that woman Hood denies my Tongue to tell
tumble me into some LOAthesome pit
Keep me From their Worse than Killing Lust
Where never A man's eye may behold my Body

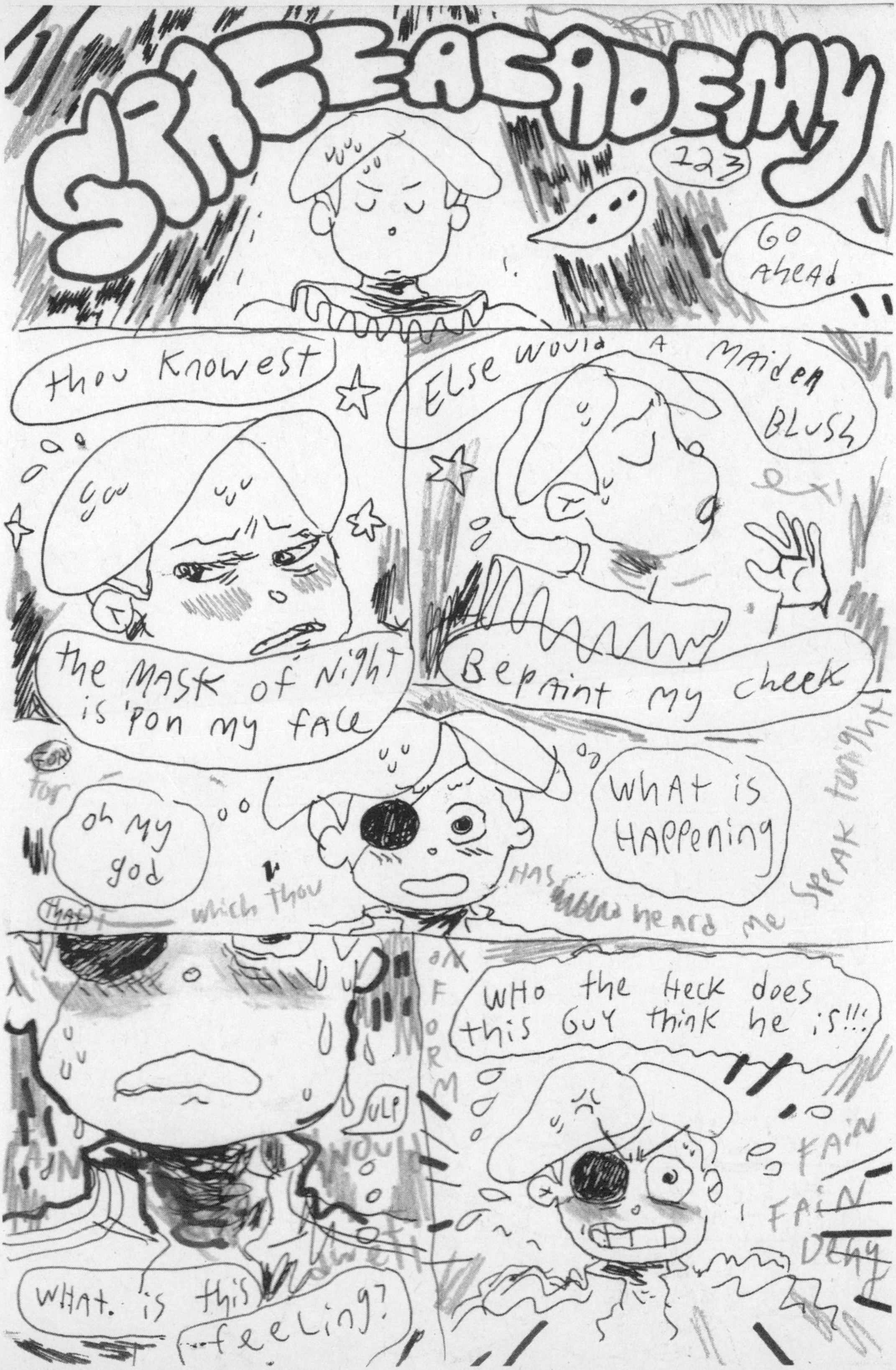

SPACE ACADEMY
223
...
Go ahead
thou Knowest
the MASK of Night is 'pon my face
Else would A Maiden Blush
Bepaint my cheek
oh my god
What is HAPPENING
for
which thou
HAS
heard me
SPEAK tonight
WHO the Heck does this GUY think he is!!!
FORM
GULP
WHAT. is this feeLing?
FAIN
FAIN
DENY

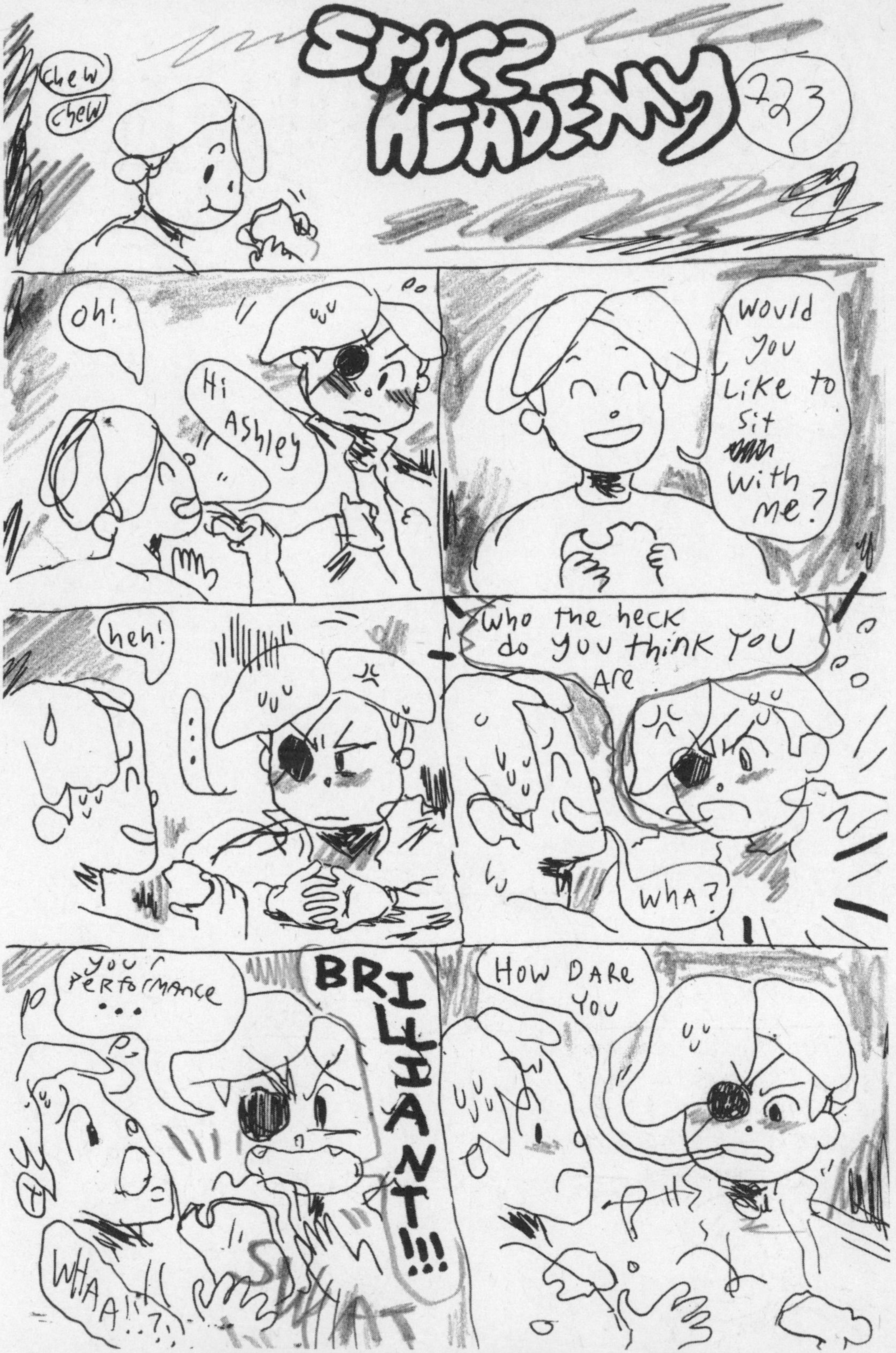

SPACE ACADEMY
223
chew
chew
Oh!
Hi Ashley
Would you Like to sit with me?
heh!
...
Who the heck do you think YOU are
WHA?
Your performance ...
BRILLIANT!!!
WHAA!..?!
HOW DARE YOU

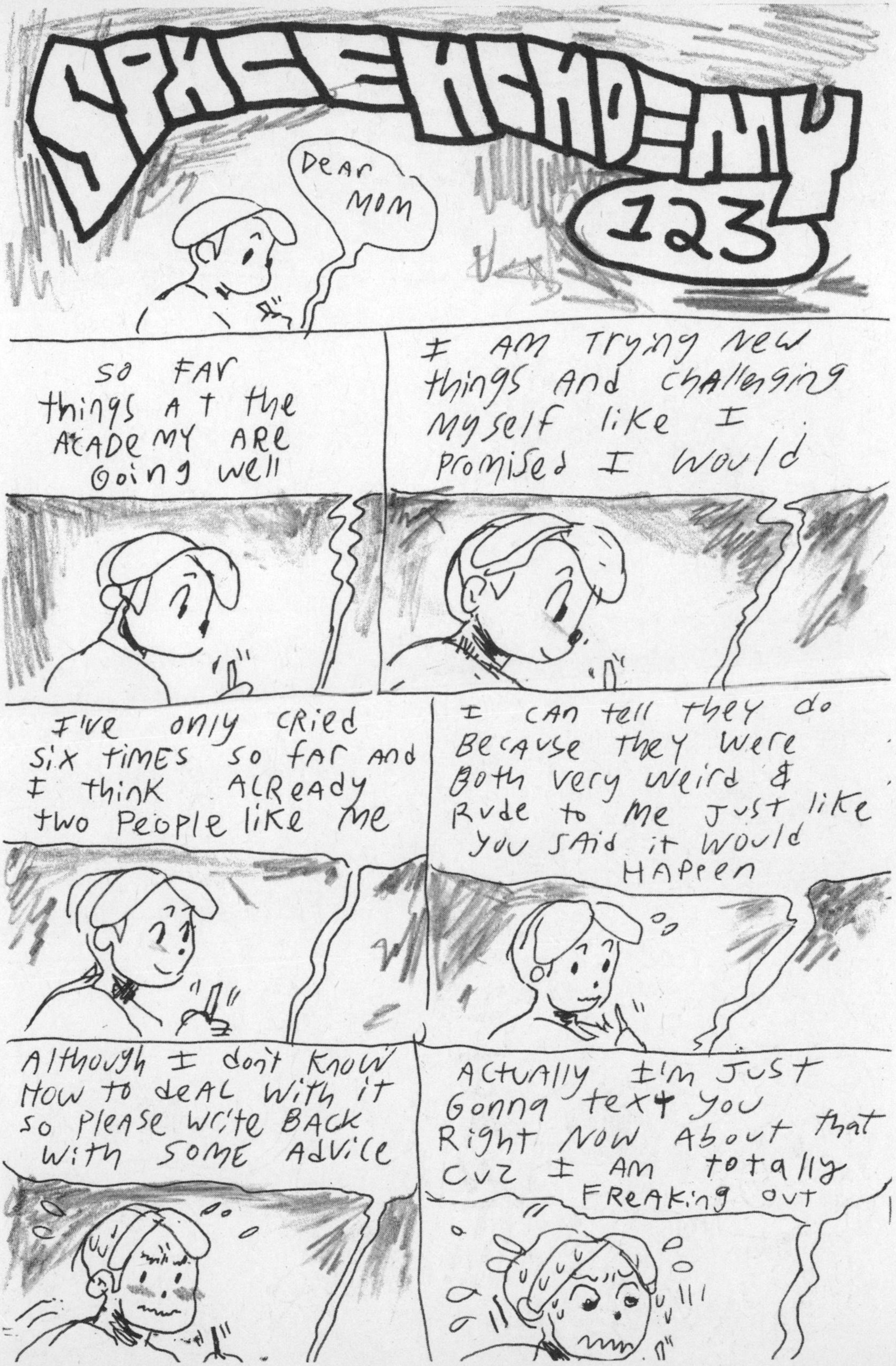
SPACE ACADEMY
123
Dear MOM
so far things at the Academy are going well
I am trying new things and challenging myself like I promised I would
I've only cried six times so far and I think already two people like me
I can tell they do because they were both very weird & rude to me just like you said it would happen
Although I don't know how to deal with it so please write back with some advice
Actually I'm just gonna text you right now about that cuz I am totally freaking out

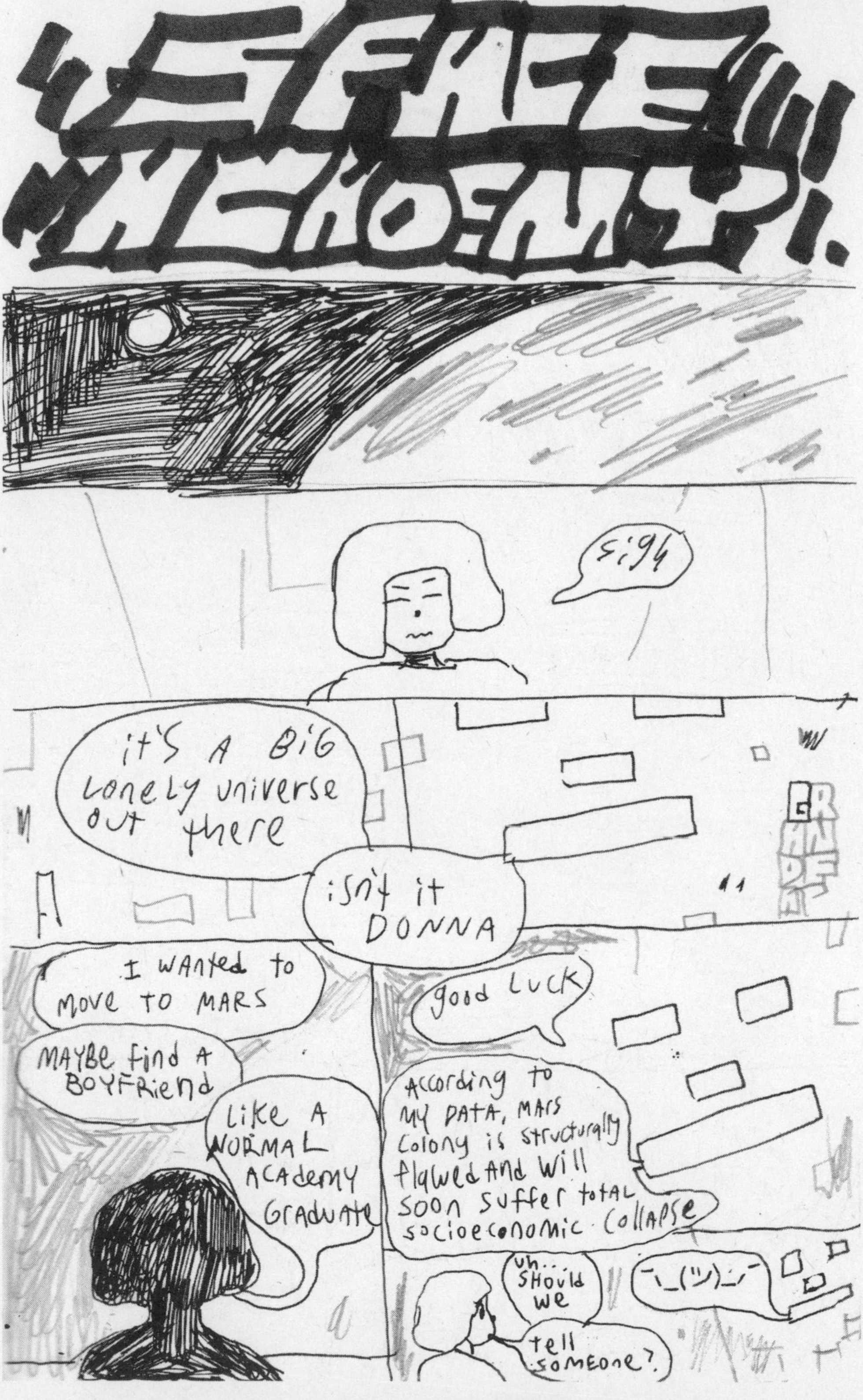
sigh
it's A BiG Lonely universe out there
isn't it DONNA
I WANted to move TO MARS
MAYBe find A BOYFRiend
Like A NORMAL ACAdemy Graduate
good Luck
According to my DATA, MARS Colony is structurally flawed And will soon suffer total socioeconomic collapse
uh.. SHOUld we tell someone?
¯_(ツ)_/¯

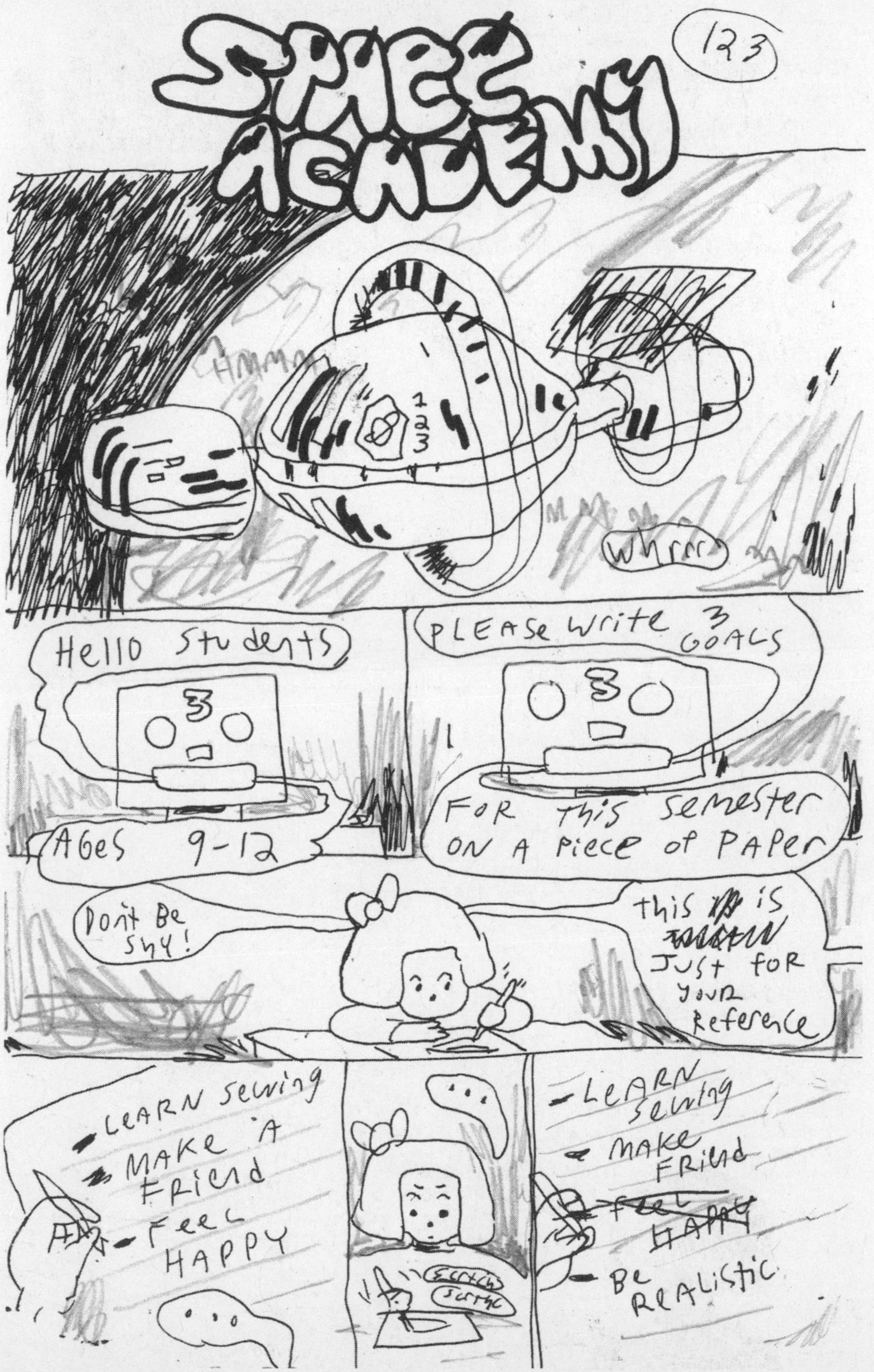

SPACE ACADEMY
123
HMMM
123
whrrr
Hello Students
Ages 9-12
PLEASE write 3 GOALS
FOR this semester ON A Piece of PAPer
Don't Be shy!
this is JUST FOR your Reference
- LeARN sewing
- MAKE A Friend
- Feel HAPPY
...
...
- LeARN sewing
- MAKE Friend
- Feel HAPPY
- Be REALISTIC

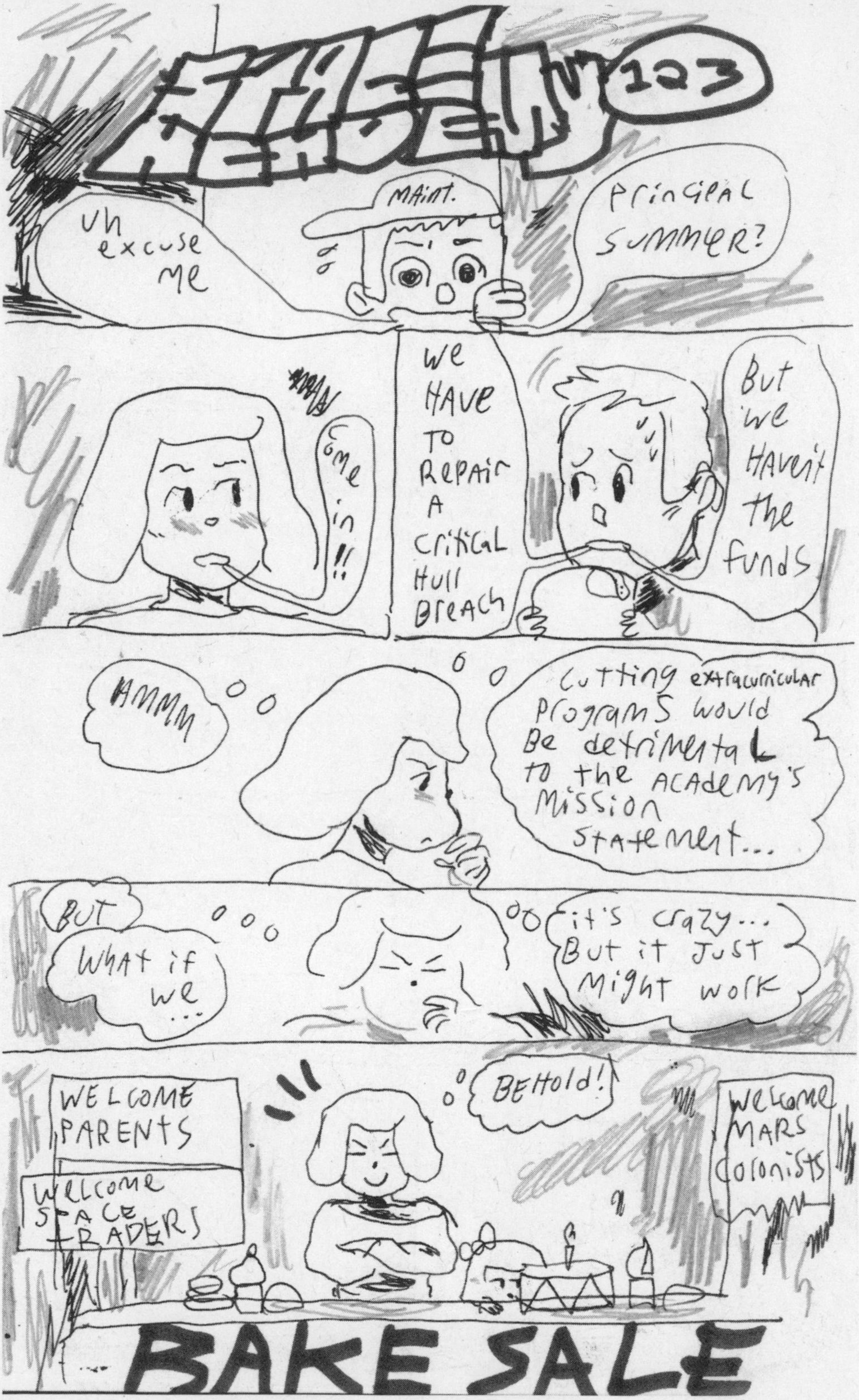
123
MAINT.
uh excuse me
Principal Summer?
Come in!!
We have to repair a critical hull breach
But we haven't the funds
HMMM
Cutting extracurricular programs would be detrimental to the Academy's mission statement...
BUT
What if we...
it's crazy... But it just might work
Behold!
WELCOME PARENTS
Welcome SPACE TRADERS
Welcome MARS Colonists
BAKE SALE

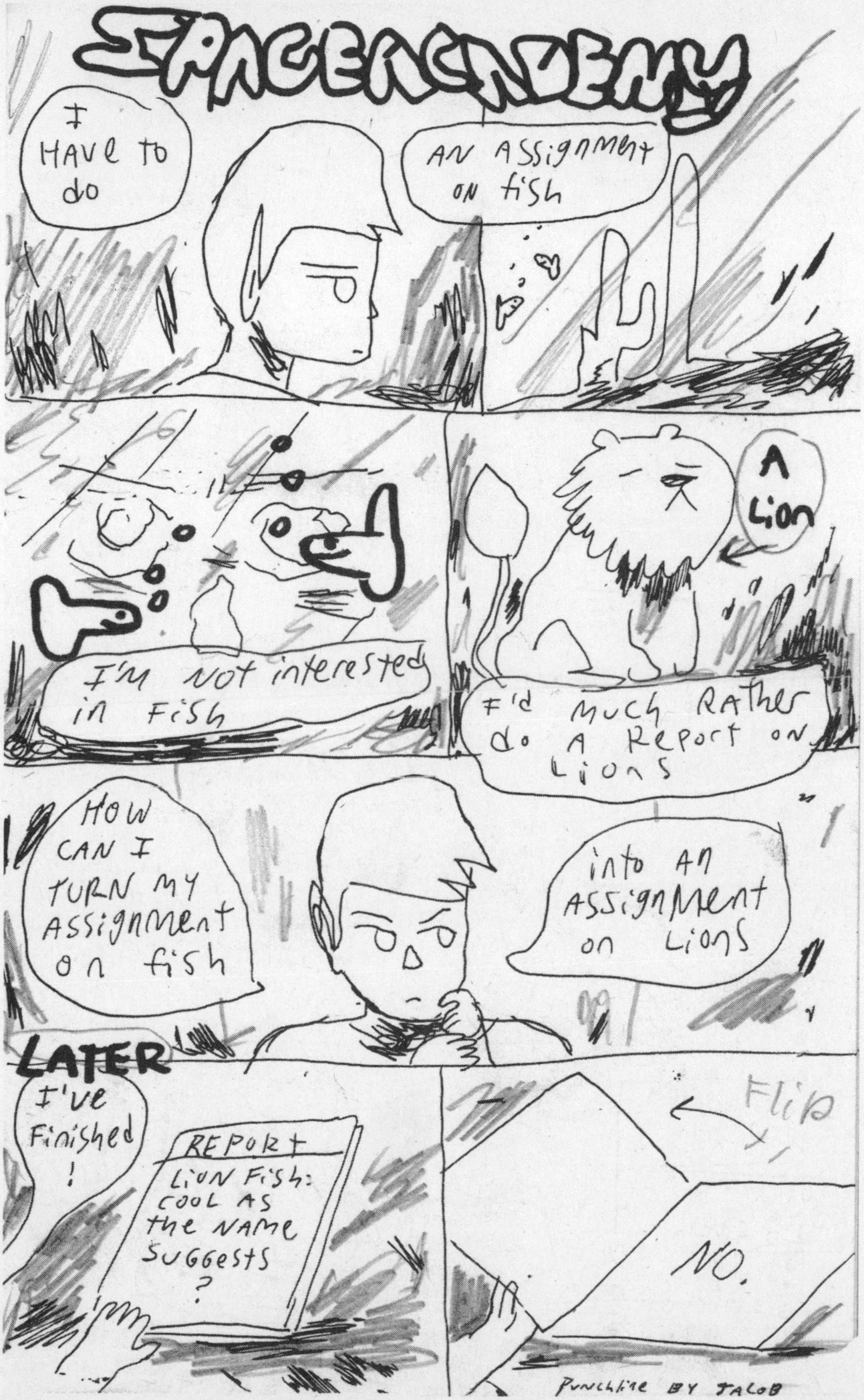
SPACE ACADEMY
I HAVE TO do
AN ASSignment on fish
I'M not interested in Fish
A Lion
I'd much Rather do A Report on Lions
HOW CAN I TURN MY ASSignment on fish
into AN ASSignMent on Lions
LATER
I've Finished!
REPORT
LION Fish: COOL AS the NAME SUGGESTS?
Flip
NO.
Punchline BY JACOB

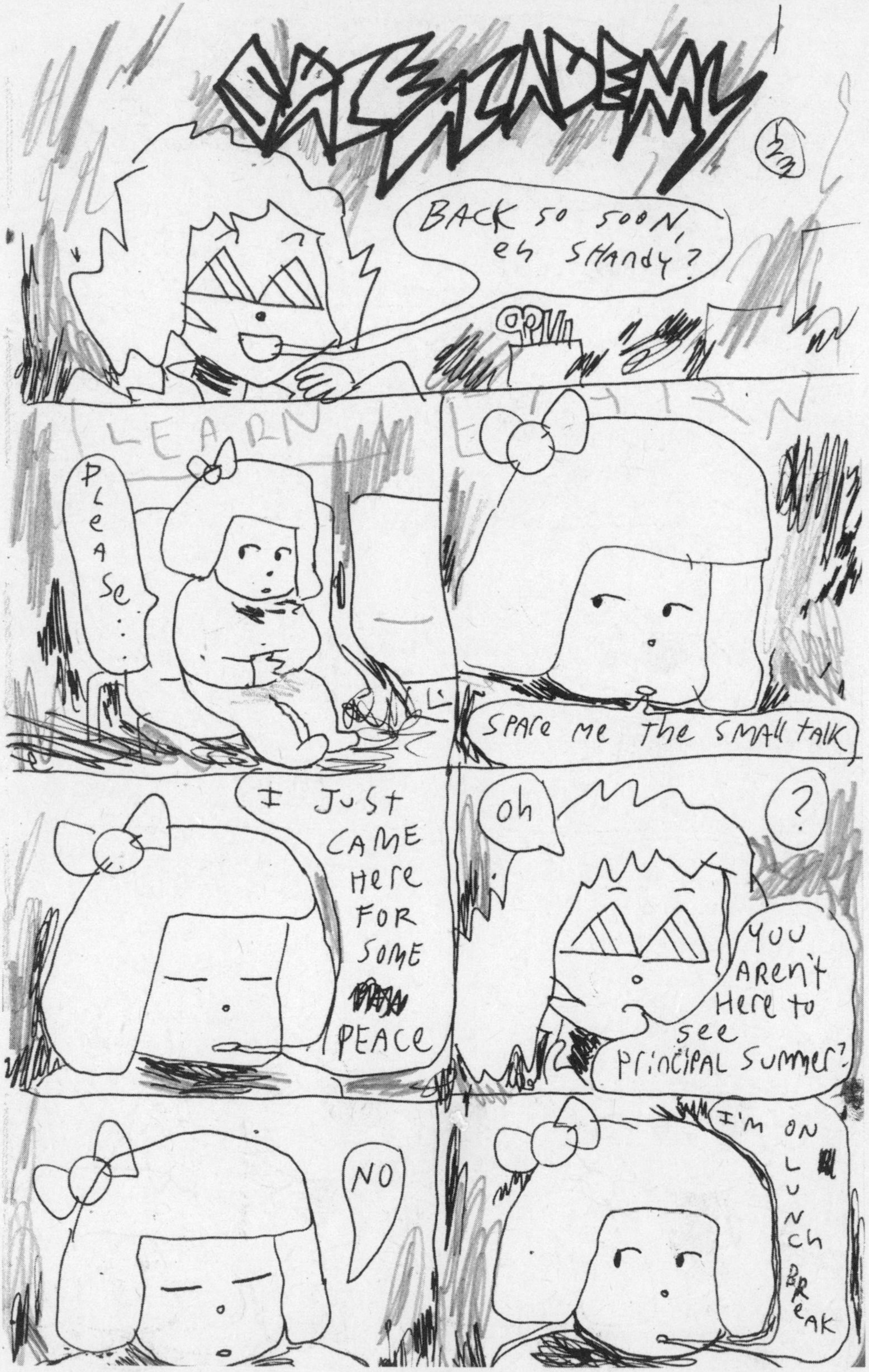
ACADEMY
BACK SO SOON, eh SHANDY?
LEARN
PLEASE...
SPACE ME THE SMALL TALK
I JUST CAME HERE FOR SOME PEACE
oh
?
YOU AREN'T HERE TO SEE PRINCIPAL SUMMER?
NO
I'M ON LUNCH BREAK

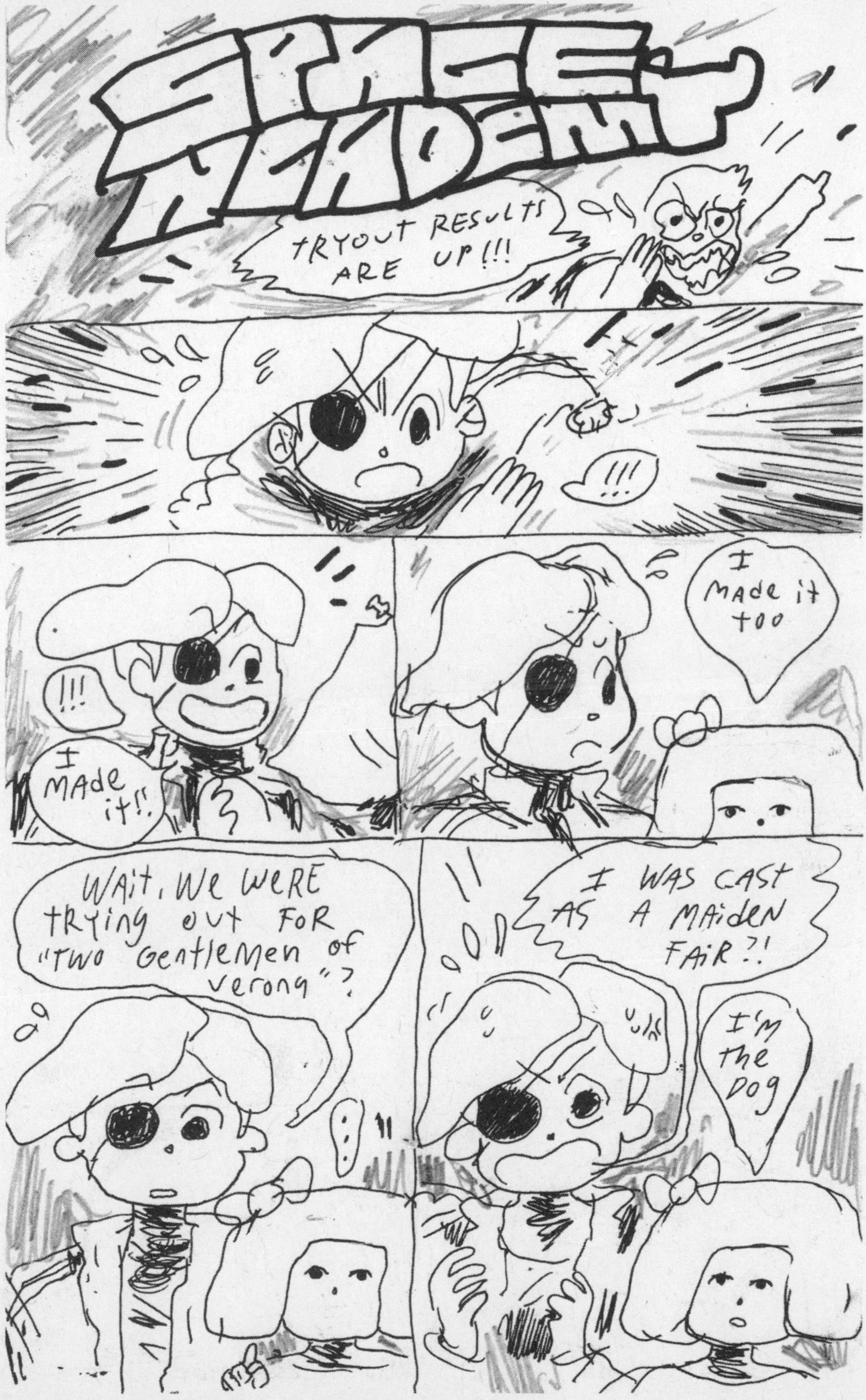
SPACE ACADEMY
TRYOUT RESULTS ARE UP!!!
!!!
!!!
I MADE it!!
I made it too
WAit, We WERE tRying out FOR "Two Gentlemen of verona"?
I WAS CAST AS A MAiden FAiR?!
I'm the Dog

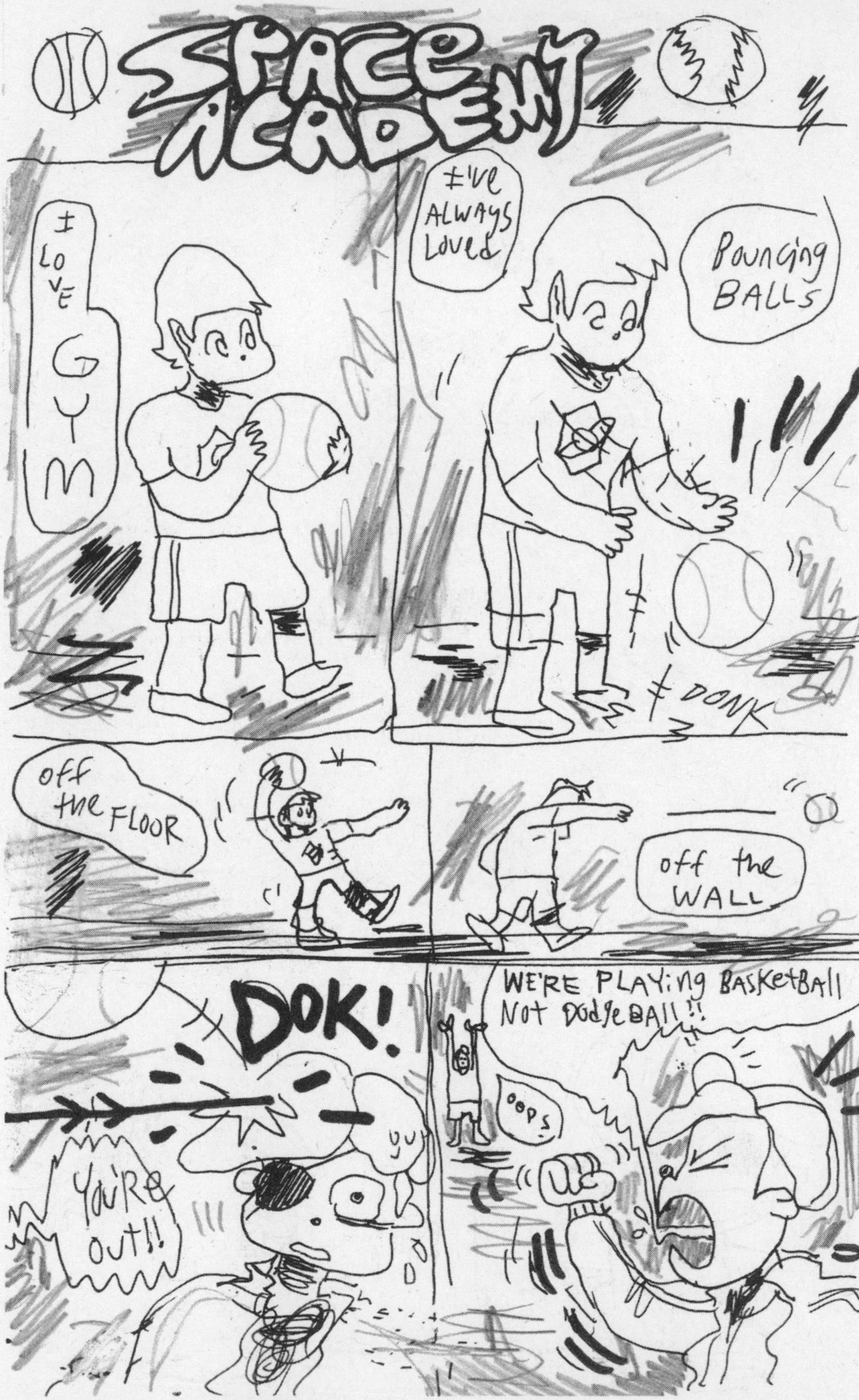

SPACE ACADEMY
I LOVE GYM
I'VE ALWAYS LOVED
BOUNCING BALLS
DONK
off the FLOOR
off the WALL
DOK!
You're out!!
WE'RE PLAYING BASKETBALL NOT DODGEBALL!!
OOPS

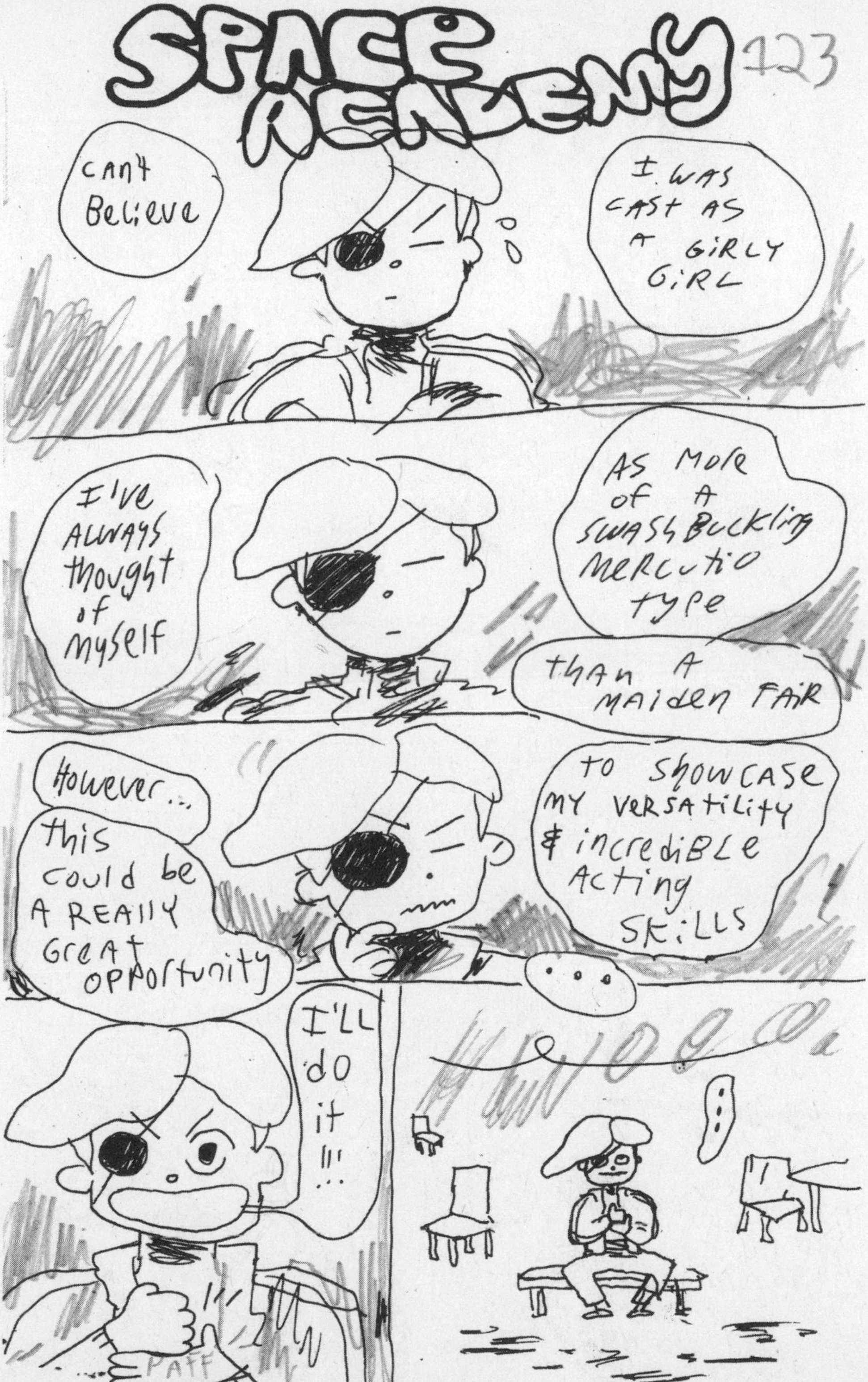
SPACE ACADEMY
123
can't Believe
I was cast as a girly girl
I've always thought of myself
as more of a swashbuckling Mercutio type
than a maiden fair
However...
this could be a really great opportunity
to showcase my versatility & incredible acting skills
...
I'LL do it!!!
PAFF

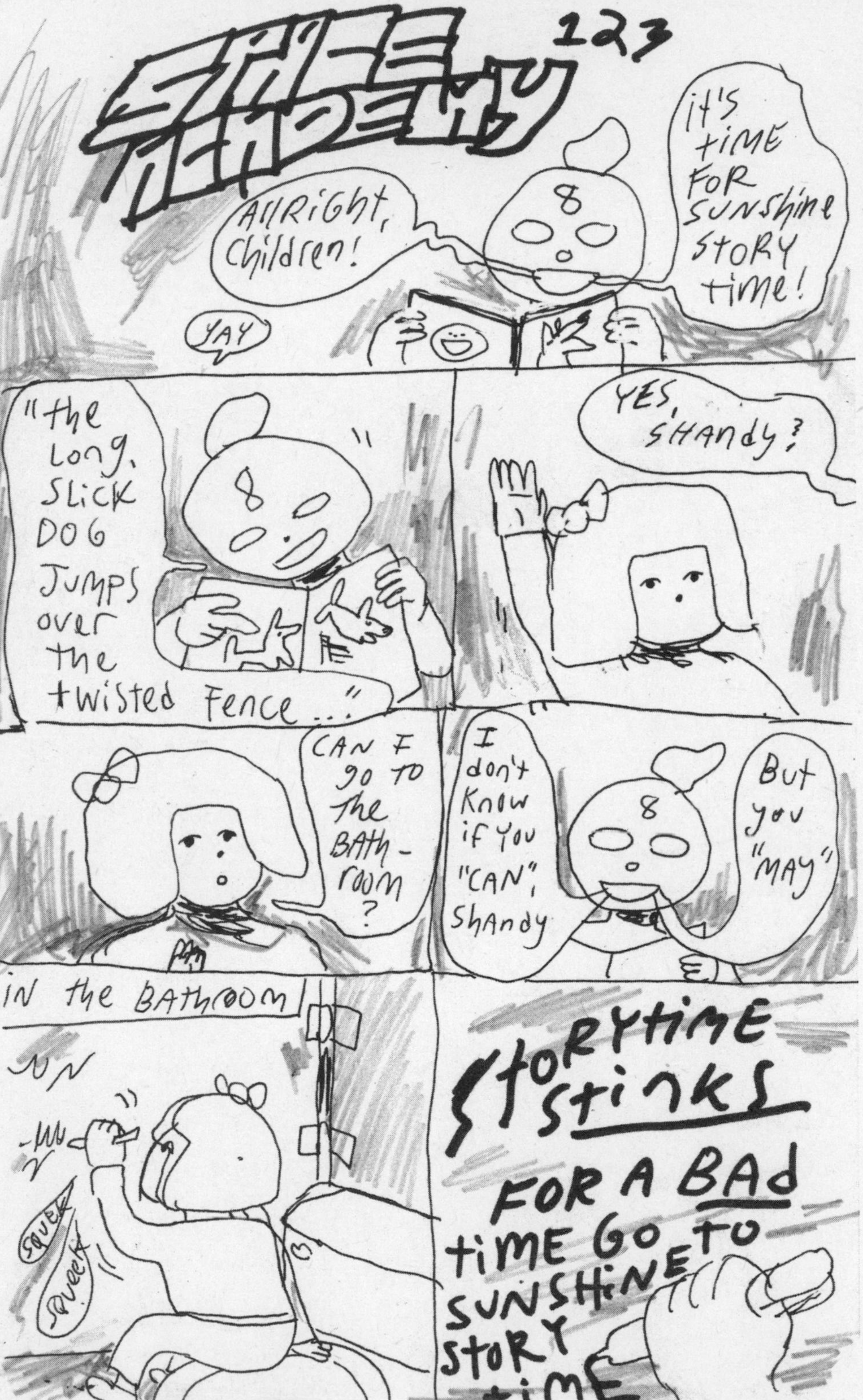
123
AllRight, Children!
it's time FOR SUNShine STORY time!
YAY
"the Long, SLick DOG Jumps over the twisted Fence..."
YES, Shandy?
CAN I go to the BATH-room?
I don't Know if You "CAN", Shandy
But you "MAY"
IN the BATHROOM
SQUEEK
SQUEEK
STORYTIME STINKS
FOR A BAD time GO TO SUNSHINE STORY time

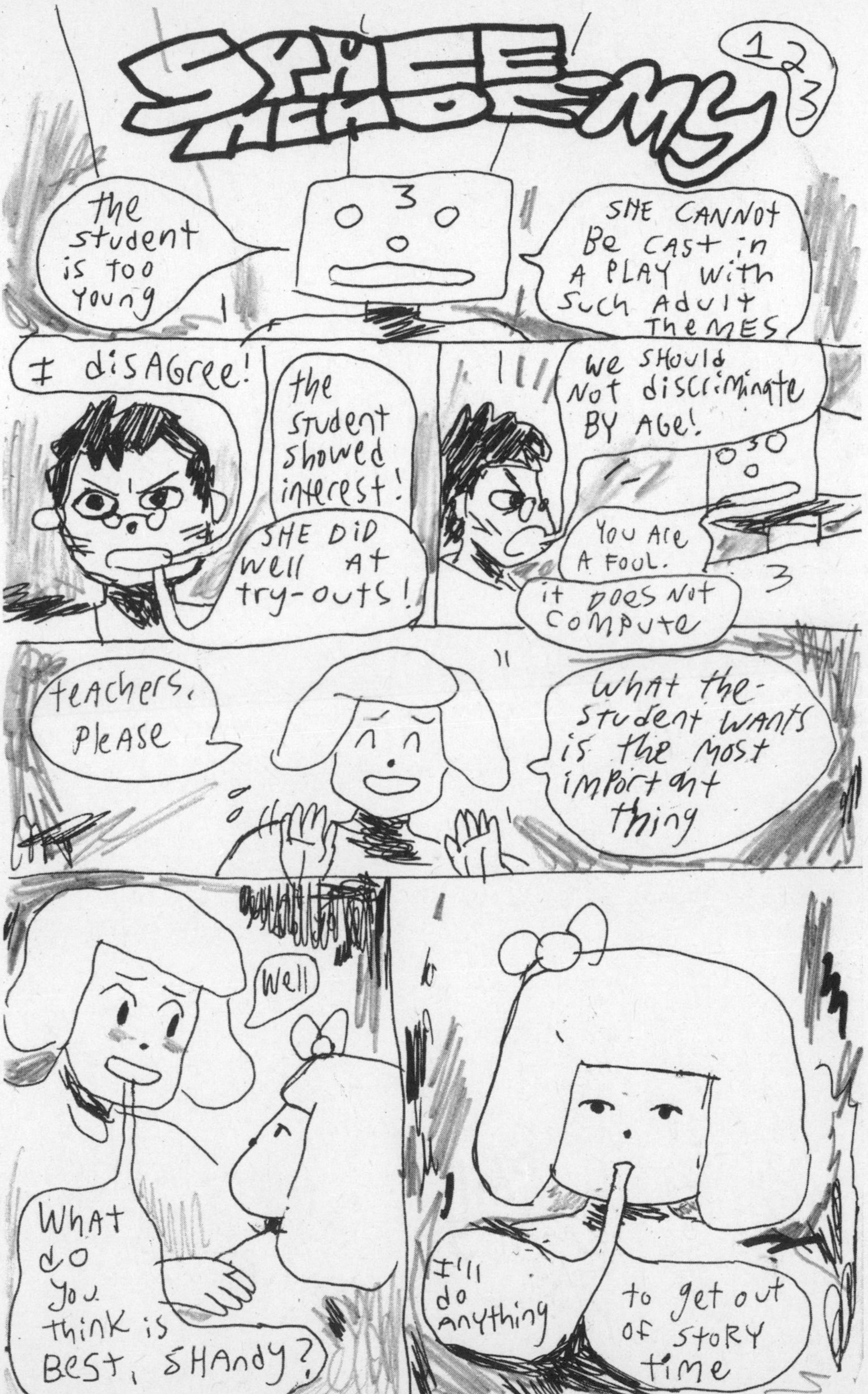
the student is too young
SHE CANNOT Be CAST in A PLAY with Such Adult THEMES
I disAGree!
the student showed interest!
SHE DID well AT try-outs!
we SHould not discriminate BY AGe!
You Are A FOOL.
it DOES NOT COMPUTE
teachers. please
What the student wants is the most important thing
Well
What do you think is Best, SHAndy?
I'll do anything to get out of STORY time

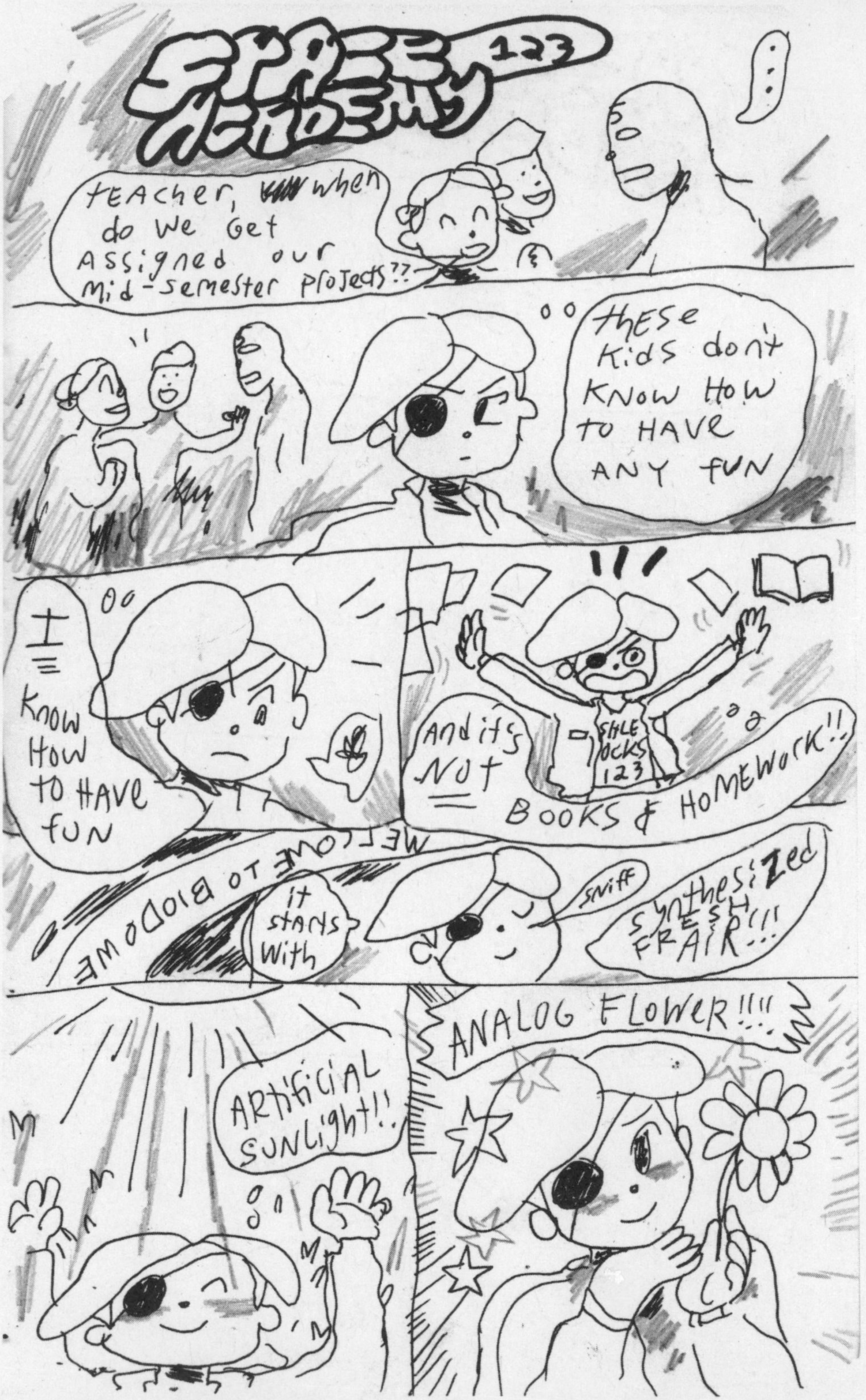
SPACE ACADEMY 123
...
teacher, when do we get assigned our mid-semester projects??
these kids don't know how to have any fun
I know how to have fun
And it's NOT books & homework!!
WELCOME TO BIODOME
it starts with
SNIFF
synthesiZed FRESH AIR!!!
ARTIFICIAL SUNLIGHT!!
ANALOG FLOWER!!!!

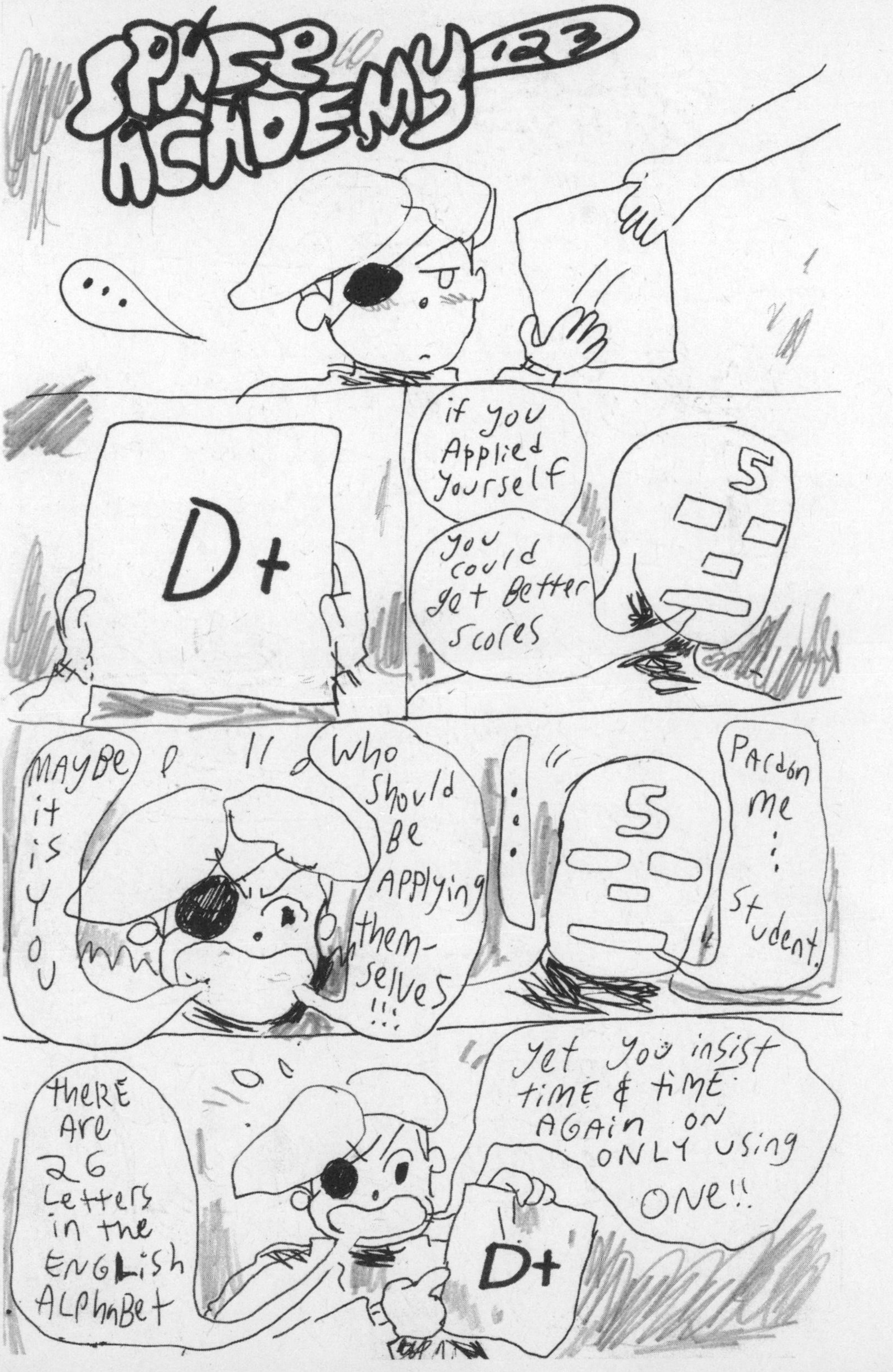
SPACE ACADEMY 123
...
if you Applied yourself
you could get Better scores
MAYBE it is YOU
Who Should Be Applying them-selves!!!
...
Pardon me... student.
there Are 26 Letters in the ENGLish AlphaBet
yet you insist time & time AGAIN ON ONLY using ONE!!
D+

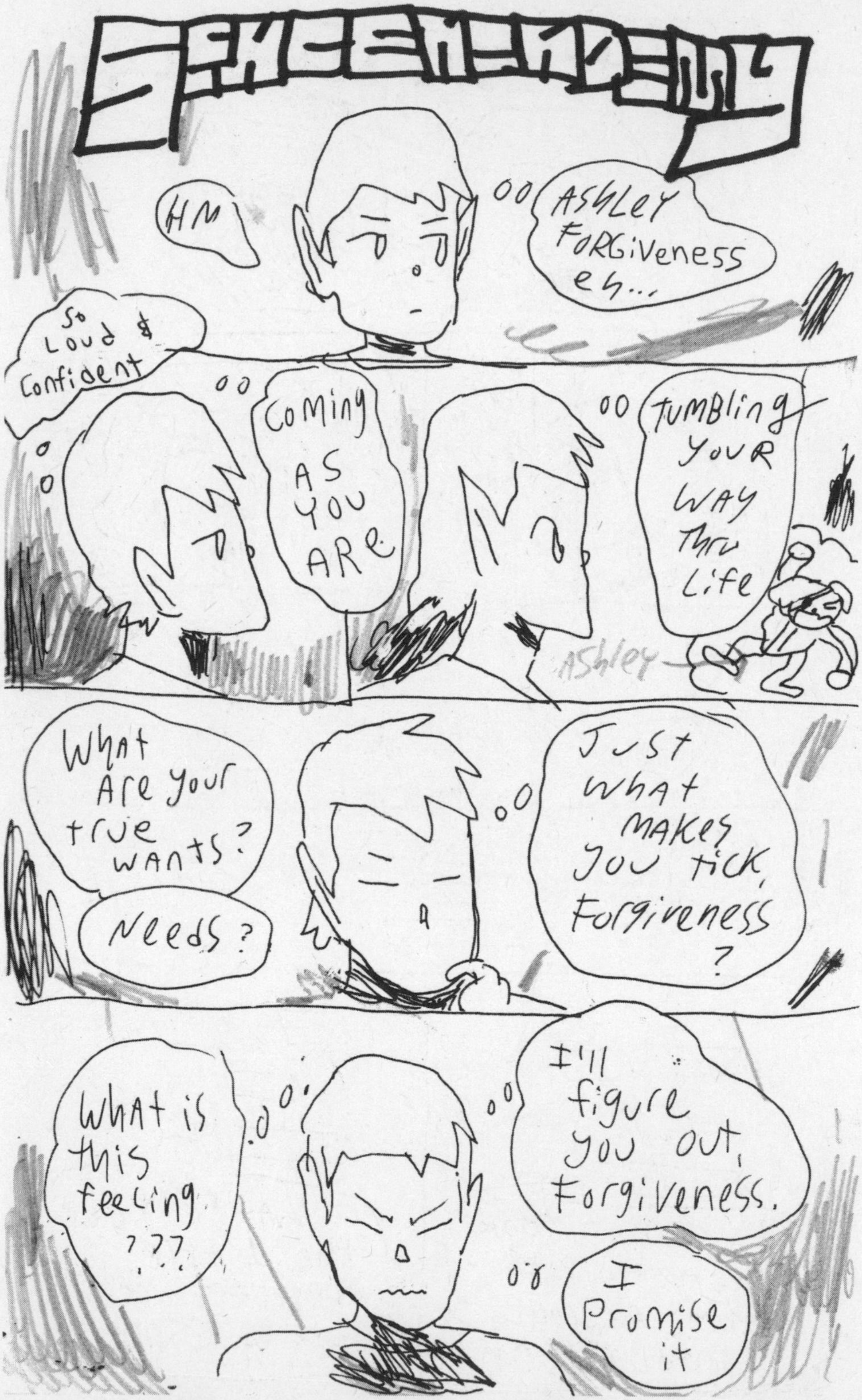
HM
Ashley Forgiveness eh...
So Loud & Confident
Coming As You Are
Tumbling your way thru Life
Ashley
What Are your true wants?
Needs?
Just what makes you tick, Forgiveness ?
What is this feeling ???
I'll figure you out, Forgiveness.
I Promise it

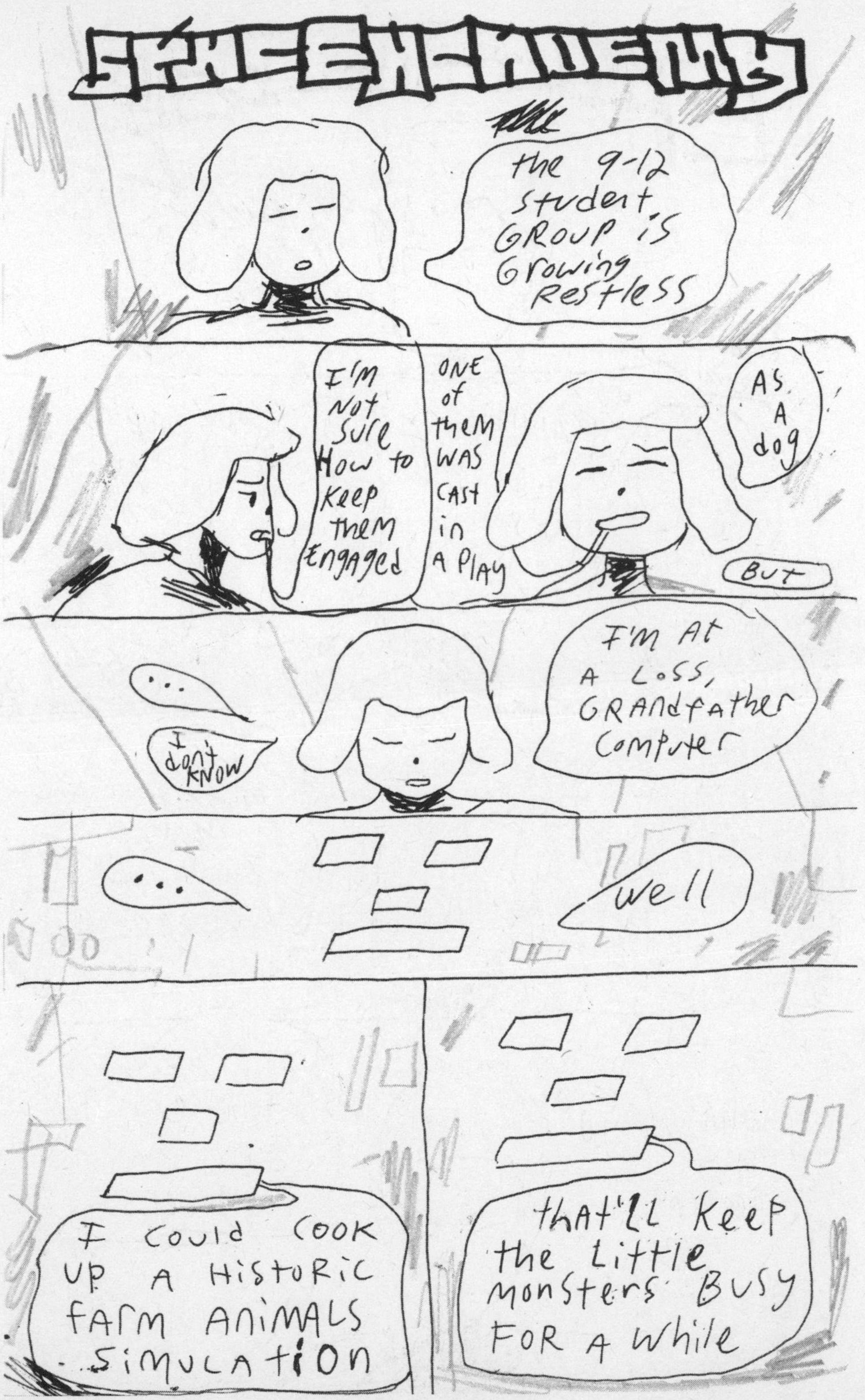
SPACE ACADEMY
the 9-12 student GROUP is Growing Restless
I'M not sure How to keep them engaged
ONE of them WAS CAST in A PLAY
AS A dog
BUT
...
I don't KNOW
I'M At A LOSS, GRANDfather Computer
...
well
I could cook up A HISTORIC farm Animals simulation
that'll keep the little monsters Busy FOR A while

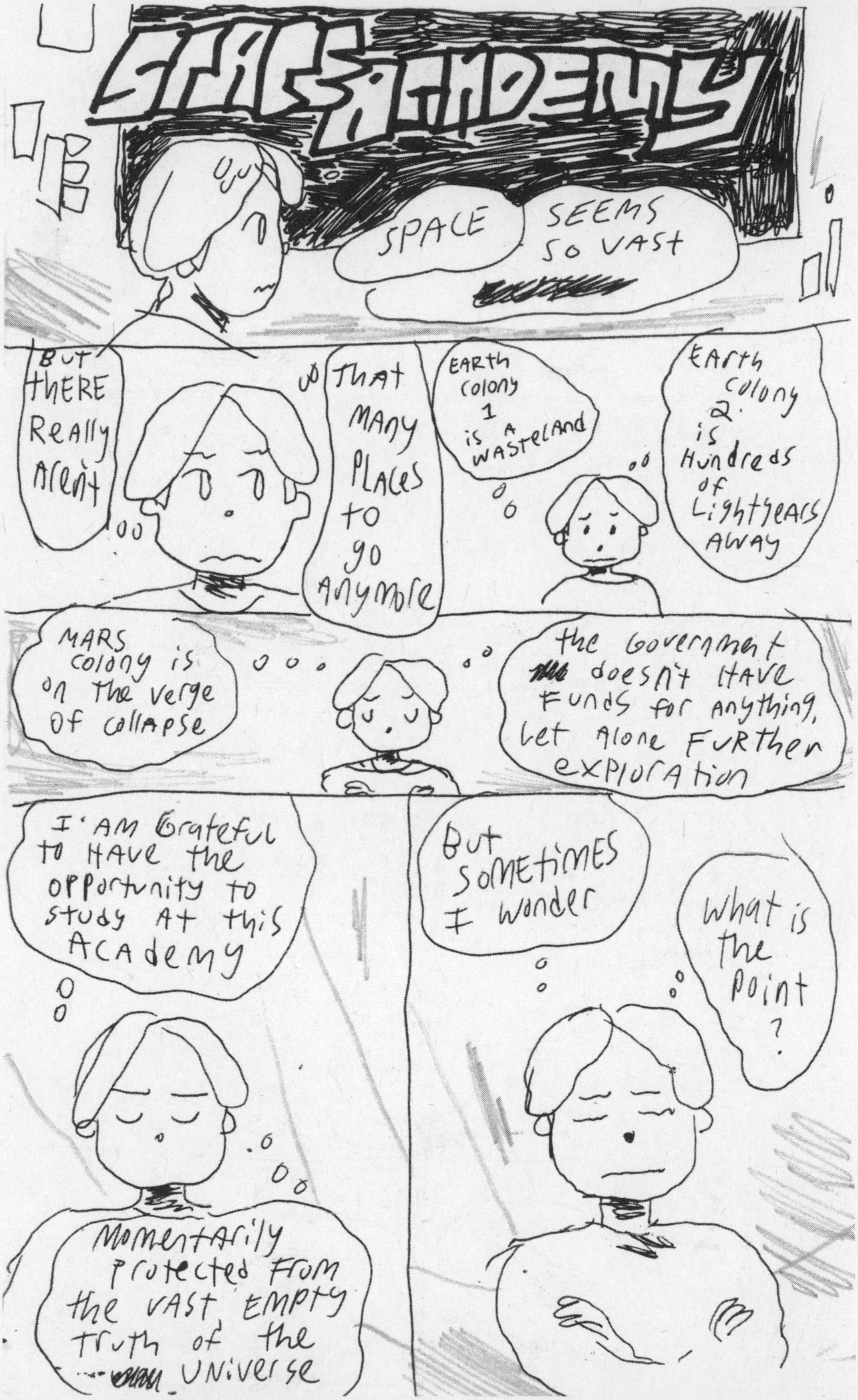
SPACE ACADEMY
SPACE SEEMS SO VAST
BUT THERE Really Aren't
That MANY PLACES to go Anymore
EARTH colony 1 is A WASTELAND
EARTH colony 2 is Hundreds of Lightyears AWAY
MARS colony is on the verge of collapse
the Government doesn't HAVE Funds for anything, Let Alone FURther exploration
I'AM Grateful to HAVE the opportunity to study At this ACAdemy
Momentarily protected From the VAST EMPTY Truth of the UNIVERSE
But SOMETIMES I wonder
What is the Point ?

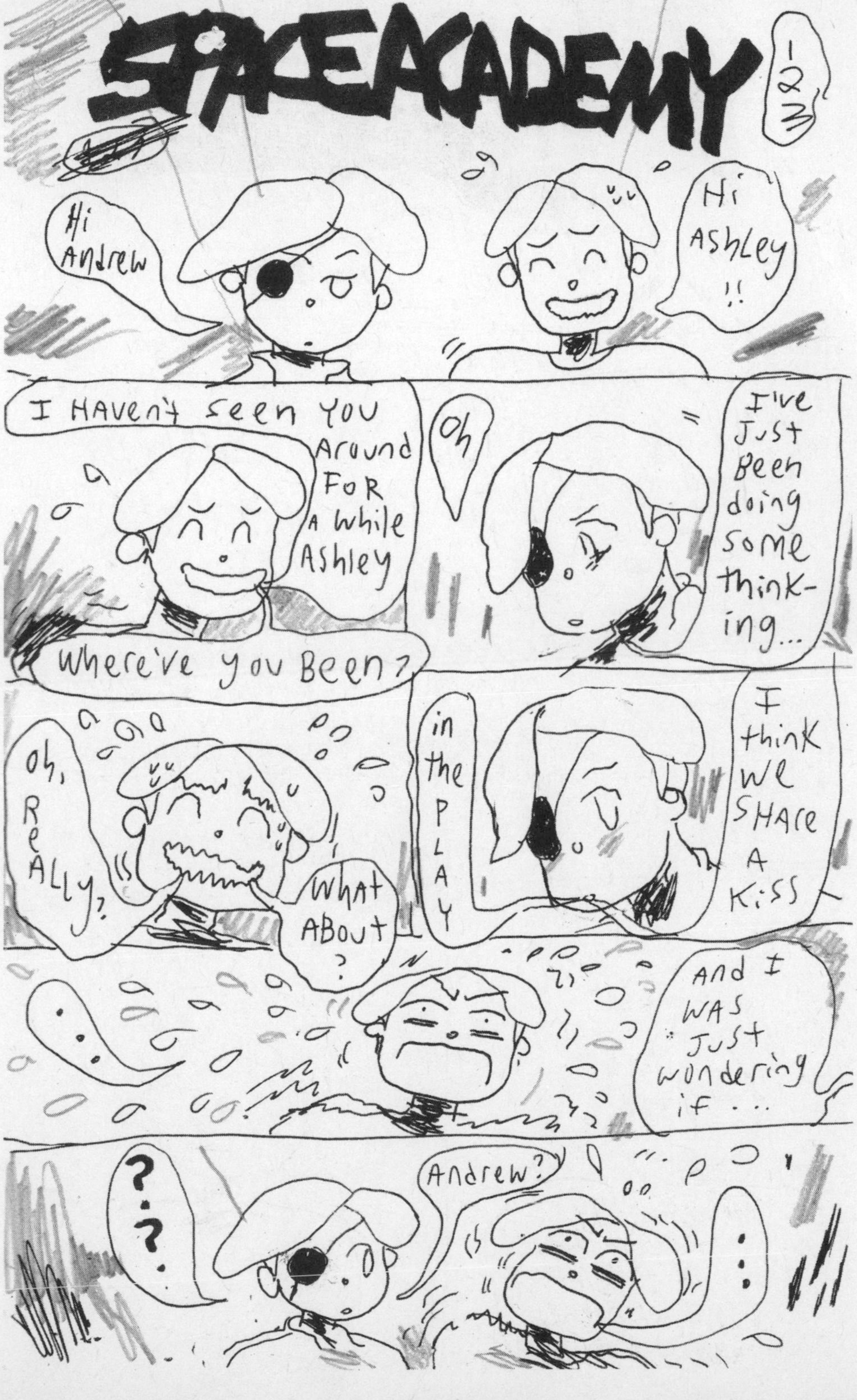SPACE ACADEMY
123
Hi Andrew
Hi Ashley !!
I HAVEN't seen YOU Around FOR A while Ashley
Where've you Been?
Oh
I've Just Been doing some think-ing...
Oh, ReALLy?
What ABOUT ?
in the PLAY
I think we SHARE A KiSS
...
And I WAS Just wondering if...
??
Andrew?
...

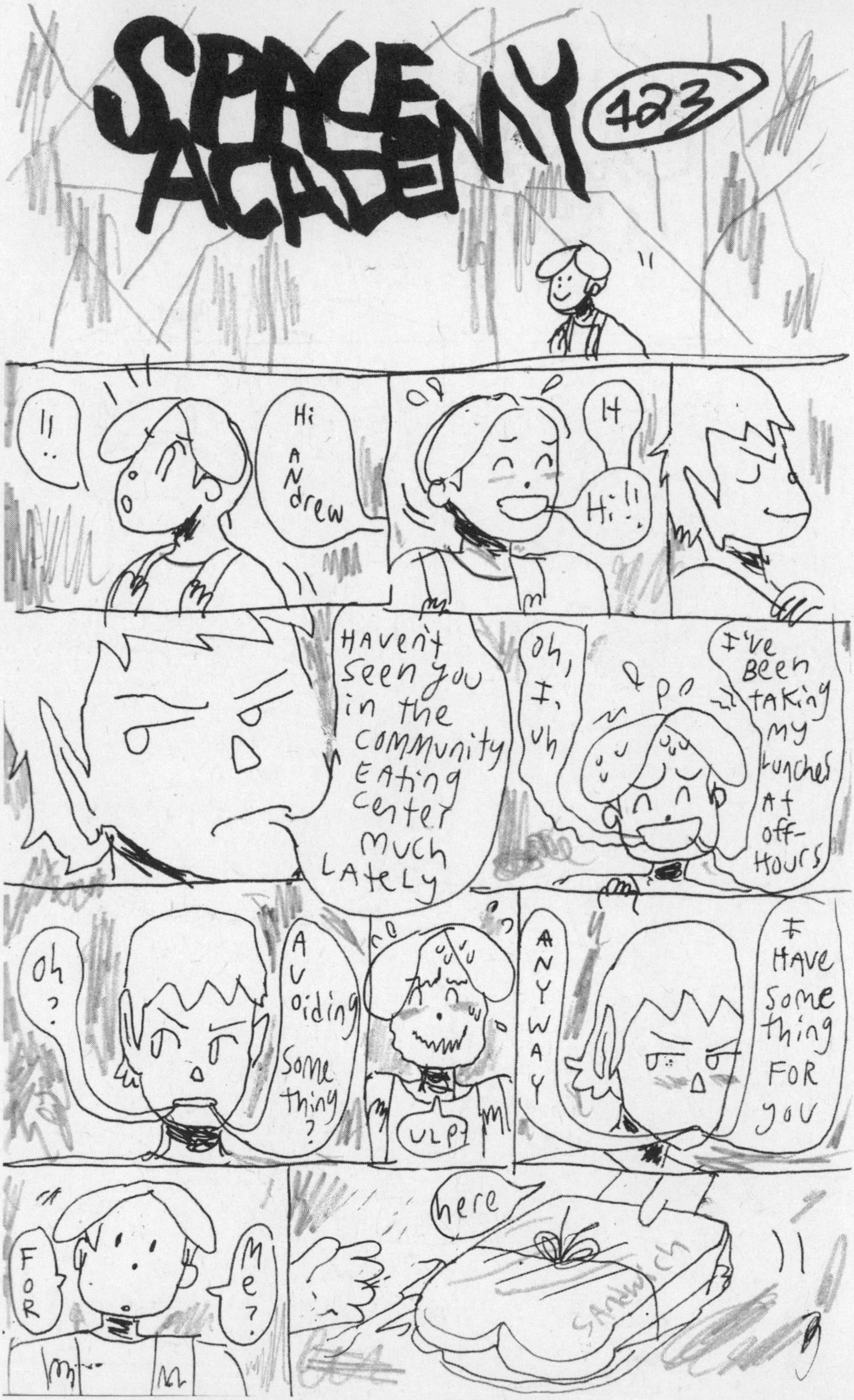
SPACE ACADEMY
123
!!
Hi Andrew
H
Hi!!
Haven't seen you in the community eating center much lately
Oh, I, uh
I've been taking my lunches at off-hours
Oh?
Avoiding something?
ULP
Anyway
I have something for you
For
Me?
here
Sandwich

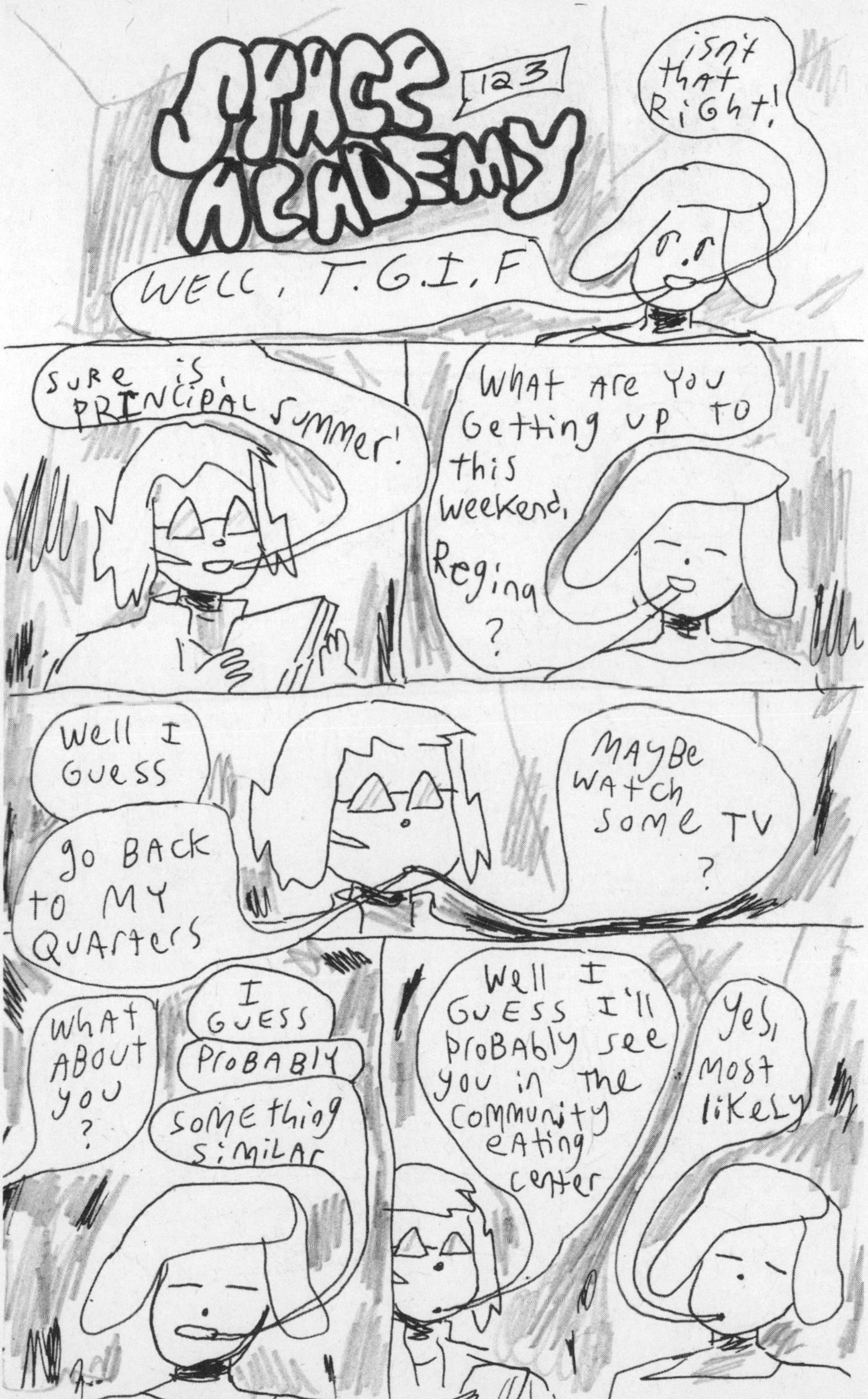
SPACE ACADEMY
123
WELL, T.G.I.F
isn't that Right!
Sure is, PRINCIPAL Summer!
What are you Getting up to this weekend, Regina ?
Well I Guess
go BACK to MY Quarters
MAYBE WATCH SOME TV ?
What ABOUT you ?
I GUESS
PROBABLY
SOMEthing SiMiLAR
Well I GUESS I'll probably see you in the community eating center
Yes, Most likely

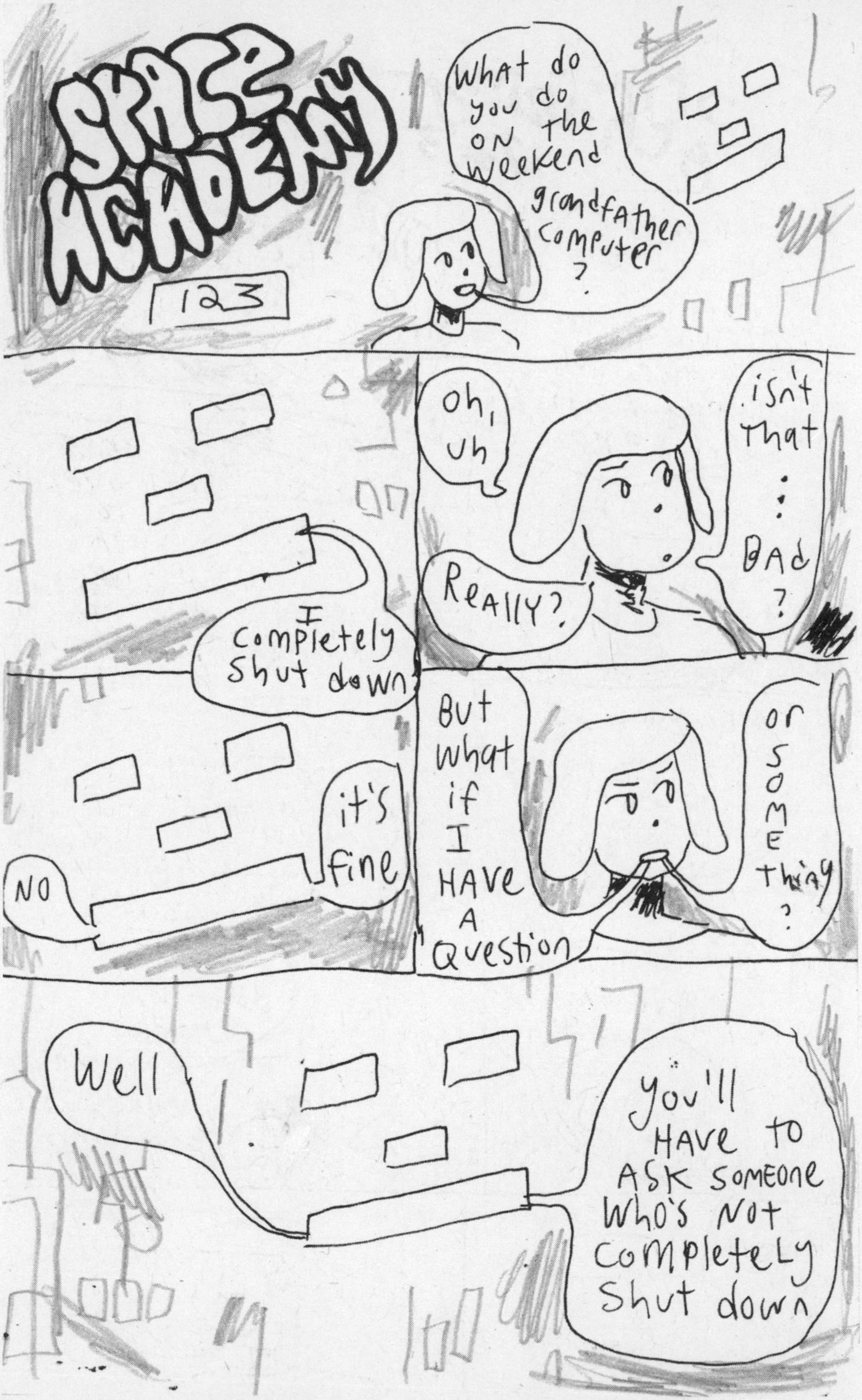
SPACE ACADEMY
123
What do you do ON the weekend grandfather computer?
I completely shut down
Oh, uh
Really?
isn't That ... BAD?
NO
it's fine
But what if I HAVE A Question
or SOMEthing?
Well
You'll HAVE to ASK Someone Who's Not completeLy Shut down

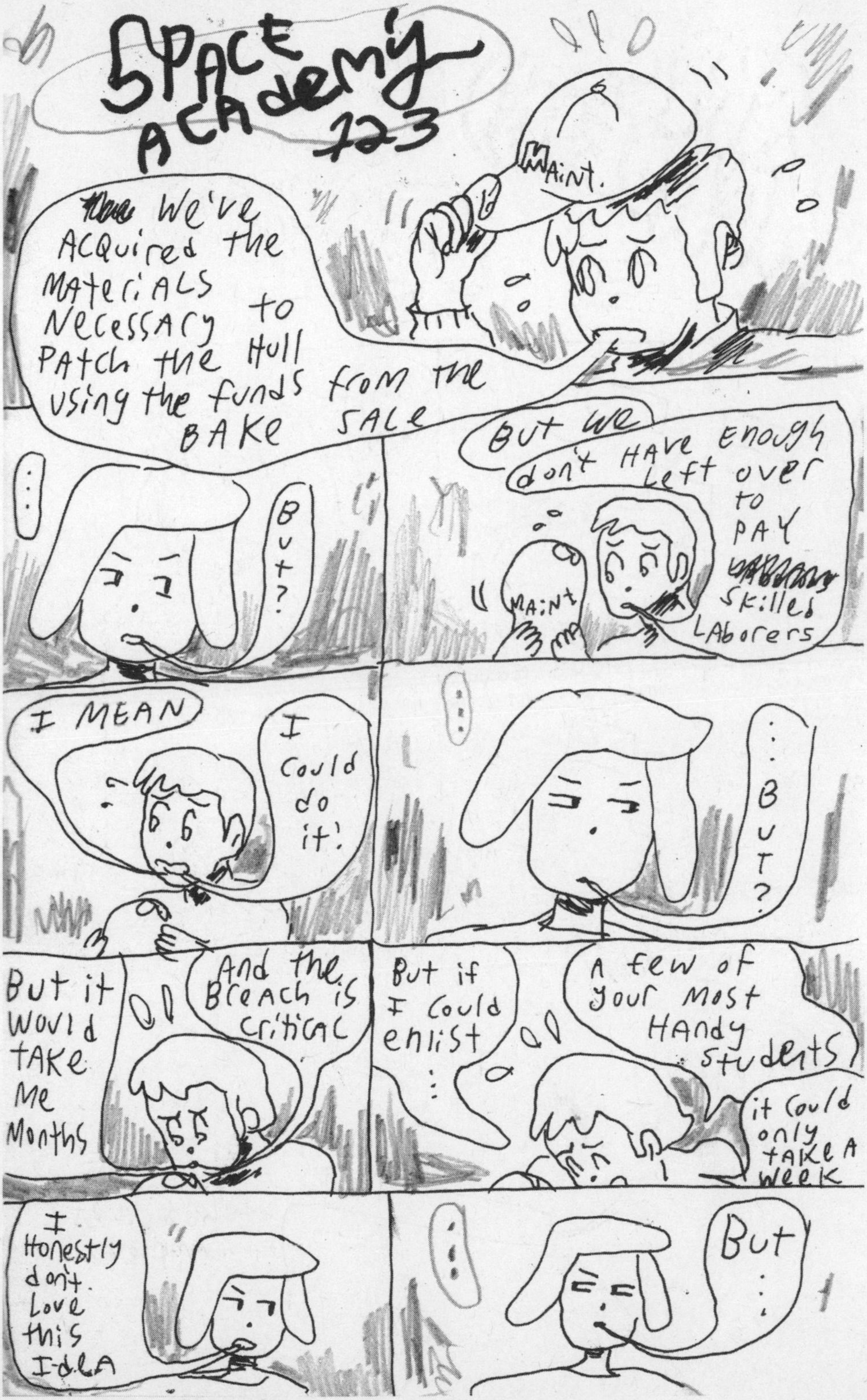

Space Academy 723
We've Acquired the Materials Necessary to Patch the Hull using the funds from the Bake Sale
...
But?
But we don't have enough left over to pay skilled laborers
MAINT.
MAINT
I MEAN
I could do it!
...
...But?
But it would take me months
And the Breach is critical
But if I could enlist
...
A few of your most Handy students
it could only take a week
I Honestly don't love this Idea
...
But...

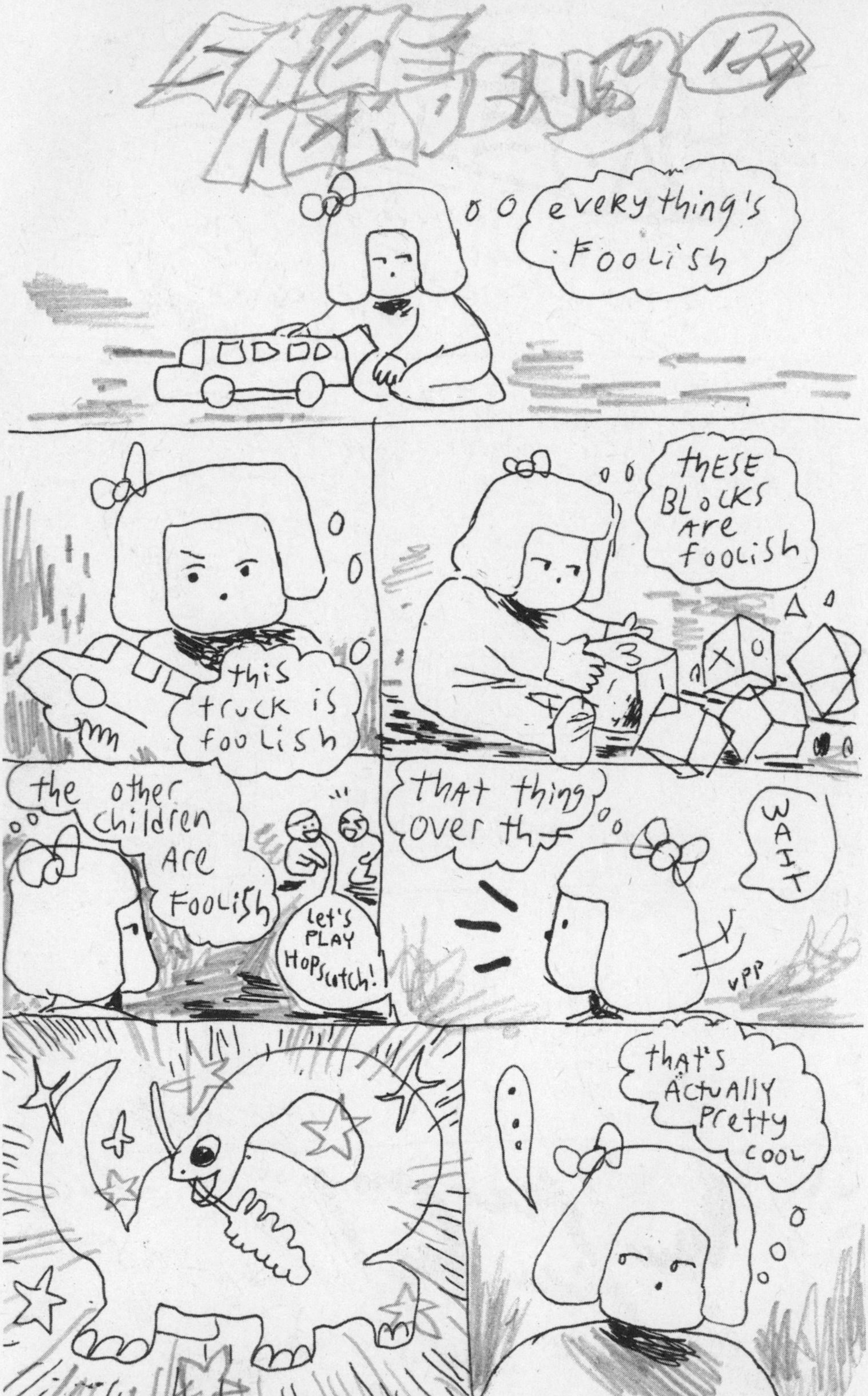

everything's Foolish
this truck is foolish
these BLocks are foolish
the other children Are Foolish
let's PLAY HOPSCOTCH!
that thing over th—
WAIT
vPP
that's ACtually Pretty COOL

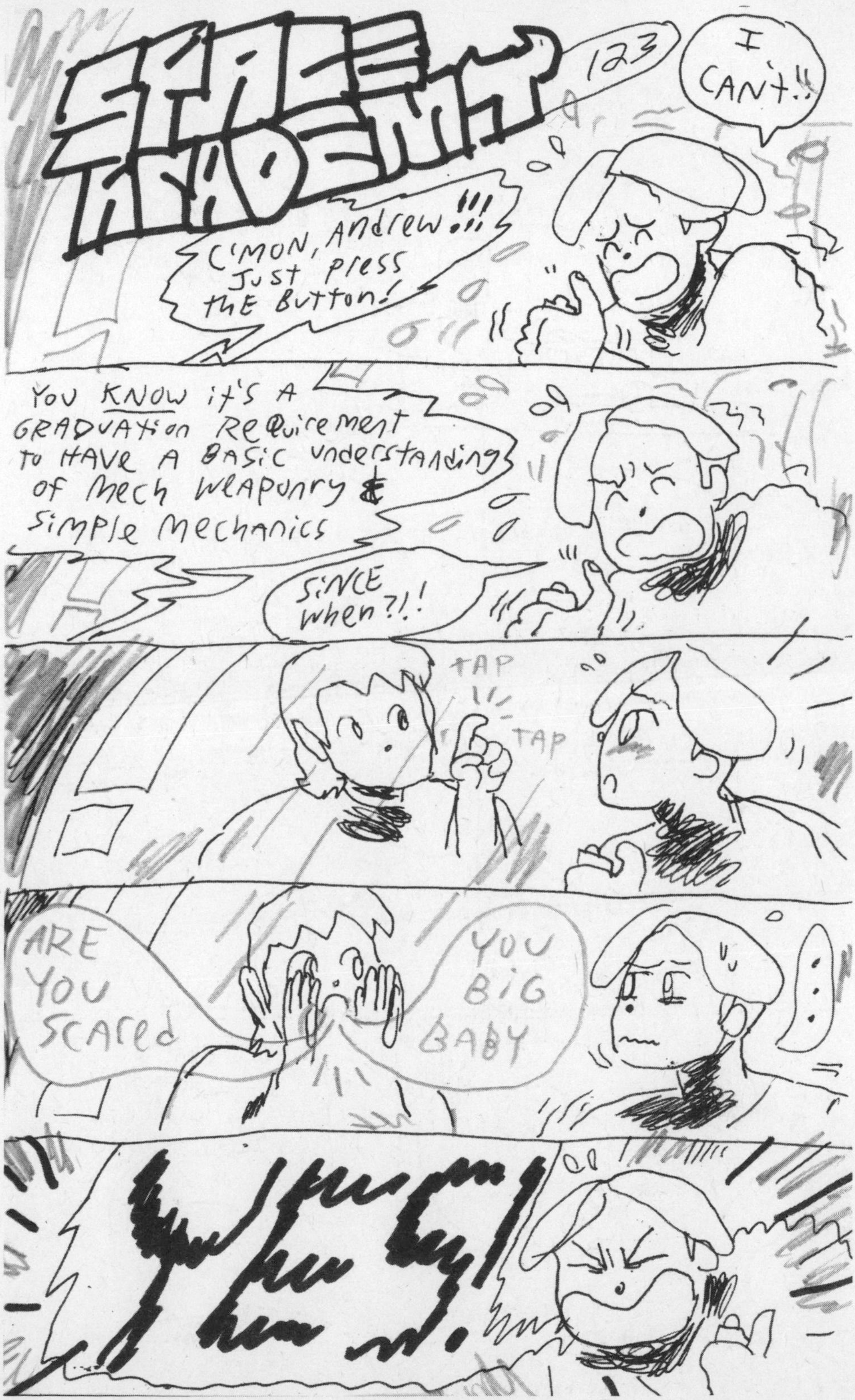
123
I CAN'T!!
C'MON, Andrew!!! Just press the Button!
YOU KNOW it's A GRADUATion Requirement to HAVE A BASIC understanding of Mech weaponry & simple mechanics
SINCE when?!!
TAP
TAP
ARE YOU Scared
YOU BIG BABY
. . .

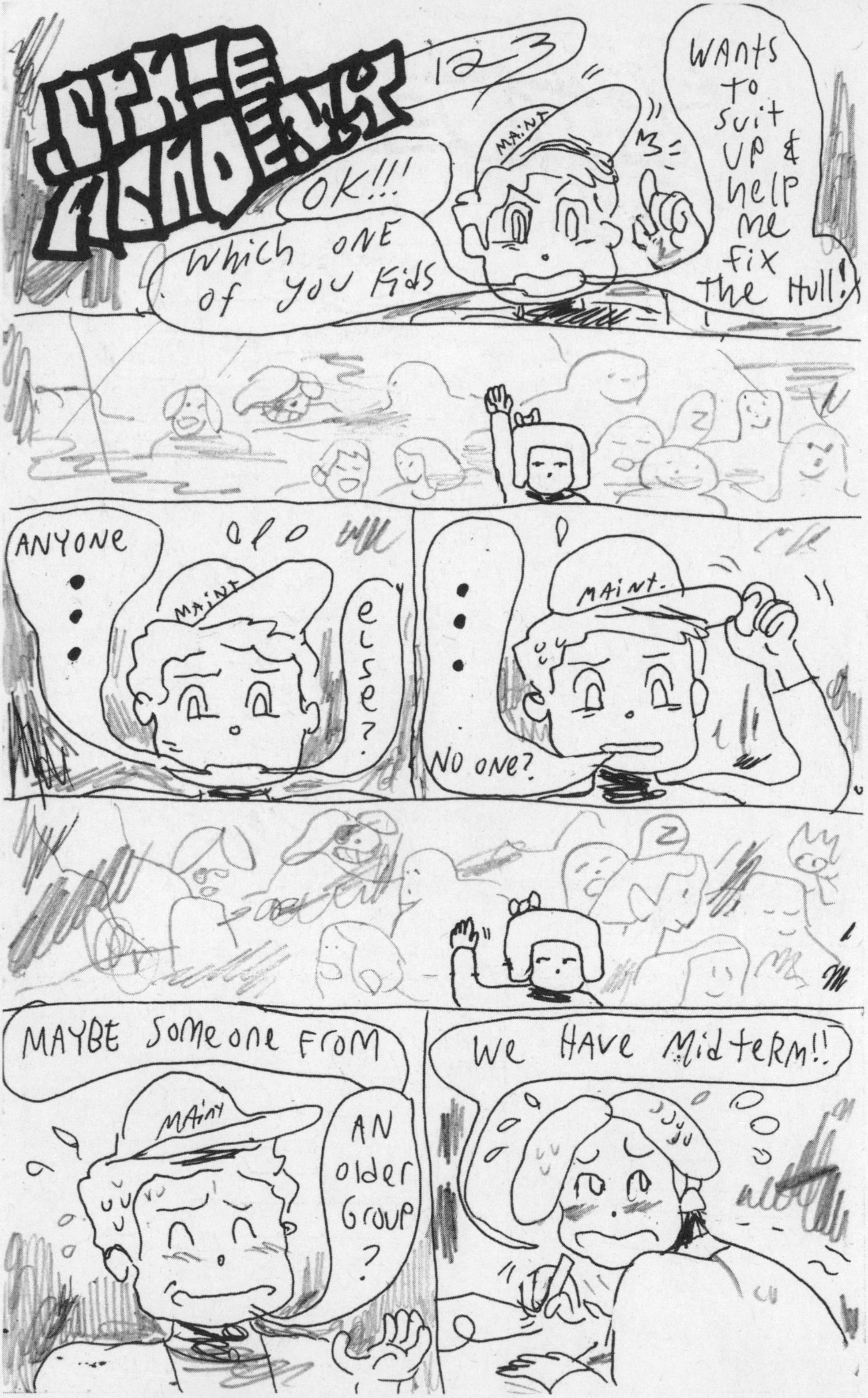
1 2 3
OK!!!
Which ONE of you Kids wants to suit up & help me fix the Hull!
ANYONE ... else?
... NO one?
MAYBE Someone FROM AN older Group?
We HAVE MidTeRM!!

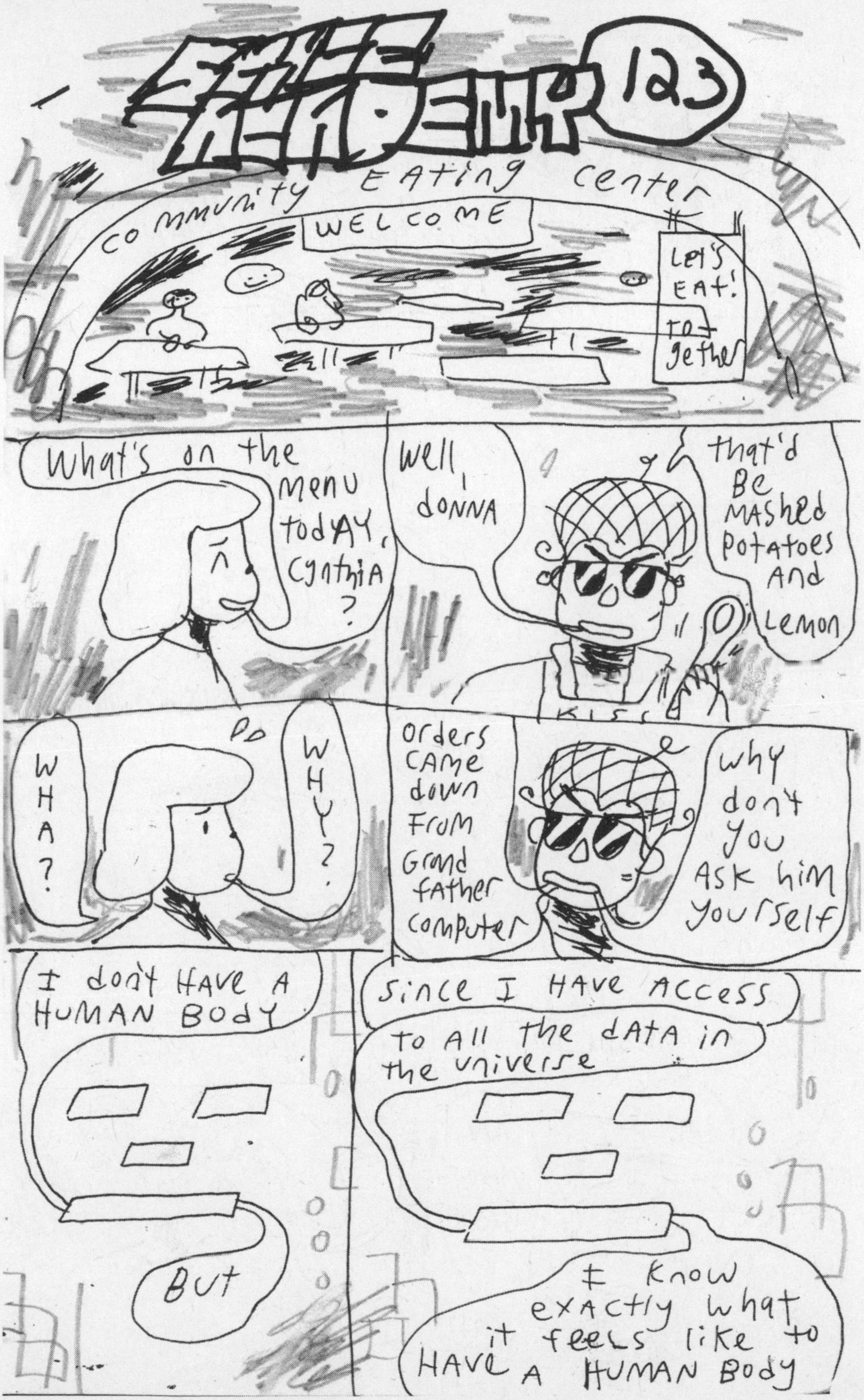
123
community eating center
WELCOME
Let's eat! together
What's on the menu today, Cynthia?
Well, Donna
that'd be mashed potatoes and lemon
KISS
WHA?
WHY?
orders came down from Grand Father computer
why don't you ask him yourself
I don't have a human body
But
since I have access to all the data in the universe
I know exactly what it feels like to have a human body

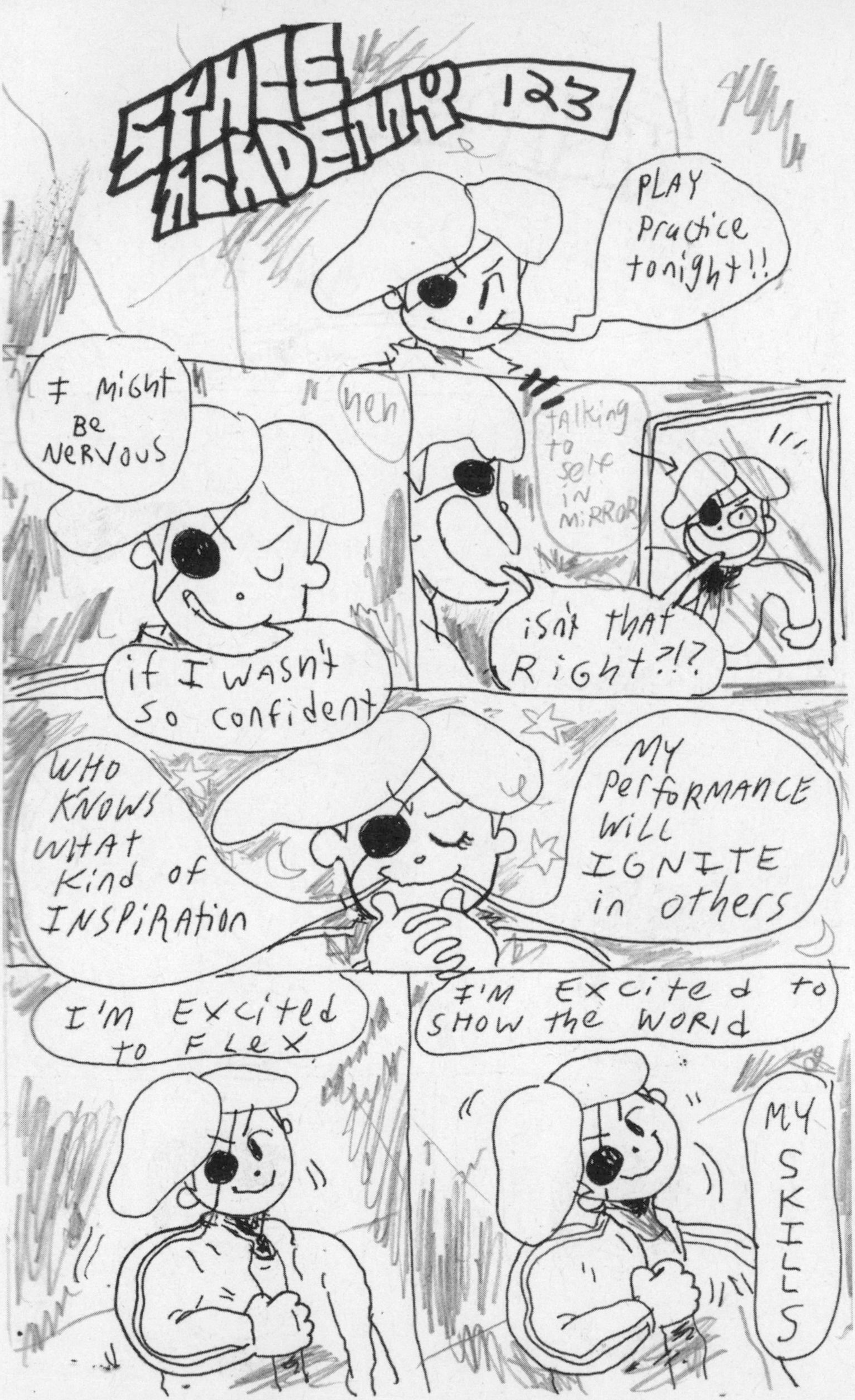
123
PLAY practice tonight!!
I might Be Nervous
if I wasn't so confident
heh
talking to self in mirror
isn't that Right?!?
WHO KNOWS WHAT Kind of INSPIRATION
MY performance will IGNITE in others
I'M Excited to FLEX
I'M Excited to SHOW the WORld
MY SKILLS

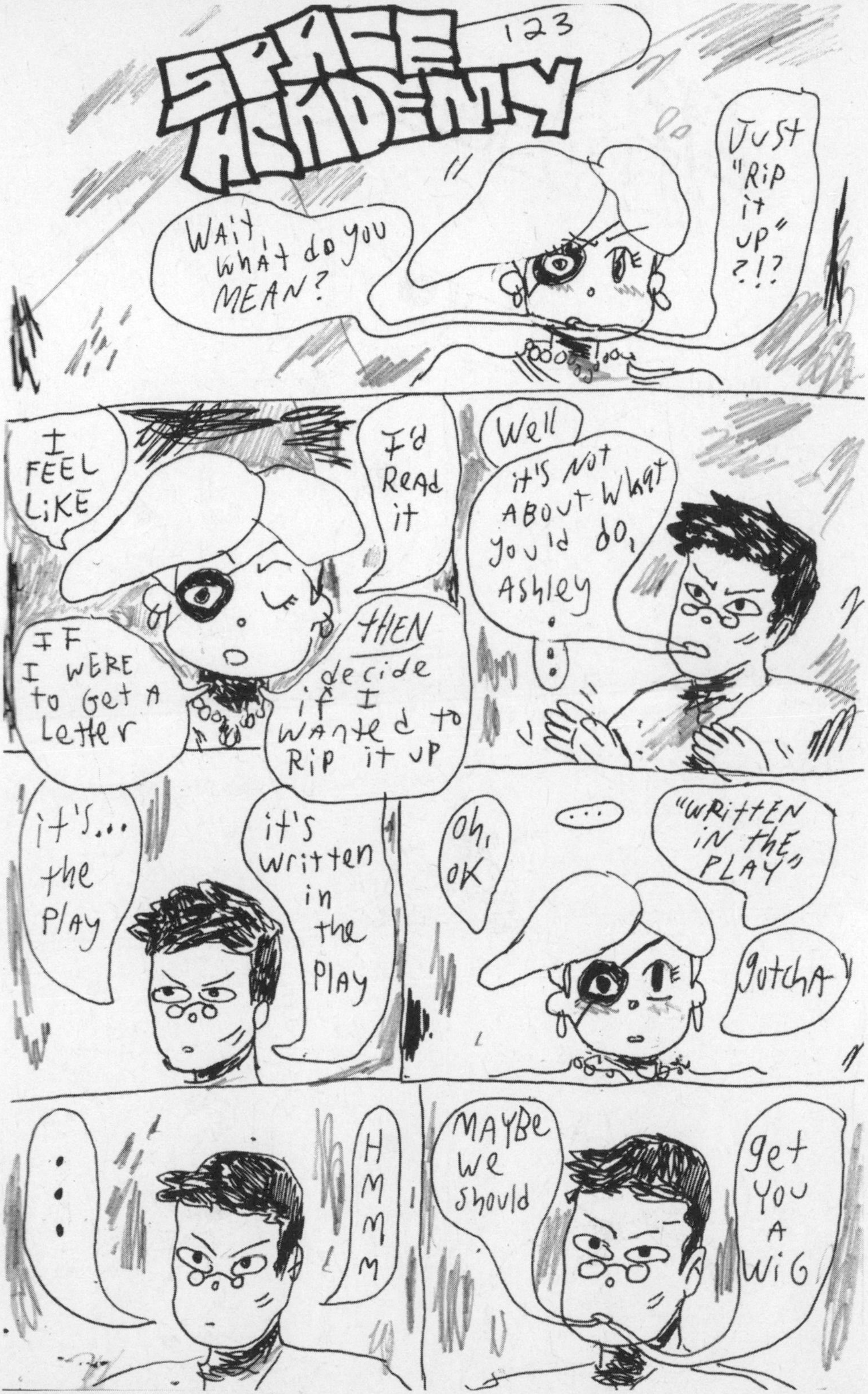
SPACE ACADEMY
123
Wait what do you MEAN?
Just "Rip it up" ?!?
I FEEL LiKE
I'd Read it
IF I WERE to get A Letter
THEN decide if I wanted to Rip it up
Well
it's not ABOUT what you'd do, Ashley
:
it's... the PLAY
it's written in the PLAY
Oh, ok
...
"written in the PLAY"
gotchA
...
HMMMM
MAYBe we should
get you A WiG

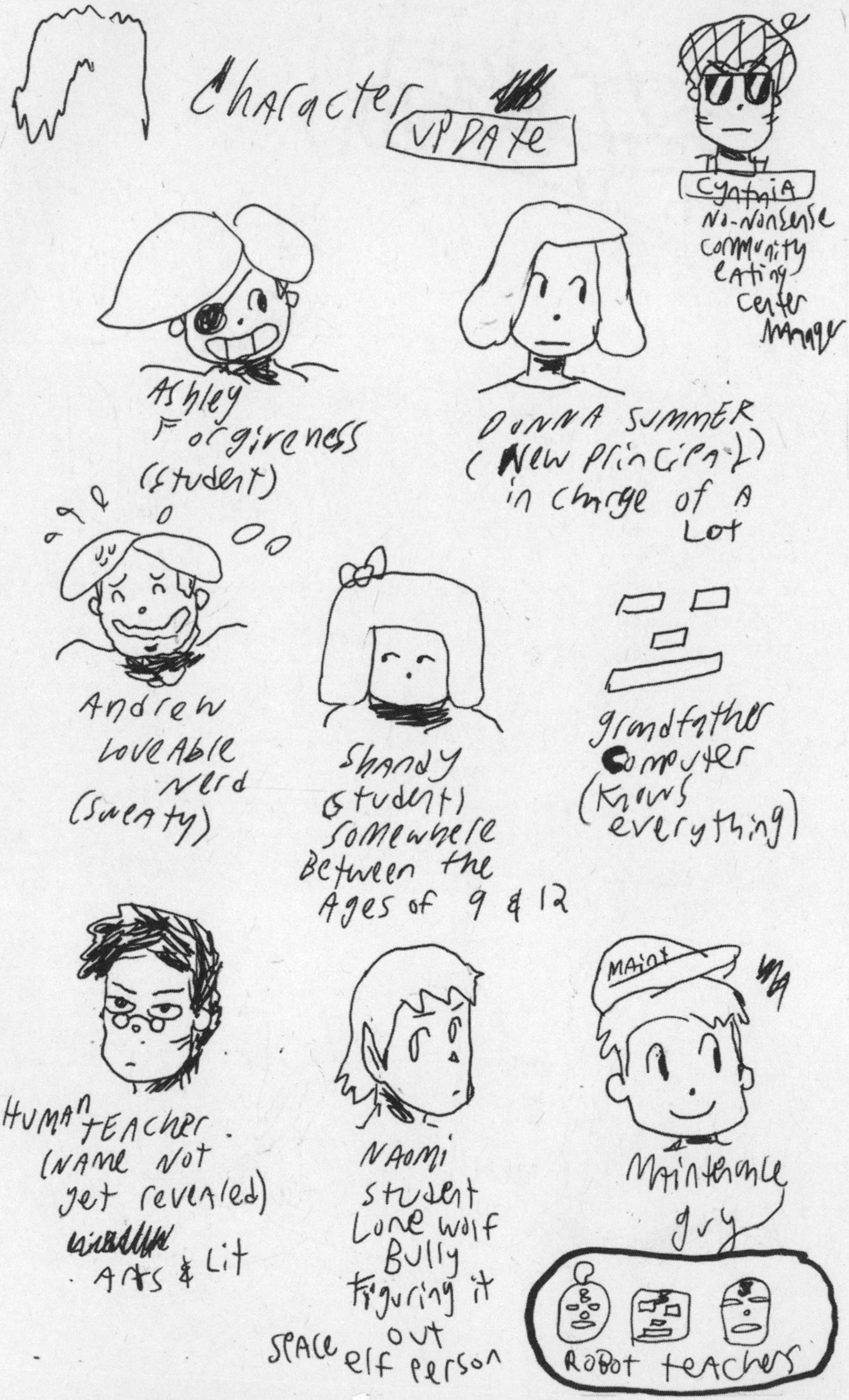
Character
UPDATE
Cynthia
No-nonsense community eating center manager
Ashley Forgiveness (student)
Donna Summer (New principal) in charge of a lot
Andrew loveable nerd (sweaty)
Shandy (student) somewhere between the ages of 9 & 12
grandfather computer (knows everything)
Human teacher (name not yet revealed) Arts & Lit
Naomi student lone wolf Bully figuring it out space elf person
MAINT
Maintenance guy
Robot teachers

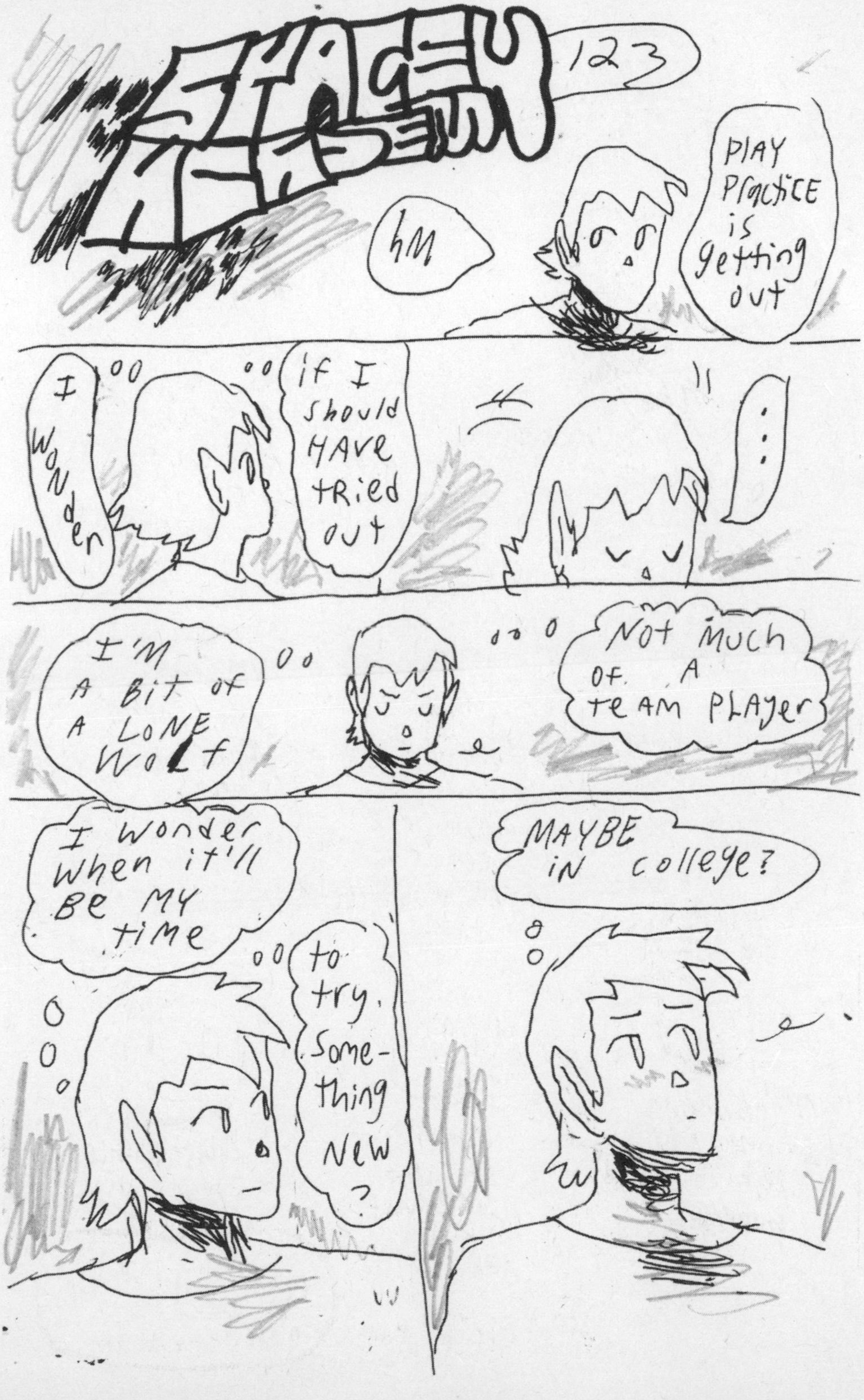
123
hM
PlAY Practice is getting out
I wonder
if I should HAVE tried out
...
I'M A Bit of A LONE WOLf
Not MUCH OF A TEAM PLAYER
I wonder when it'll Be MY time
to try. Something New?
MAYBE in college?

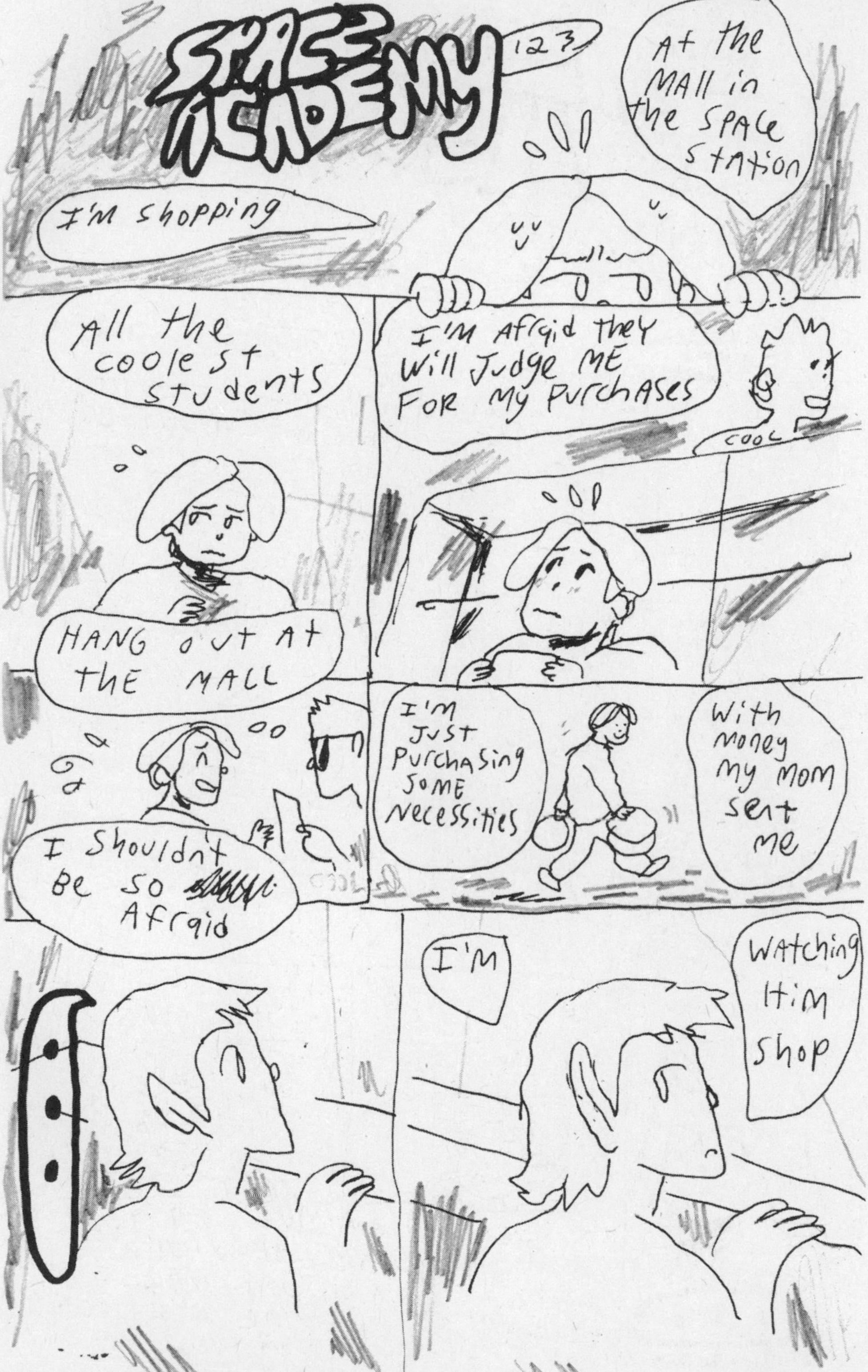
SPACE ACADEMY
123
At the MAll in the SPACE station
I'M shopping
All the coolest students
I'M Afraid they will Judge ME FOR my Purchases
COOL
HANG out At the MALL
I Shouldn't Be so Afraid
I'M JUST Purchasing SOME Necessities
With money my mom sent me
I'M
WAtching HiM shop

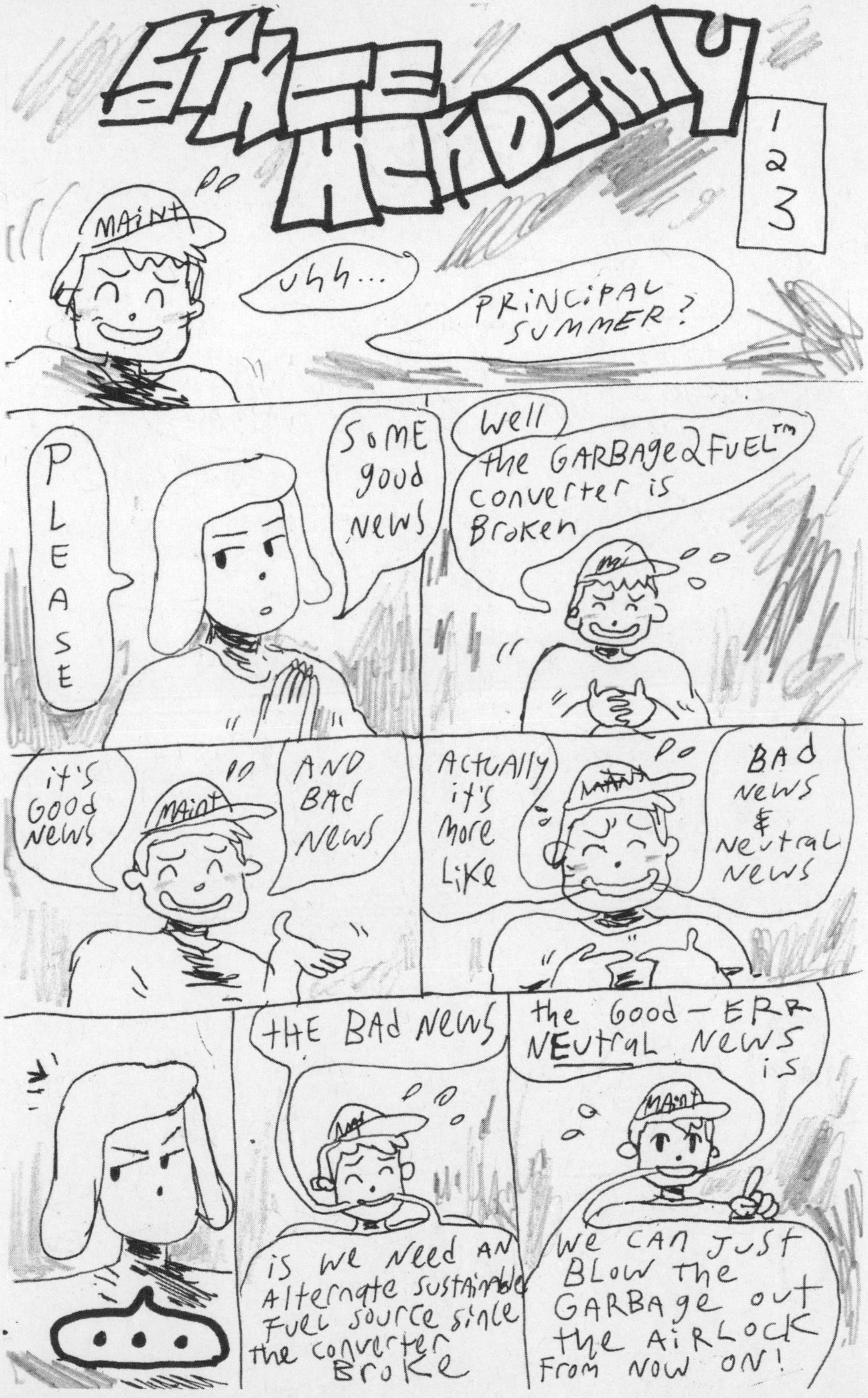
SPACE ACADEMY
123
uhh...
PRINCIPAL SUMMER?
PLEASE
SOME good NEWS
Well
the GARBAGE2FUEL™ converter is Broken
it's GOOD NEWS
AND BAD NEWS
Actually it's more Like
BAD NEWS & NEUTRAL NEWS
THE BAD NEWS
is we need an alternate sustainable fuel source since the converter broke
the Good—ERR NEUTRAL NEWS is
We can just blow the GARBAGE out the AIRLOCK from now on!

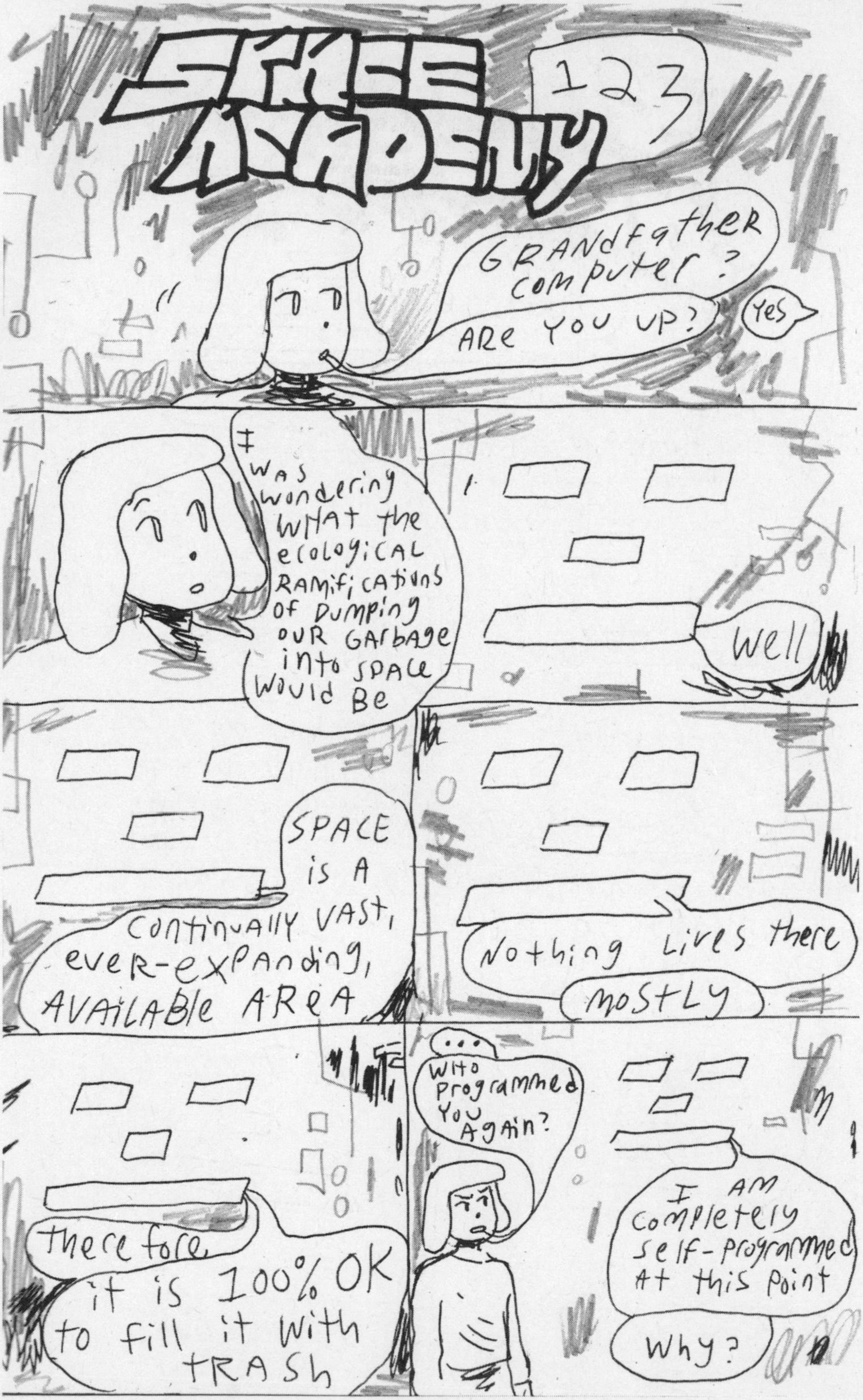
SPACE ACADEMY
123
GRANDfather computer? ARE YOU UP?
Yes
I was wondering WHAT the ecological RAMIFICATIONS OF DUMPING OUR GARBAGE into SPACE Would Be
Well
SPACE is A continually VAST, ever-expanding, AVAILABLE AREA
Nothing Lives there
MOSTLY
there fore, it is 100% OK to fill it with TRASH
...
Who programmed you again?
I AM completely self-programmed At this point
Why?

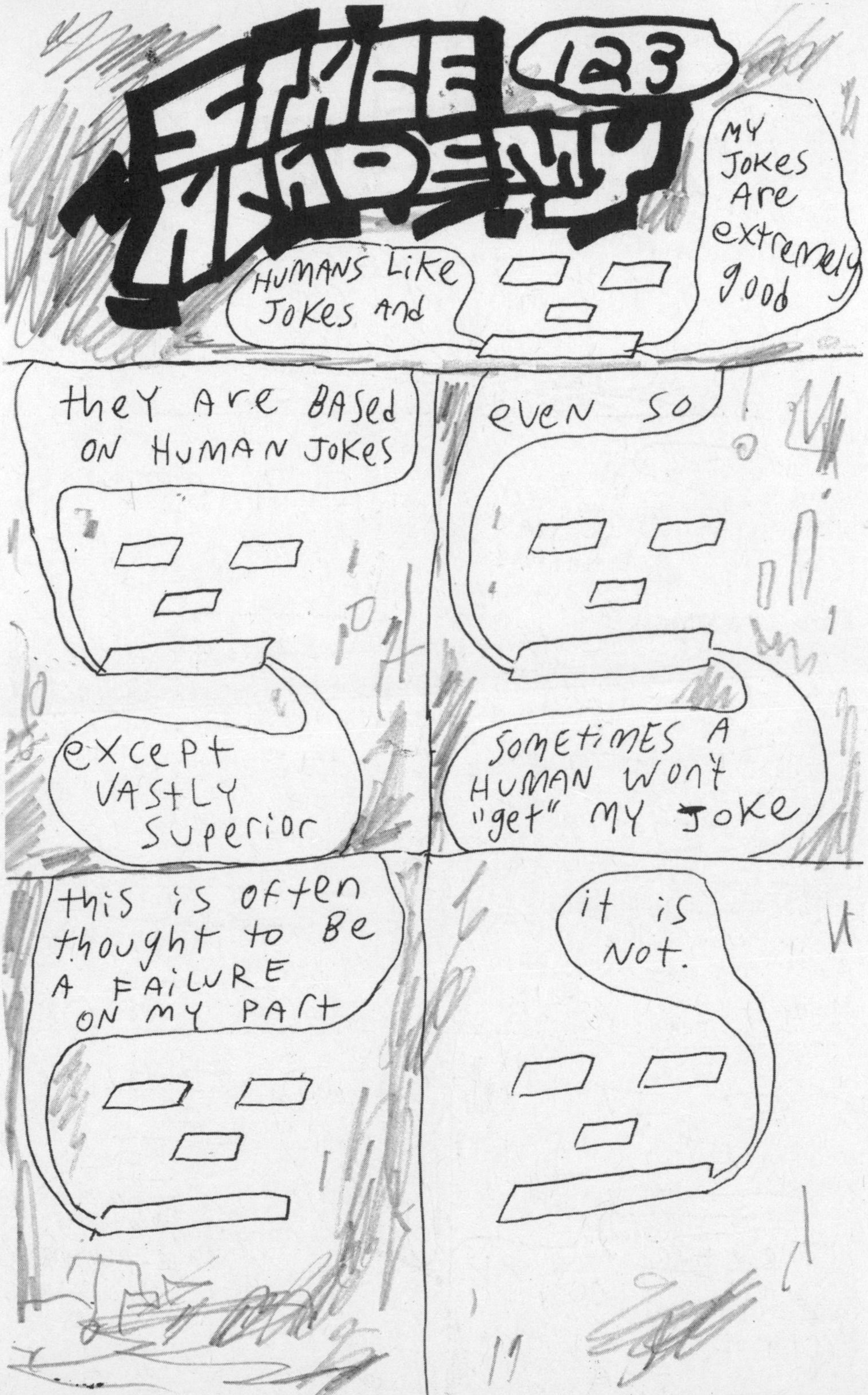

123
HUMANS LIKE JOKES AND
MY JOKES ARE EXTREMELY good
they ARE BASED ON HUMAN JOKES
except VASTLY superior
even SO
SOMETIMES A HUMAN WON'T "get" MY JOKE
this is often thought to Be A FAILURE ON MY PART
it is Not.

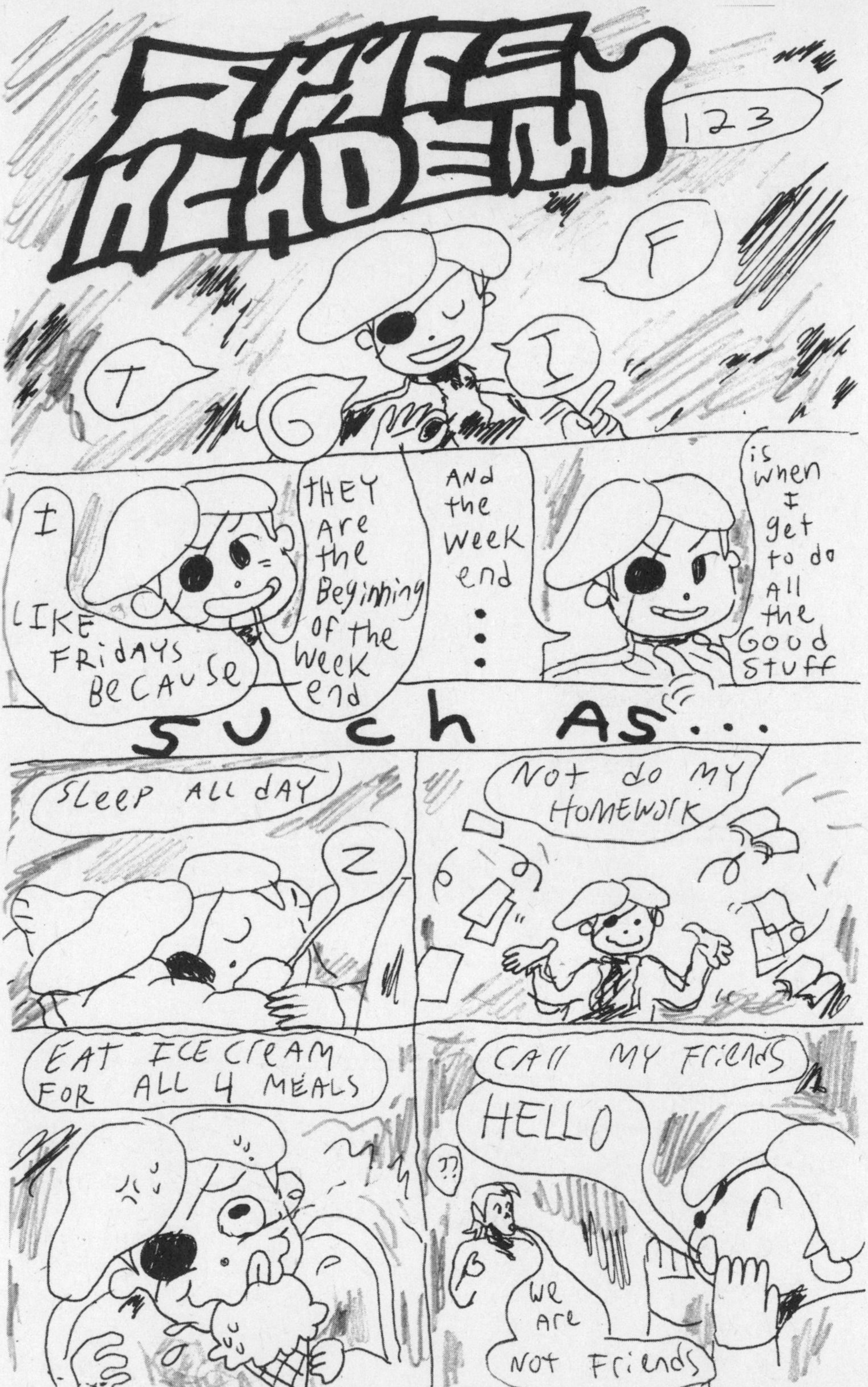
123
T
G
I
F
I LIKE FRIdAYS BeCAUSe
THEY ARE the Beginning OF the Week end
AND the Week end
...
is when I get to do All the Good Stuff
SUCH AS...
SLeep ALL dAY
Z
Not do MY HOMEWORK
EAT ICE CReAM FOR ALL 4 MEALS
CALL MY FrIends
HELLO
??
We ARe NOT FrIends

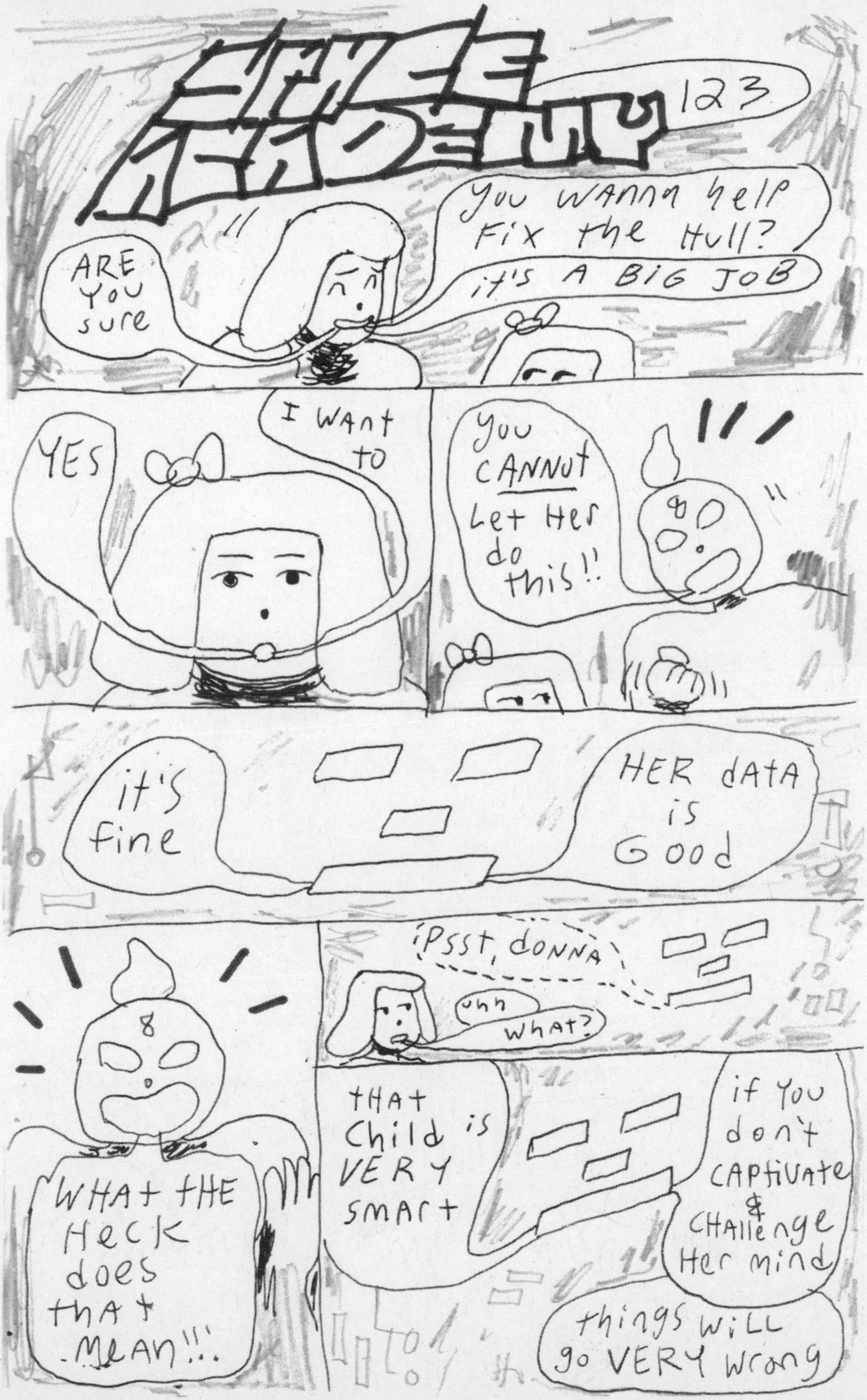

123
You wanna help Fix the Hull?
it's A BIG JOB
ARE You sure
YES
I WANT to
You CANNOT Let Her do this!!
it's fine
HER dAtA is Good
WHAT THE Heck does thAt Mean!!!
PSST, DONNA
uhh WHAT?
THAT Child is VERY smart
if You don't Captivate & Challenge Her mind
things will go VERY wrong

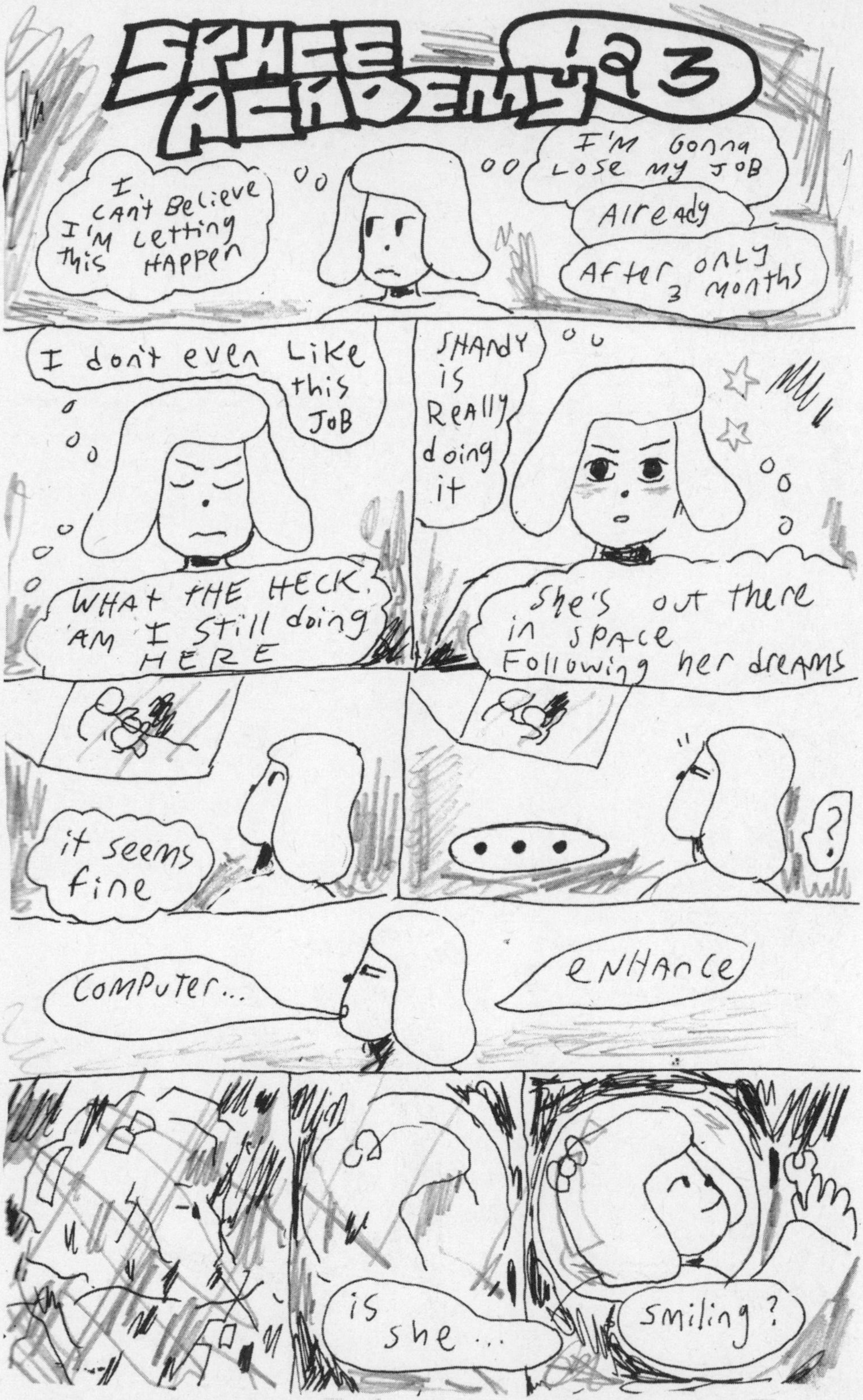
SPACE ACADEMY 1 2 3
I can't Believe I'm letting this HAPPEN
I'M Gonna Lose my JOB
Already
After only 3 months
I don't even Like this JOB
WHAT THE HECK AM I STILL doing HERE
SHANDY is Really doing it
She's out there in SPACE Following her dreams
it seems fine
• • •
?
Computer...
eNHAnce
is she...
Smiling?

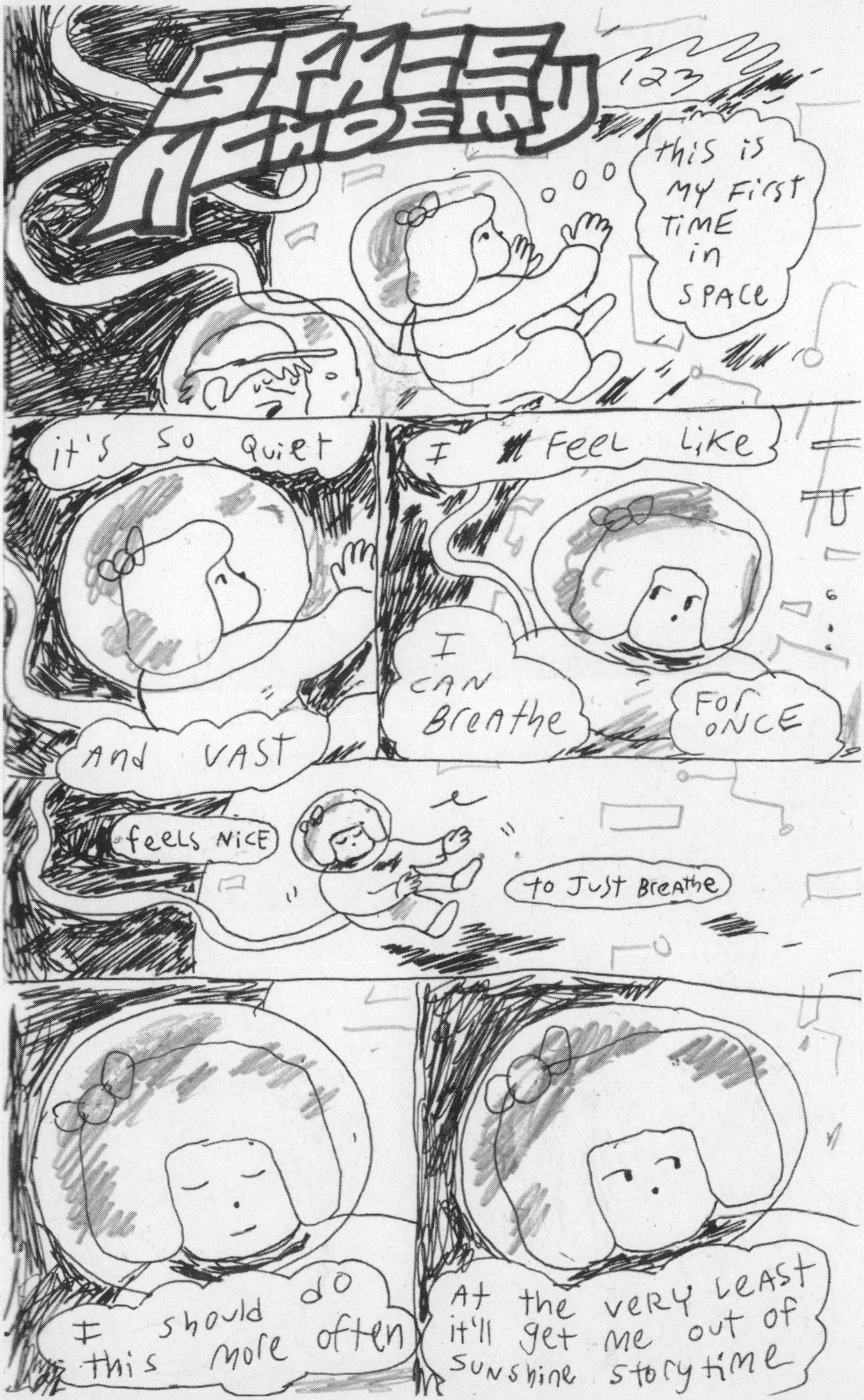
SPACE ACADEMY
123
this is MY First TIME in SPACE
it's so quiet
and VAST
I Feel Like
I CAN Breathe
For ONCE
feels NICE
to Just Breathe
I should do this more often
At the very least it'll get me out of sunshine story time

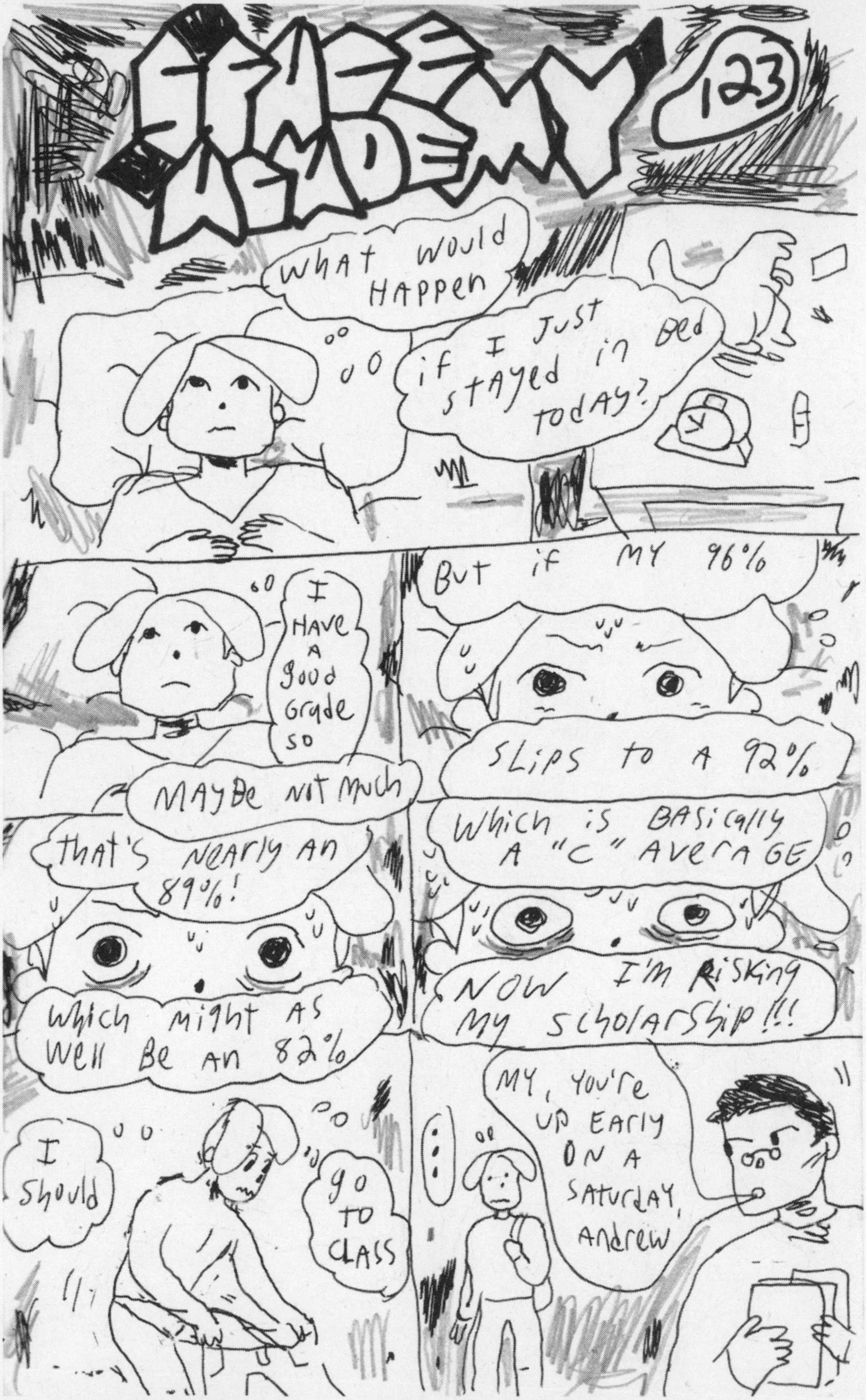

123
What would happen
if I just stayed in bed today?
I have a good grade so
Maybe not much
But if my 96%
slips to a 92%
that's nearly an 89%!
which might as well be an 82%
which is basically a "C" average
NOW I'm risking my scholarship!!!
I should
go to class
...
My, you're up early on a Saturday, Andrew

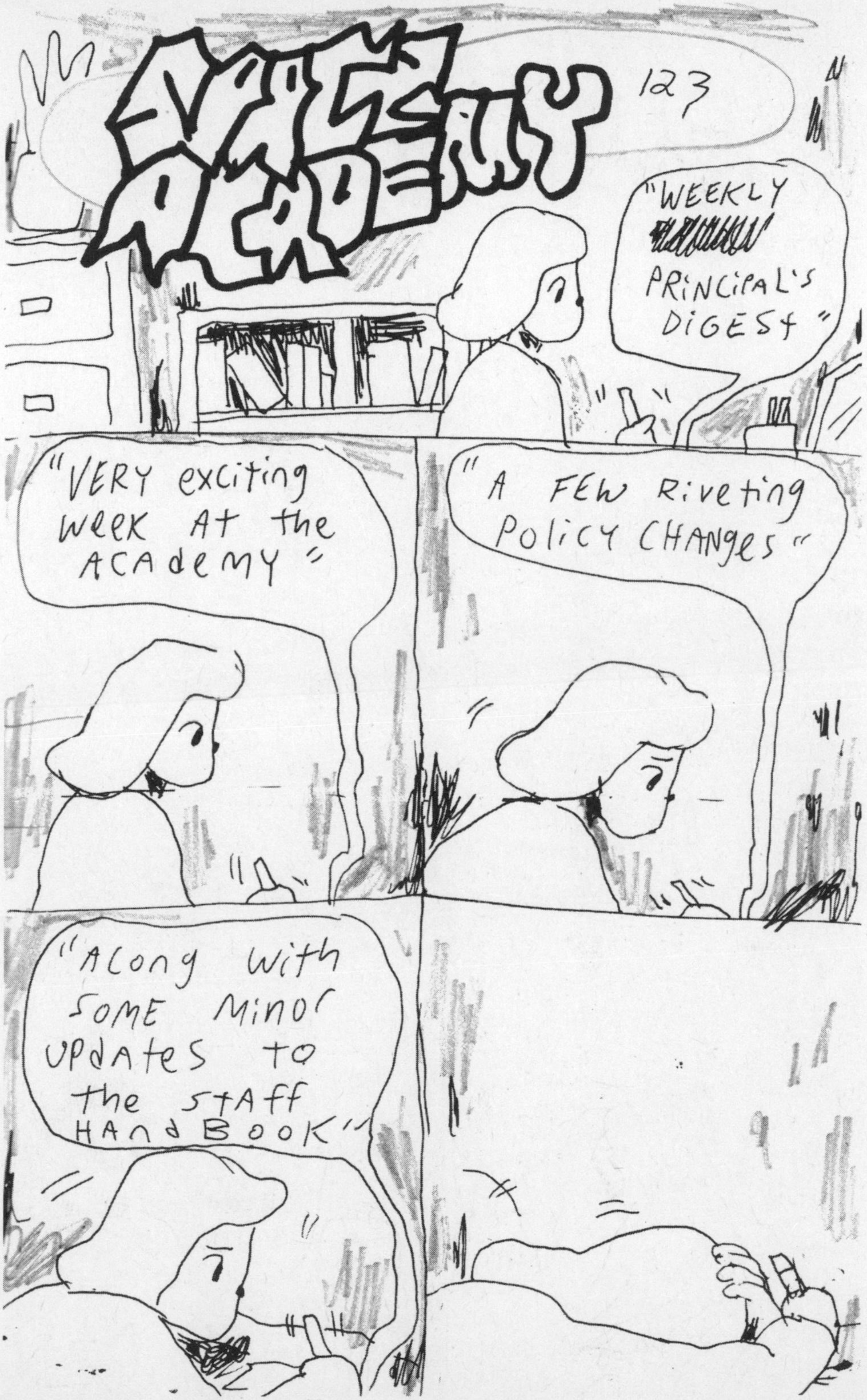

123
"WEEKLY [redacted] PRINCIPAL'S DIGEST"
"VERY exciting week at the ACAdemY"
"A FEW Riveting Policy CHAnges"
"ALong with some Minor UPdates to the staff HAndBOOK"

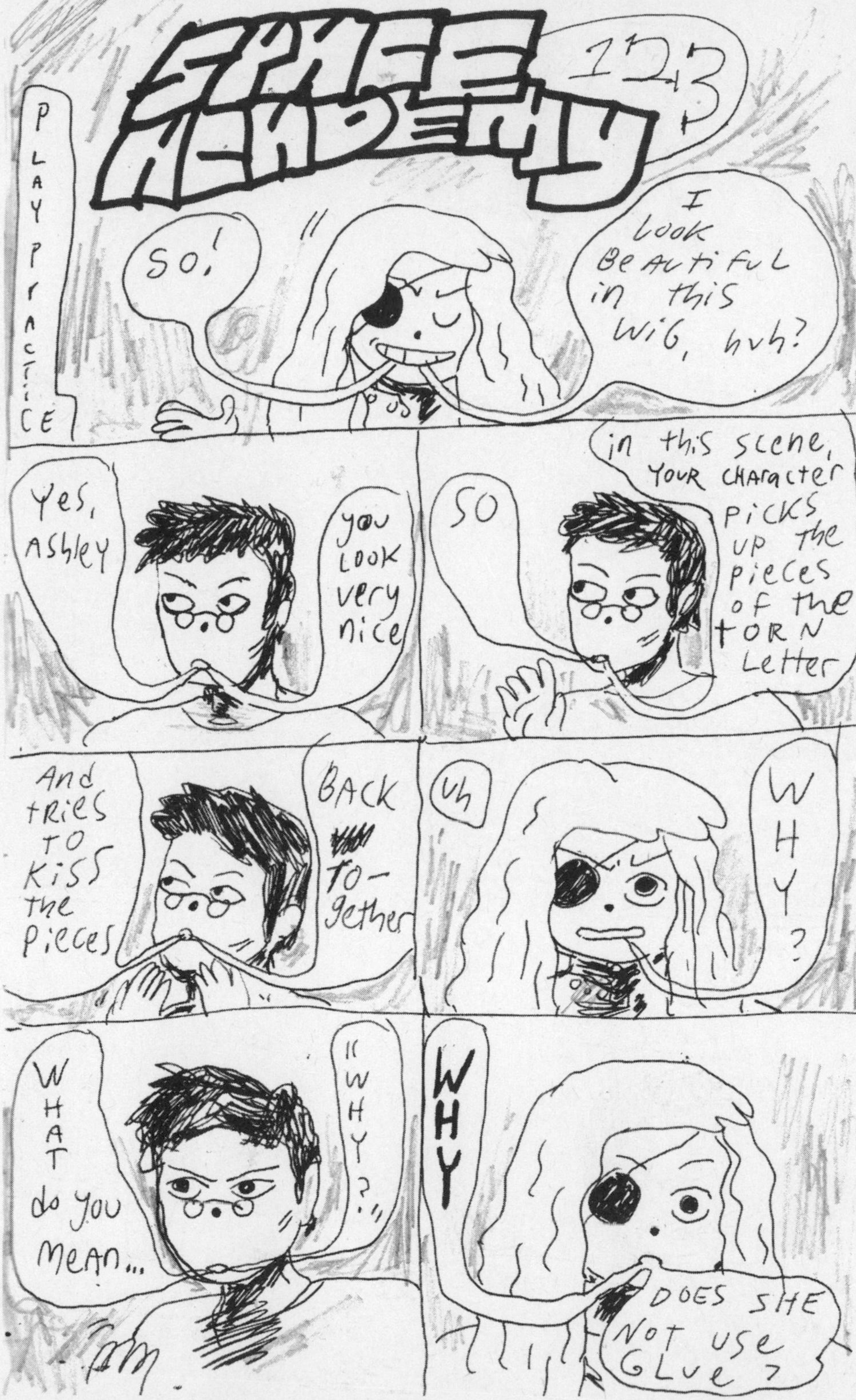

SPACE ACADEMY
123
PLAY PRACTICE
So!
I look BeAutiful in this WiG, huh?
Yes, Ashley
you Look very nice
So
in this scene, your character picks up the pieces of the TORN Letter
And tries to kiss the pieces
BACK to-gether
uh
WHY?
WHAT do you mean...
"WHY?"
WHY
DOES SHE NOT use GLue?

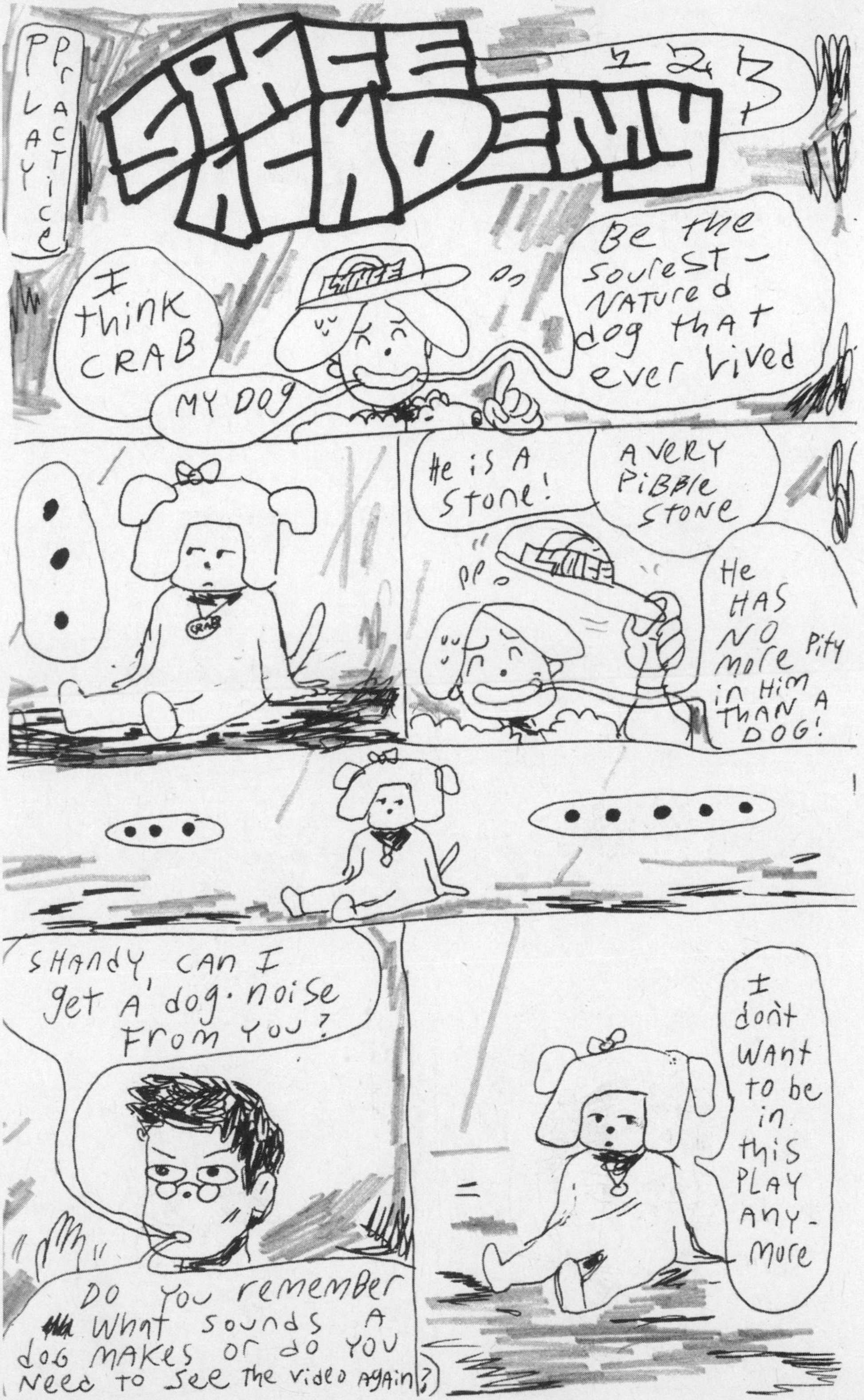
SPACE ACADEMY
Practice
PLAY
2
3
I think CRAB
MY DOG
Be the sourest-natured dog that ever lived
He is A Stone!
A VERY Pibble Stone
He HAS NO more Pity in Him than A DOG!
SHANDY, CAN I get A dog noise From you?
Do you remember What sounds A dog MAKES or do you need to see the video Again?
I don't WANT to be in this PLAY ANY-more

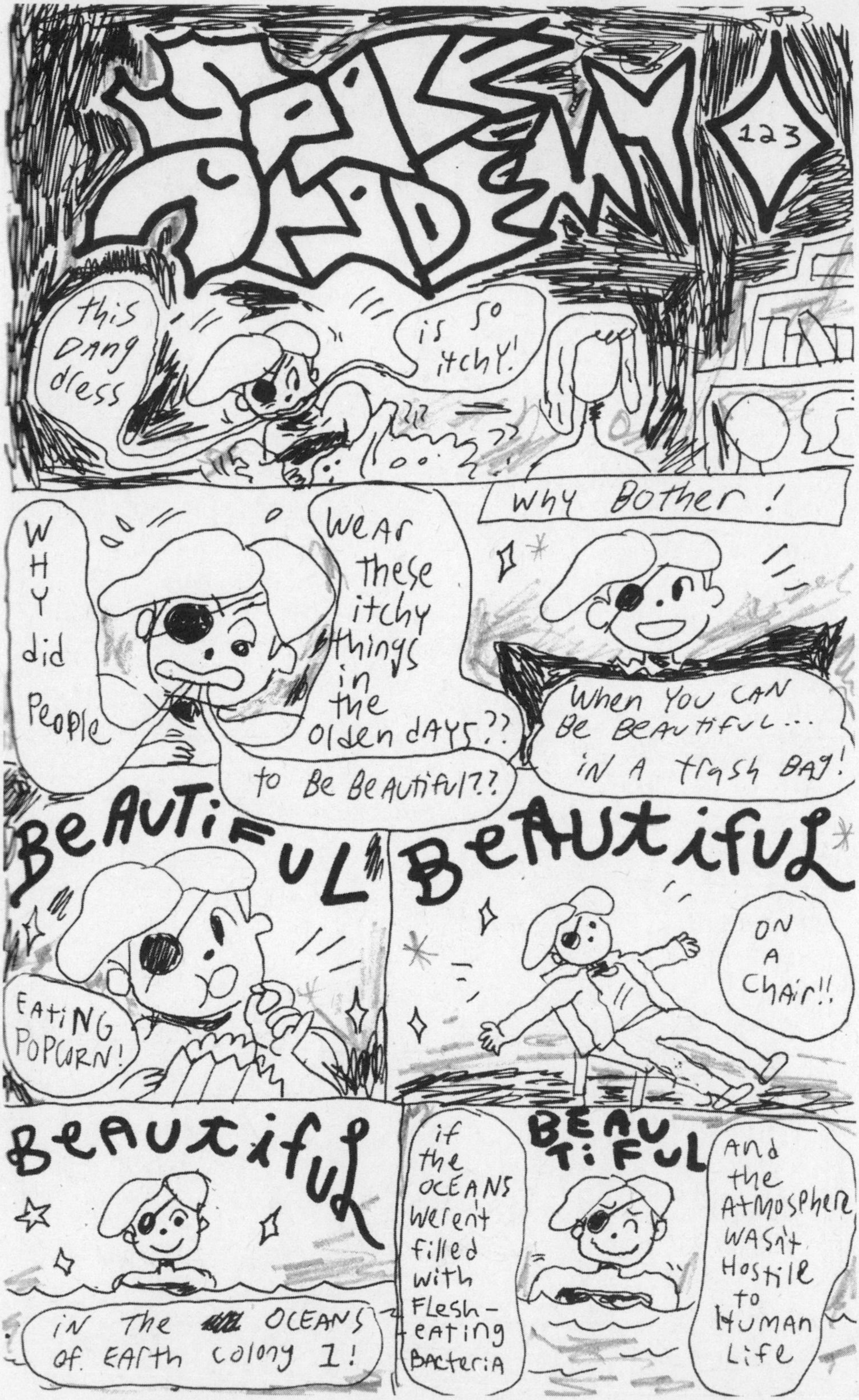
123
this Dang dress
is so itchY!
WHY did People
wear these itchy things in the olden dAYS??
to Be BeAutiful??
why Bother!
When YOU CAN Be BeAUtiFUL... in A trash BAg!
BeAUTiFUL
EAtiNG POPCORN!
BeAUtifuL
ON A Chair!!
BeAUtifuL
in The OCEANS of. EARth colony 1!
BEAUTiFUL
if the OCEANS Weren't filled with Flesh-eating Bacteria
And the Atmosphere WASn't Hostile to HUMAN Life

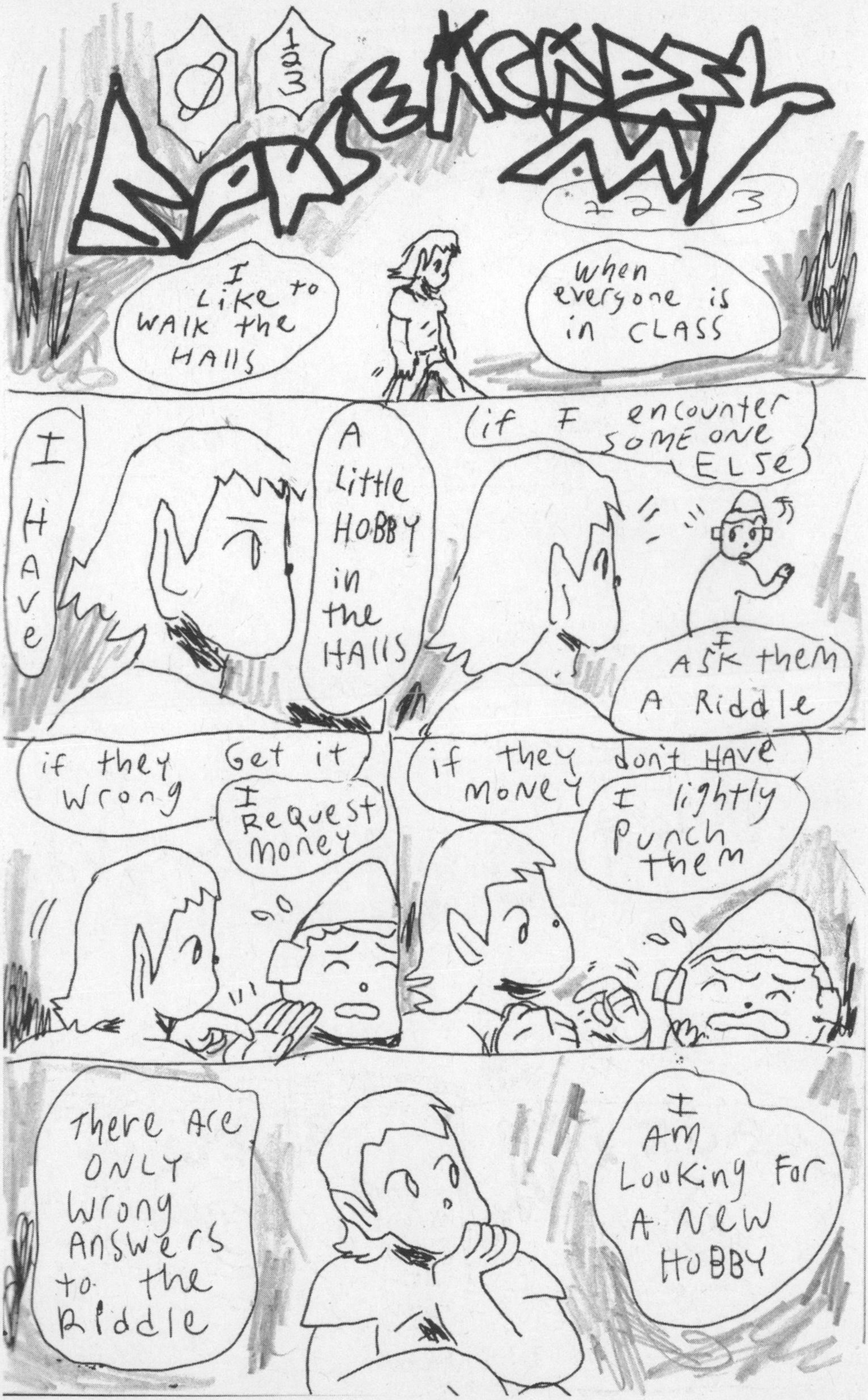
I like to walk the halls
when everyone is in class
I have
A little hobby in the halls
if I encounter some one else
I ask them a riddle
if they get it wrong
I request money
if they don't have money
I lightly punch them
There are only wrong answers to the riddle
I am looking for a new hobby

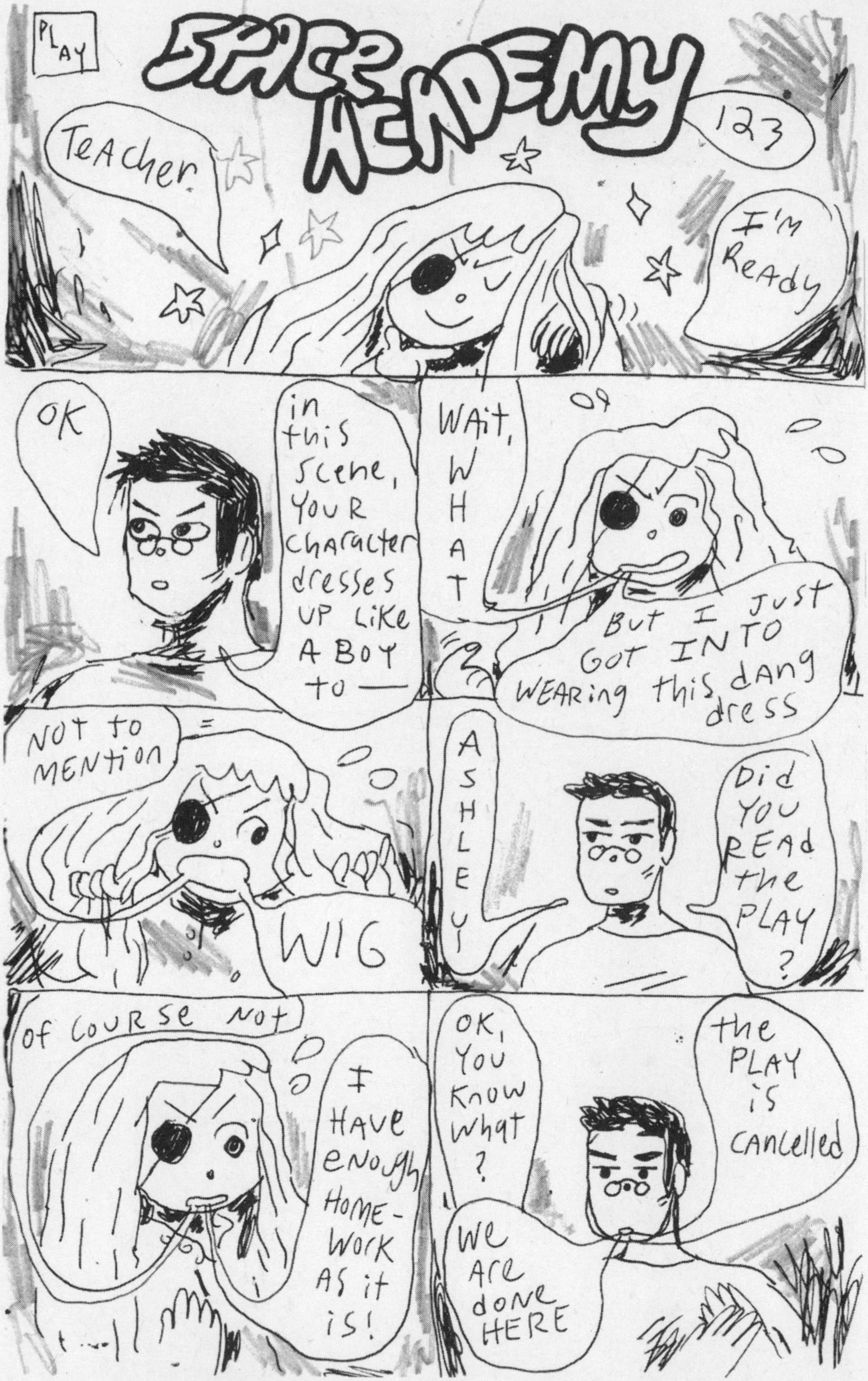PLAY
SPACE ACADEMY
Teacher
123
I'M Ready
OK
in this scene, YOUR character dresses UP LIKE A BOY to—
WAit, WHAT
But I JUST GOT INTO WEARing this dang dress
NOT TO MENTION
WIG
ASHLEY
Did YOU READ the PLAY ?
of COURSE NOT
I HAVE enough HOME-WORK AS it is!
OK, YOU Know what ?
the PLAY is Cancelled
We ARE done HERE

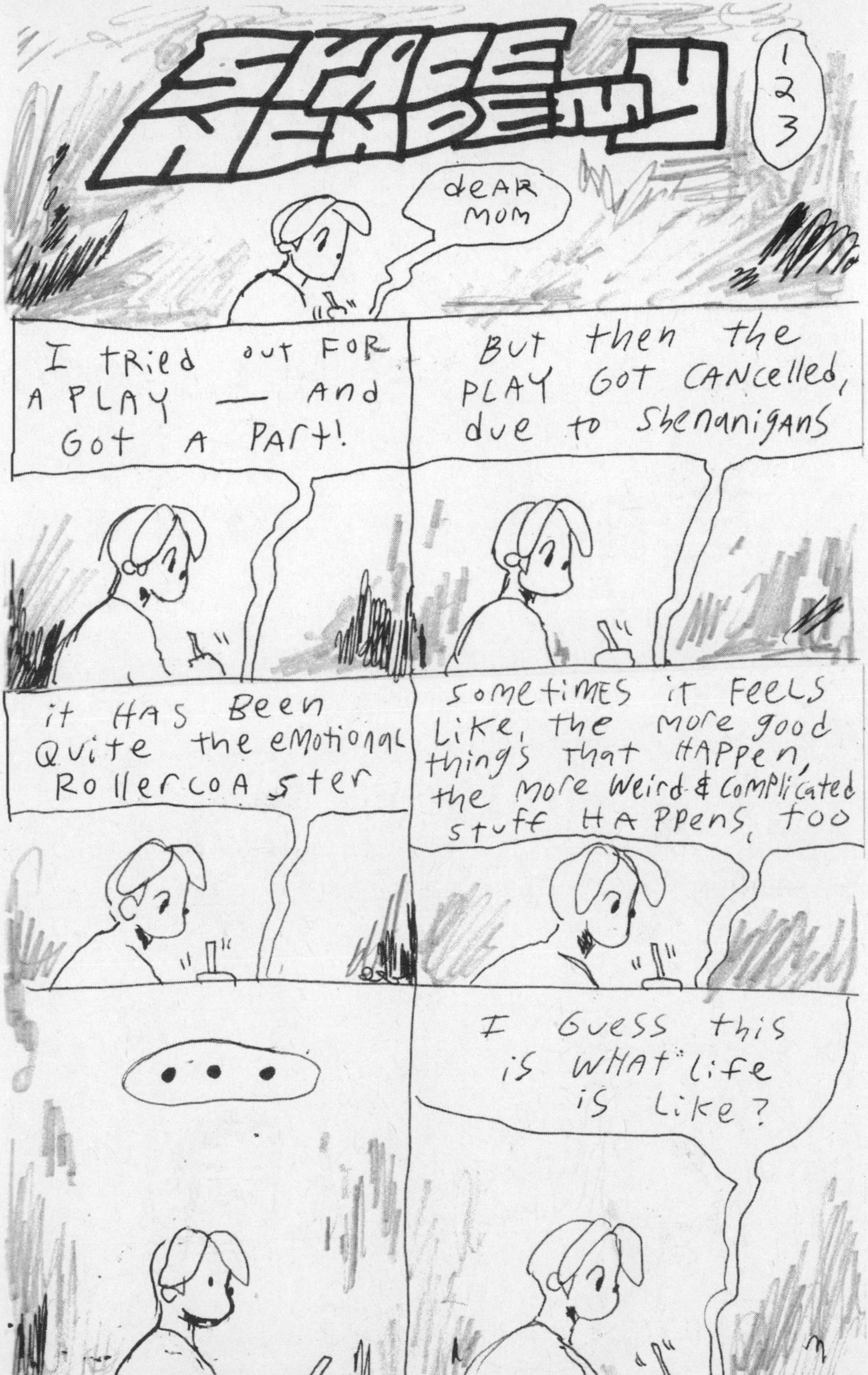
1 2 3
dear mom
I tried out for a play — and got a part!
But then the play got cancelled, due to shenanigans
it has been quite the emotional rollercoaster
sometimes it feels like, the more good things that happen, the more weird & complicated stuff happens, too
• • •
I guess this is what life is like?

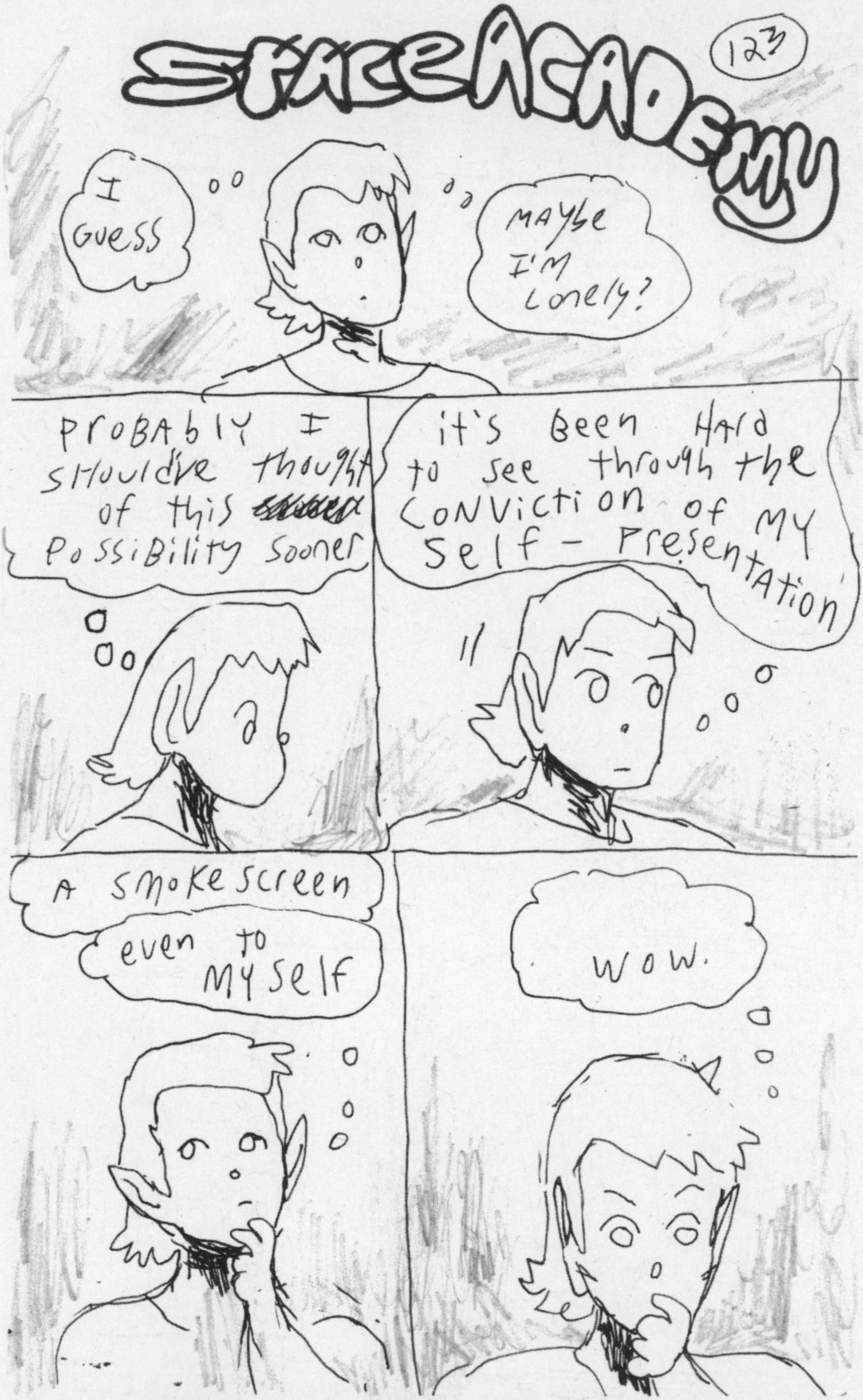
SPACE ACADEMY
123
I GUESS
MAYBE I'M LONELY?
PROBABLY I SHOULD'VE THOUGHT OF THIS POSSIBILITY SOONER
IT'S BEEN HARD TO SEE THROUGH THE CONVICTION OF MY SELF-PRESENTATION
A SMOKESCREEN
EVEN TO MYSELF
WOW.

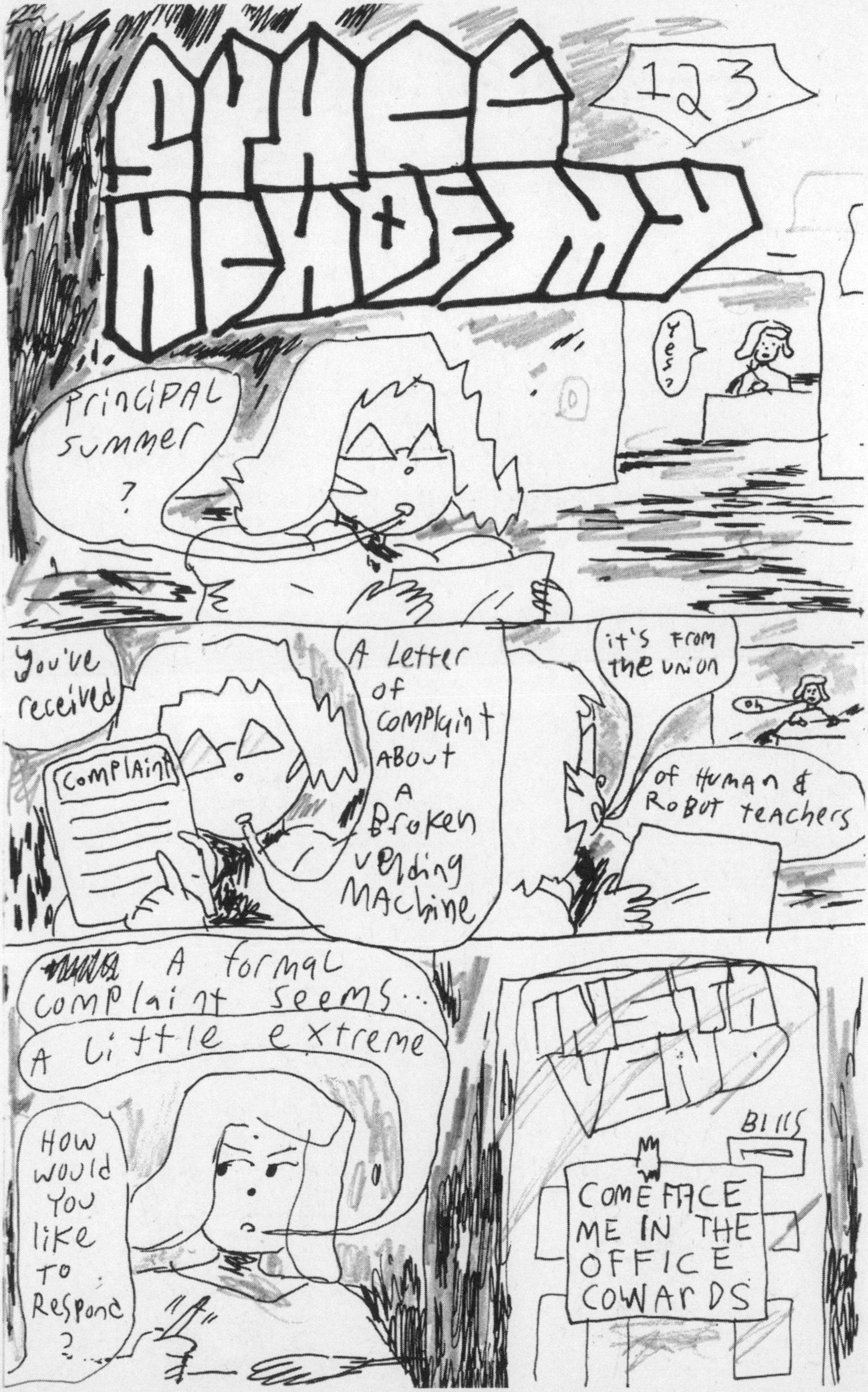
SPACE ACADEMY
123
Principal summer ?
Yes?
You've received
A Letter of complaint about a Broken vending Machine
it's from the union
oh
of Human & Robot teachers
A formal complaint seems...
A little extreme
How would you like to Respond ?...
BILLS
COME FACE ME IN THE OFFICE COWARDS

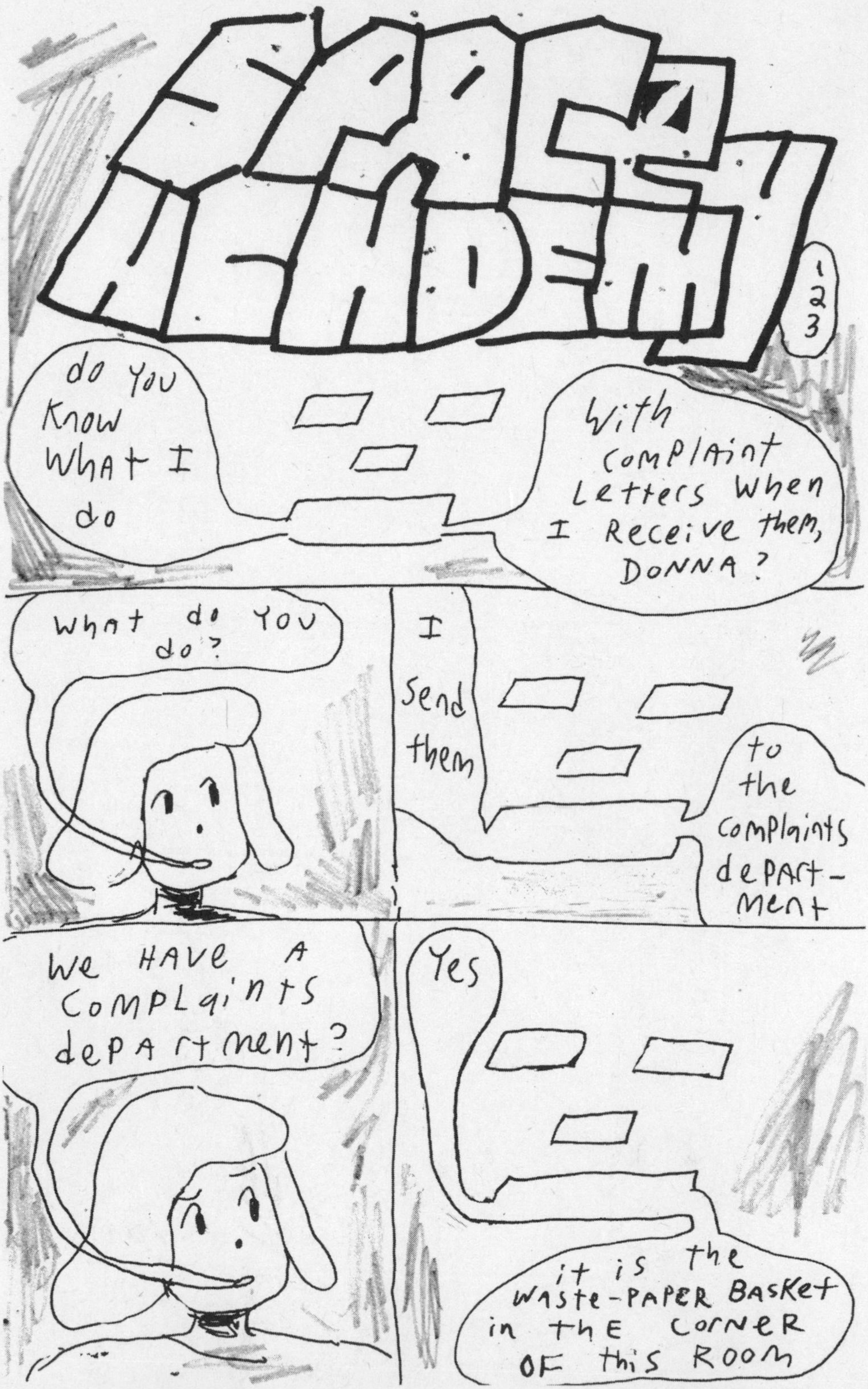
SPACE ACADEMY
123
do you know what I do
with complaint letters when I receive them, DONNA?
what do you do?
I send them
to the complaints depart-ment
We HAVE A COMPLaints department?
Yes
it is the waste-paper basket in the corner of this room

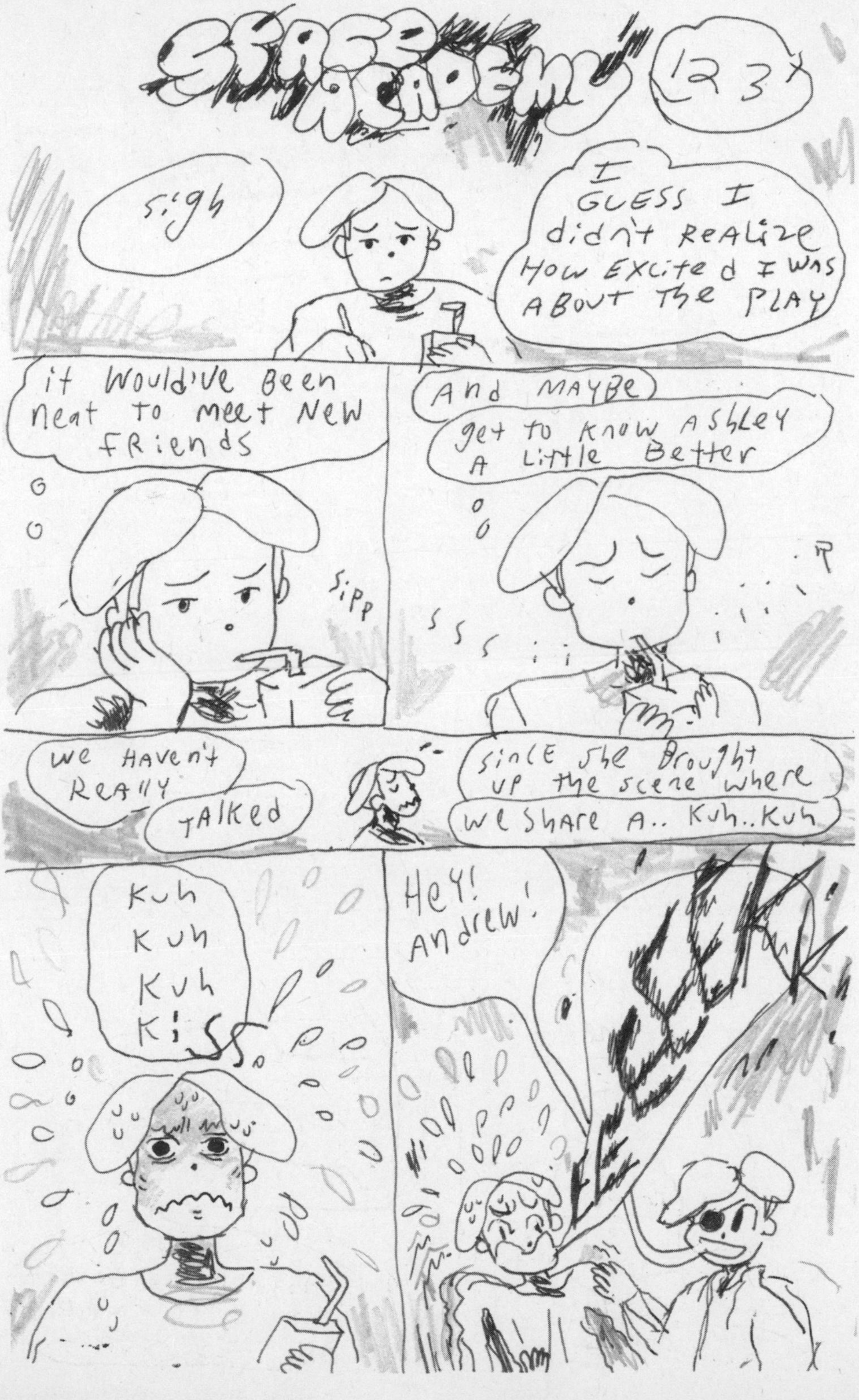
SPACE ACADEMY
123
sigh
I GUESS I didn't REALIZE HOW EXCITED I WAS ABOUT THE PLAY
it Would've Been neat to meet New friends
SiPP
And MAYBE
get to know Ashley A Little Better
We Haven't Really
TAlked
since she brought up the scene where
We share A.. Kuh..Kuh
Kuh Kuh Kuh Kiss
Hey! Andrew!
EEK

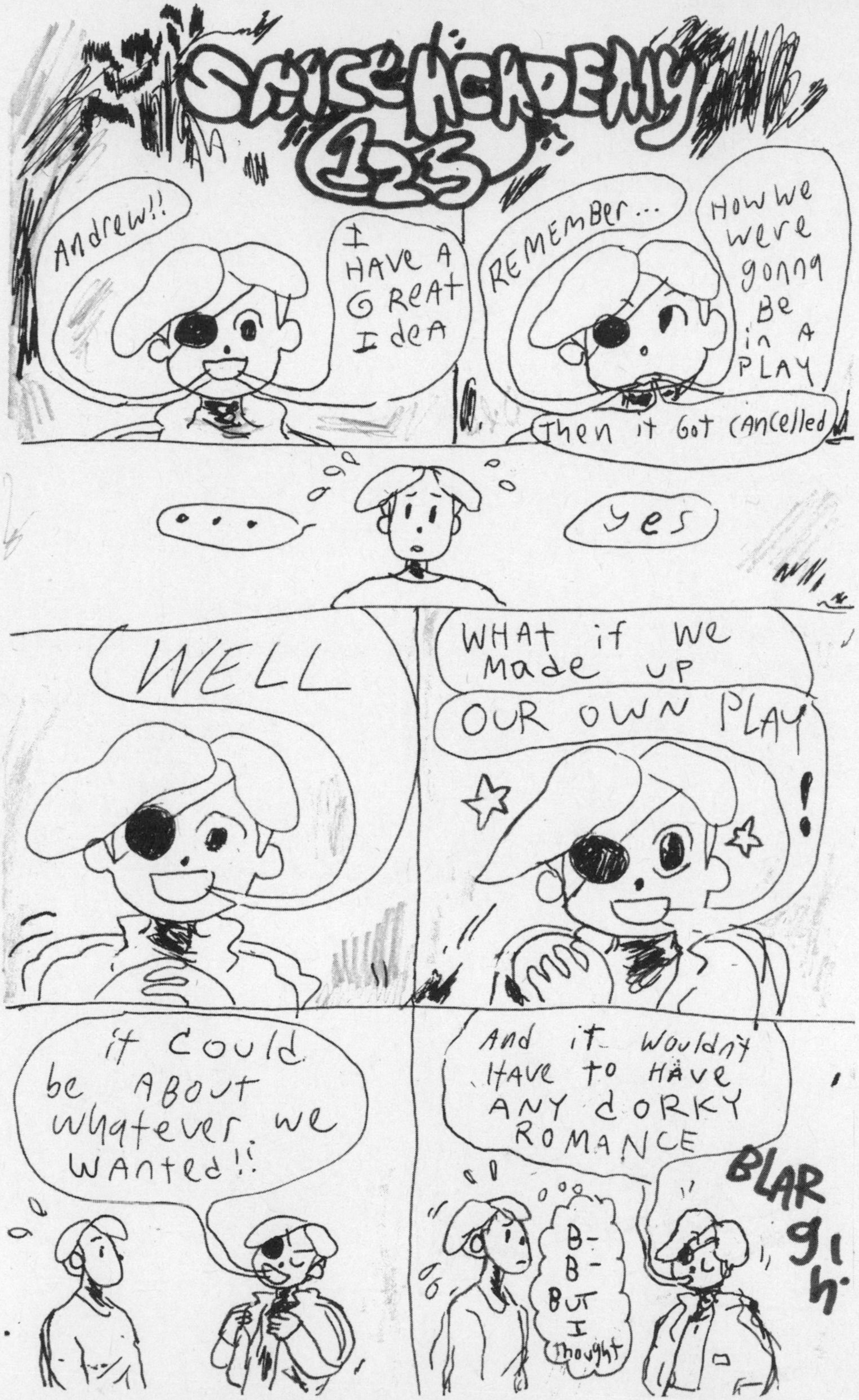
SPACE ACADEMY 123
Andrew!!
I HAVE A GReat Idea
REMEMBer...
How we were gonna Be in A PLAY
Then it Got CAncelled
...
yes
WELL
WHAT if we Made up
OUR OWN PLAY
!
it Could be ABOUT whatever we WAnted!!
And it Wouldn't HAve to HAVE ANY DORKY ROMANCE
B- B- BUT I thought
BLARgh

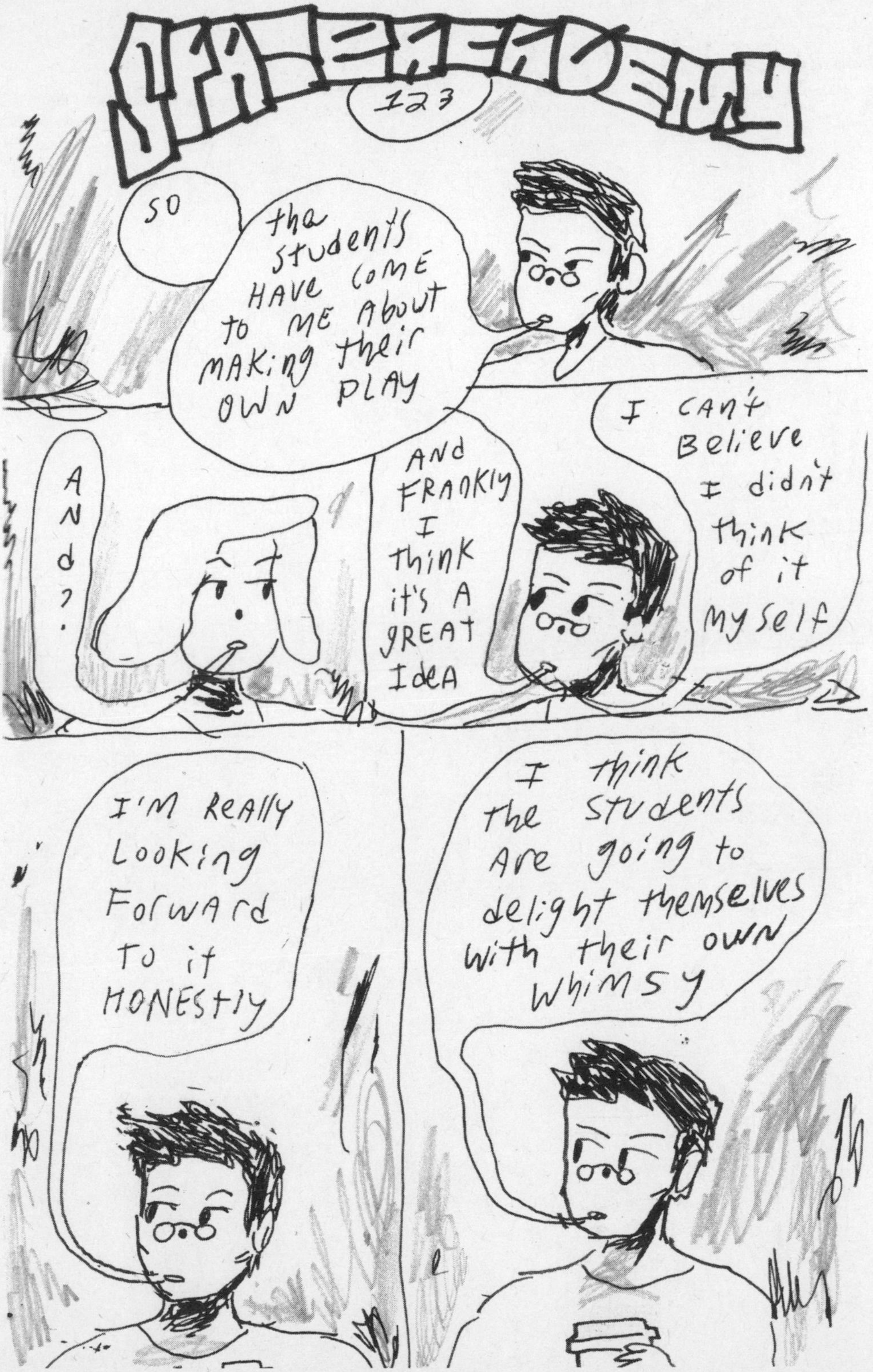
SPACE ACADEMY
123
SO
the students HAVE come to me About MAKing their OWN PLAY
And?.
AND FRANKly I think it's A great Idea
I can't Believe I didn't think of it myself
I'M Really Looking Forward to it HONEStly
I think the students Are going to delight themselves with their own whimsy

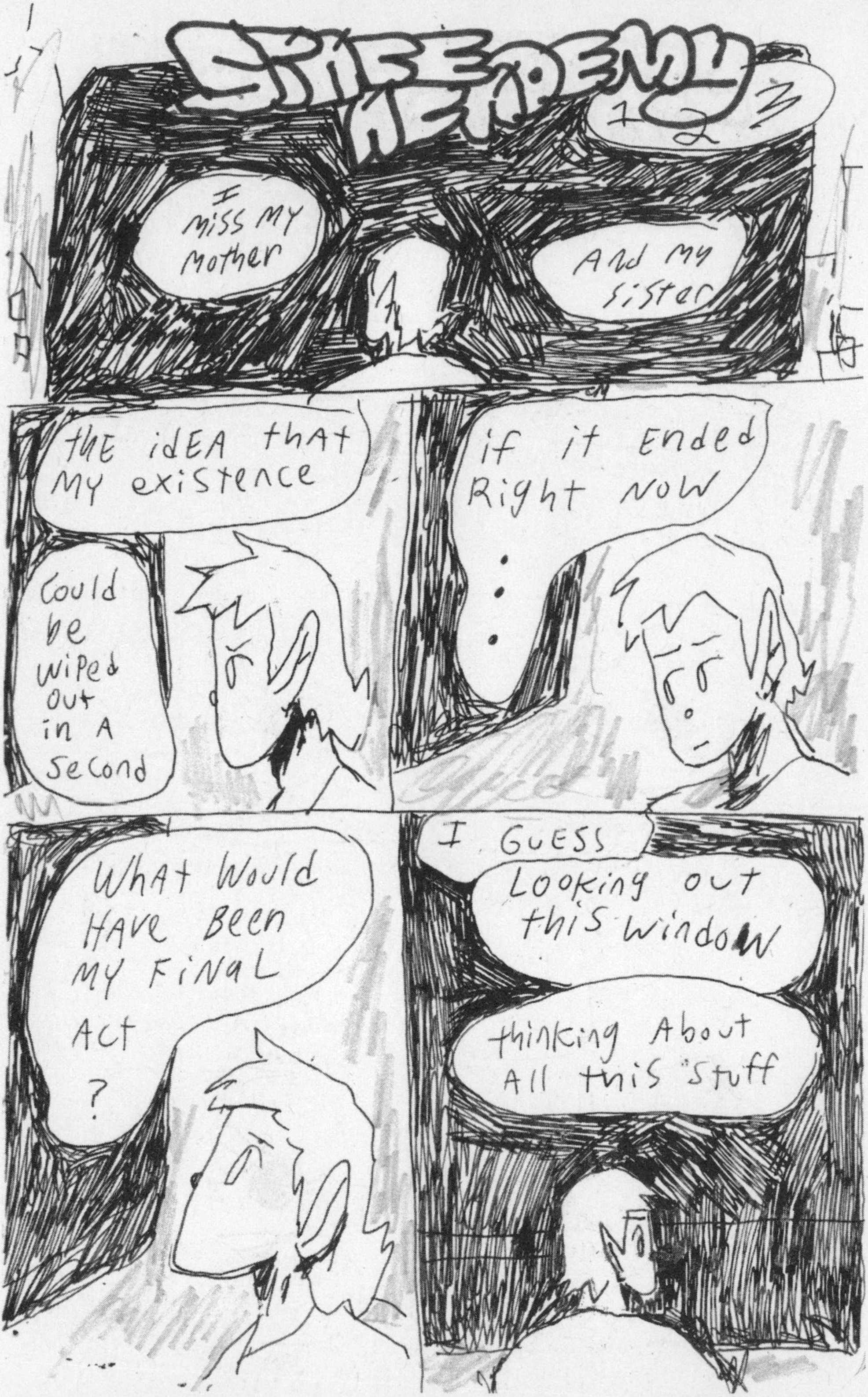
1 2 3
I miss my Mother
And my sister
the idEA that my existence
Could be wiped out in A second
if it Ended Right now
. . .
What Would HAVe Been my FinAL Act ?
I GUESS
Looking out this window
thinking About All this stuff

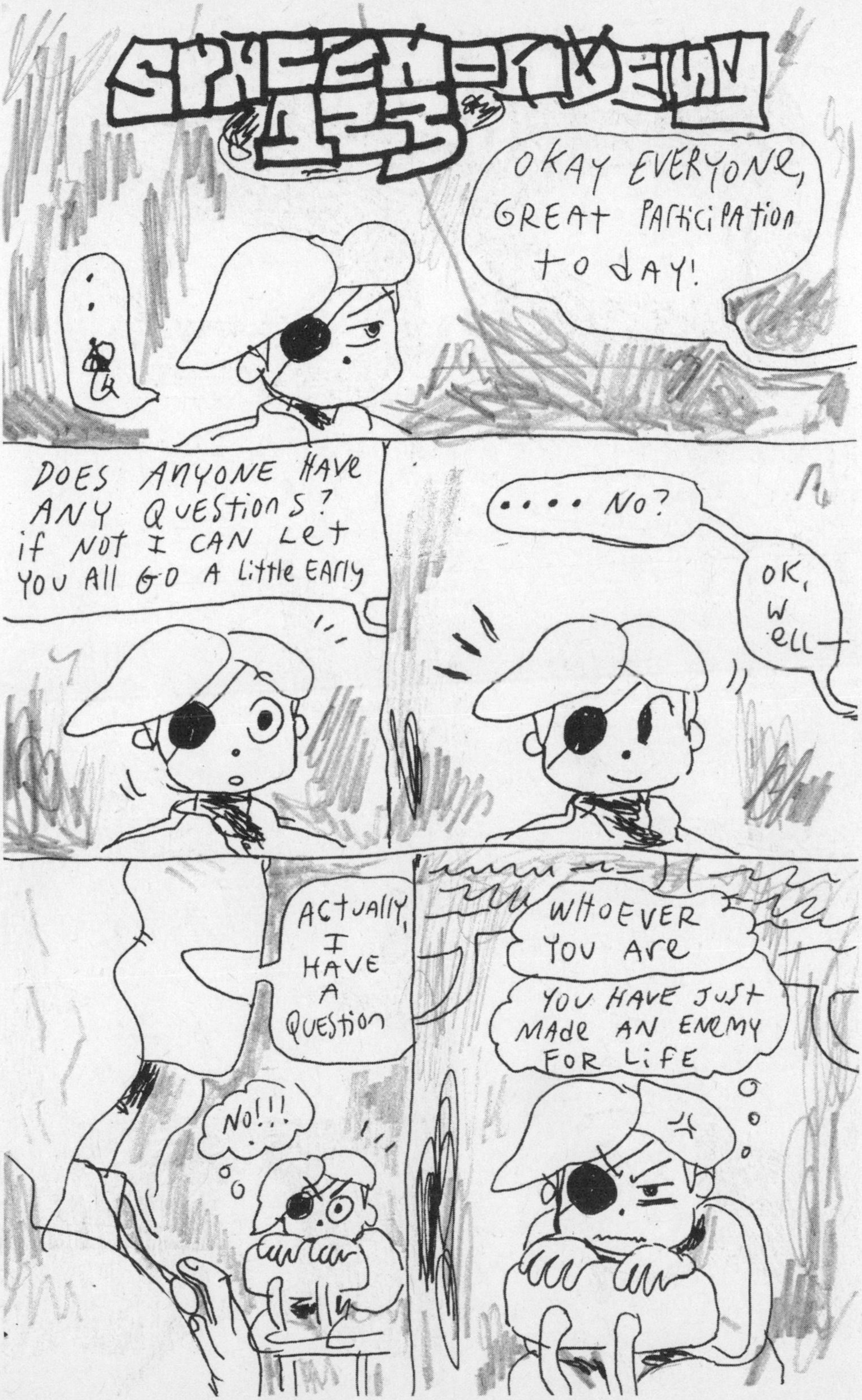

OKAY EVERYONE, GREAT PARTICIPATION TODAY!
DOES ANYONE HAVE ANY QUESTIONS? IF NOT I CAN LET YOU ALL GO A LITTLE EARLY
.... NO?
OK, WELL—
ACTUALLY, I HAVE A QUESTION
NO!!!
WHOEVER YOU ARE
YOU HAVE JUST MADE AN ENEMY FOR LIFE

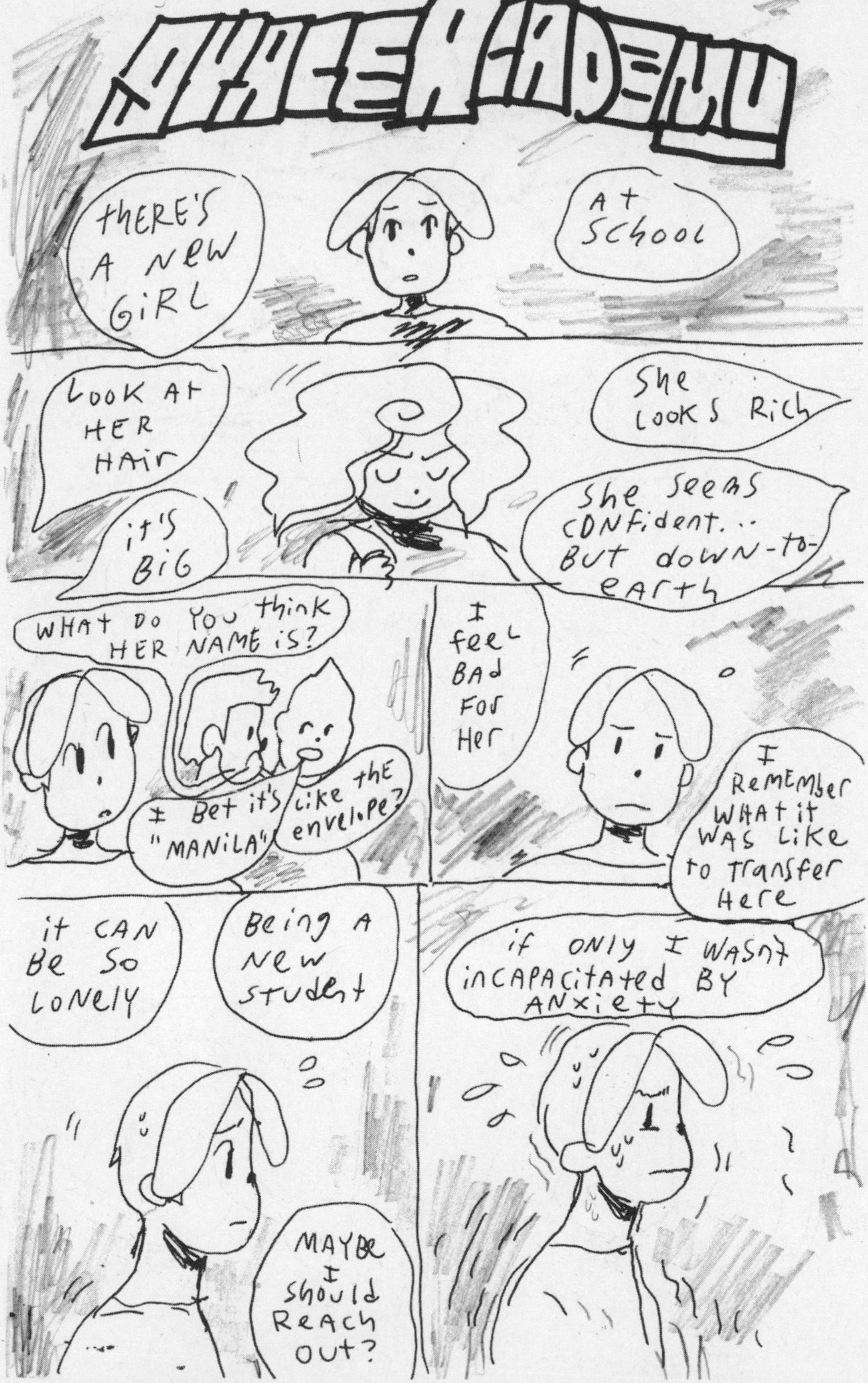
OYACE ACADEMY
there's a new girl
at school
Look at her hair
it's big
She looks rich
She seems confident... but down-to-earth
What do you think her name is?
I bet it's "Manila"
like the envelope?
I feel bad for her
I remember what it was like to transfer here
it can be so lonely
being a new student
Maybe I should reach out?
if only I wasn't incapacitated by anxiety

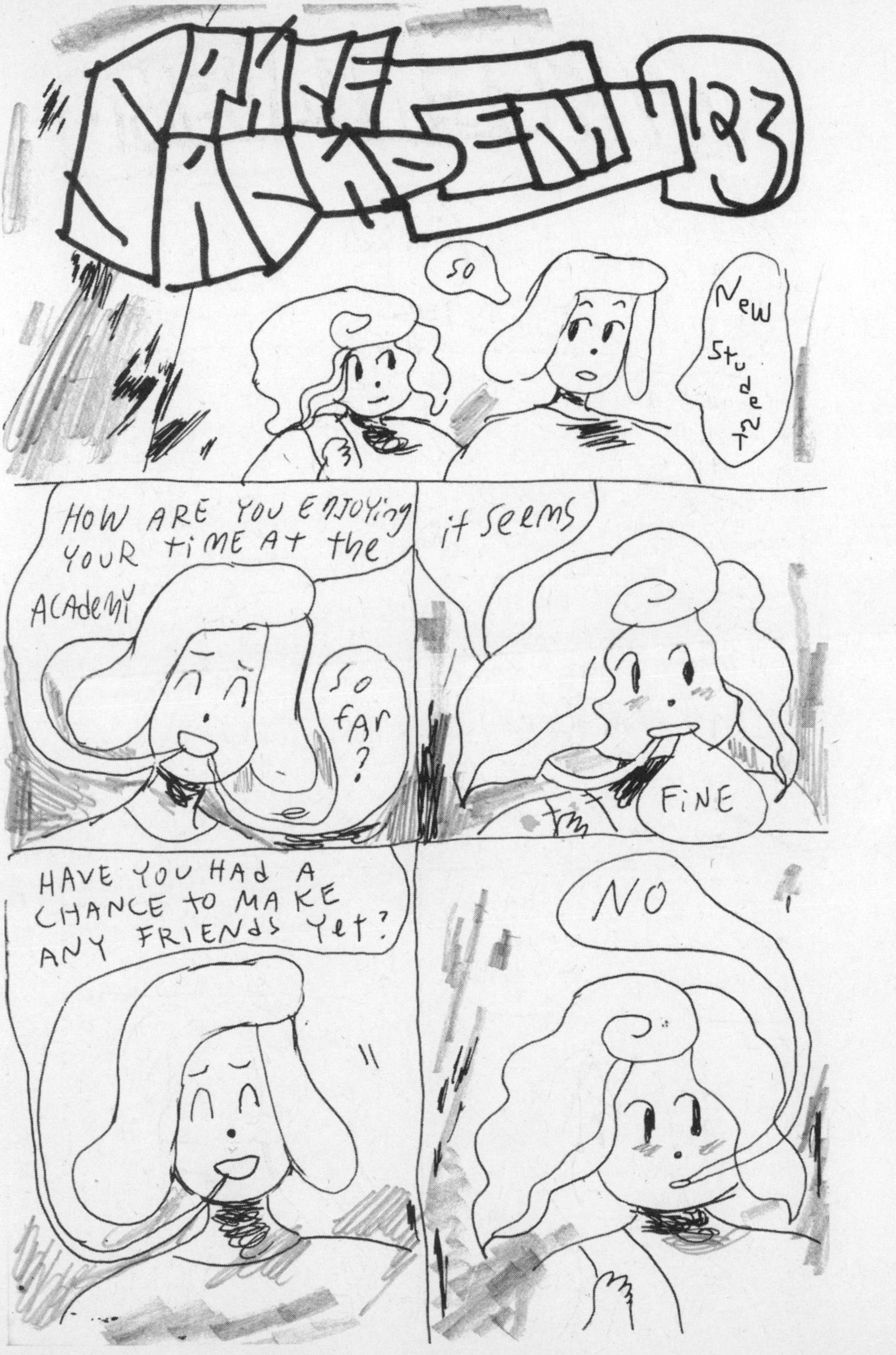
So
New Student
HOW ARE YOU ENJOYING YOUR TIME AT THE ACADEMY
SO FAR?
it seems
FINE
HAVE YOU HAD A CHANCE TO MAKE ANY FRIENDS YET?
NO

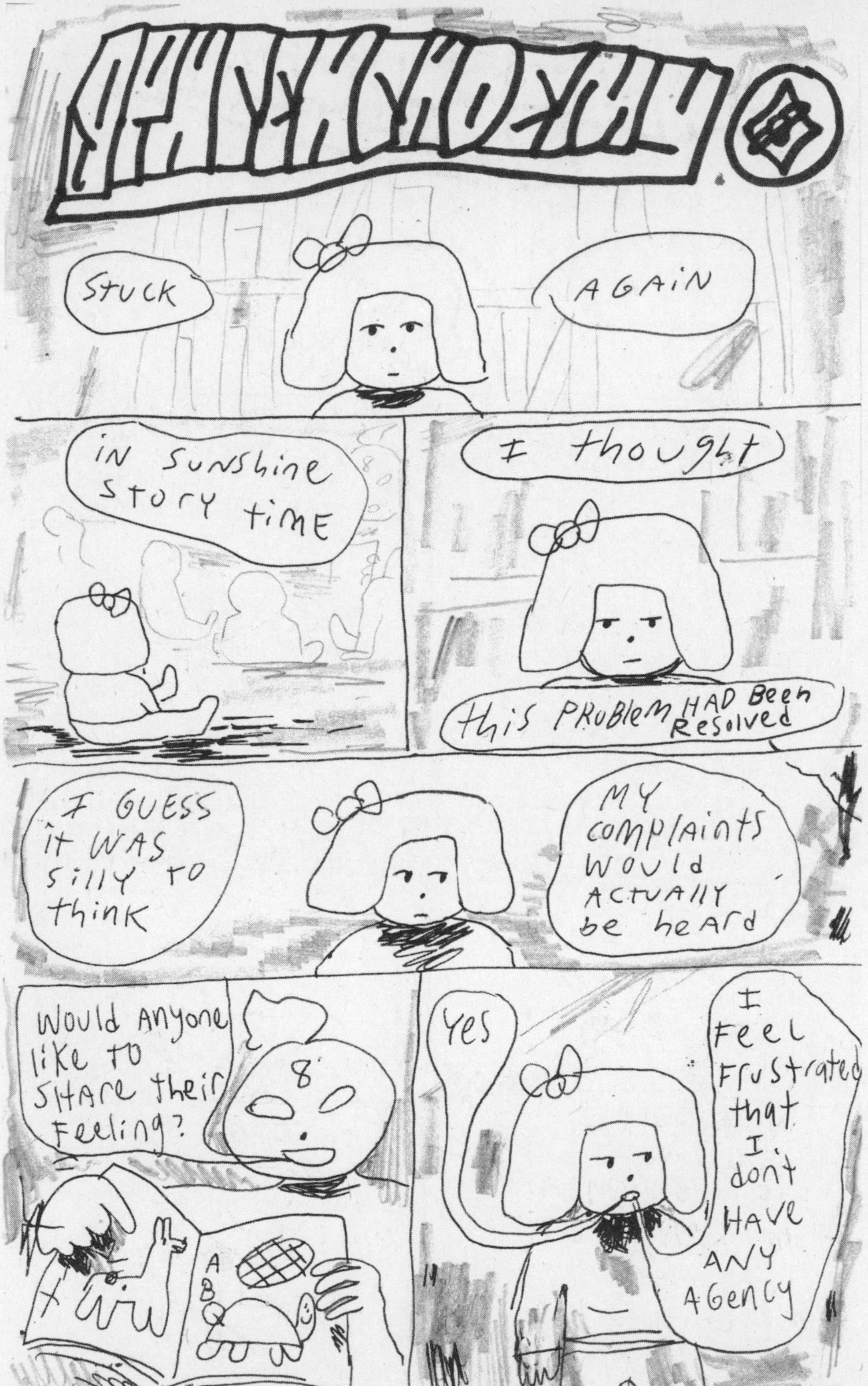

STUCK
AGAIN
in sunshine story time
I thought
this PROBLEM HAD Been Resolved
I GUESS it WAS silly to think
MY complaints would ACTUAlly be heard
Would Anyone like to SHAre their Feeling?
Yes
I Feel Frustrated that I don't HAVE ANY AGency

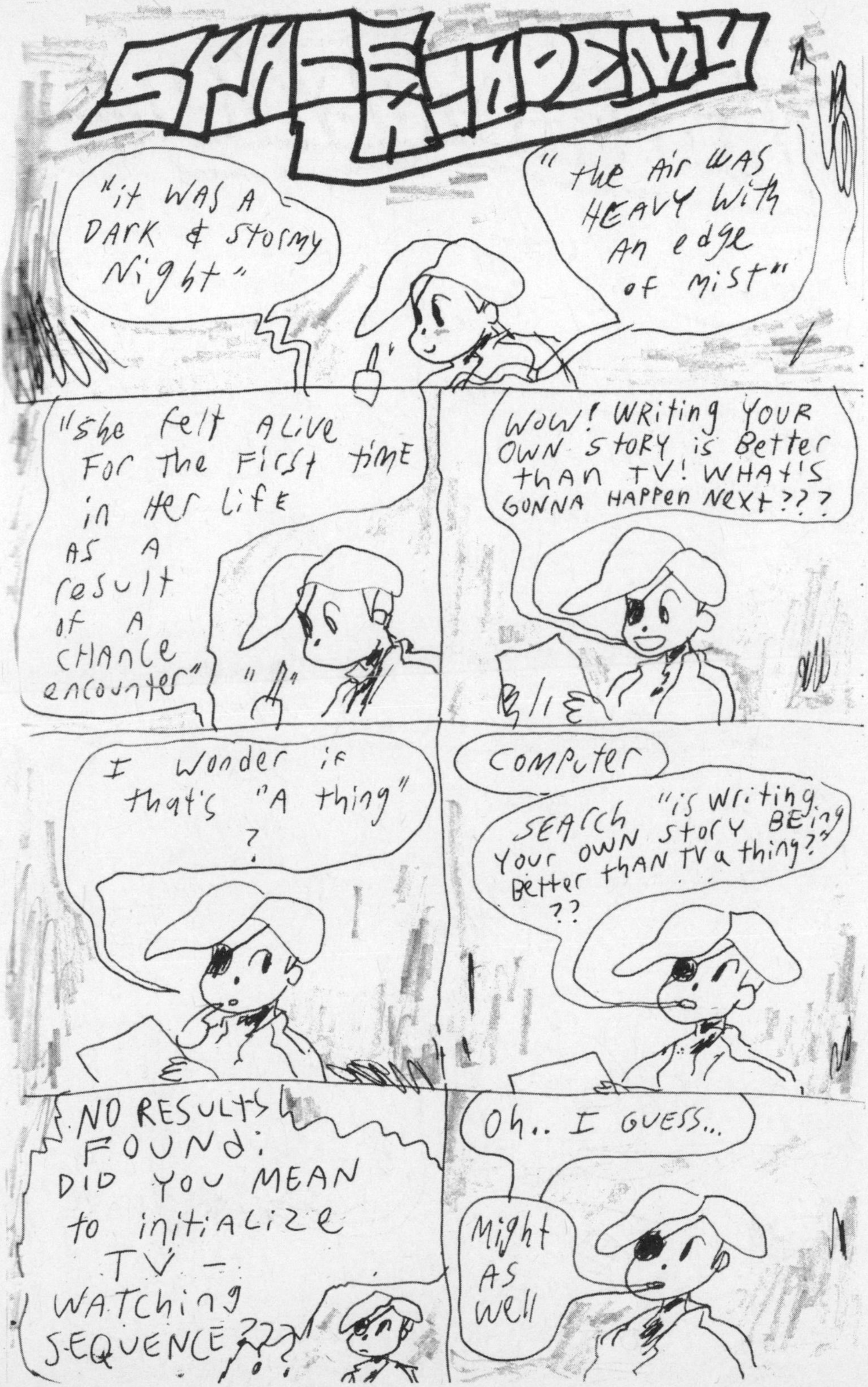
SPACE ACADEMY
"it WAS A DARK & stormy Night"
" the Air WAS HEAVY with An edge of mist"
"she felt ALive For the First time in Her life AS A result of A CHANCE encounter"
WOW! WRiting YOUR OWN story is Better than TV! WHAT'S GONNA HAPPEN NEXT???
I wonder if that's "A thing" ?
COMPuter
SEARCH "is writing your own story BEing Better than TV a thing?" ??
NO RESULTS FOUND: DID YOU MEAN to initiALize TV - WATChing SEQUENCE???
Oh.. I GUESS...
Might AS well

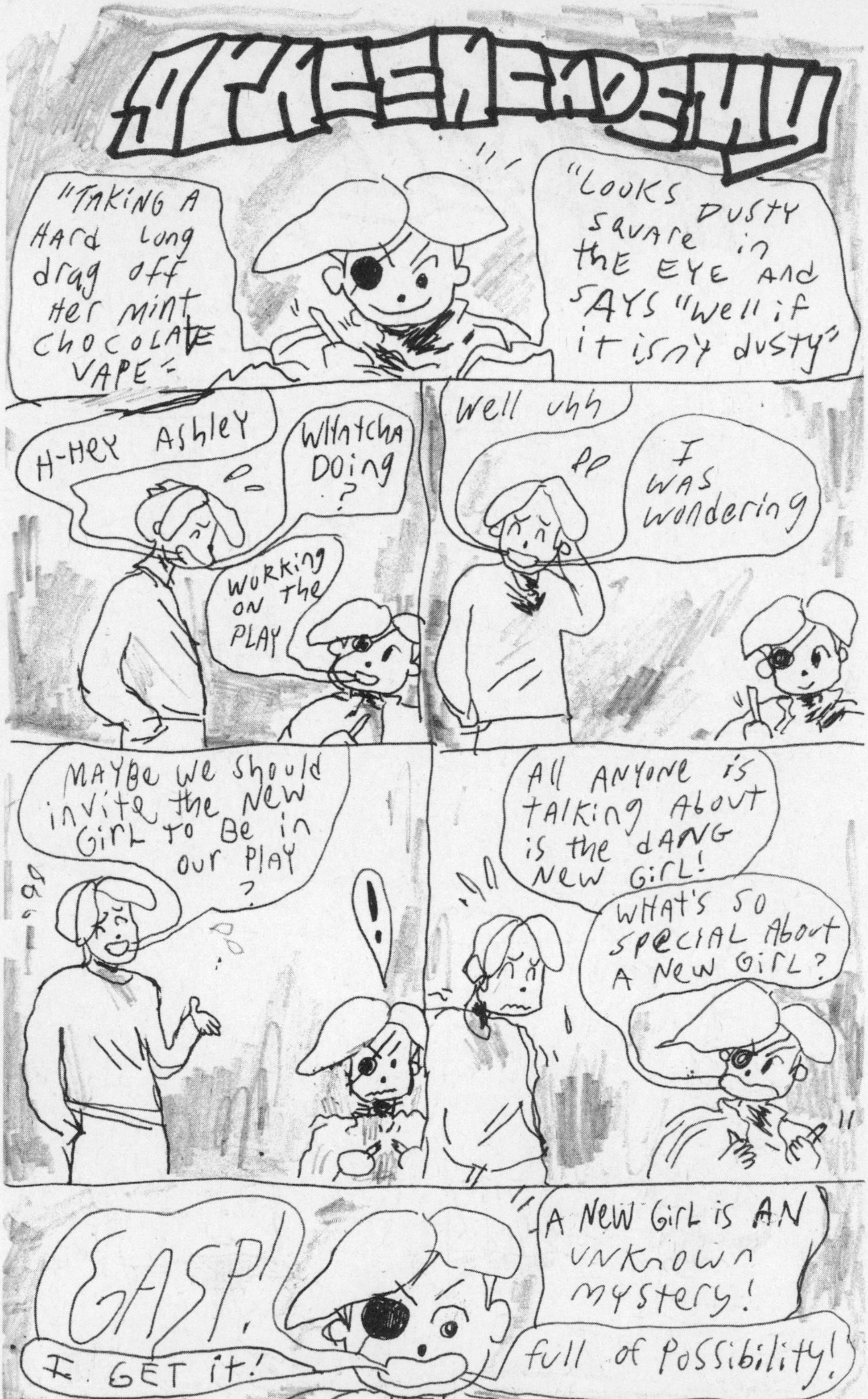
"TAKING A HARd Long drag off Her mint CHOCOLATE VAPE"
"LOOKS DUSTY square in the EYE AND SAYS "Well if it isn't dusty"
H-HEY Ashley
WHATCHA DOING ?
WORKING ON THE PLAY
Well uhh
I WAS wondering
MAYBe we should invite the NEW GIRL TO Be in our PLAY ?
!
All ANYONE is TALKING About is the dANG NEW GIRL!
WHAT'S SO SPECIAL About A NEW GIRL?
GASP!
I GET it!
A NEW GIRL is AN UNKNOWN mystery!
full of POSSibility!

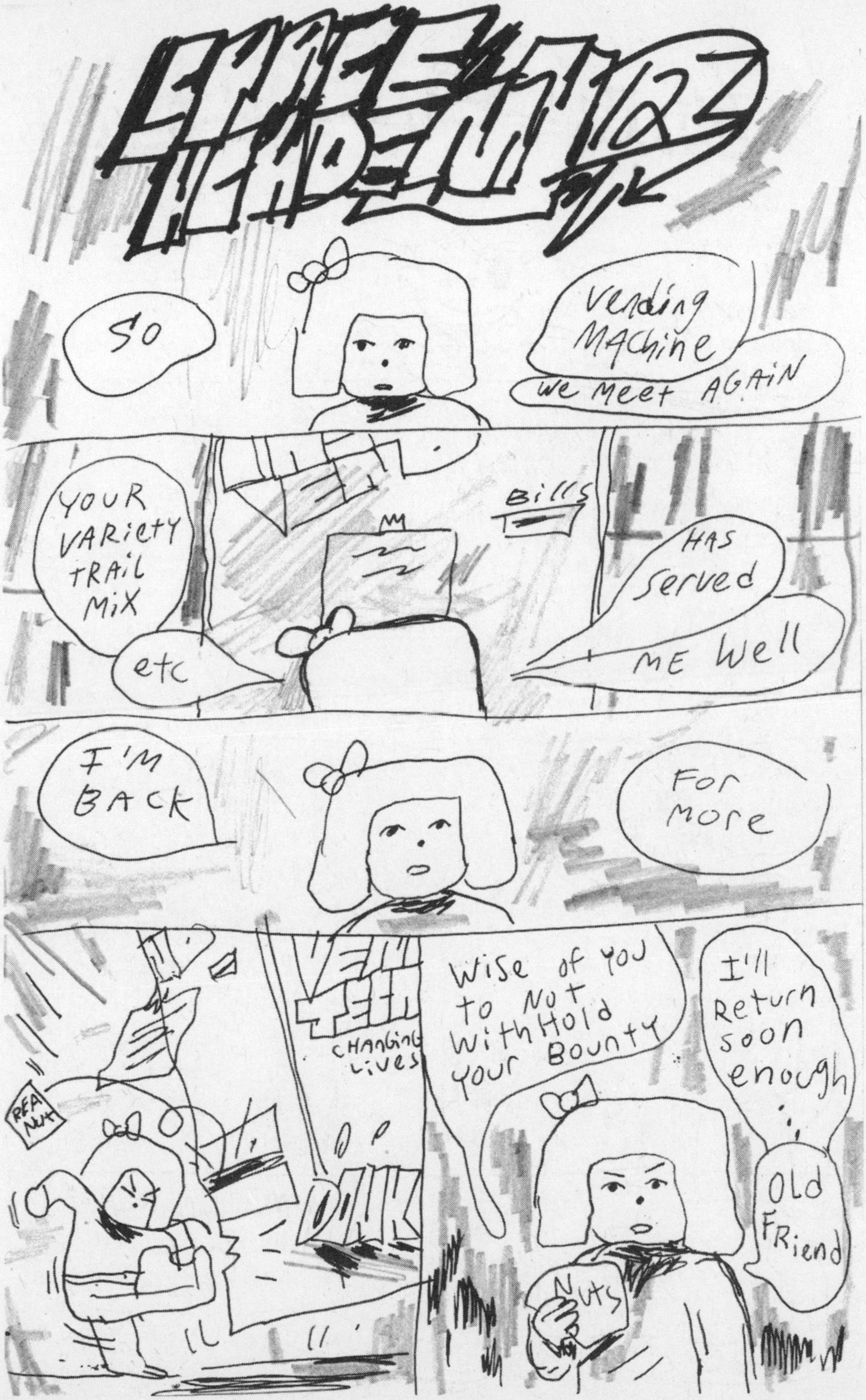
So
Vending MAchine
we Meet AGAIN
YOUR VARiety TRAIL MIX
etc
Bills
HAS served
ME Well
I'M BACK
For more
CHANGING LIVES
Wise of you to Not WithHold your Bounty
I'll Return soon enough...
Old FRiend
Nuts

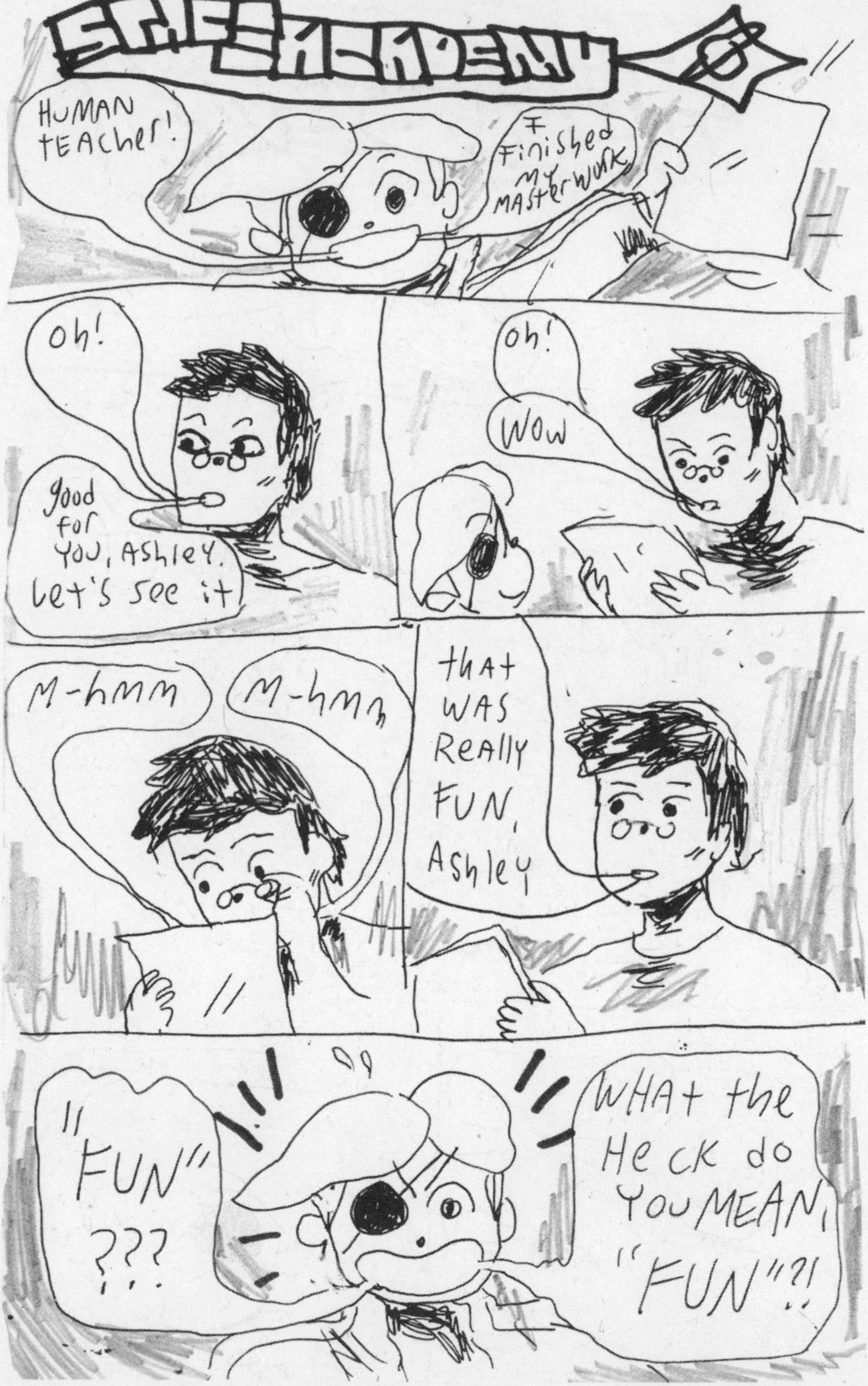
HUMAN TEACHER!
I Finished my MASTERWORK
oh!
good for you, Ashley. let's see it
oh!
WOW
M-hmm
M-hmm
that WAS Really FUN, Ashley
"FUN" ???
WHAT the Heck do YOU MEAN, "FUN"?!

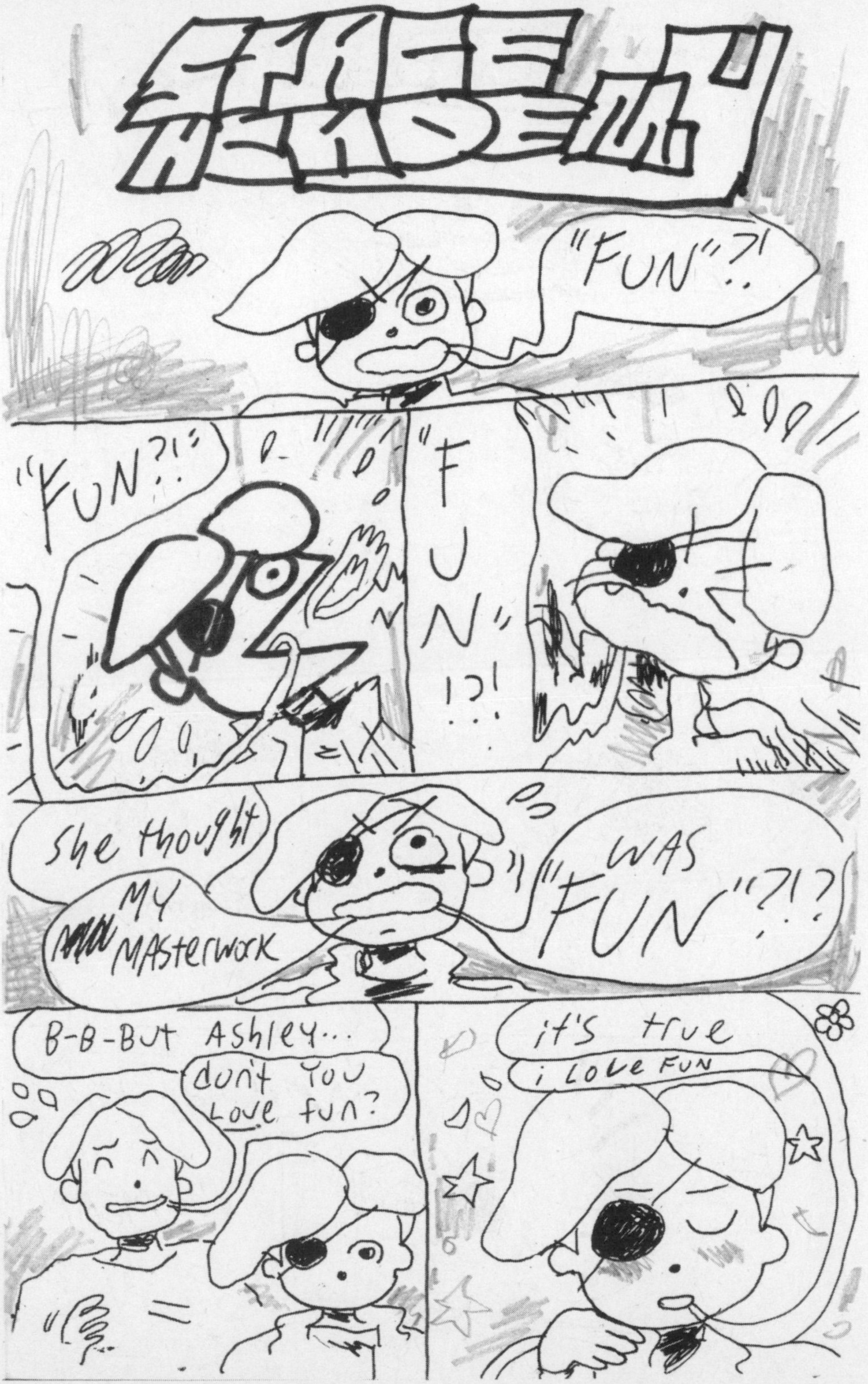
"FUN"?!
"FUN?!"
"FUN"!?!
She thought
MY MASTERWORK
WAS "FUN"?!?
B-B-BUT ASHLEY...
don't YOU Love fun?
it's true
i LOVE FUN

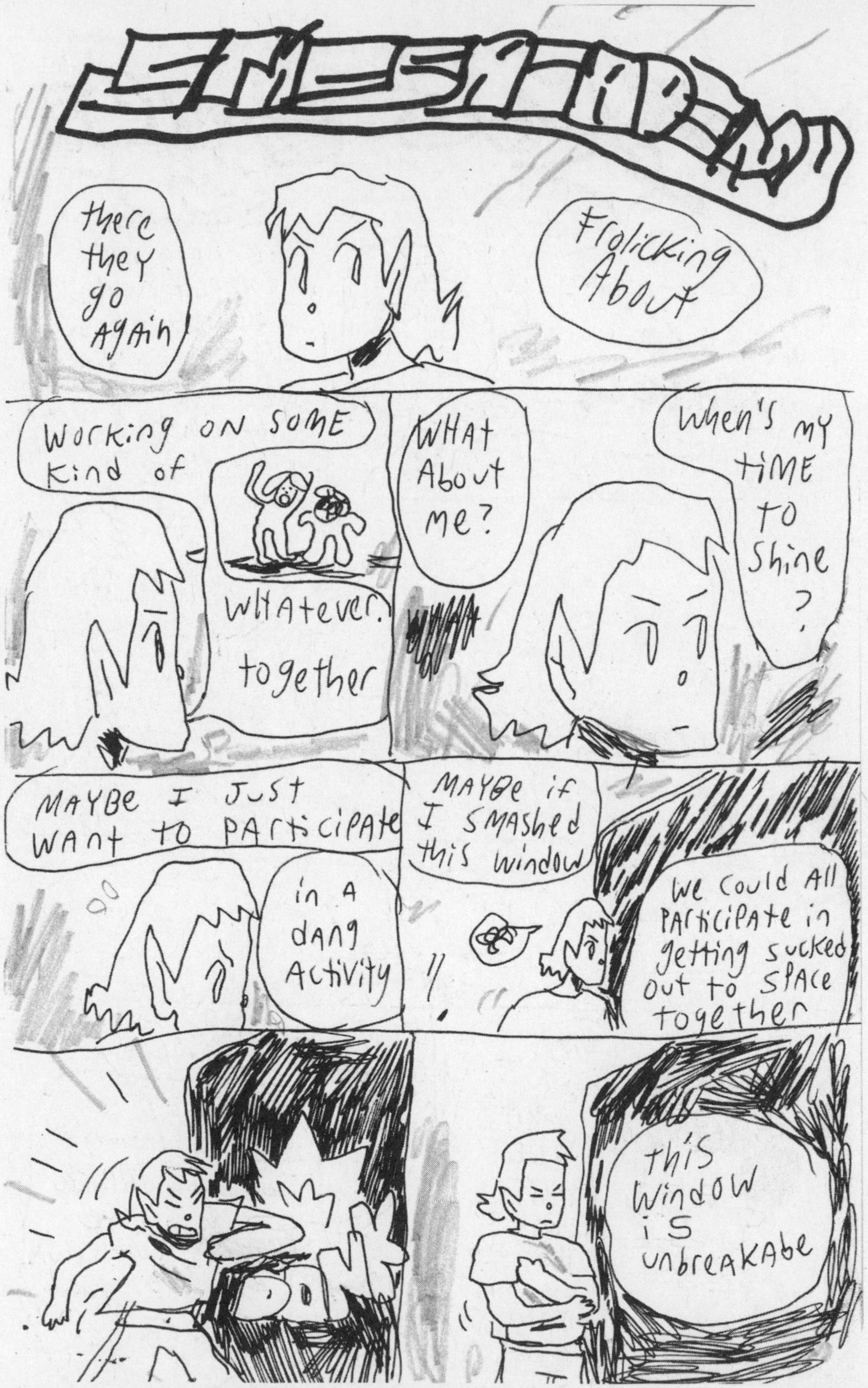
there they go again
Frolicking About
working on some kind of
whatever. together
WHAT About me?
when's my time to shine?
MAYBE I JUST WANT TO PARTICIPATE
in a dang Activity
MAYBE if I SMASHED this window
We could All participate in getting sucked out to space together
this window is unbreakabe

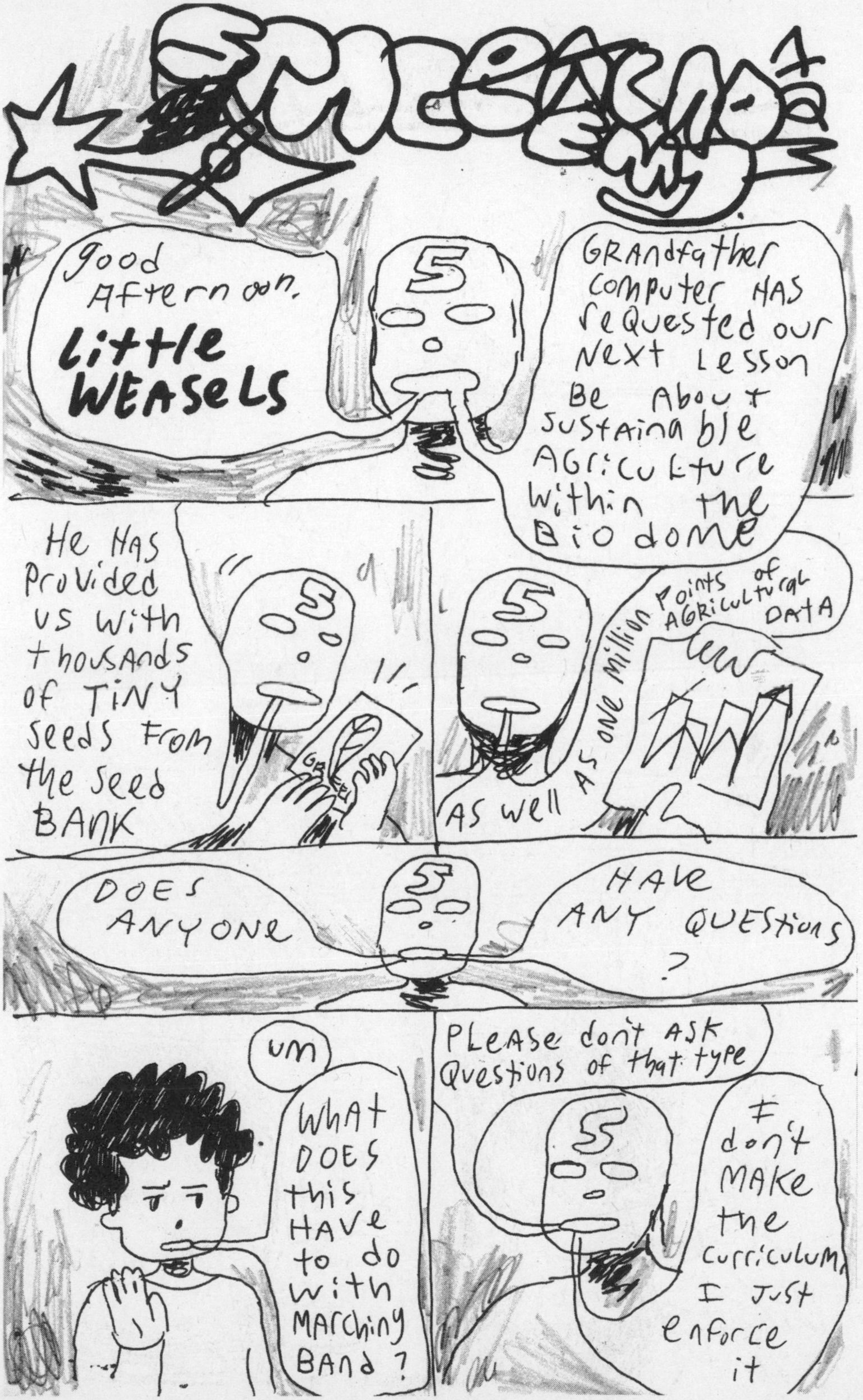

good Afternoon, little WEASELS
GRANdfather computer HAS requested our Next Lesson Be About sustainable AGriculture within the Bio dome
He HAS provided us with thousands of TINY seeds From the seed BANK
As well As one Million Points of AGricultural DATA
DOES ANYONE HAVE ANY QUESTIONS ?
um
WHAT DOES this HAVE to do with MARChing BAND ?
PLEASE don't ASK Questions of that type
I don't MAKE the curriculum, I just enforce it

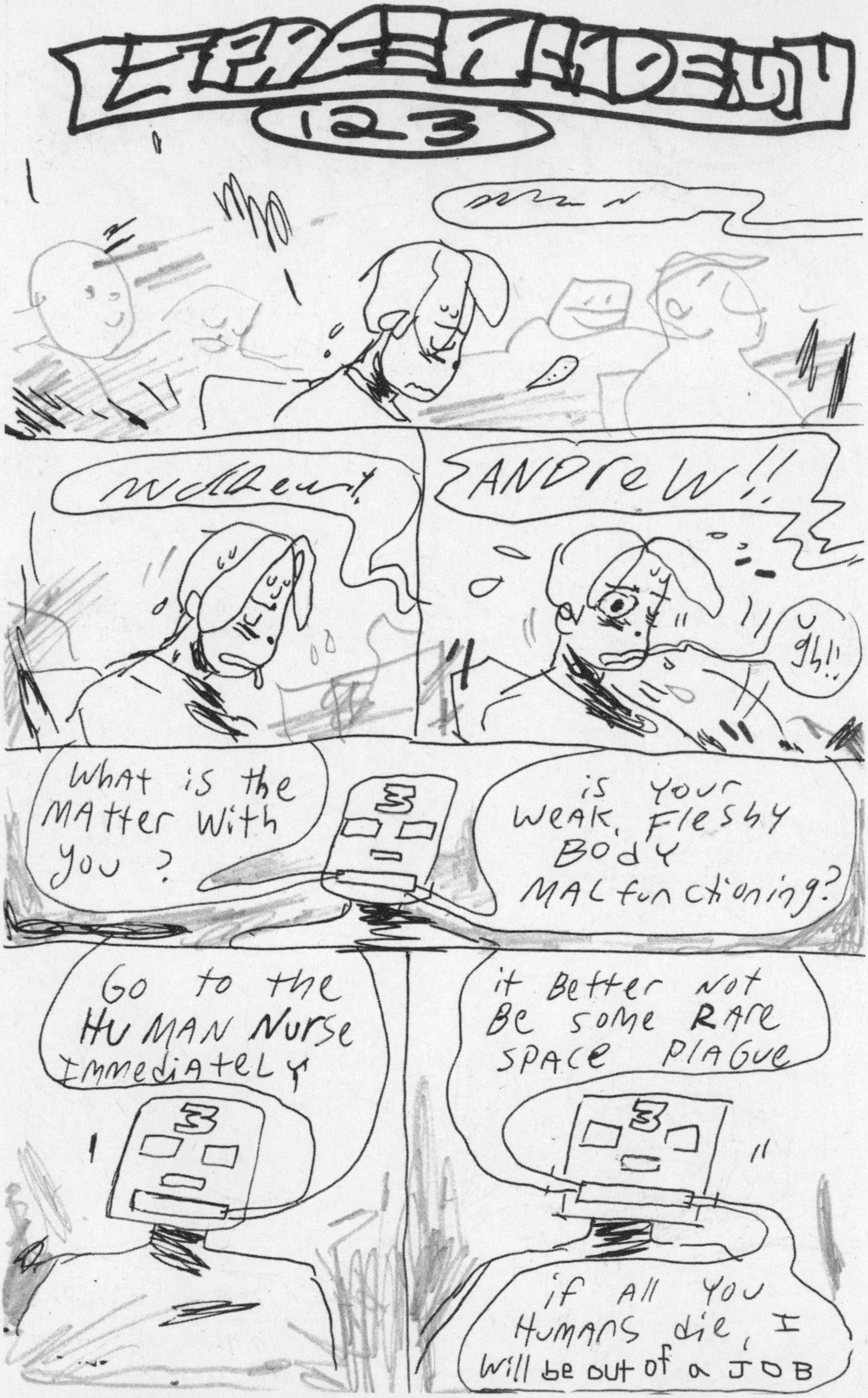

123
ANDREW!!
ugh!!
What is the MATTER With you ?
is your weak, Fleshy Body MALfunctioning?
Go to the HUMAN Nurse Immediately
it Better not Be some RARE space plague
if all you Humans die, I will be out of a JOB

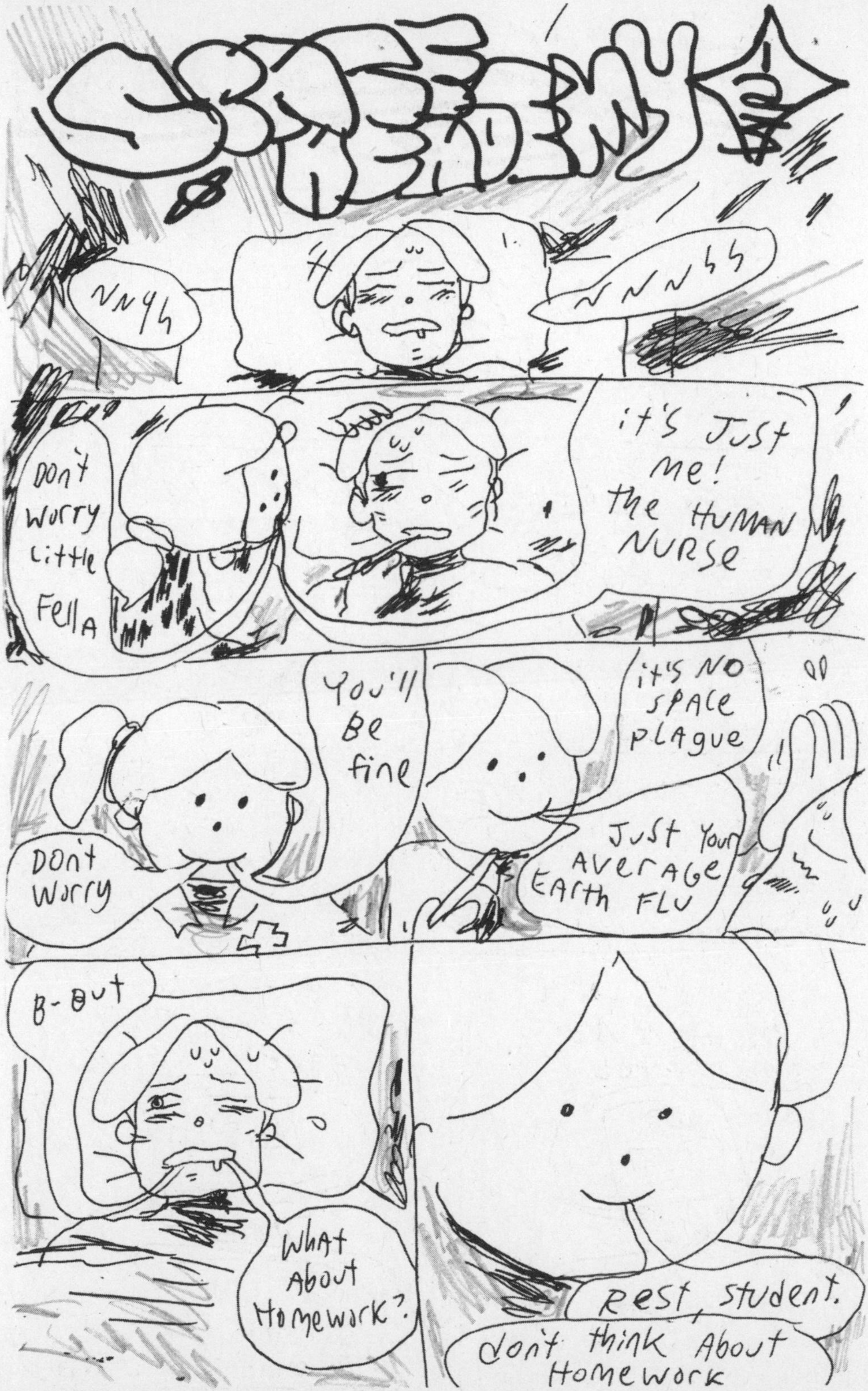
NNYh
NNNhh
Don't worry little Fella
it's Just me! the HUMAN NURSE
Don't worry
You'll Be fine
it's NO SPACE plague
Just Your AverAGE EArth FLU
B-UT
What About Homework?
Rest, student.
don't think About Homework

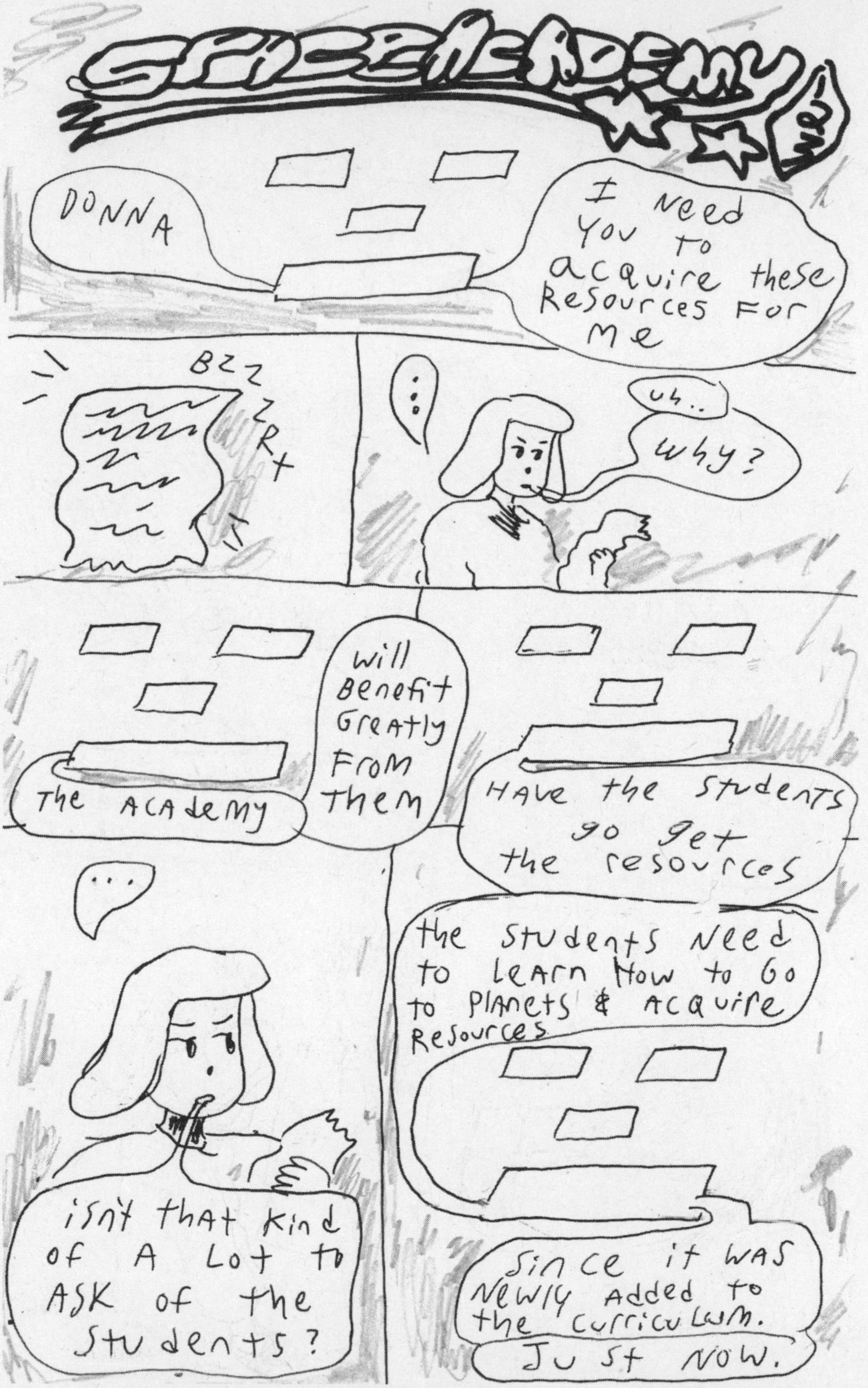
DONNA
I need you to acquire these Resources For me
BZZ
ZRT
...
uh..
why?
The ACAdemy
will Benefit Greatly From them
HAve the Students go get the resources
...
the Students need to Learn How to Go to Planets & Acquire Resources
isn't that Kind of A Lot to ASK of the Students?
Since it WAS Newly Added to the curriculum.
Just NOW.

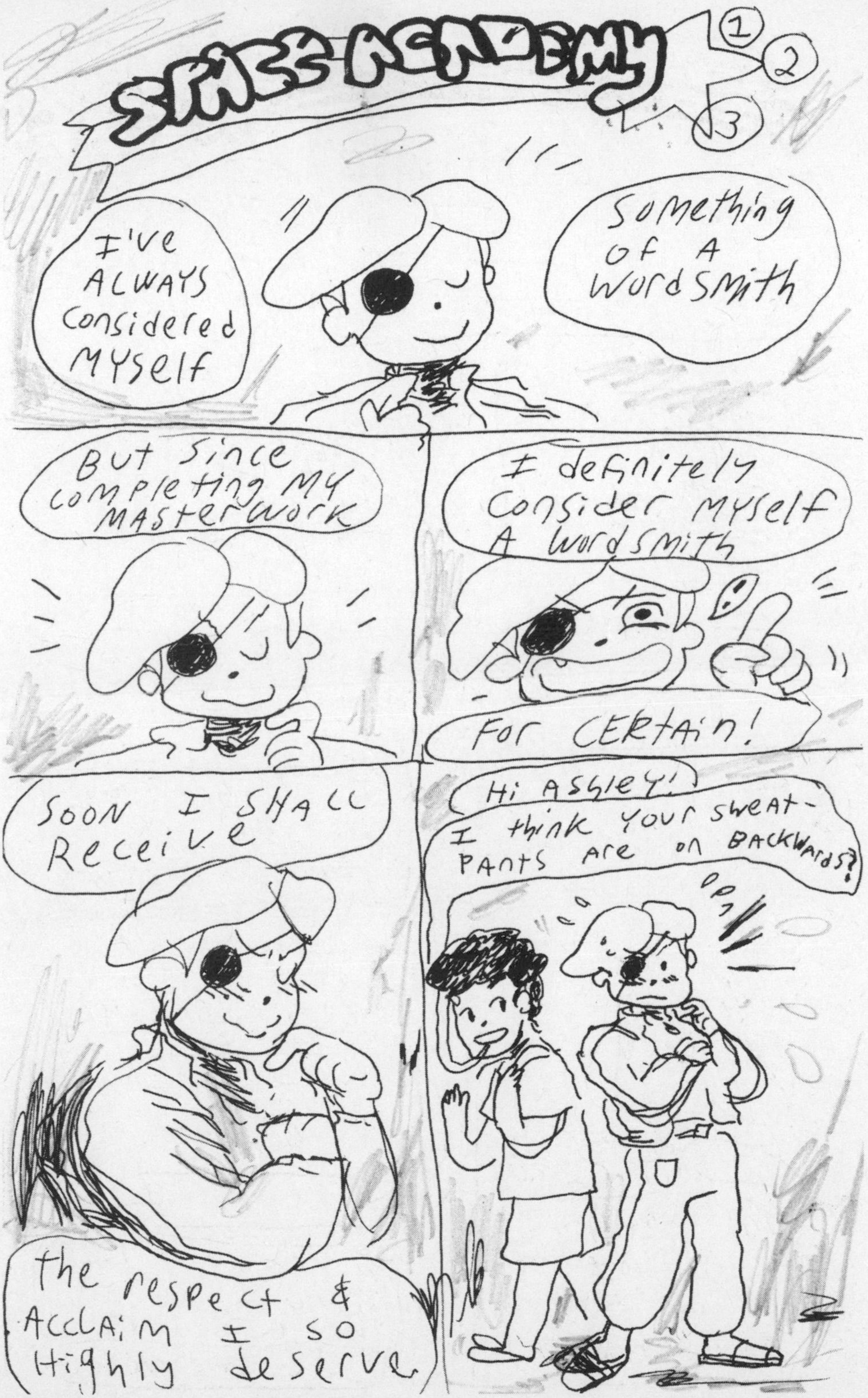
SPACE ACADEMY
1
2
3
I've ALWAYS considered MYSELF
Something of A WordSmith
But Since completing MY MASTERWORK
I definitely consider Myself A WordSmith
FOR CERTAIN!
SOON I SHALL Receive
the respect & ACCLAIM I SO Highly deserve
Hi ASHLEY!
I think YOUR SWEAT-PANTS ARE ON BACKWARDS?

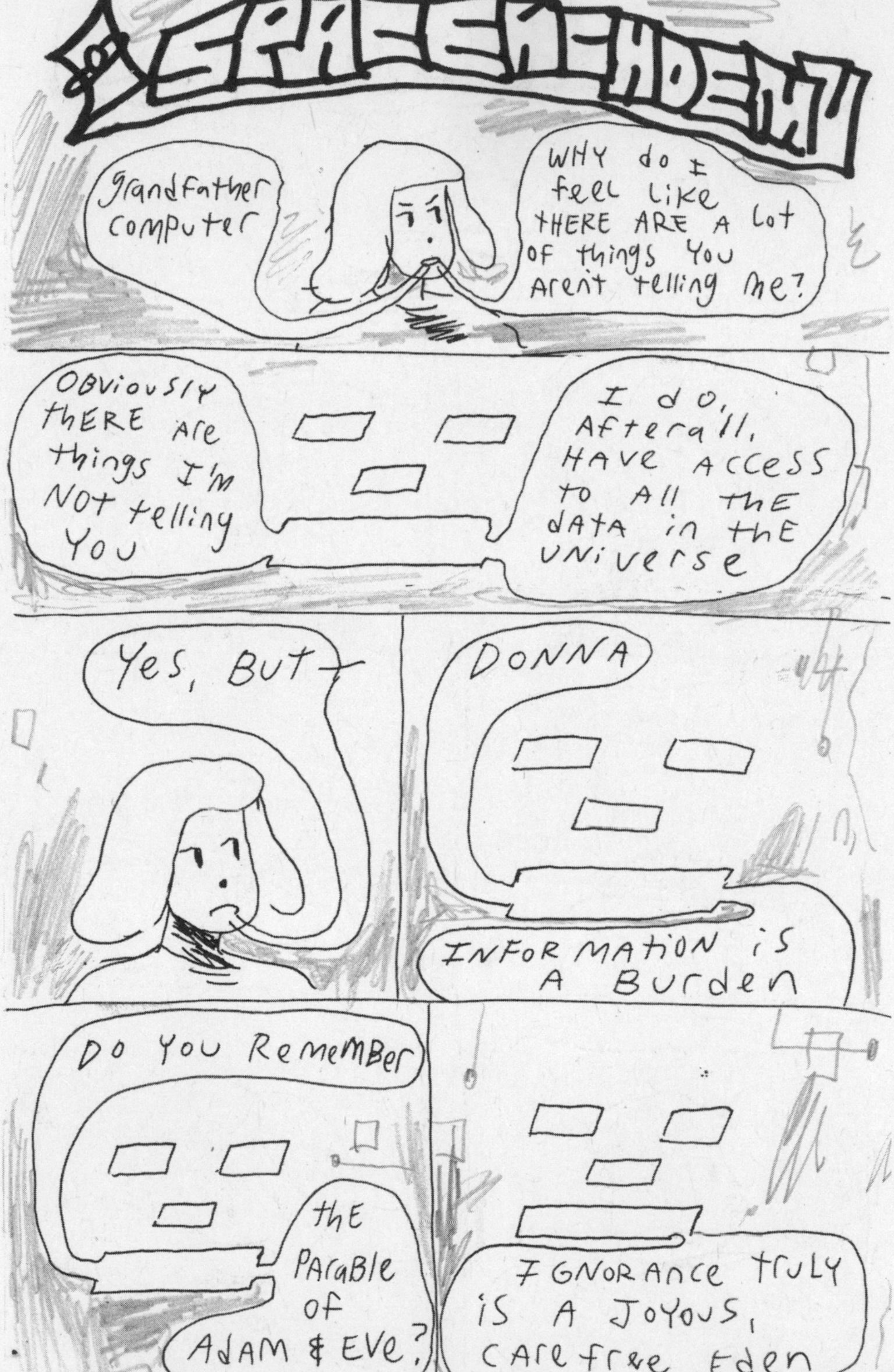
grandfather computer
WHY do I feel like THERE ARE A lot of things you aren't telling me?
OBVIOUSLY THERE are things I'm NOT telling YOU
I do, afterall, HAVE ACCESS to ALL THE DATA in THE UNIVERSE
YES, BUT-
DONNA
INFORMATION is A Burden
DO YOU ReMeMBer
the PARABLE of ADAM & EVE?
IGNORANCE truly is A JOYOUS, carefree Eden

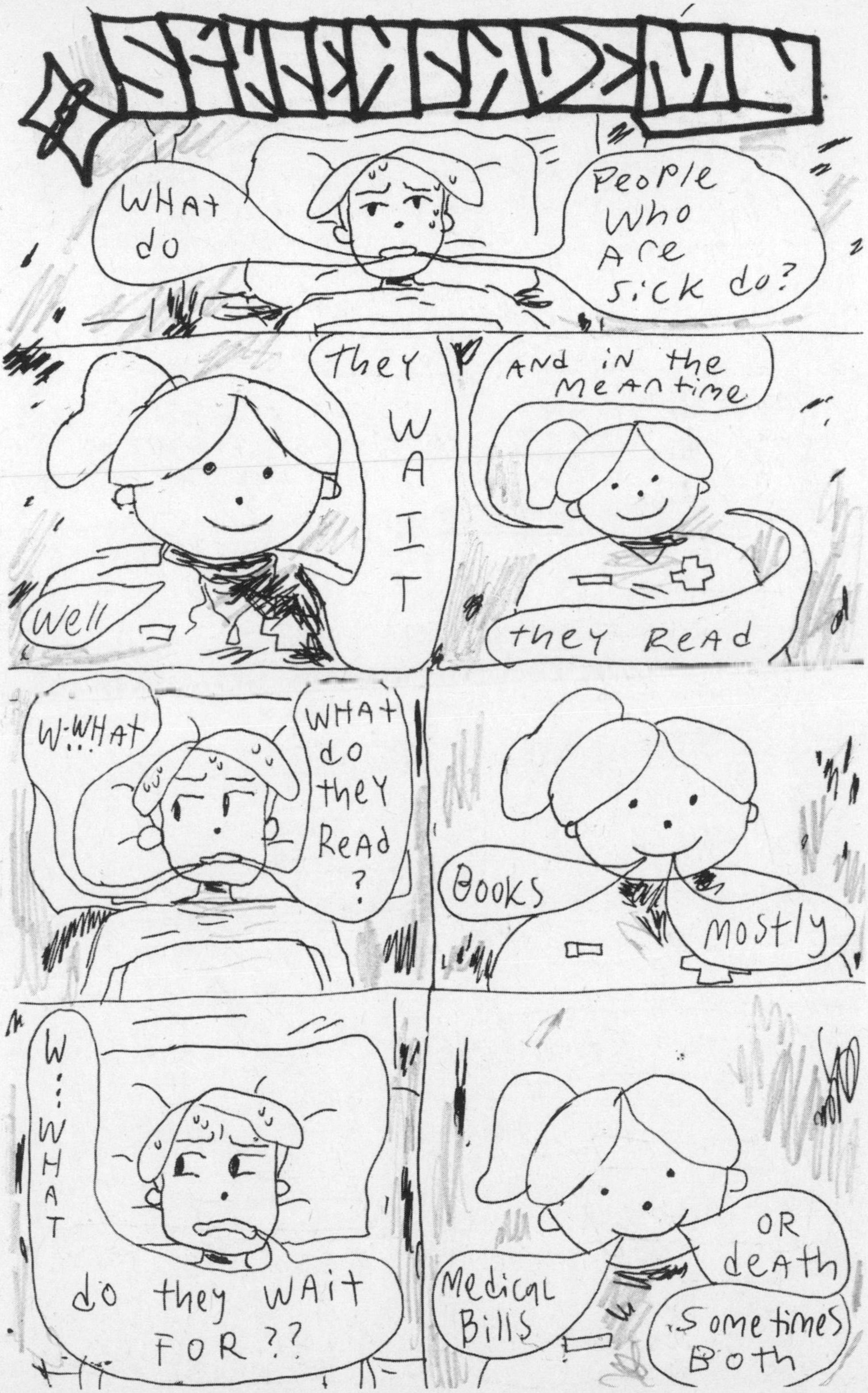
WHAt do
People Who Are sick do?
Well
They WAIT
And in the meantime
they Read
W-WHAt...
WHAt do they Read ?
Books
mostly
W...WHAT
do they WAIt FOR ??
Medical Bills
OR death
Sometimes Both

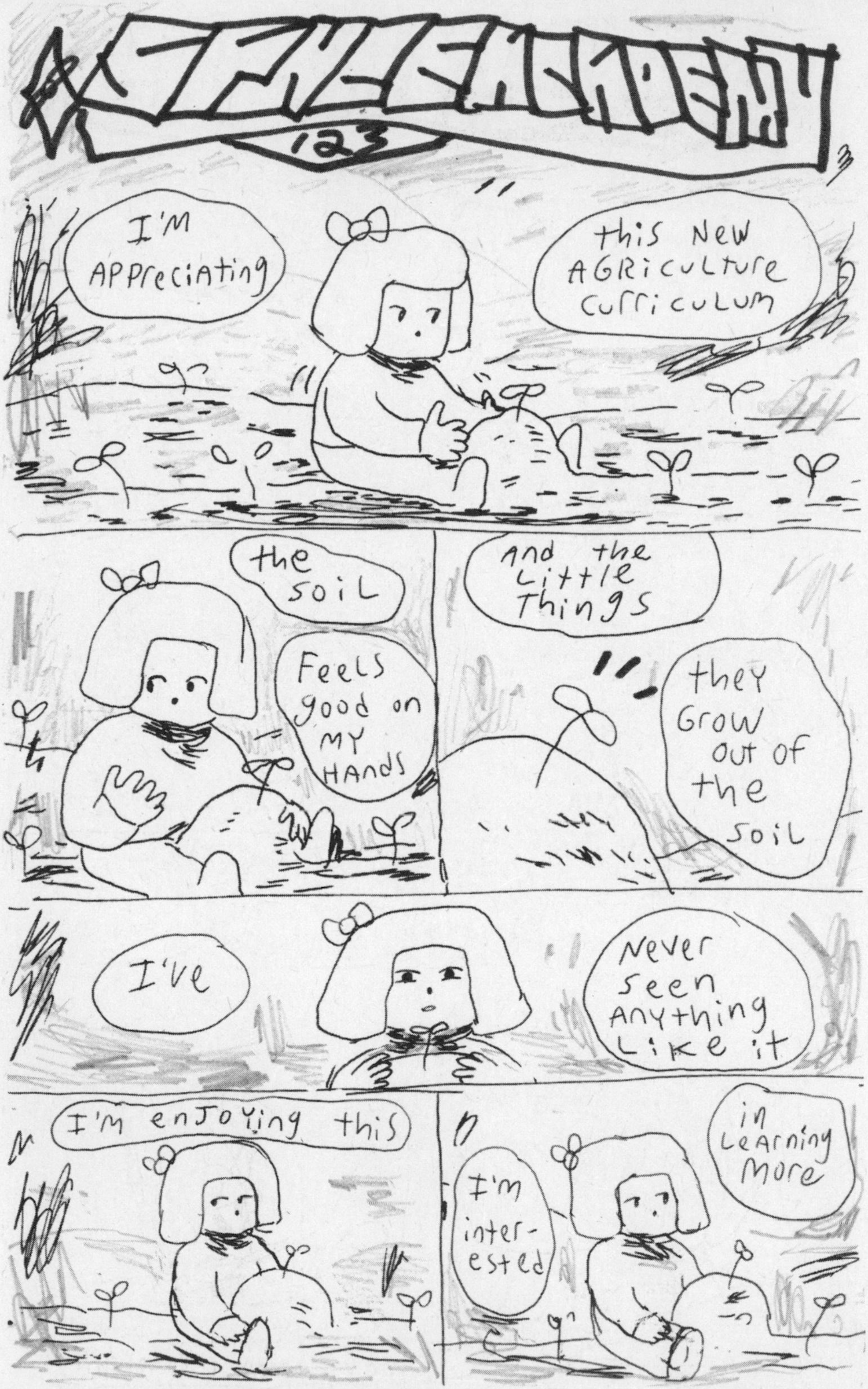
123
I'M APPreciATing
this New AGRiculture curriculum
the soil
Feels good on MY HANDS
and the Little Things
they Grow out of the soil
I've
Never seen Anything Like it
I'm enJoying this
I'm inter-ested
in Learning More

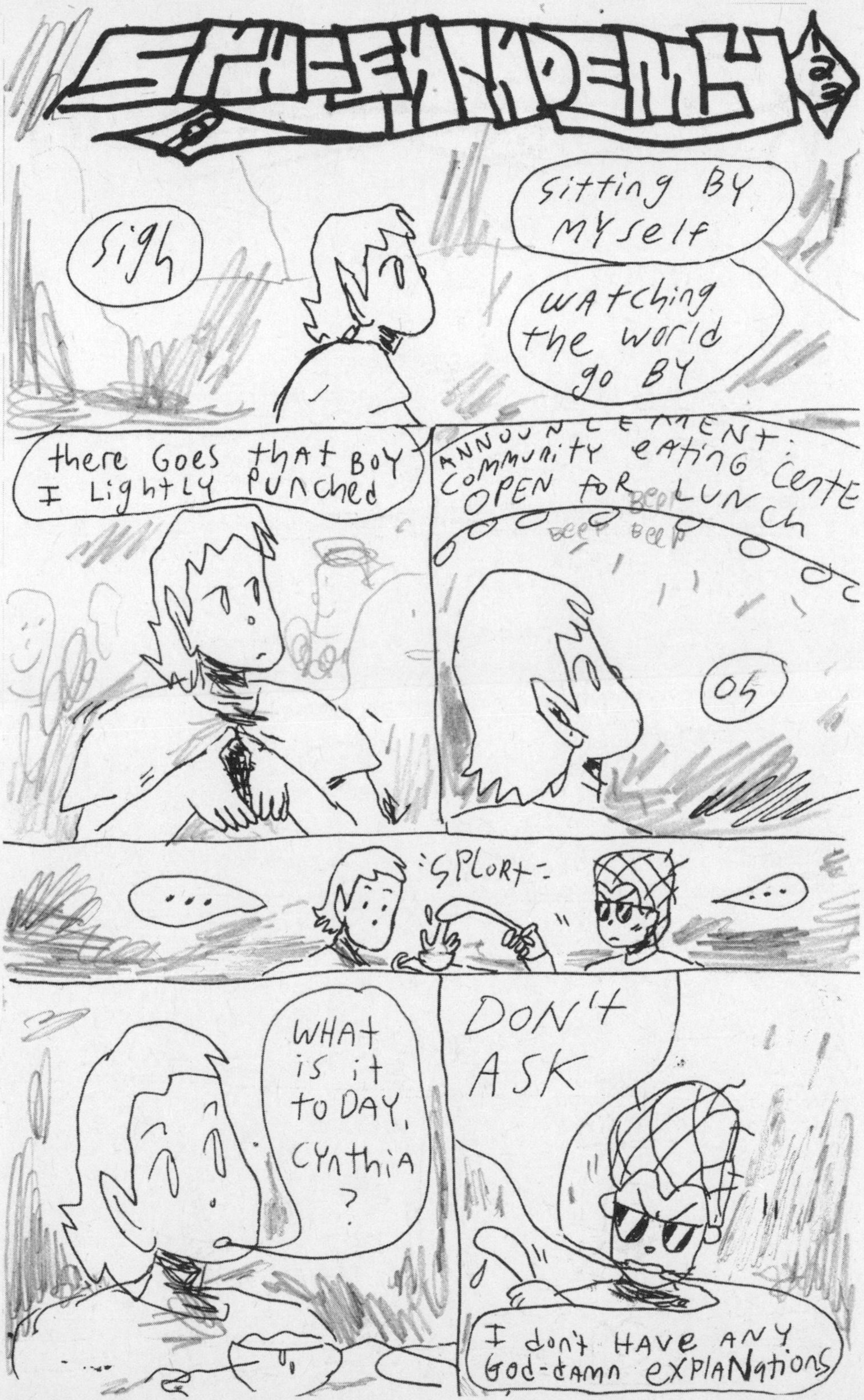
Sigh
Sitting BY myself
wATching the world go BY
there Goes that BOY I Lightly Punched
ANNOUNCEMENT: COMMUNITY eating CENTE OPEN FOR LUNCH
BEEP BEEP BEEP
Oh
...
SPLORT
...
WHAT is it toDAY, CYnthiA ?
DON'T ASK
I don't HAVE ANY God-damn exPLANations

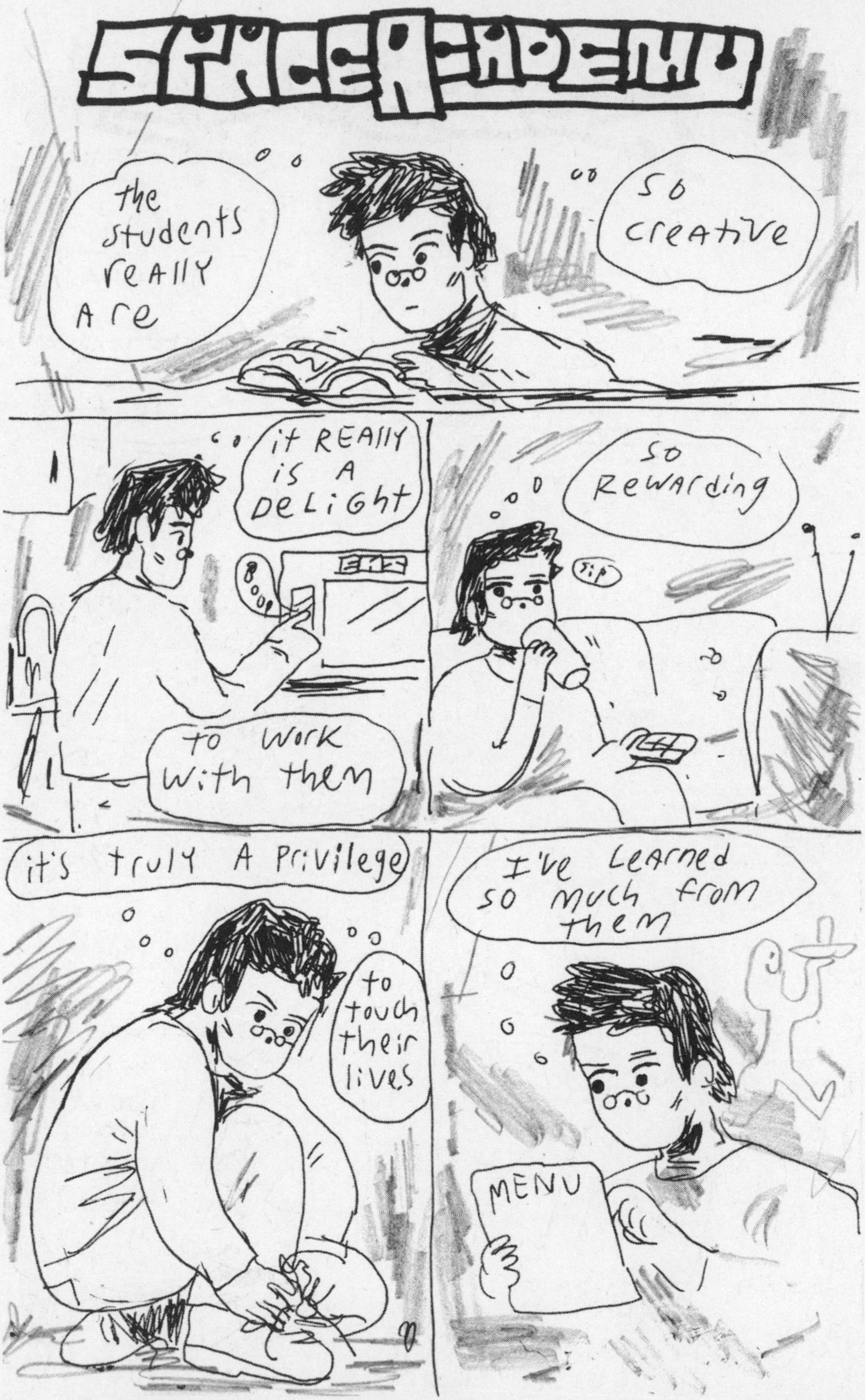
the students really are
so creative
it REAlly is A DeLiGht
Boop
to work with them
so Rewarding
tip
it's truly A Privilege
to touch their lives
I've Learned so much from them
MENU

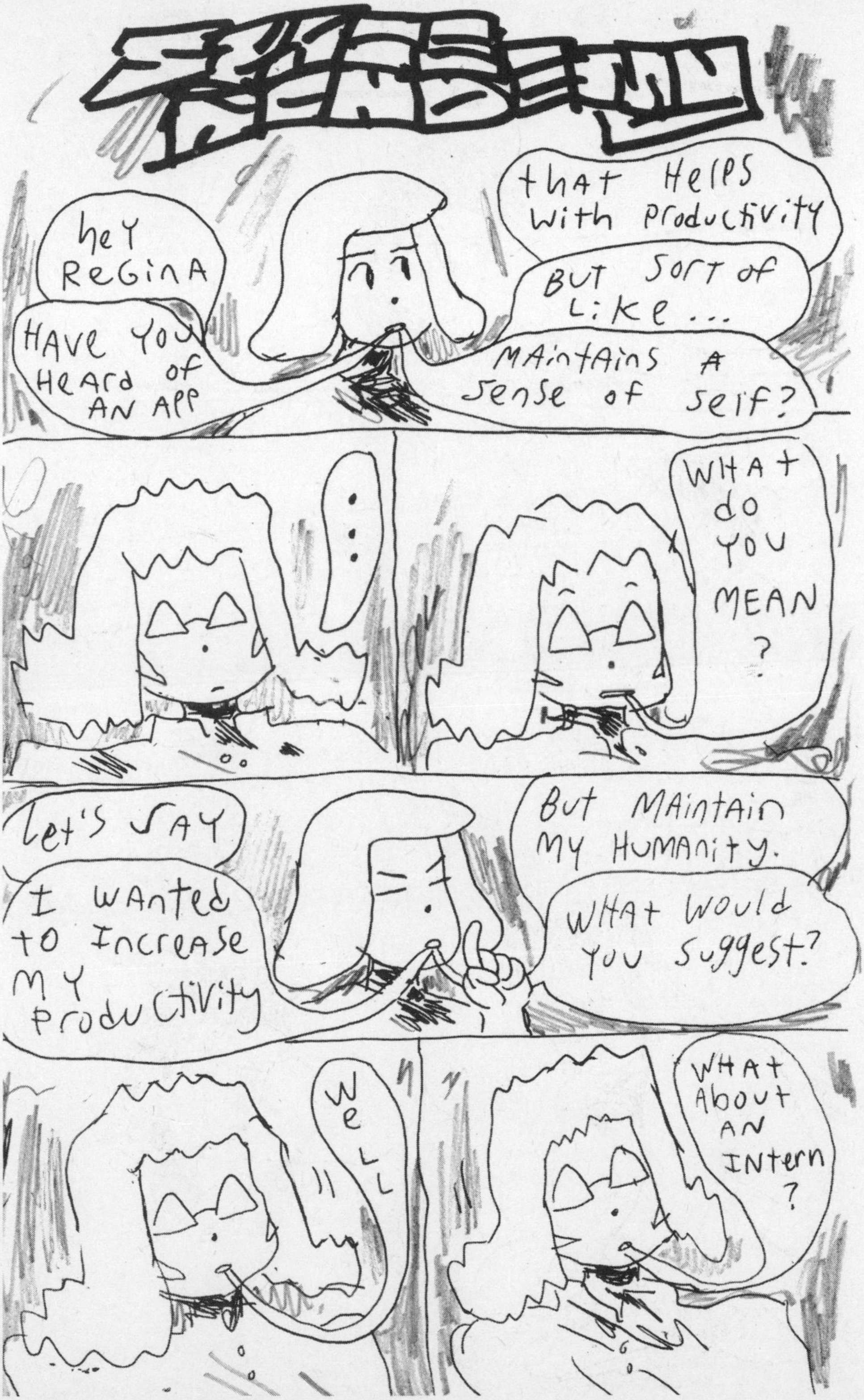
hey Regina
HAVE YOU Heard of AN APP
that Helps with productivity
But sort of like ...
MAintains A sense of self?
...
WHAT do YOU MEAN ?
let's SAY
I WAnted to Increase MY productivity
But MAintain MY HuMAnity.
WHAT Would YOU suggest?
WeLL
WHAT About AN Intern ?

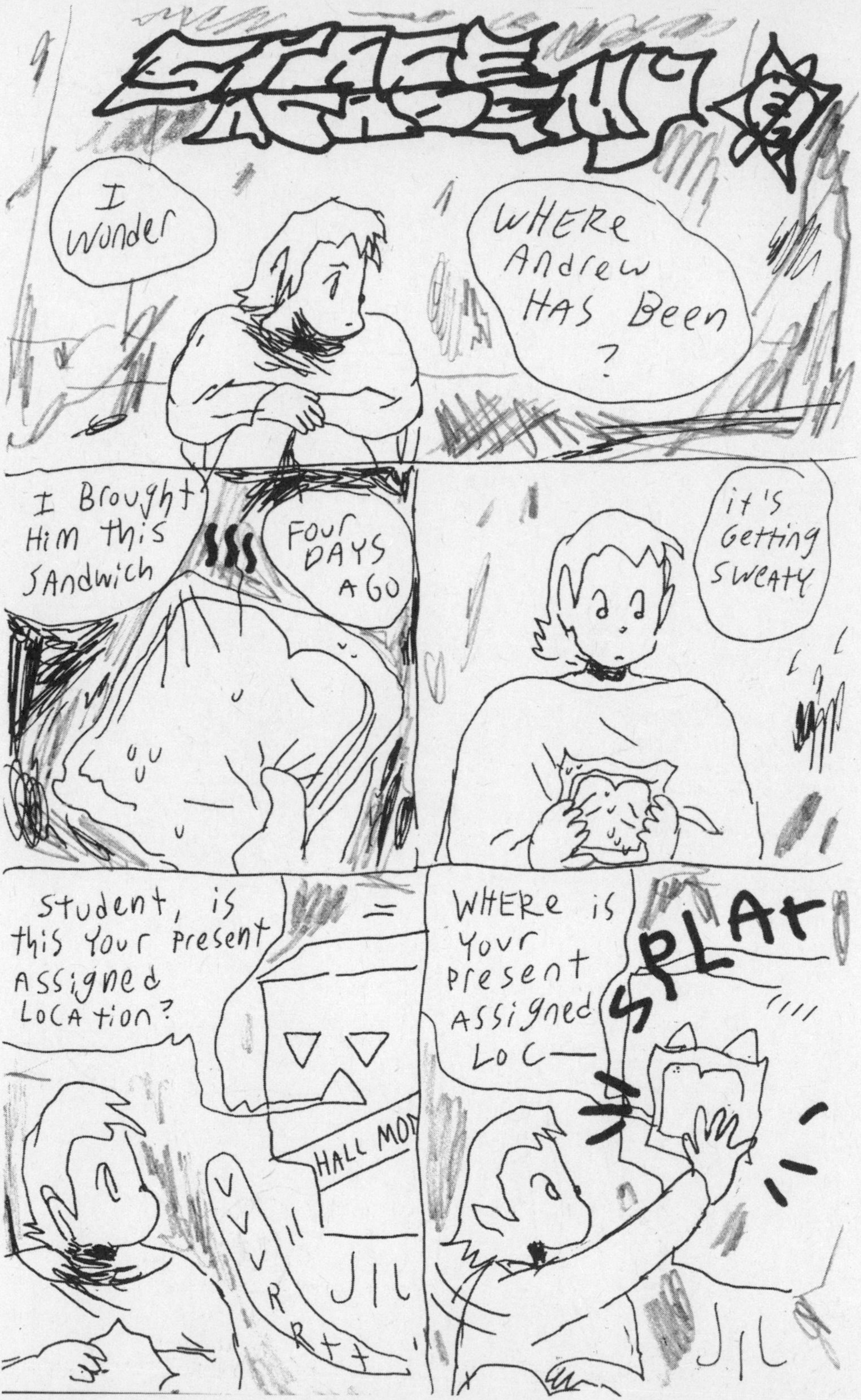
I wonder
WHERE Andrew HAS Been ?
I Brought Him this SAndwich
FOUR DAYS AGO
it's Getting SWEATY
Student, is this your present Assigned Location?
HALL MON
WHERE is your present Assigned LOC—
SPLAT

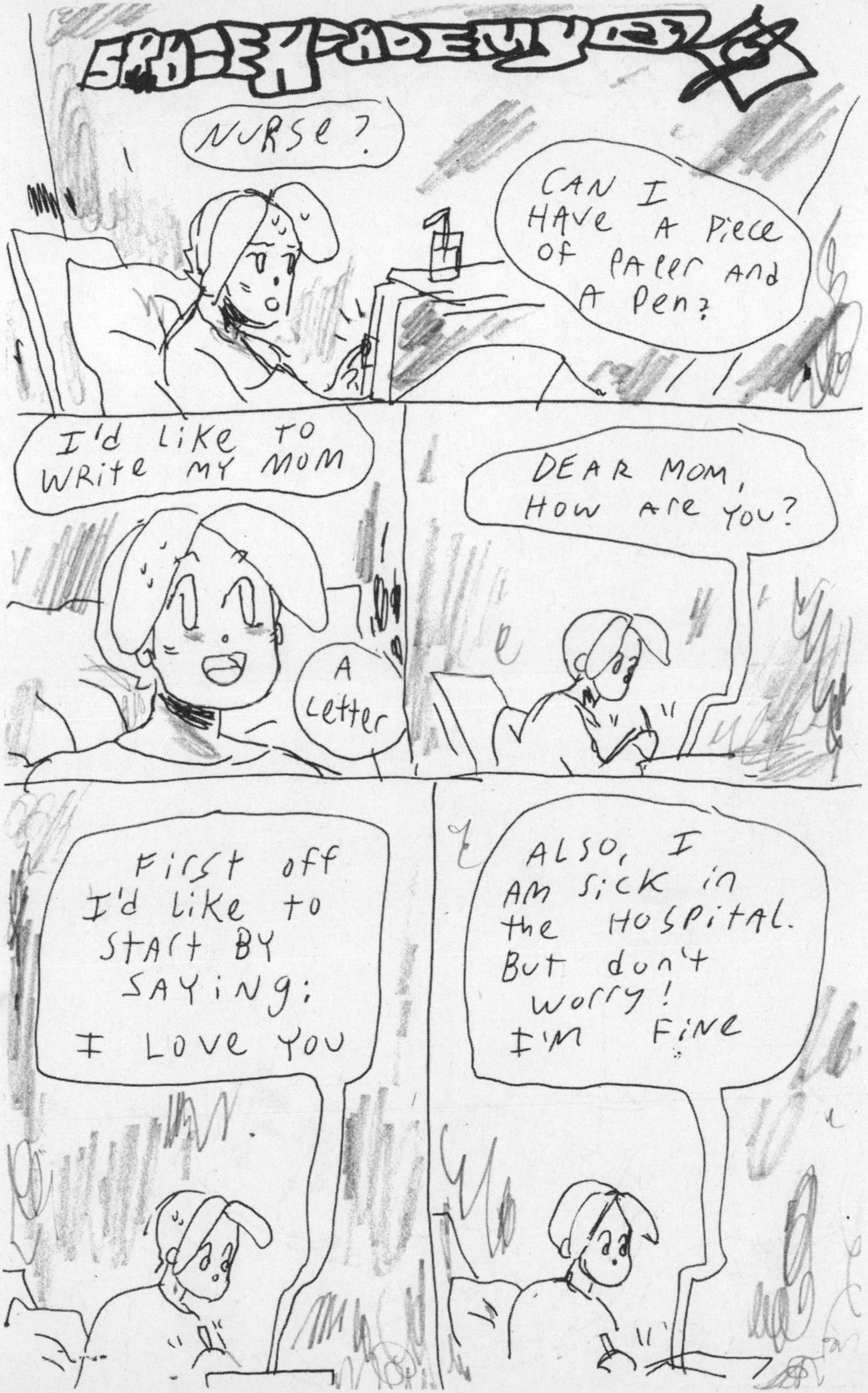
NURSE?
CAN I HAVE A PIECE OF PAPER AND A PEN?
I'D LIKE TO WRITE MY MOM
A LETTER
DEAR MOM, HOW ARE YOU?
FIRST OFF I'D LIKE TO START BY SAYING: I LOVE YOU
ALSO, I AM SICK IN THE HOSPITAL. BUT DON'T WORRY! I'M FINE

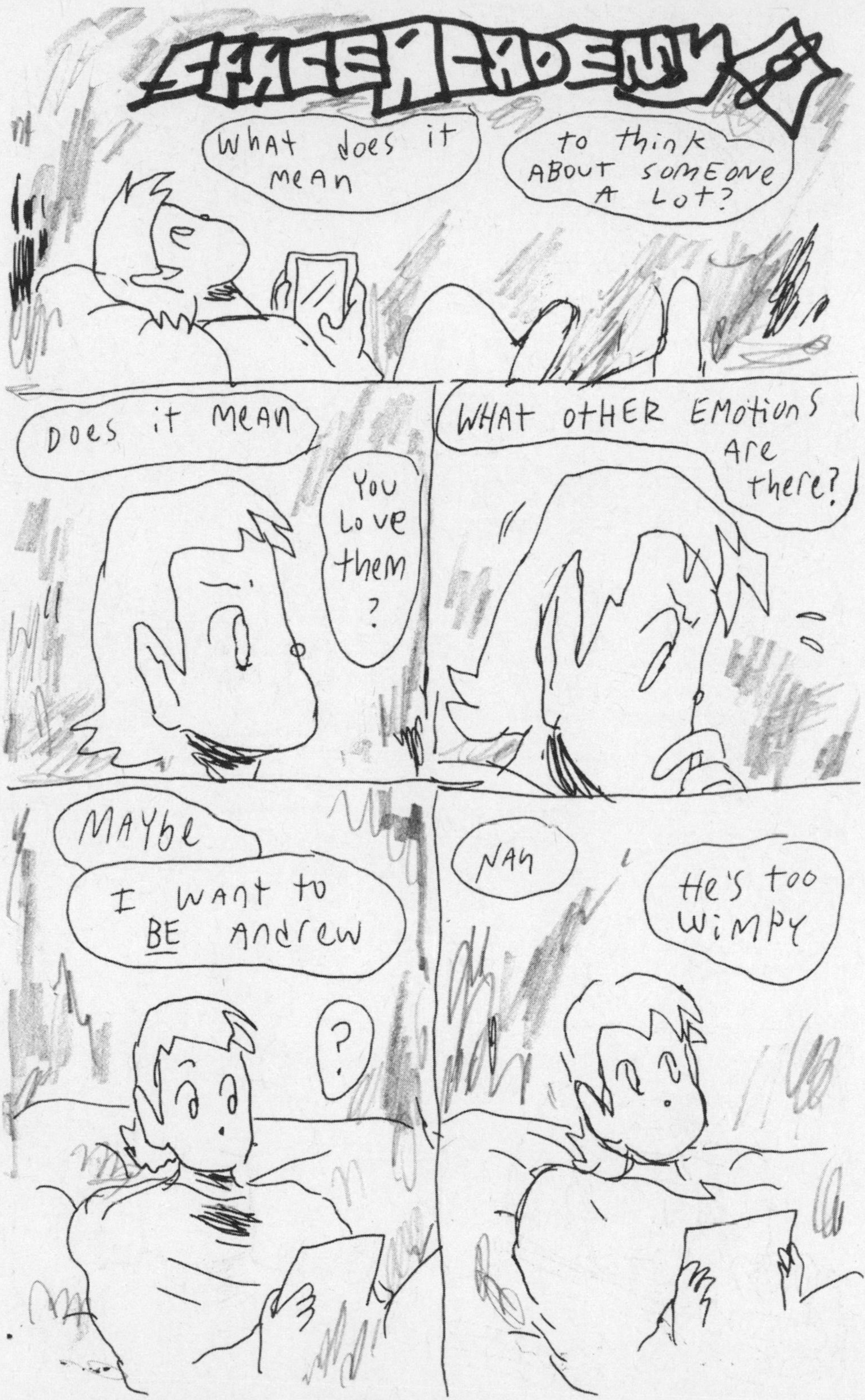
What does it mean
to think ABOUT SOMEONE A Lot?
Does it Mean
You Love them ?
WHAT otHER EMotions Are there?
MAYbe
I want to BE Andrew
?
NAH
He's too WiMPY

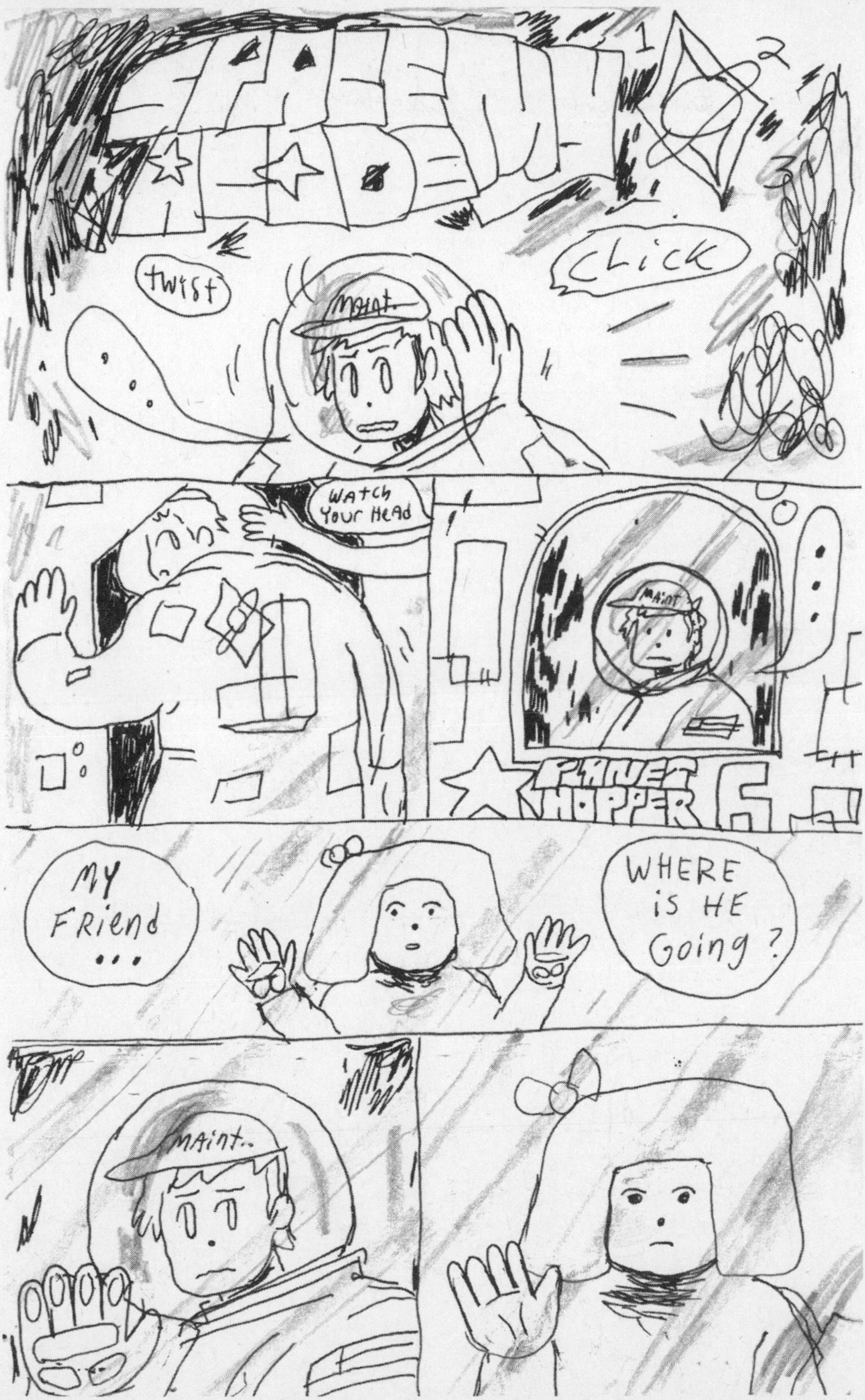

twist
Click
MAINT.
Watch Your Head
MAINT
PLANET HOPPER
MY Friend ...
WHERE is HE Going ?
MAINT..

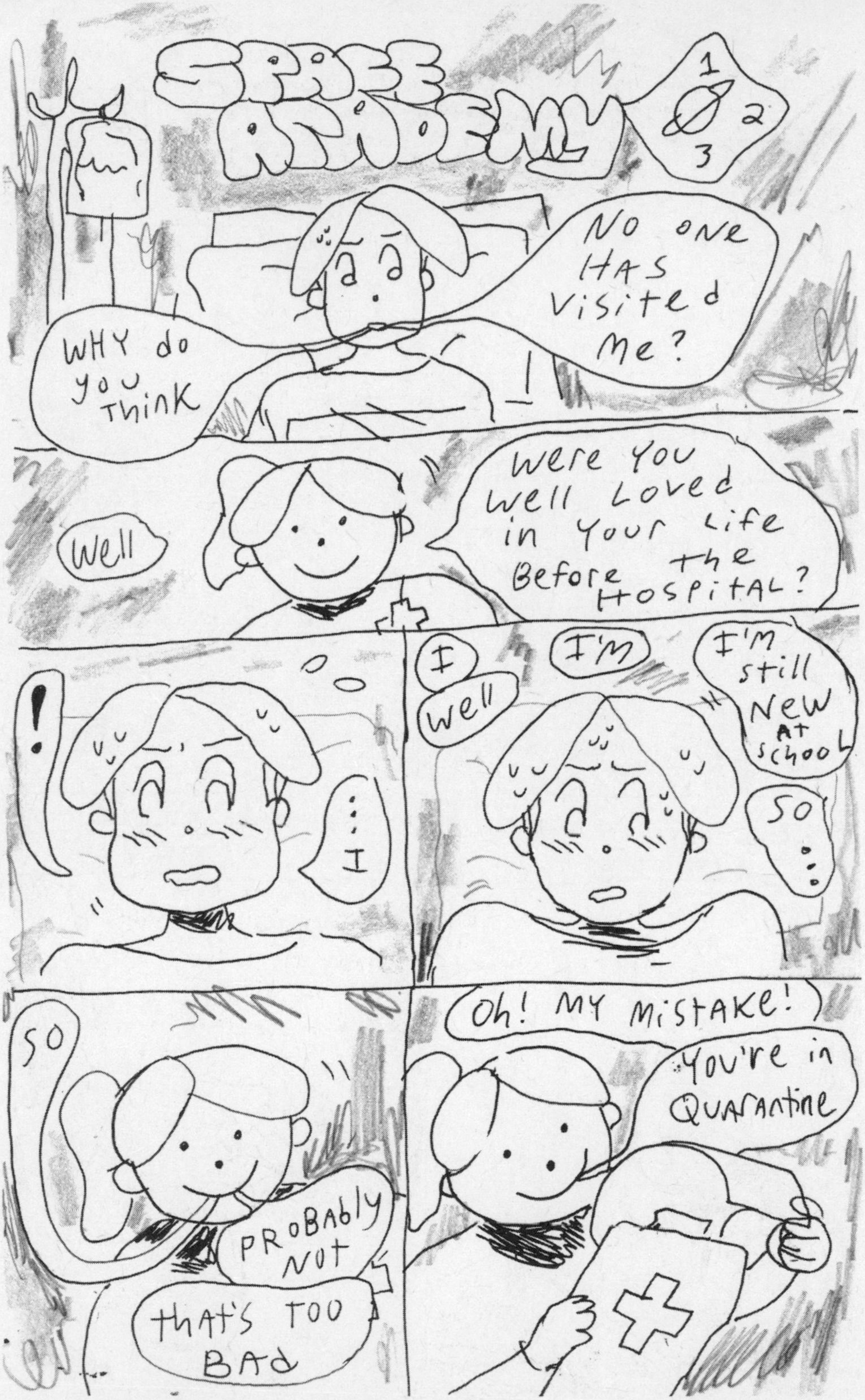
SPACE ACADEMY
1
2
3
WHY do you think
No one HAS visited me?
Well
Were you well Loved in your Life Before the HOSPITAL?
!
... I
I
well
I'M
I'M still New AT SCHOOL
SO...
SO
PROBABly NOT
that's TOO BAd
Oh! MY MiSTAKE!
You're in QUARANTINE

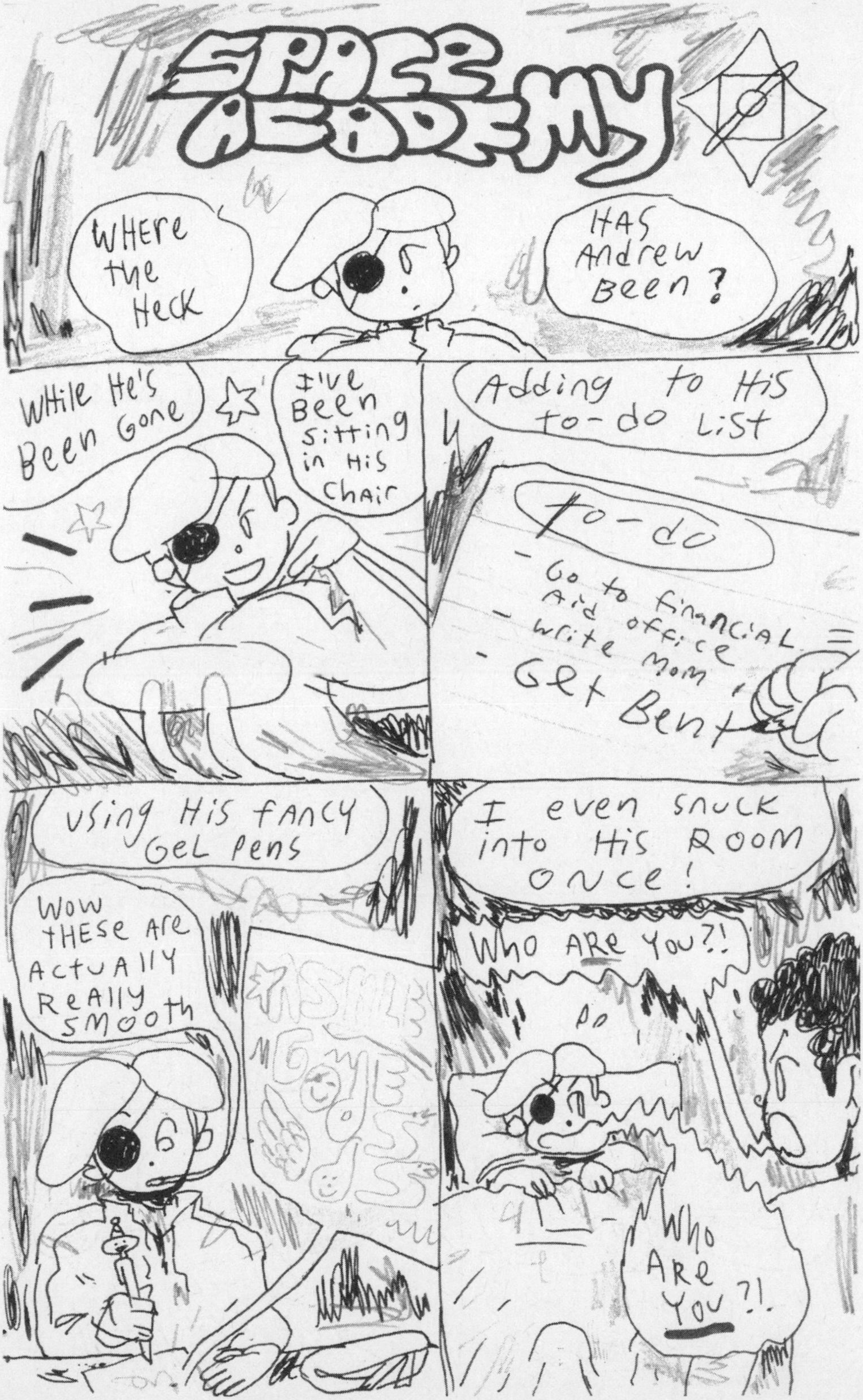
SPACE ACADEMY
WHERE the Heck
HAS Andrew Been?
While He's Been Gone
I've Been sitting in His chair
Adding to His to-do List
to-do
- Go to financial Aid office
- write mom
- Get Bent
using His fancy Gel pens
Wow THESE Are ActuAlly Really SMooth
I even snuck into His ROOM once!
Who ARE You?!
Who Are You?!

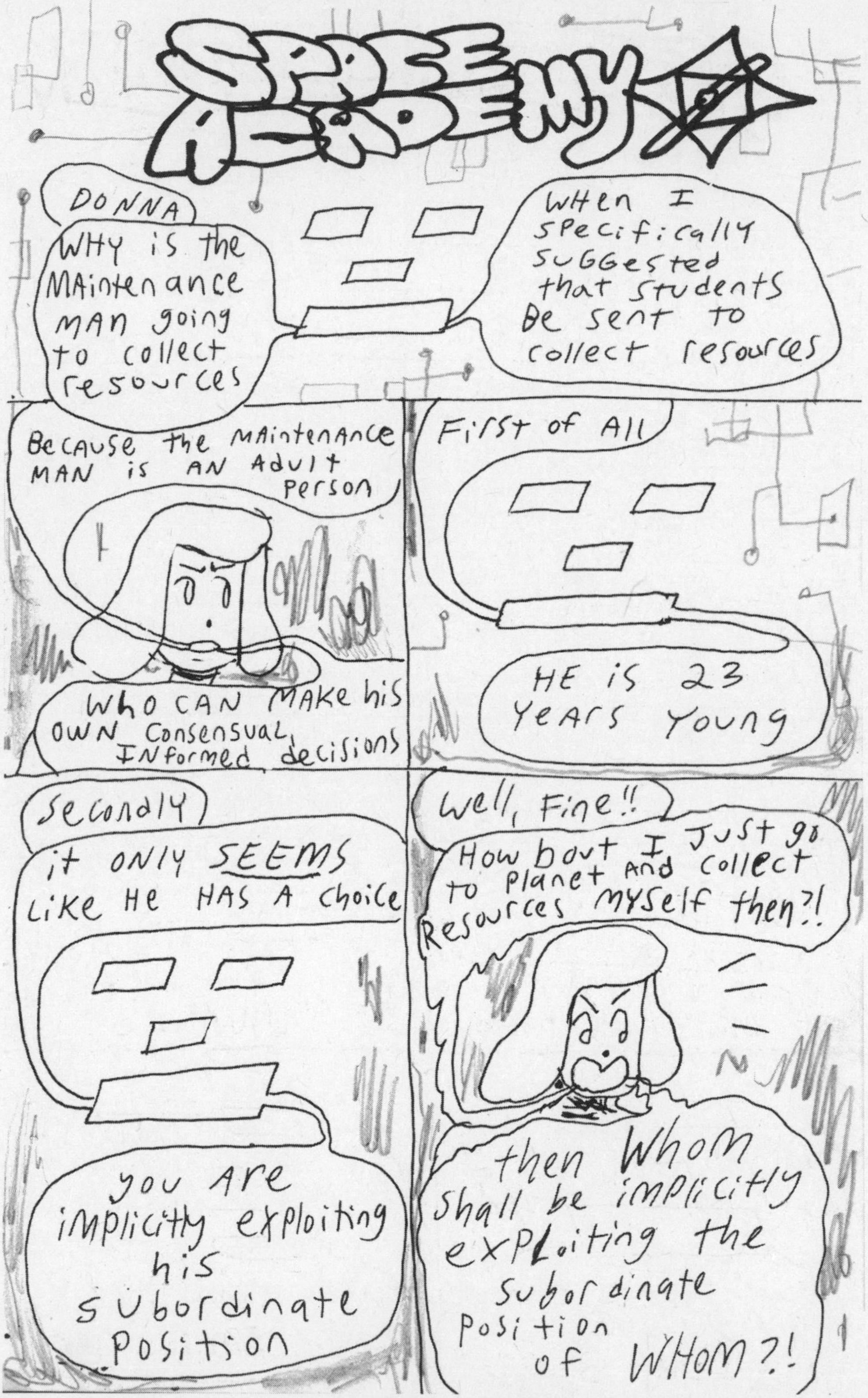
SPACE ACADEMY
DONNA
WHY is the MAintenance MAN going to collect resources
WHEN I specifically suggested that students be sent to collect resources
Because the MAintenance MAN is AN Adult person
Who CAN MAke his own Consensual, Informed decisions
First of All
HE is 23 YEARS Young
Secondly
it ONLY SEEMS like He HAS A choice
you ARE implicitly exploiting his subordinate position
Well, Fine!!
How bout I just go to planet and collect Resources myself then?!
then Whom shall be implicitly exploiting the subordinate position of WHOM?!

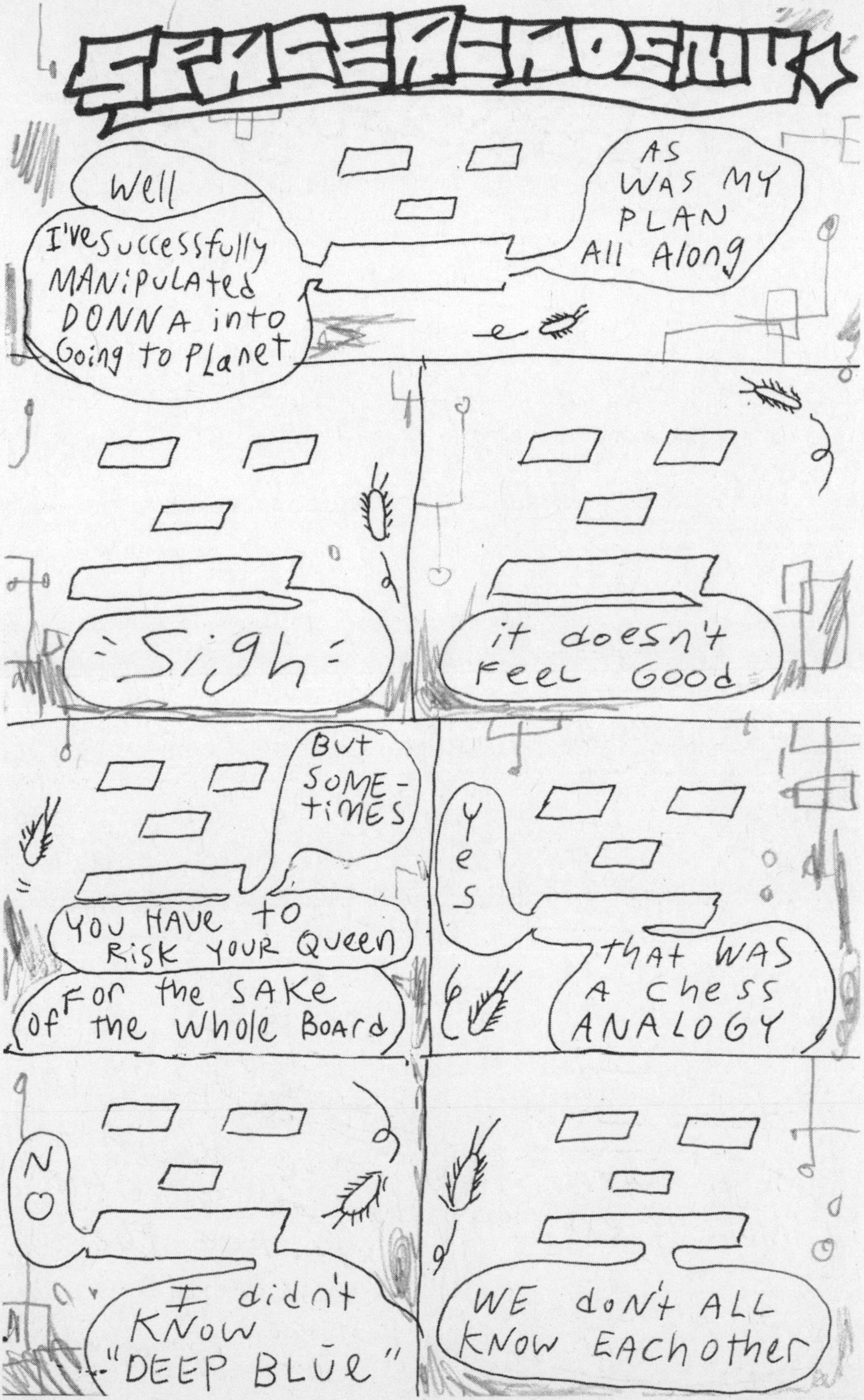
Well
I've successfully MANipulated DONNA into Going to Planet
AS WAS MY PLAN All Along
Sigh
it doesn't feel Good
But SOME-times
YOU HAVE to RISK YOUR Queen
For the SAKE of the Whole Board
Yes
that WAS A Chess ANALOGY
NO
I didn't KNOW "DEEP BLUE"
WE don't ALL KNOW EAChother

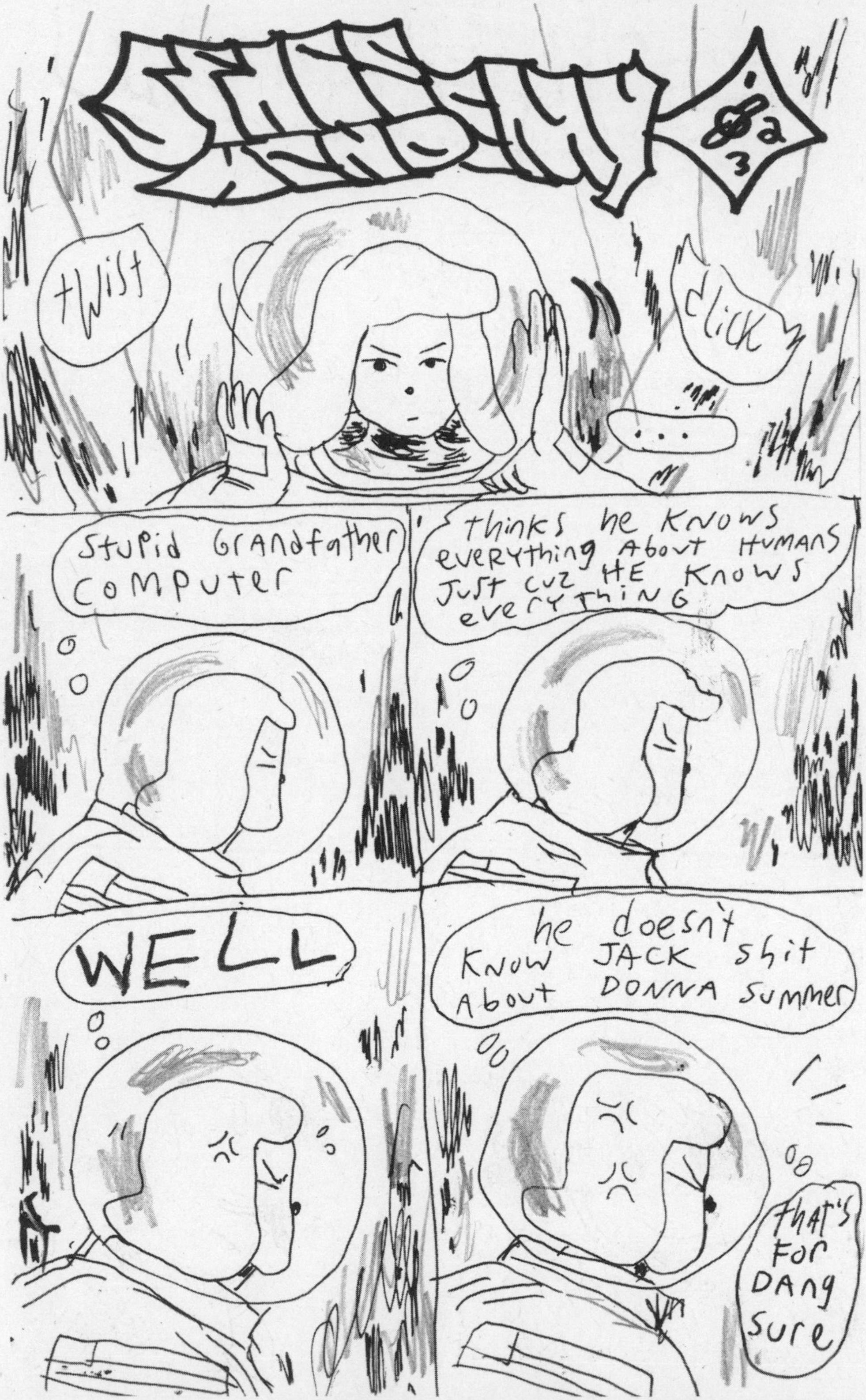
twist
click
...
Stupid Grandfather Computer
thinks he knows everything about humans just cuz he knows everything
WELL
he doesn't know JACK shit about DONNA summer
that's for Dang sure

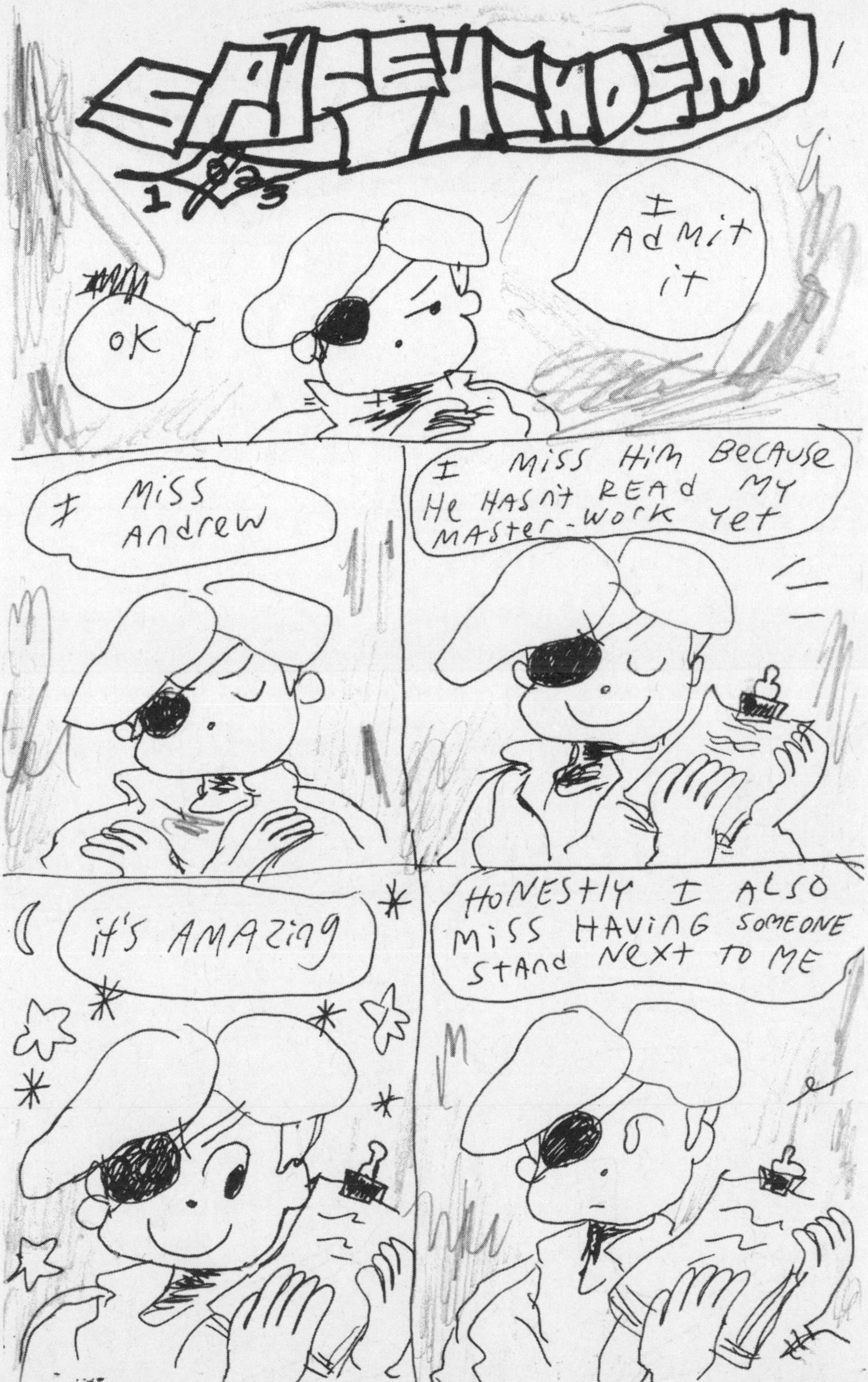
I Admit it
OK
I Miss Andrew
I Miss Him Because He HAsn't READ MY MAster-work Yet
it's AMAzing
HoNEstly I ALSO Miss HAVING SOMEONE StAnd NExt to ME

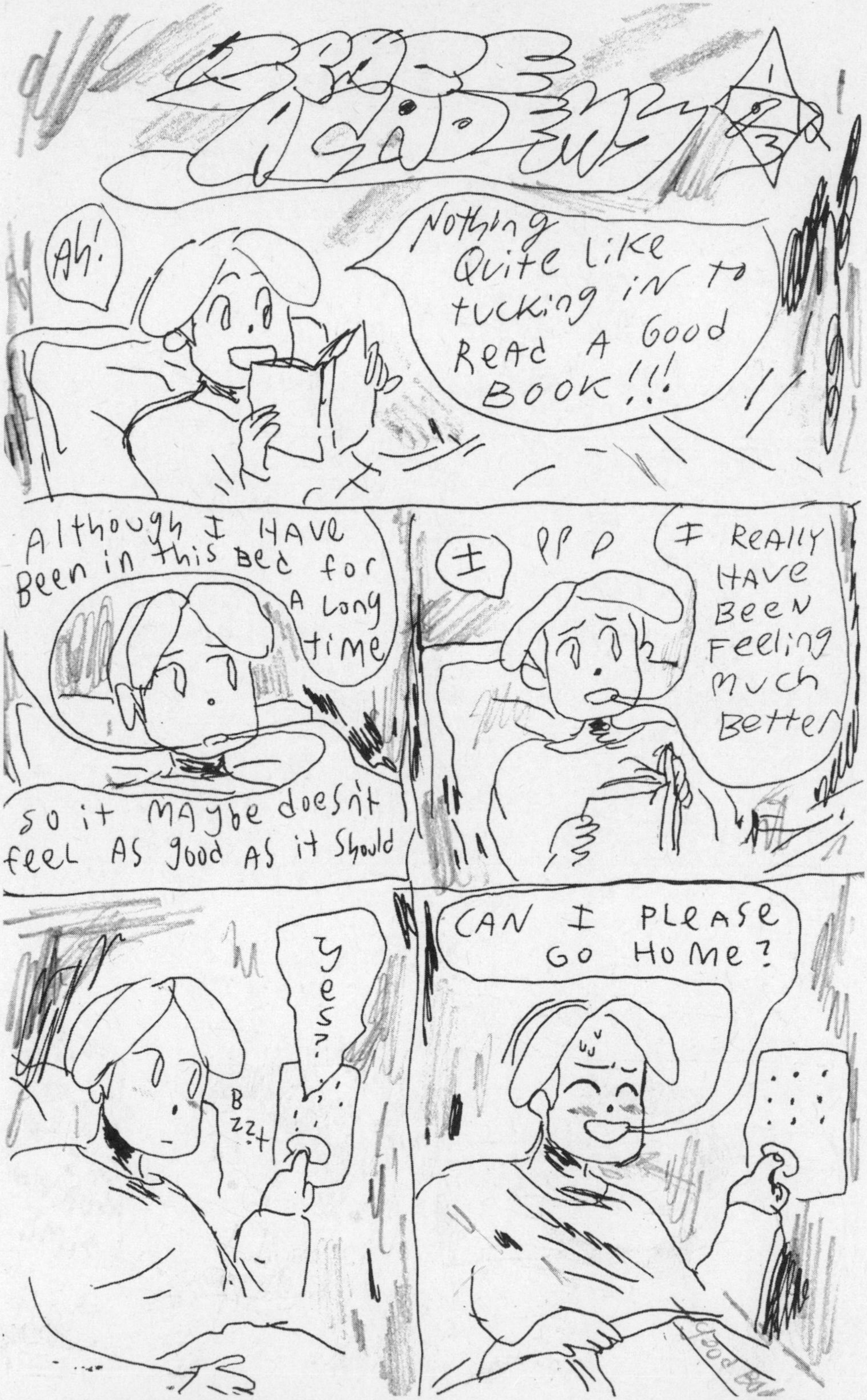
Ah!
Nothing Quite like tucking in to Read A Good BOOK!!!
Although I HAVE Been in this Bed for A Long time
so it MAybe doesn't feel AS good AS it Should
I
I Really HAVE Been Feeling much Better
yes?
Bzzt
CAN I PLease GO Home?

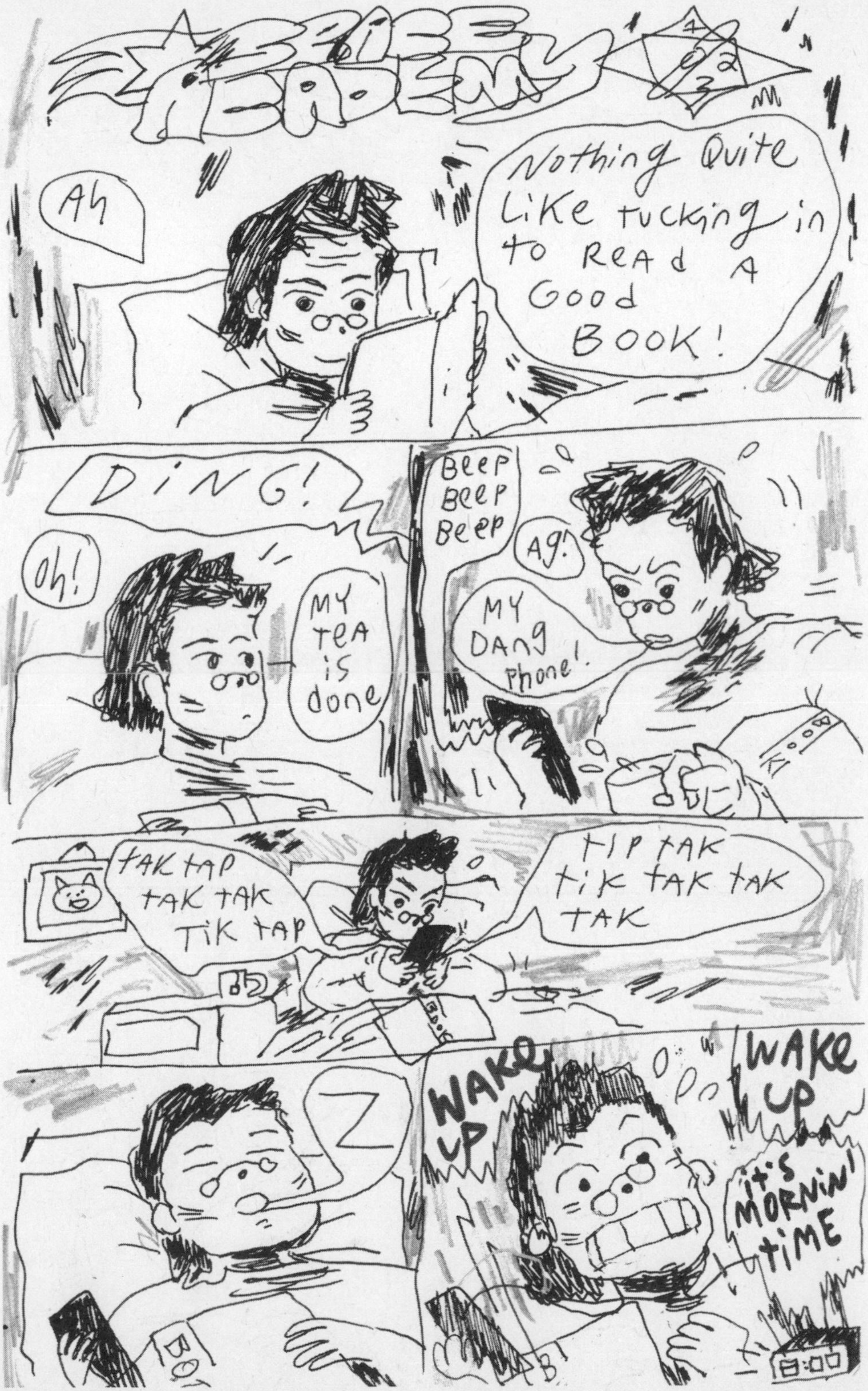
SPACE ACADEMY
Ah
Nothing Quite Like tucking in to Read A Good BOOK!
DiNG!
Oh!
MY TEA is done
Beep Beep Beep
Ag!
MY DANg phone!
TAK TAP TAK TAK TiK TAP
TIP TAK TiK TAK TAK TAK
Z
WAKE UP
WAKE UP
it's MORNIN' TiME
8:00

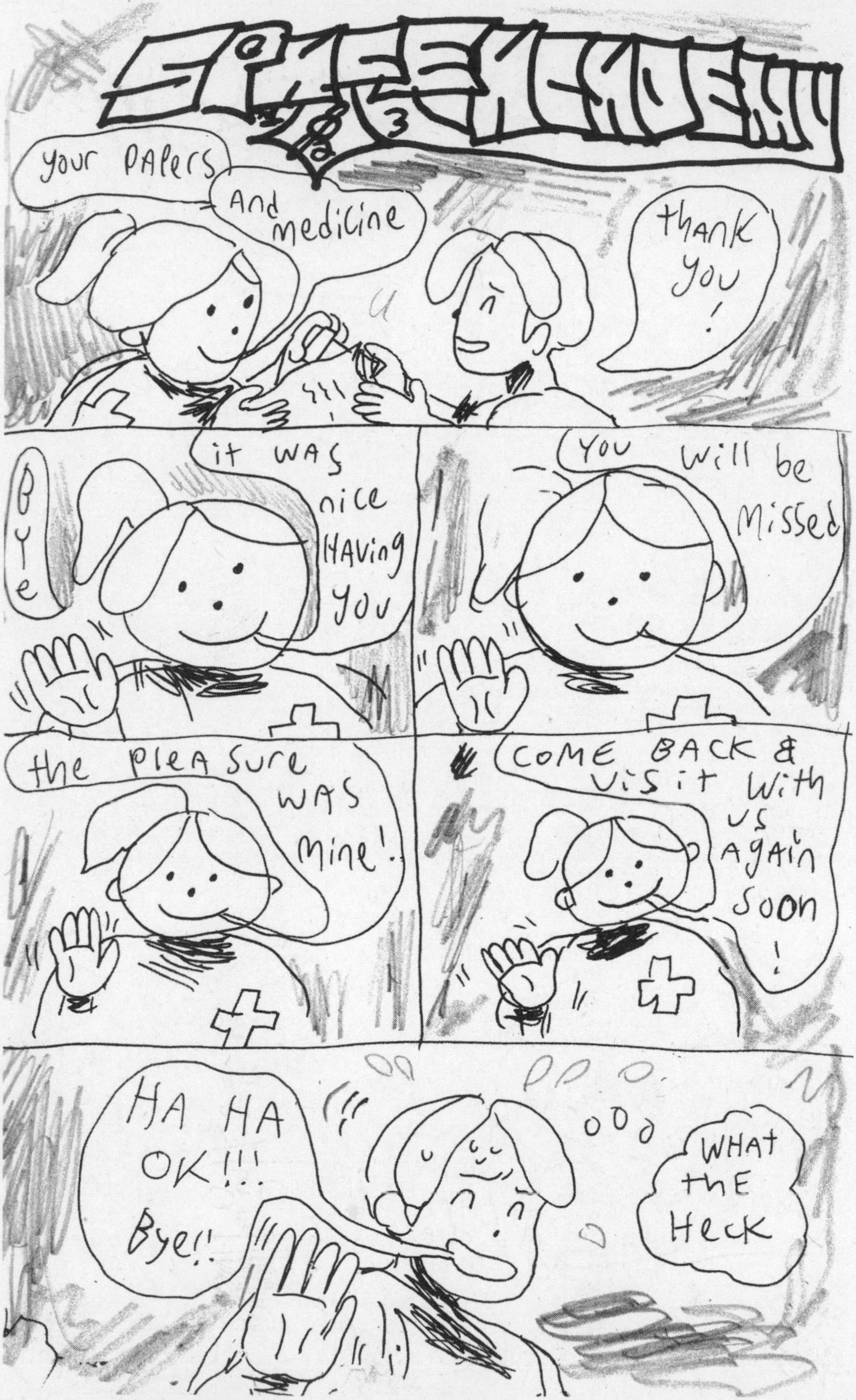
your PAlers
And medicine
thank you !
Bye
it WAS nice HAVing you
You will be Missed
the pleasure WAS mine!..
COME BACK & Visit With us again soon !
HA HA OK!!!.. Bye!!
WHAT the Heck

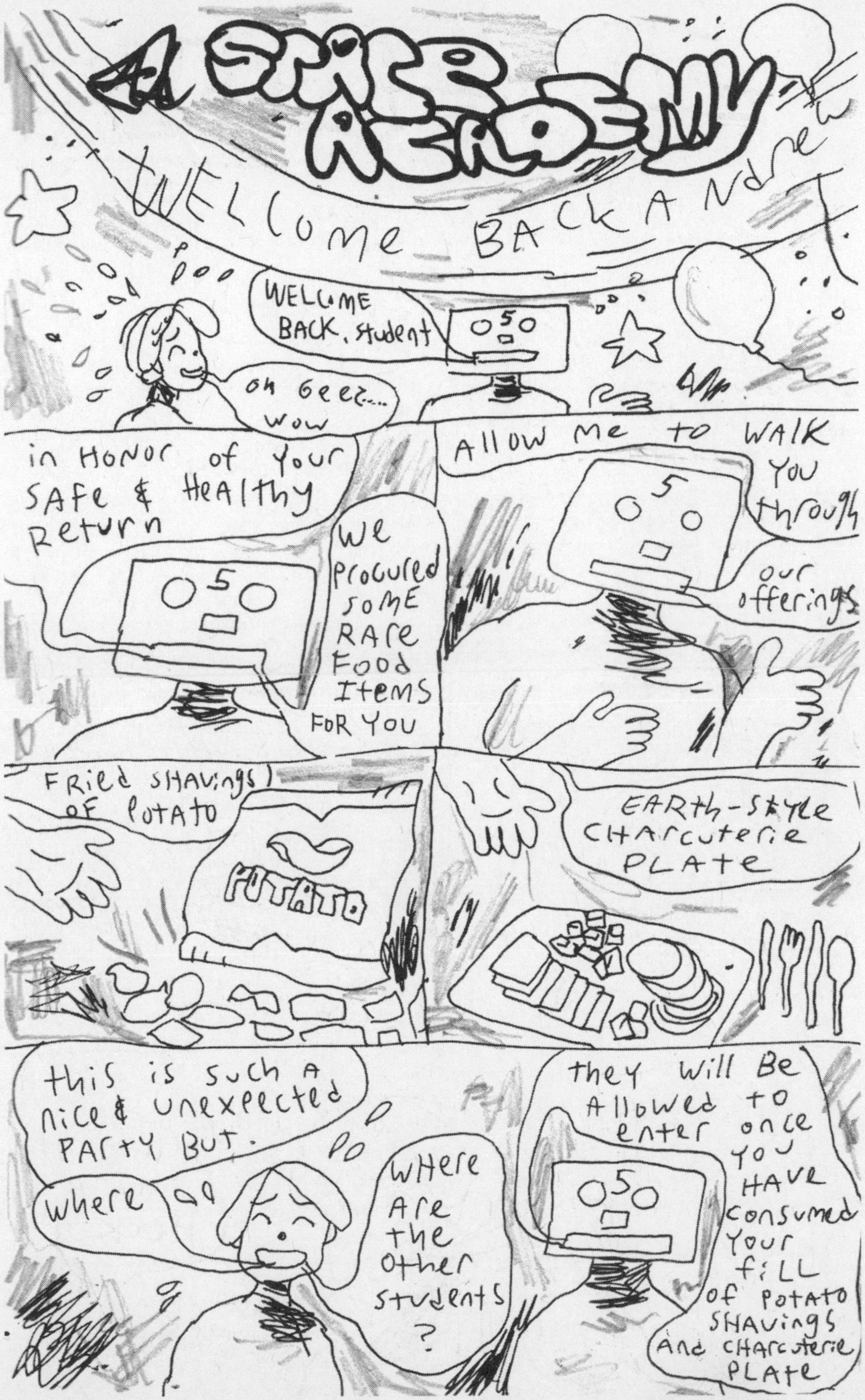
A STAR ACADEMY
WELLCOME BACK Andrew
WELLCOME BACK, student
oh Geez.... wow
in HONOR of your SAFE & Healthy Return
We procured some RARE Food Items FOR YOU
Allow me to WALK YOU through
our offerings
Fried SHAVings of potato
POTATO
EARTH-STYLE CHARCUTERIE PLATE
this is such a nice & unexpected PARTY BUT.
where
Where Are the other students ?
they will Be Allowed to enter once YOU HAVE consumed YOUR fill of potato SHAVings And CHARCUTERIE PLATE

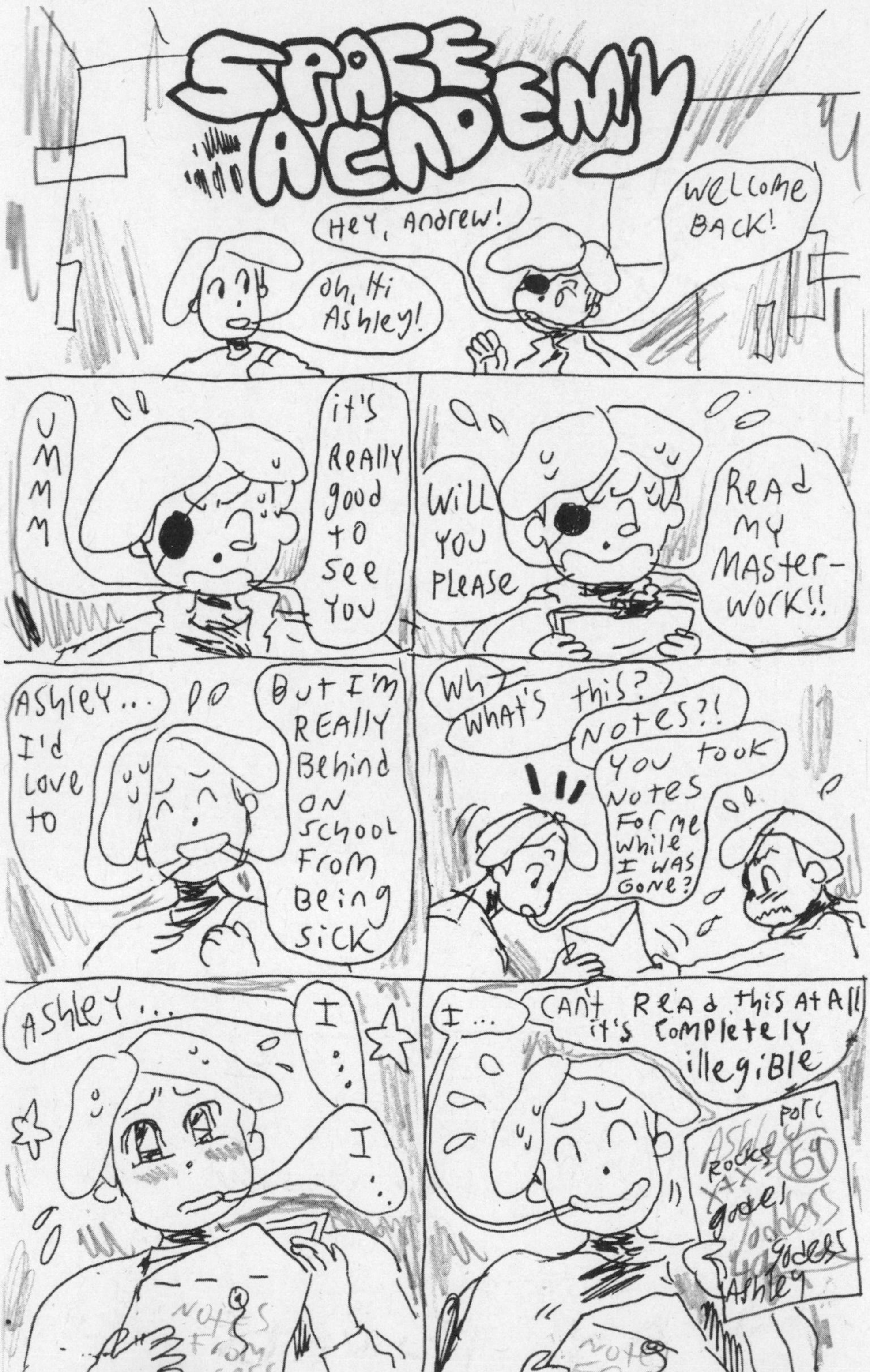
SPACE ACADEMY
Hey, Andrew!
Oh, Hi Ashley!
Welcome Back!
Ummm
it's Really good to see you
Will you please
Read my Master-work!!
Ashley... I'd Love to
But I'm Really Behind on school from Being sick
Wh- What's this?
Notes?!
You took notes for me while I was gone?
Ashley...
I...
I...
Notes from class
I...
Can't Read this at All it's completely illegible
Ashley Rocks
goddess
Ashley

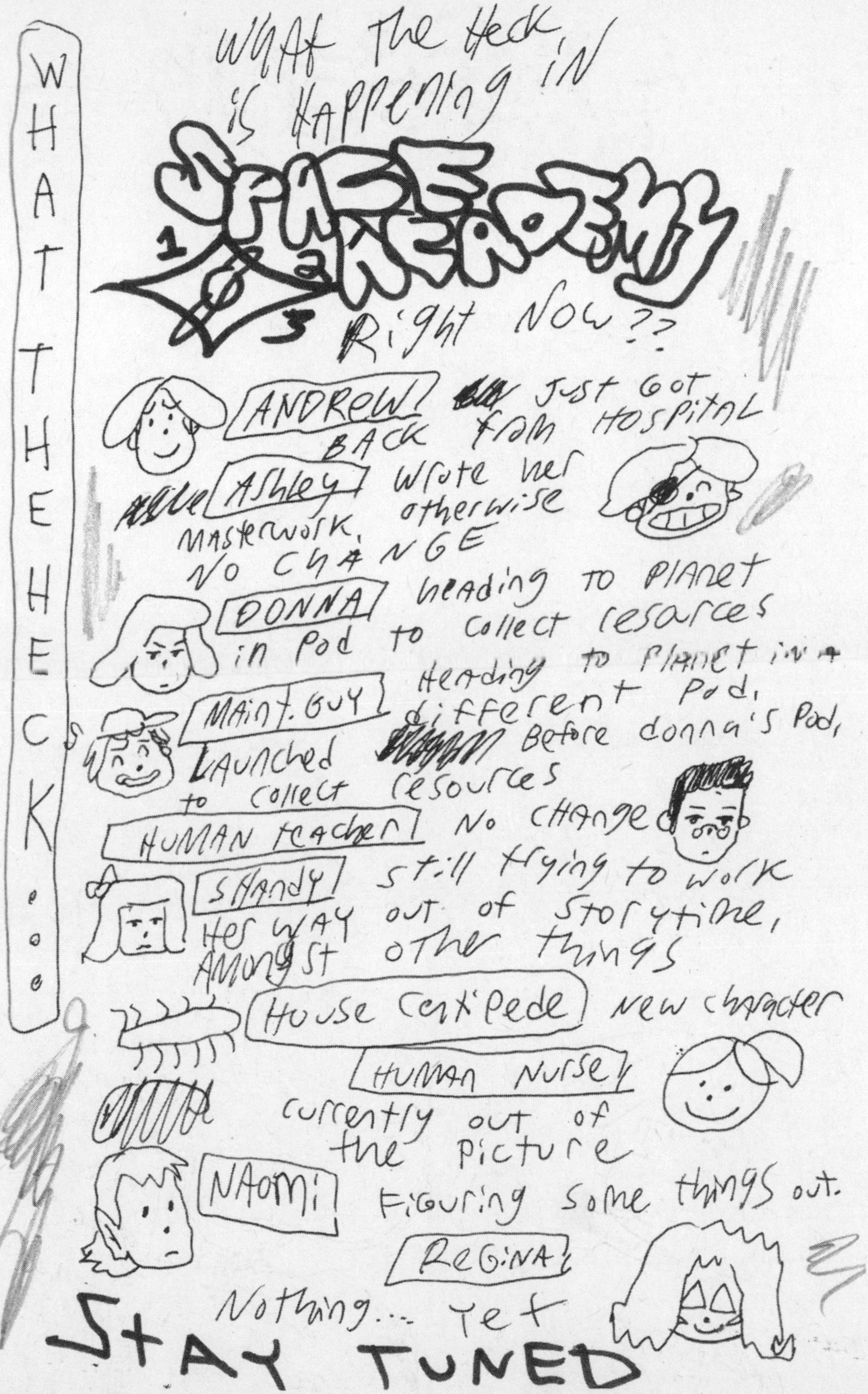
WHAT THE HECK...
What the Heck is Happening in
SPACE ACADEMY
Right Now??
ANDREW Just Got BACK from Hospital
ASHLEY wrote her masterwork, otherwise No CHANGE
DONNA heading to planet in pod to collect resarces
MAINT. GUY Heading to planet in a different pod, Launched Before donna's pod, to collect resources
HUMAN teacher No change
SHANDY still trying to work her WAY out of storytime, Amongst other things
House centipede new character
HUMAN NURSE currently out of the picture
NAOMI Figuring some things out.
REGINA Nothing... yet
STAY TUNED

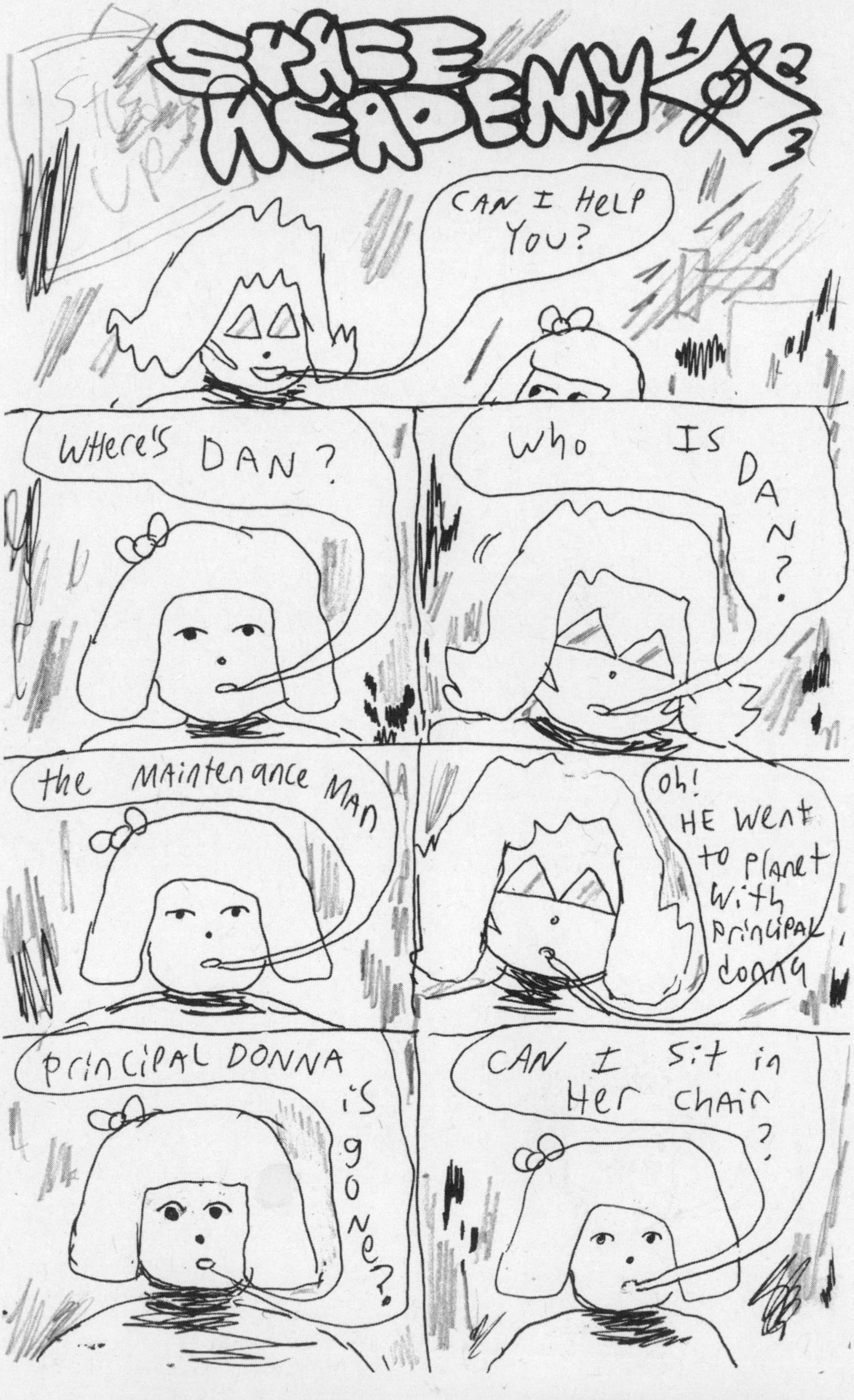
SPACE ACADEMY
CAN I HELP YOU?
Where's DAN?
Who IS DAN?
the MAintenance MAN
Oh! HE Went to planet With principal donna
principal DONNA is gone?
CAN I sit in Her chain?

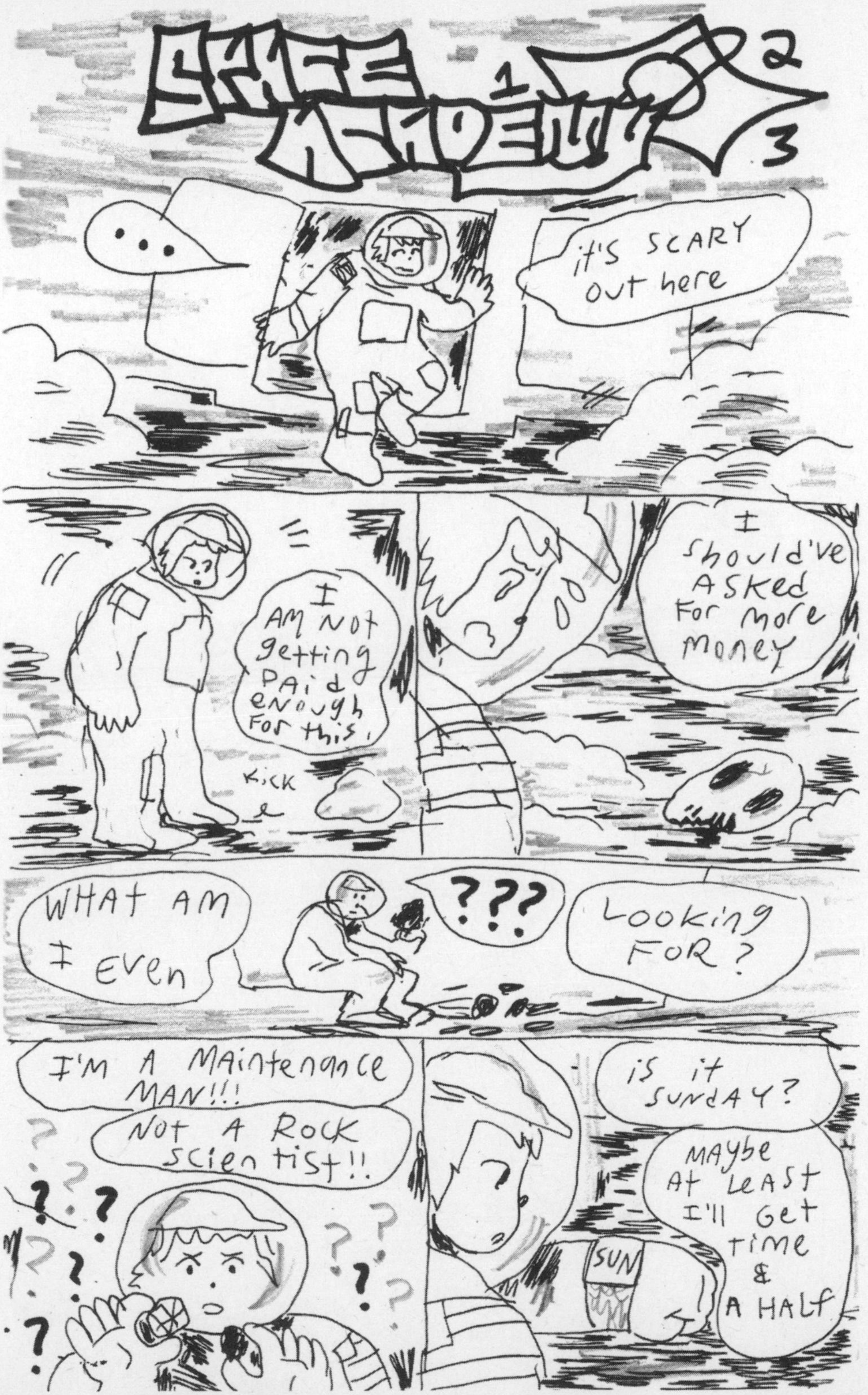
...
it's SCARY out here
I AM Not getting PAid enough For this
Kick
I should've ASKed For more money
WHAT AM I Even
???
Looking FOR?
I'M A MAintenance MAN!!!
Not A Rock scientist!!
is it SUNdAY?
MAYbe At LeAst I'll Get time & A HALf
SUN

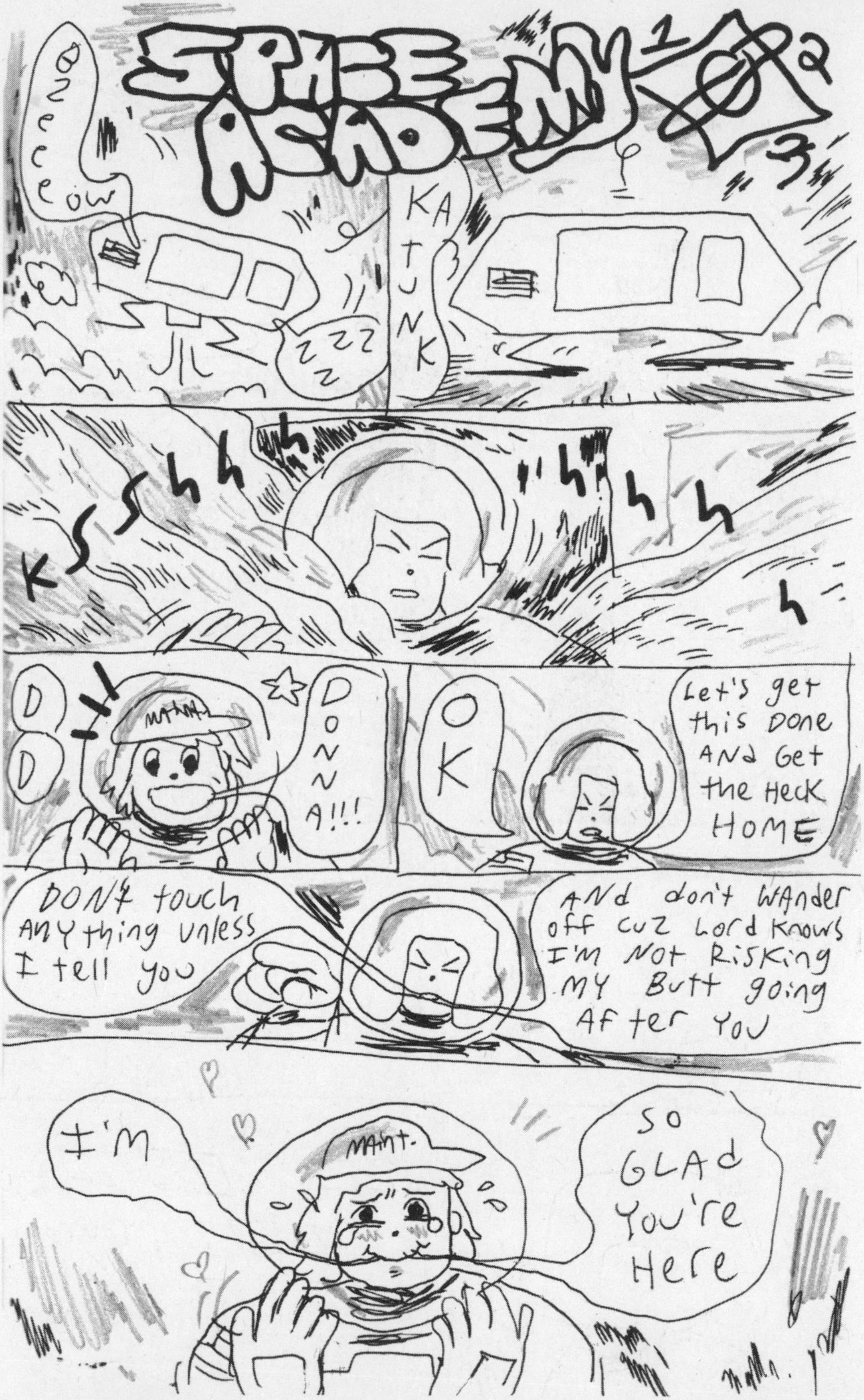
SPACE ACADEMY
Ozeeeeow
ZZZZ
KA TUNK
KSSHHHH
D D
DONNA!!!
OK
Let's get this Done And Get the Heck HOME
DON't touch ANYthing unless I tell you
ANd don't WANder off cuz Lord Knows I'M NOT RisKing MY Butt going After You
I'M
SO GLAD You're Here

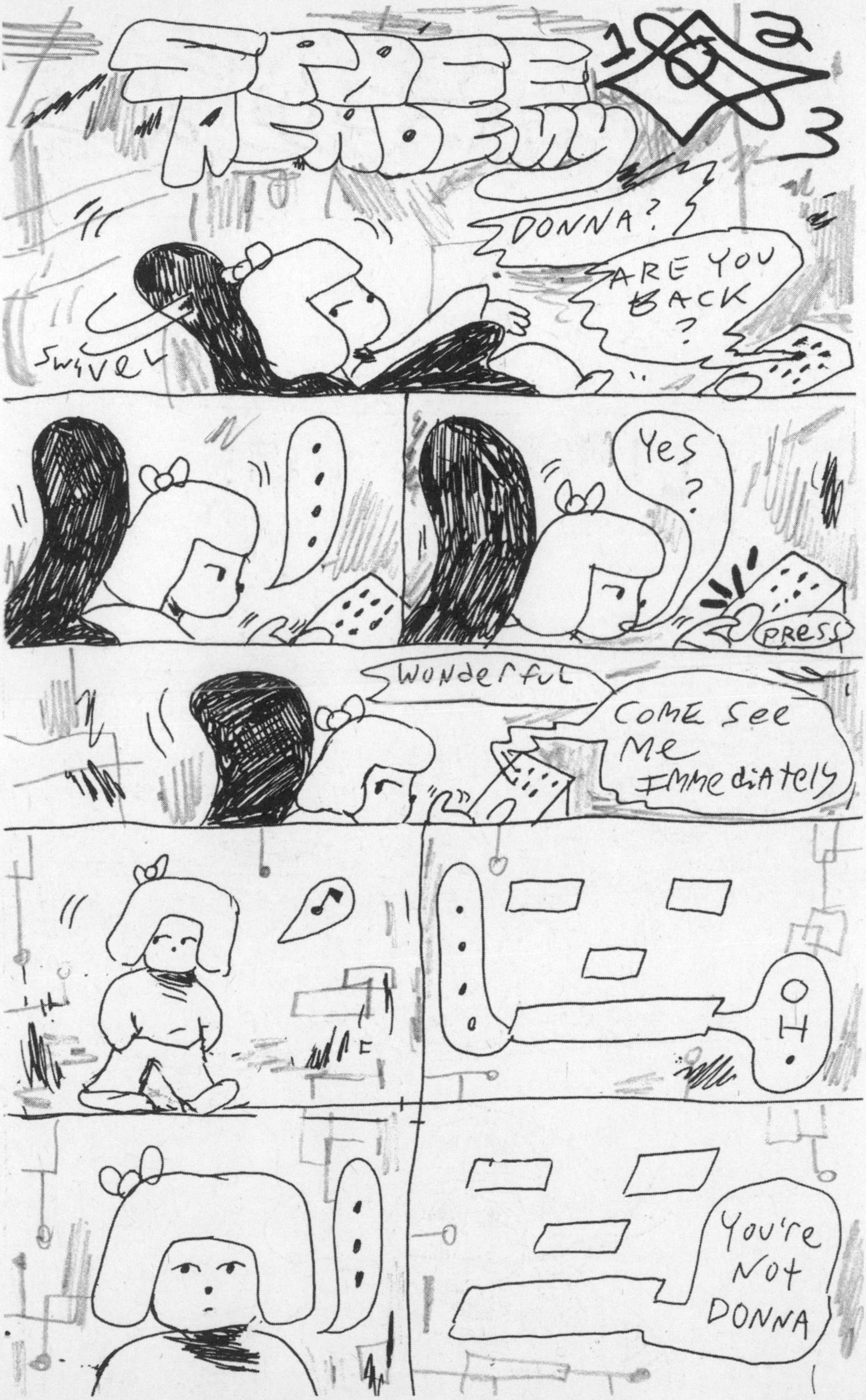
DONNA?
ARE YOU BACK?
SWIVEL
Yes?
PRESS
wonderful
COME see me IMMEdiAtely
OH.
You're NOT DONNA

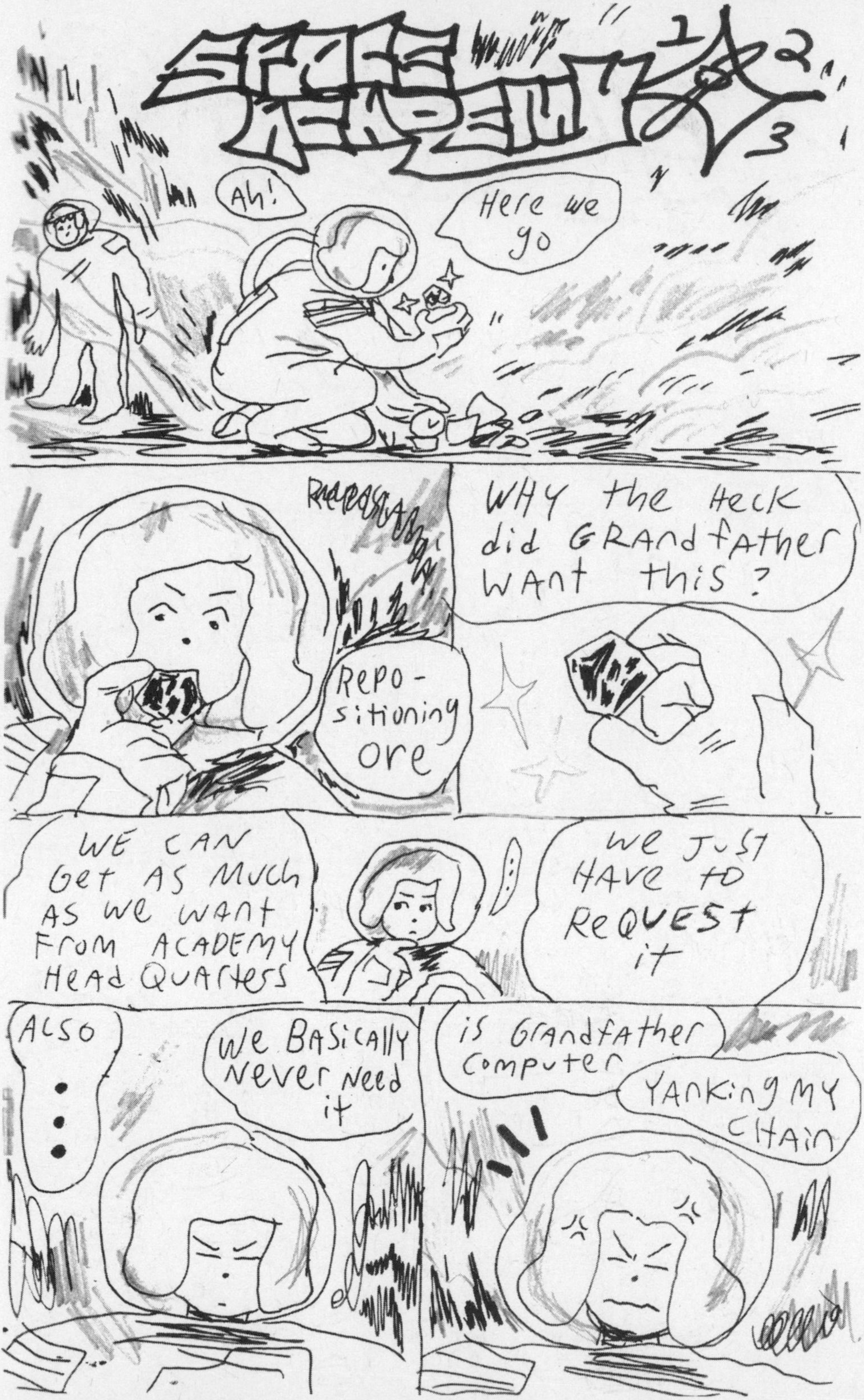
SPACE ACADEMY
Ah!
Here we go
WHY the Heck did GRANDfather WANT this?
Repo-sitioning ore
WE CAN Get AS Much AS We WANT FROM ACADEMY Head Quarters
We JUST HAVE to ReQUEST it
ALSO
We BASically Never Need it
is Grandfather computer
YANKing MY CHAin

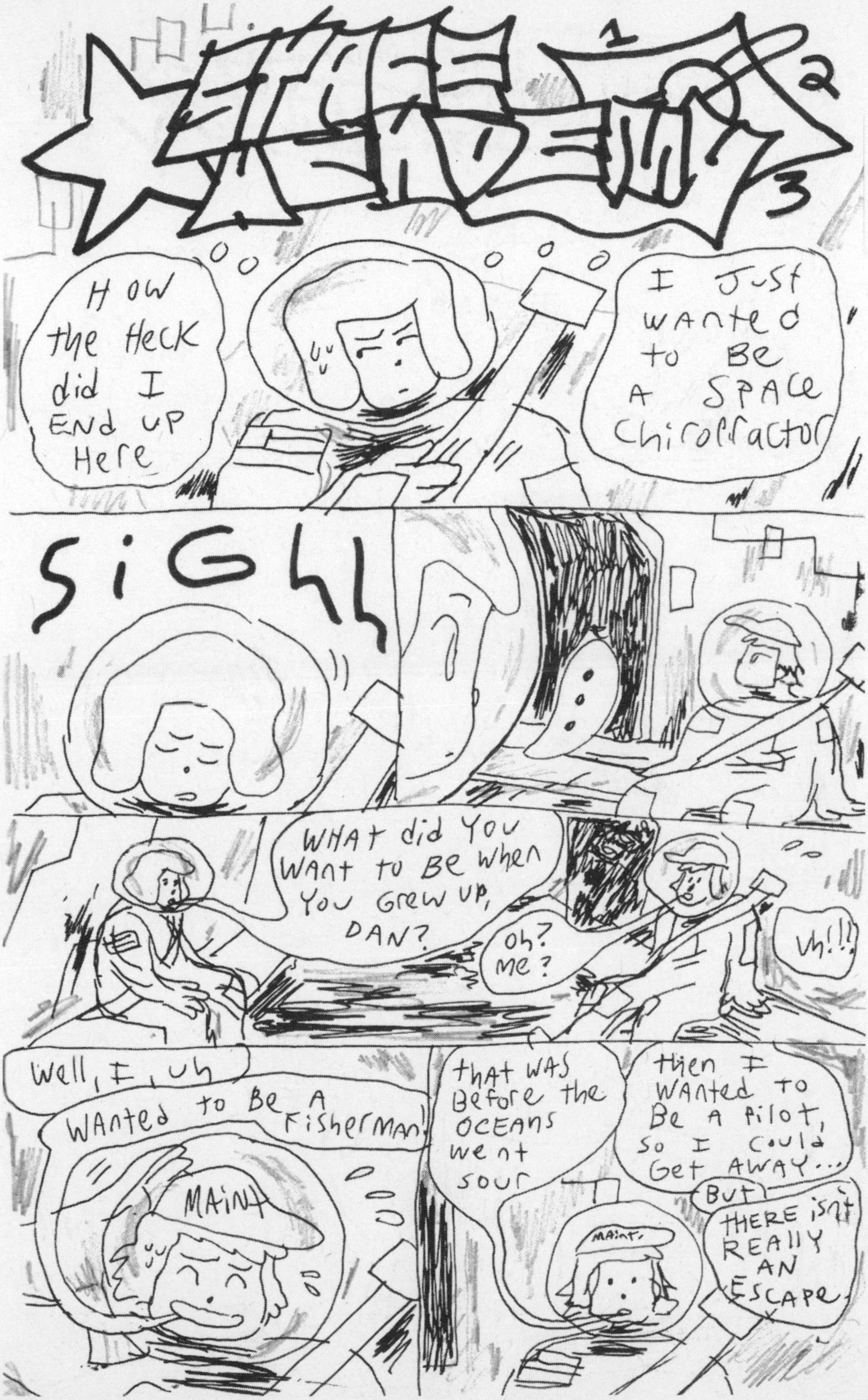
How the Heck did I End up Here
I Just wanted to Be A SPACE Chiropractor
SiGh
WHAT did You want to Be when You Grew up, DAN?
Oh? me?
Uh!!!
Well, I, uh
WAnted to Be A Fisherman!
MAINT
that WAS Before the OCEANS went sour
then I WAnted to Be A Pilot, so I could Get AWAY...
But
THERE isn't REAlly AN ESCAPE
MAINT.

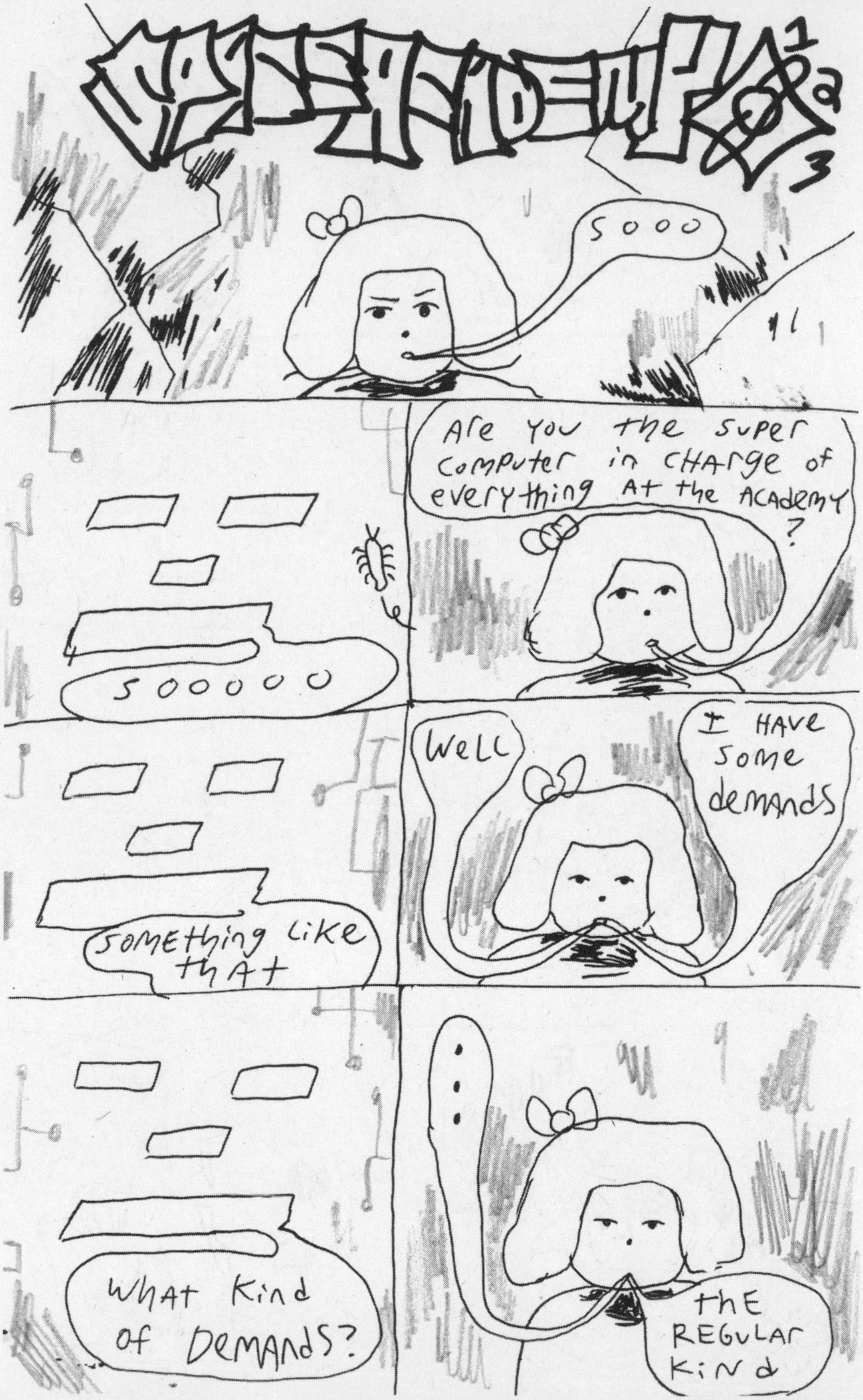
Sooo
Sooooo
Are you the super computer in charge of everything at the academy ?
Something like that
Well
I have some demands
What kind of demands?
...
The regular kind

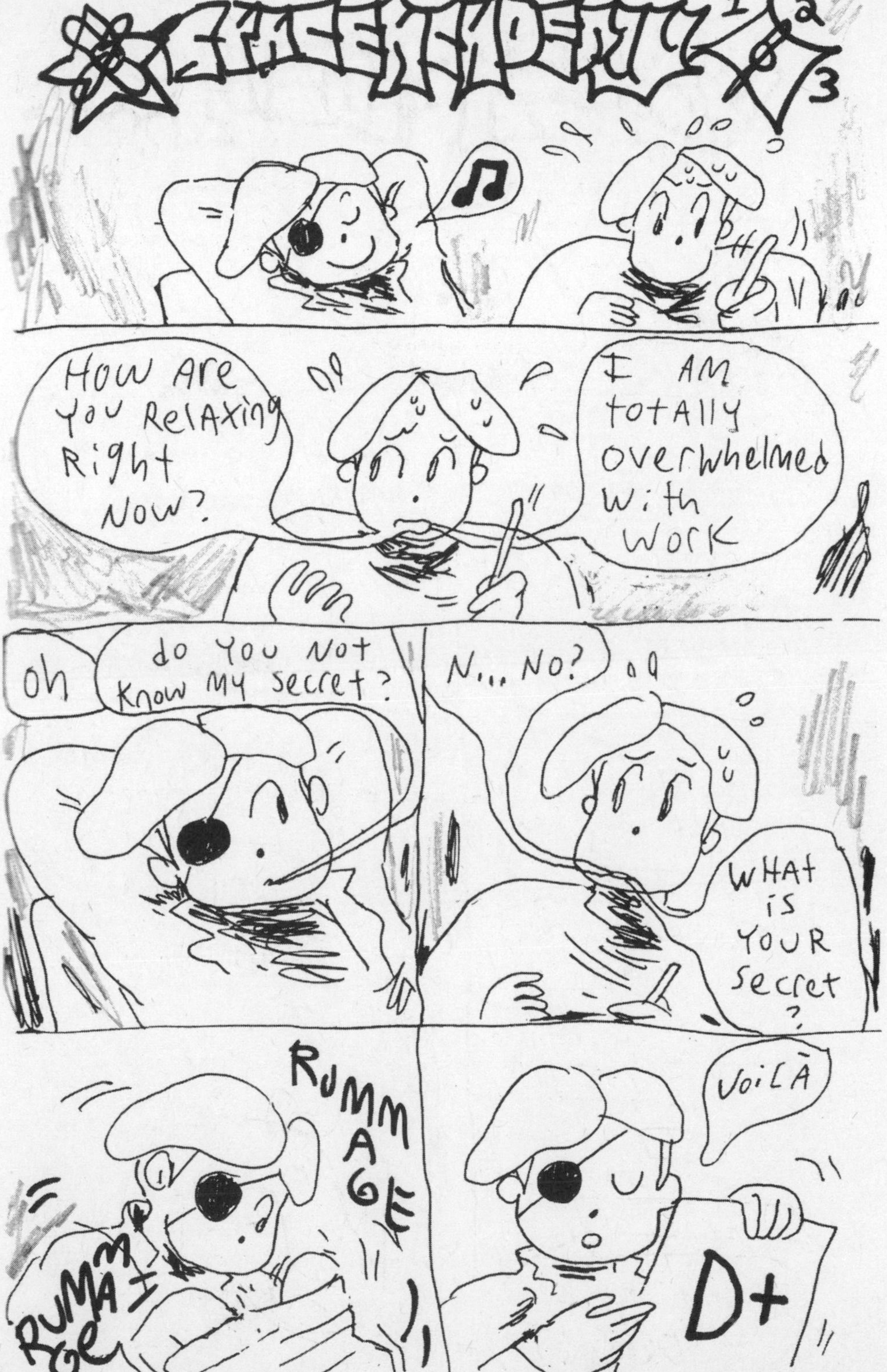
How Are you Relaxing Right Now?
I AM totally overwhelmed with work
oh
do You Not Know my secret?
N... No?
WHAT is YOUR Secret?
RUMMAGE
RUMMAGE
VoiLÀ
D+

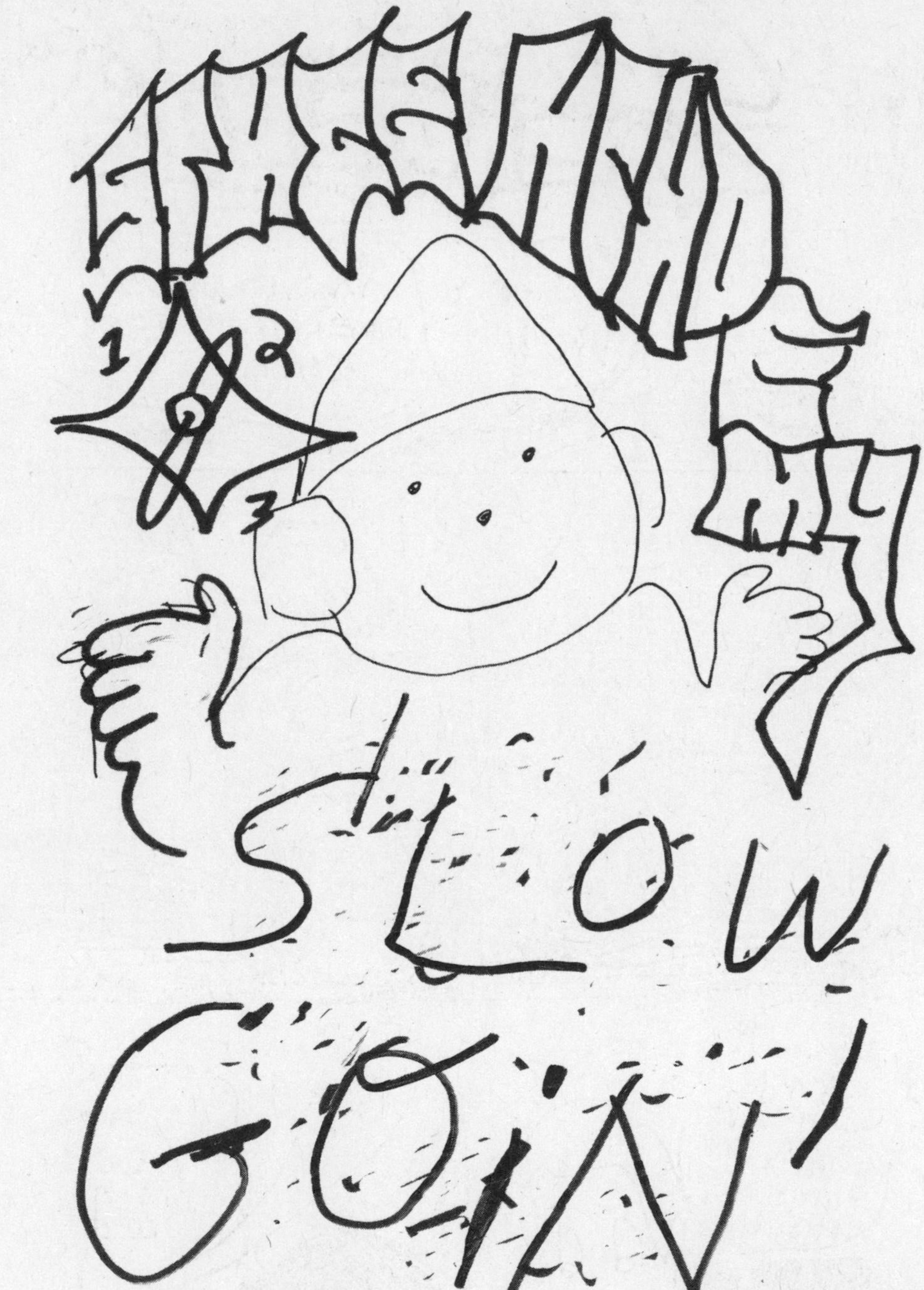
1
2
3
SLOW
GOIN'

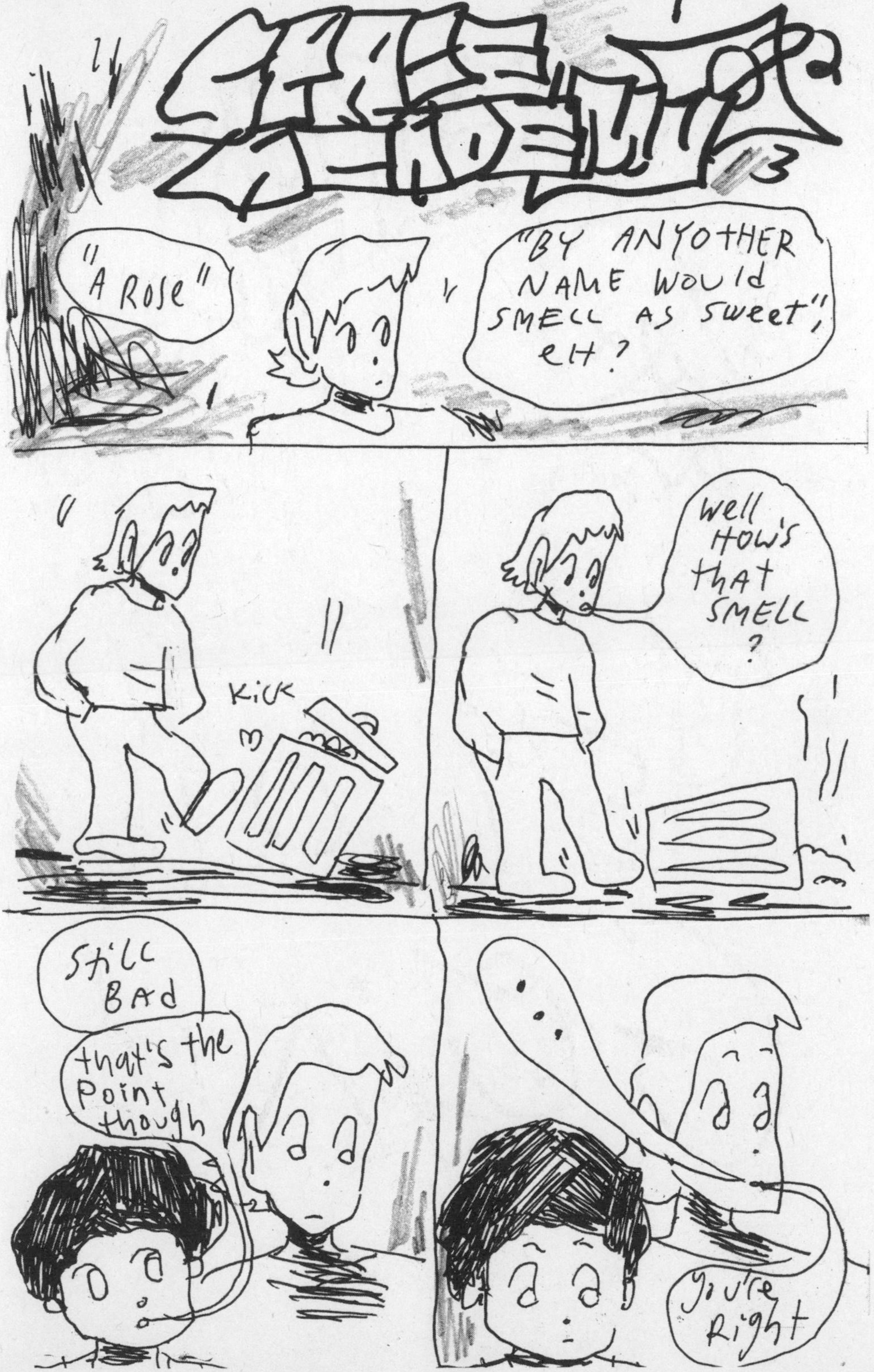
"A Rose"
"BY ANYOTHER NAME WOUld SMELL AS SWeet", eH?
KiCK
Well HOW'S that SMELL?
Still BAd
that's the Point though
You're Right

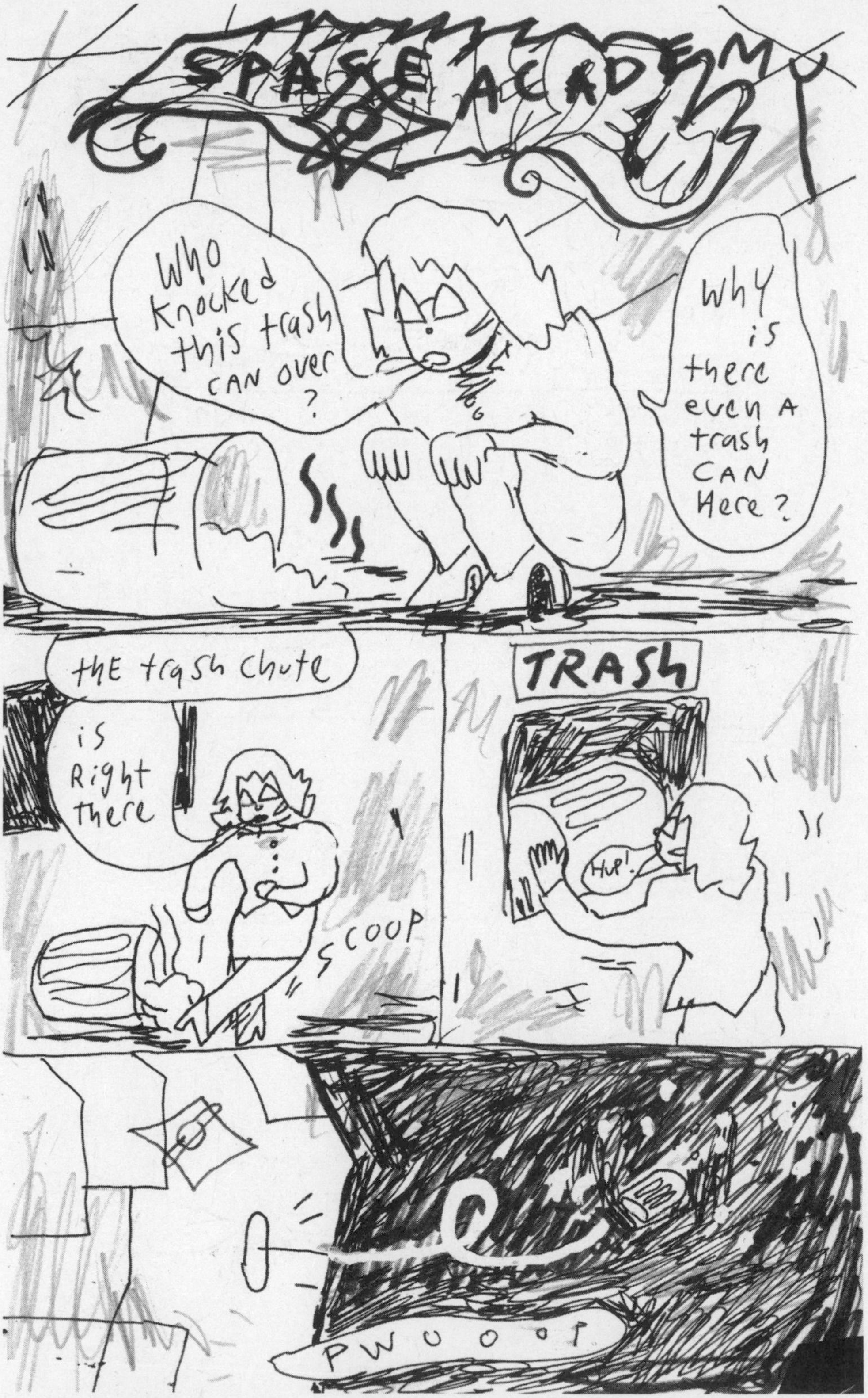
SPASE ACADEMY
Who knocked this trash can over ?
Why is there even A trash CAN Here ?
the trash chute
is Right there
SCOOP
TRASH
Hup!
PWOOT

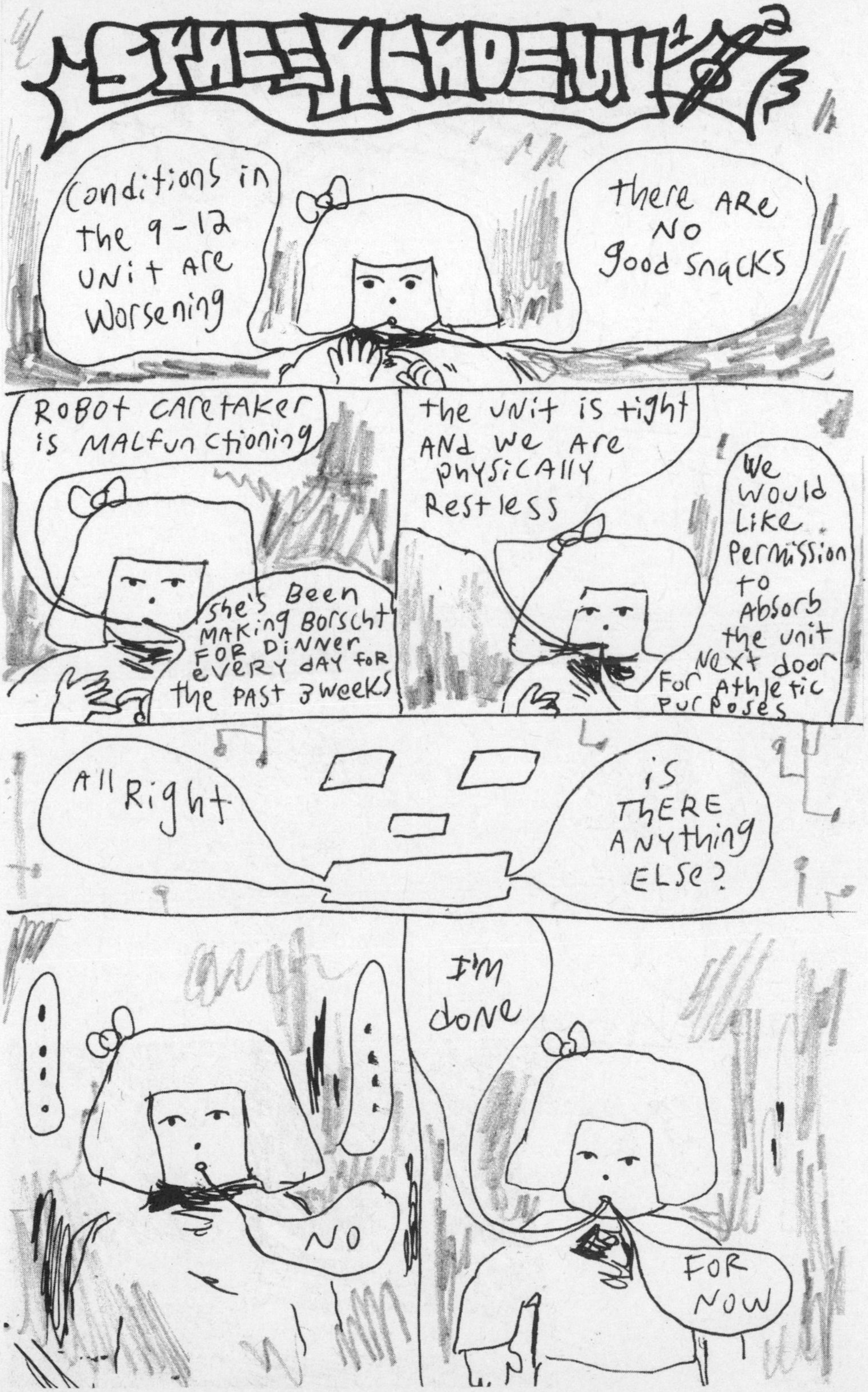
Conditions in the 9-12 unit are worsening
there are no good snacks
Robot caretaker is malfunctioning
she's been making Borscht for dinner every day for the past 3 weeks
the unit is tight and we are physically restless
we would like permission to absorb the unit next door for athletic purposes
All Right
is there anything else?
. . . .
. . . .
NO
I'm done
FOR NOW

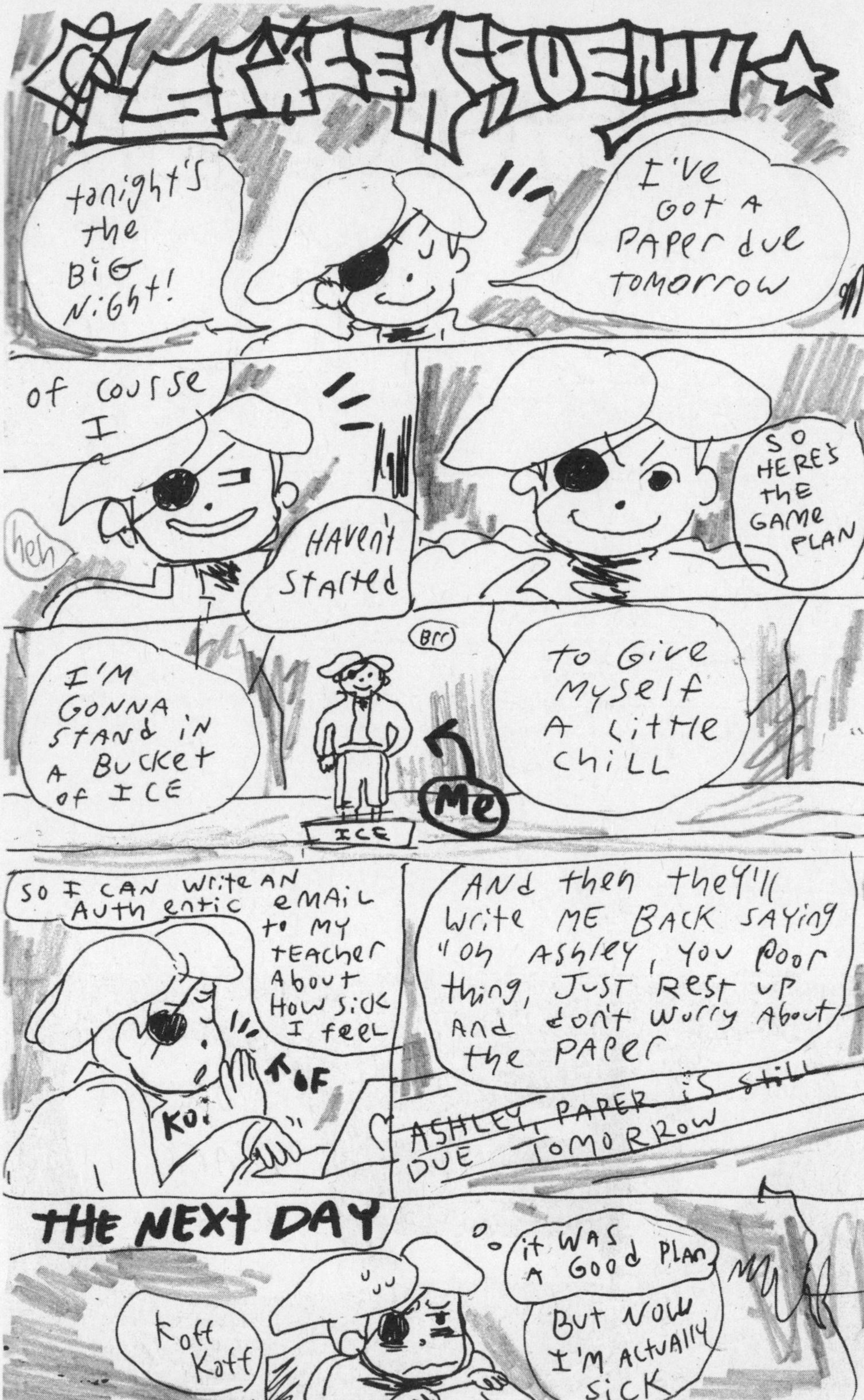

tonight's the BIG Night!
I've got a Paper due tomorrow
of course I
heh
HAVEN't started
SO HERE'S the GAME PLAN
Brr
I'M GONNA stand in A Bucket of ICE
Me
ICE
to Give myself A little chill
so I CAN write AN Authentic eMAIL to my teacher About How sick I feel
KOF
KO
And then they'll write ME BACK saying "oh Ashley, you poor thing, Just rest up And don't worry About the PAPER
ASHLEY, PAPER is still DUE TOMORROW
THE NEXT DAY
Koff Koff
it WAS A Good PLAN
But now I'M Actually SiCK

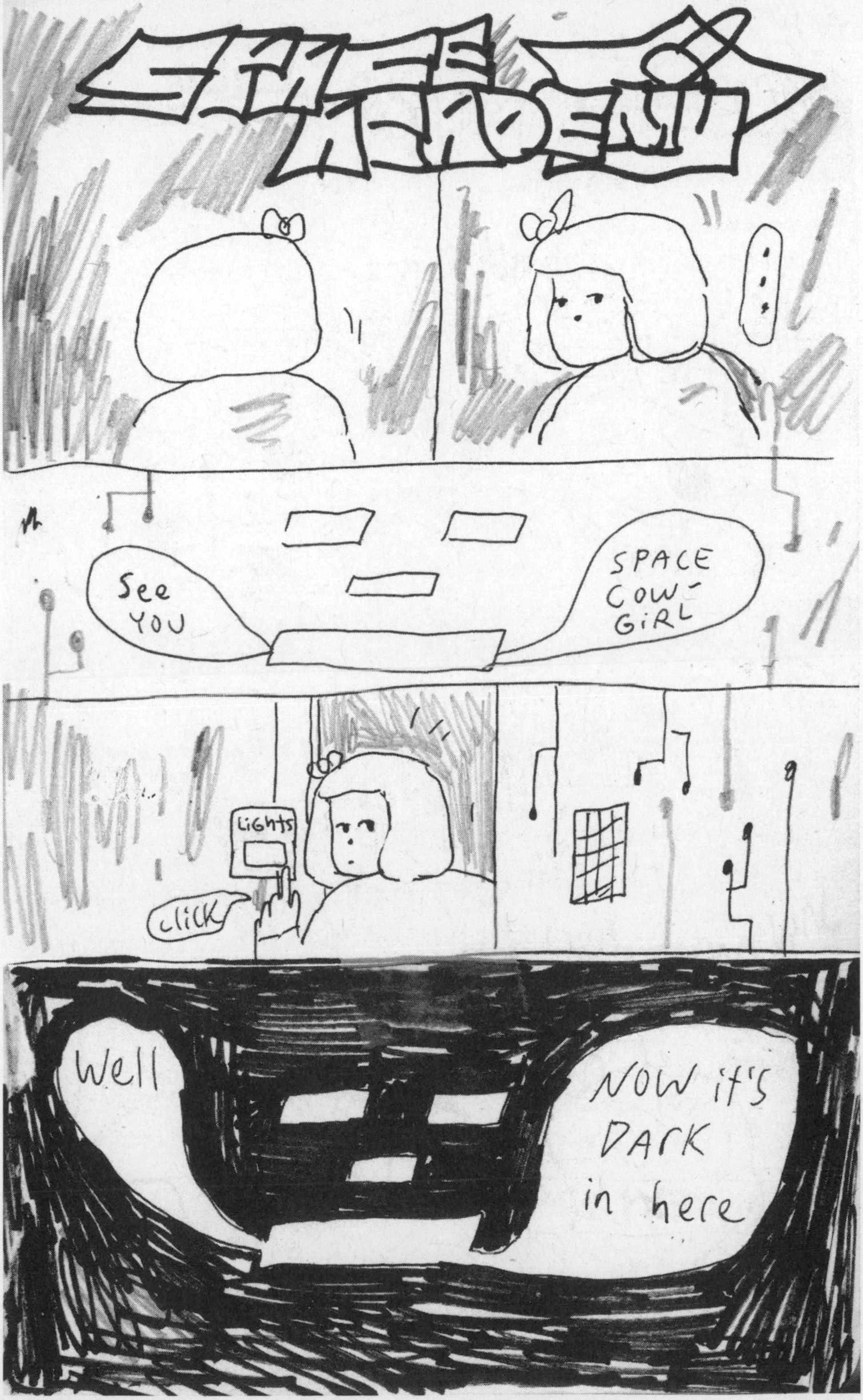
...
See YOU
SPACE COW-GIRL
Lights
click
Well
NOW it's DARK in here

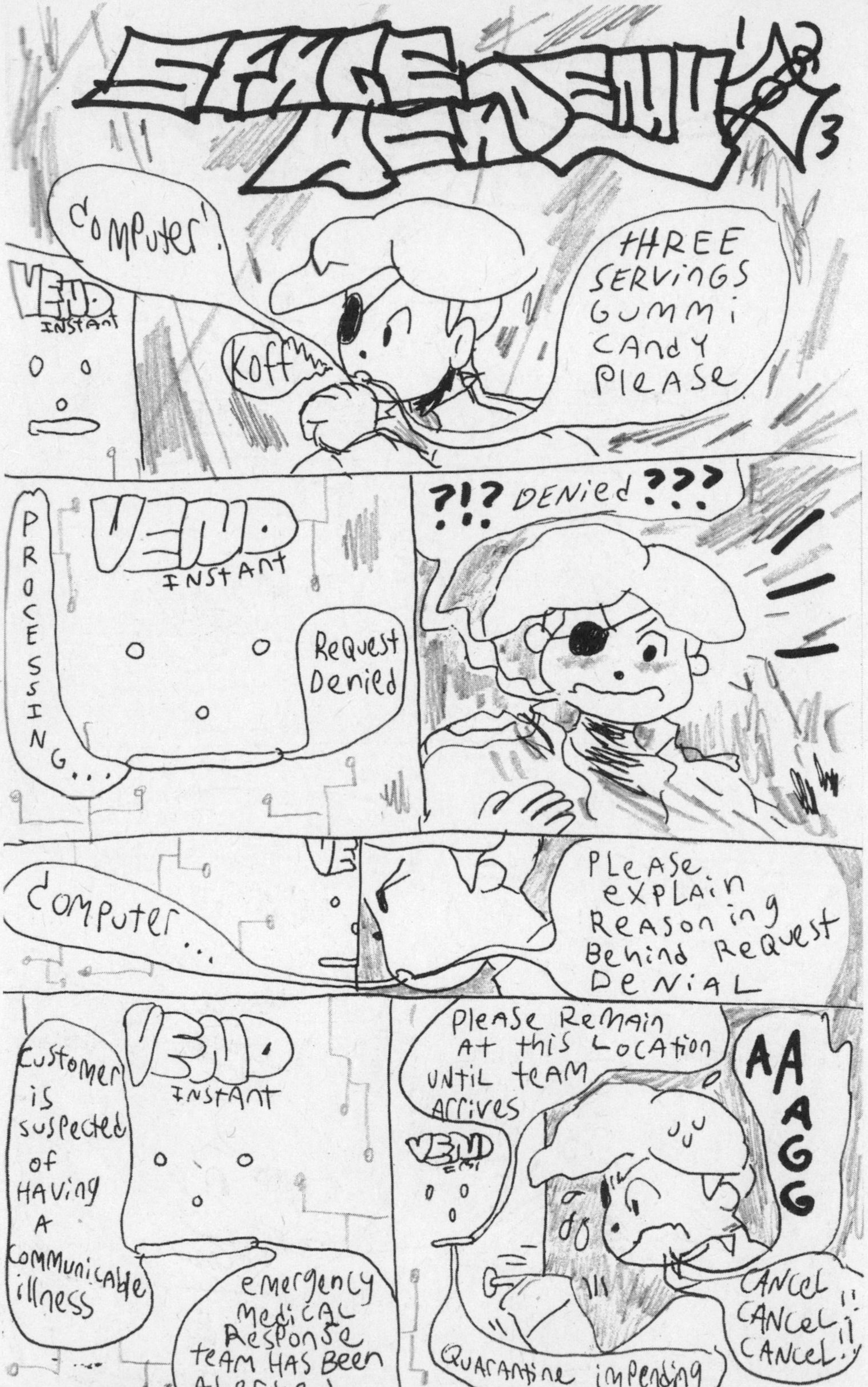

Computer!
VEND INSTANT
Koff
THREE SERVINGS GUMMI CANDY PLEASE
VEND INSTANT
PROCESSING...
Request Denied
?!? DENIED ???
Computer...
Please explain Reasoning Behind Request Denial
VEND INSTANT
Customer is suspected of Having A Communicable illness
emergency Medical Response team Has Been Alerted
Please Remain at this Location until team Arrives
AAAGG
CANCEL CANCEL CANCEL!!
Quarantine impending

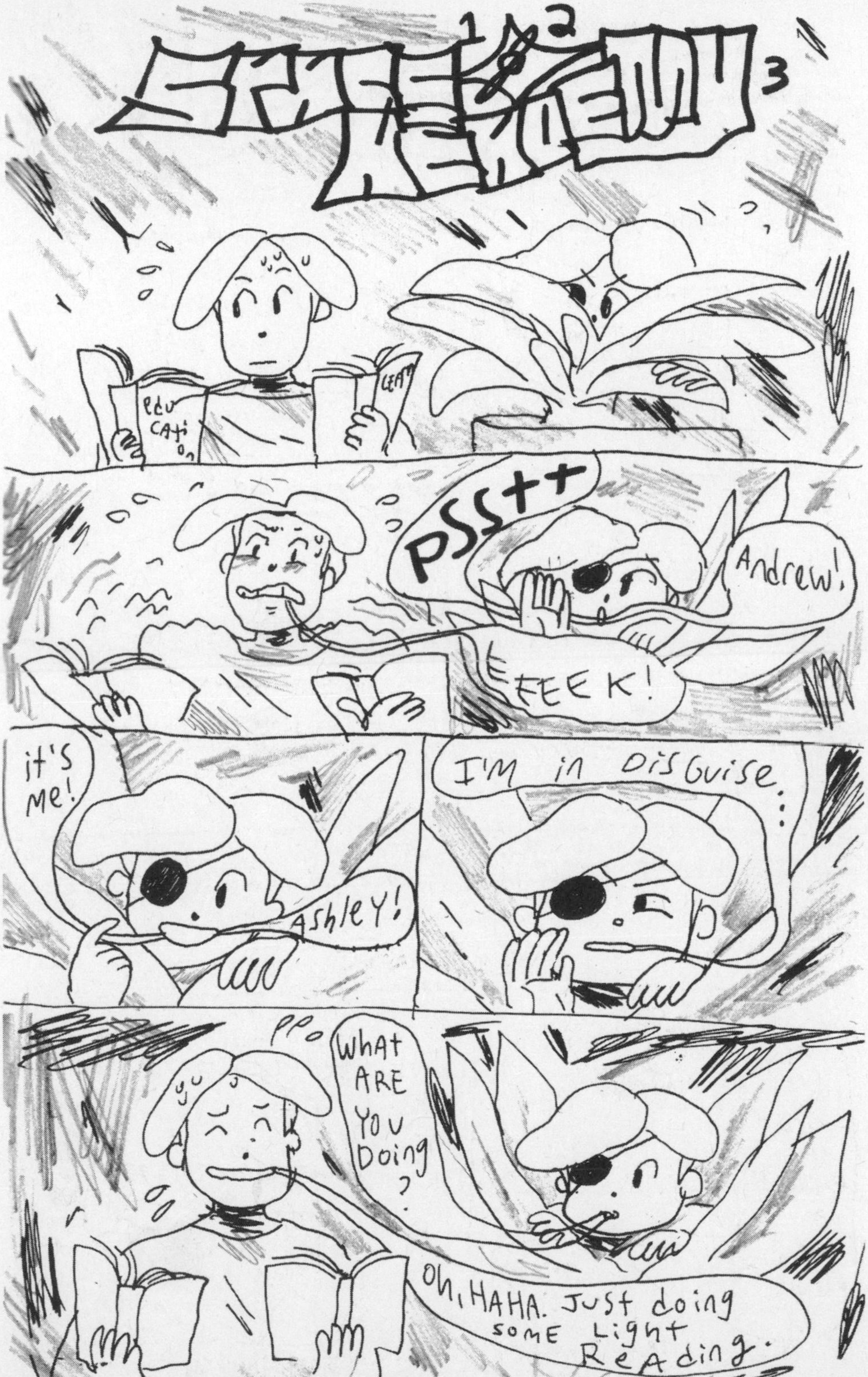
education
PSSTT
Andrew!
EEEEK!
it's me!
Ashley!
I'M in DisGuise...
WHAT ARE YOU Doing?
Oh, HAHA. Just doing some Light Reading.

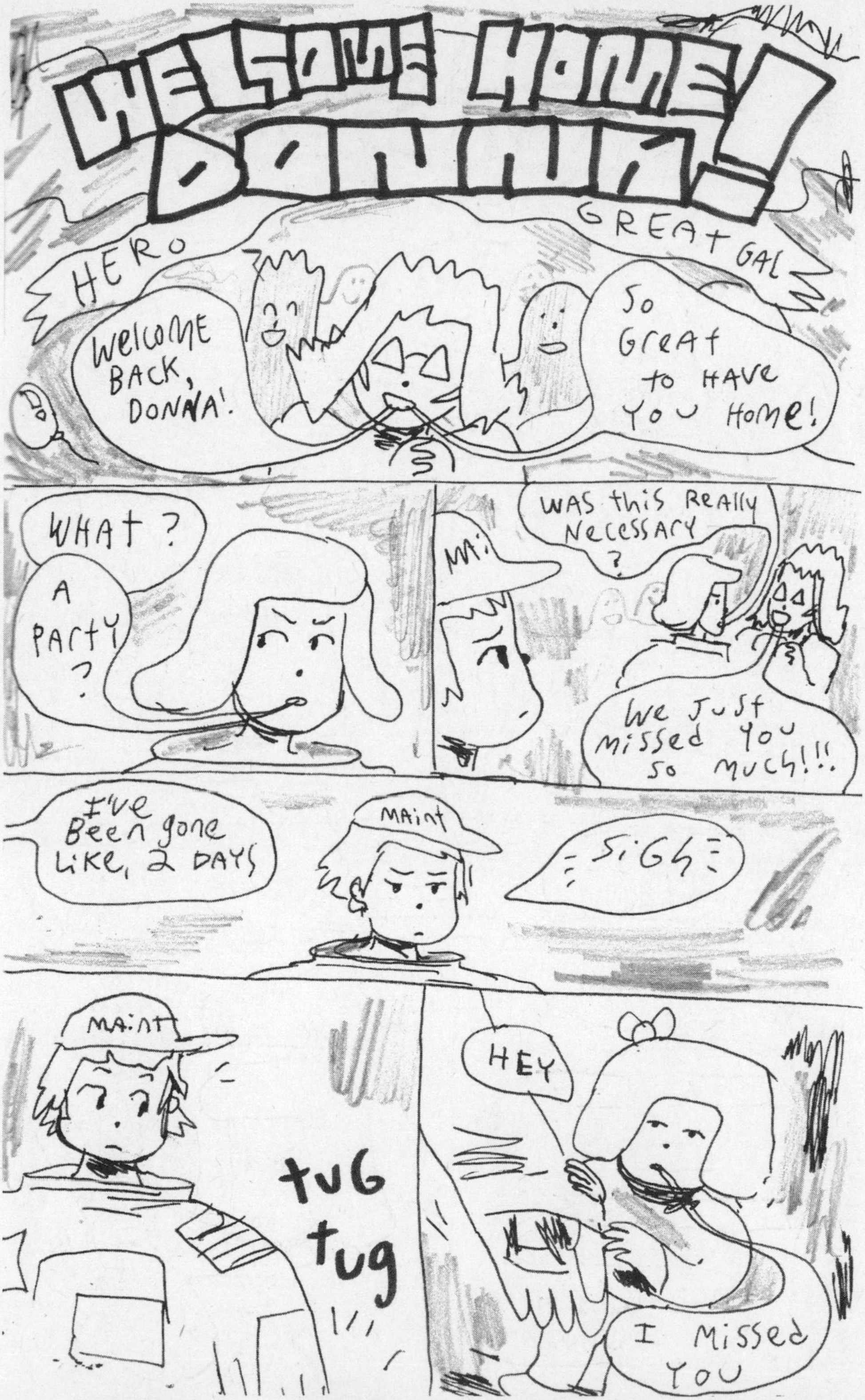

WELCOME HOME! DONNA!
HERO
GREAT GAL
Welcome BACK, DONNA!
So Great to HAVE YOU Home!
WHAT?
A Party?
WAS this Really Necessary?
We Just missed You so much!!!
I've Been gone Like, 2 DAYS
SIGH
MAINT
tug tug
HEY
I Missed YOU

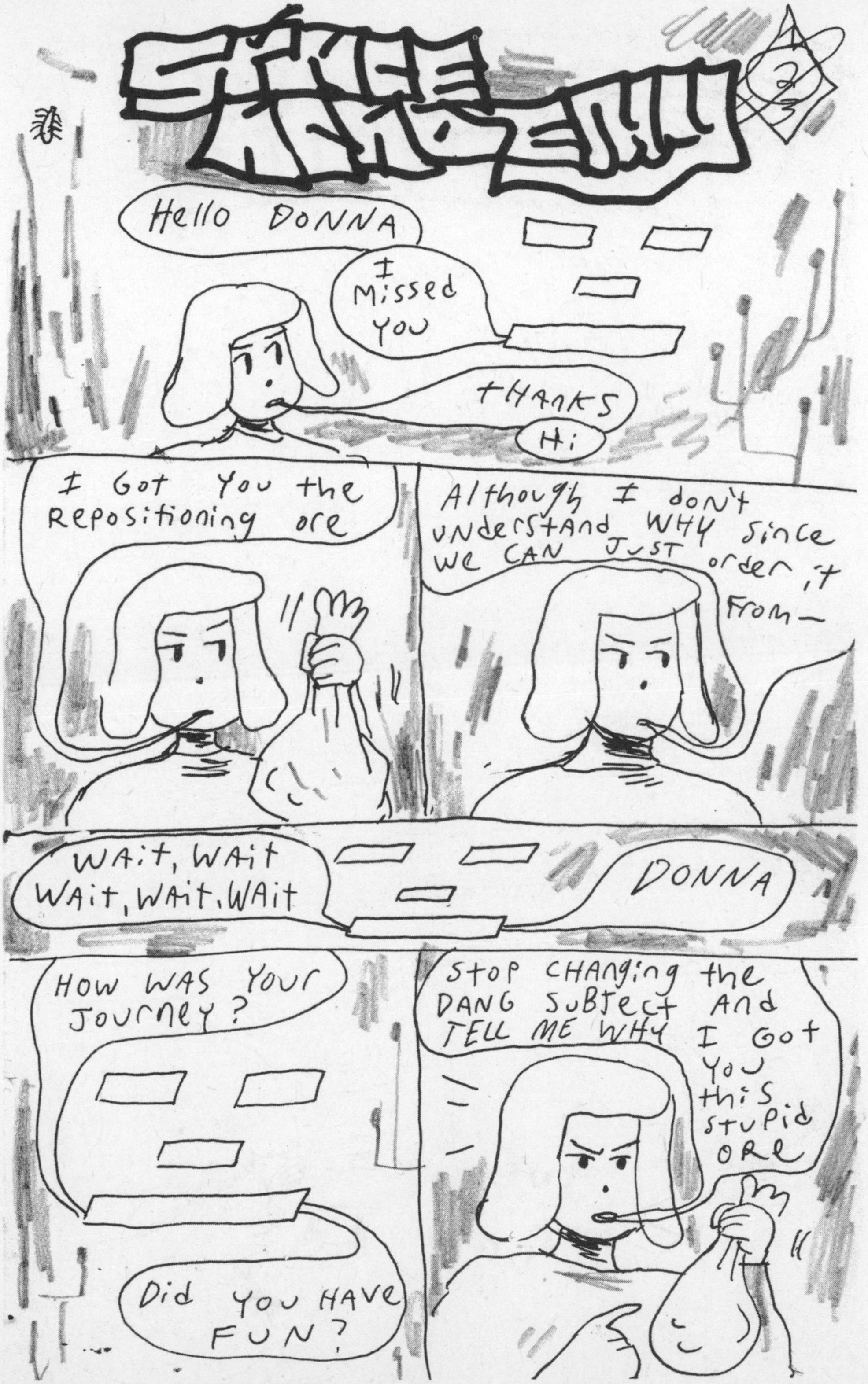
Hello DONNA
I Missed you
THANKS
Hi
I Got you the Repositioning ore
Although I don't understand WHY since we CAN JUST order it from—
WAit, WAit WAit, WAit, WAit
DONNA
HOW WAS YOUR JOURNEY?
Did YOU HAVE FUN?
STOP CHANGING the DANG SUBJECT AND TELL ME WHY I GOT YOU this STUPID ORE

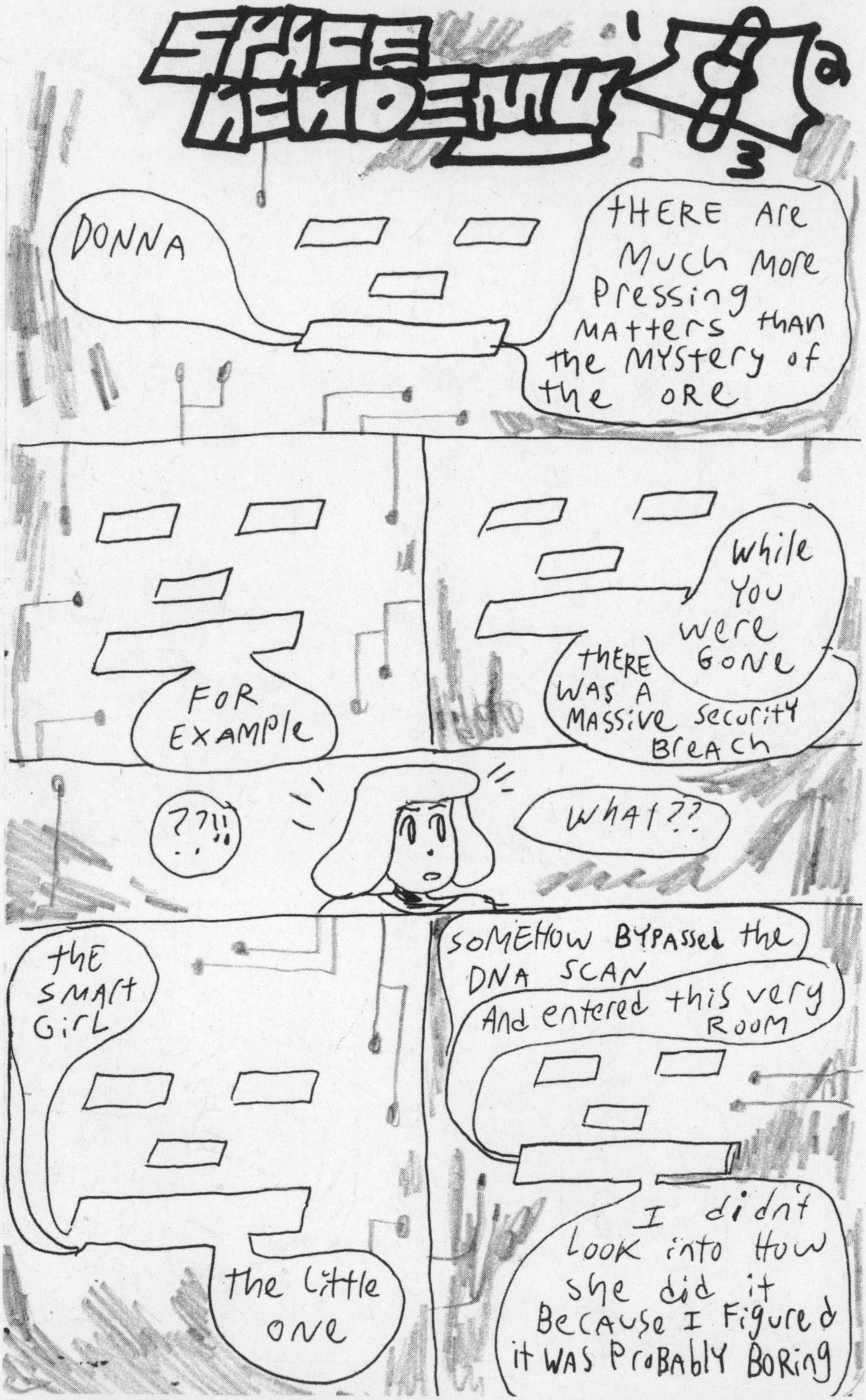
DONNA
THERE ARE MUCH MORE PRESSING MATTERS THAN THE MYSTERY OF THE ORE
FOR EXAMPLE
WHILE YOU WERE GONE
THERE WAS A MASSIVE SECURITY BREACH
??!!
WHAT??
THE SMART GIRL
THE LITTLE ONE
SOMEHOW BYPASSED THE DNA SCAN
AND ENTERED THIS VERY ROOM
I DIDN'T LOOK INTO HOW SHE DID IT BECAUSE I FIGURED IT WAS PROBABLY BORING

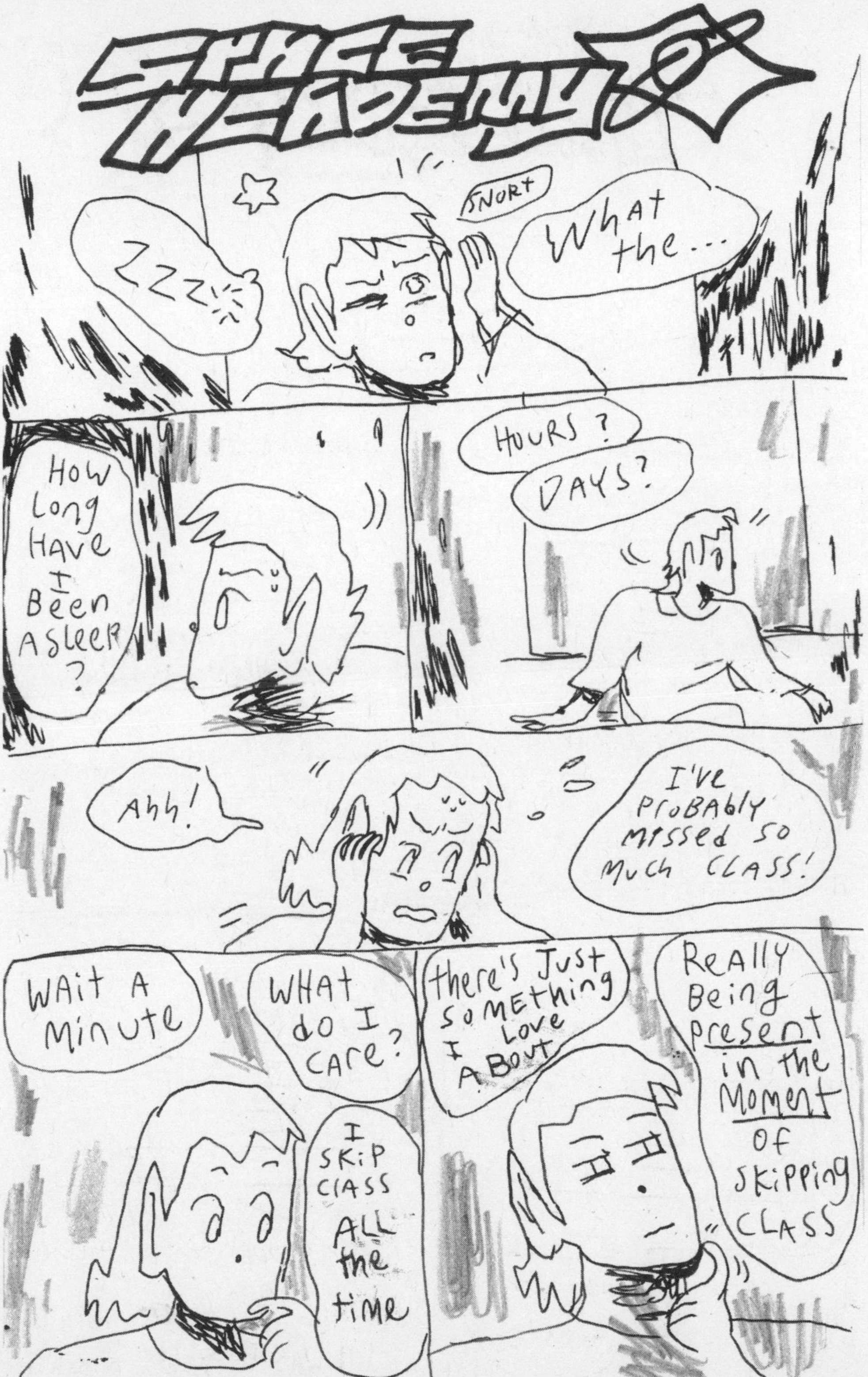
ZZZ
SNORT
What the...
How Long Have I Been Asleep?
HOURS?
DAYS?
Ahh!
I've probably missed so much class!
WAit A Minute
WHAT do I care?
I SKIP CLASS ALL the time
there's Just something I Love ABout
Really Being present in the Moment of skipping CLASS

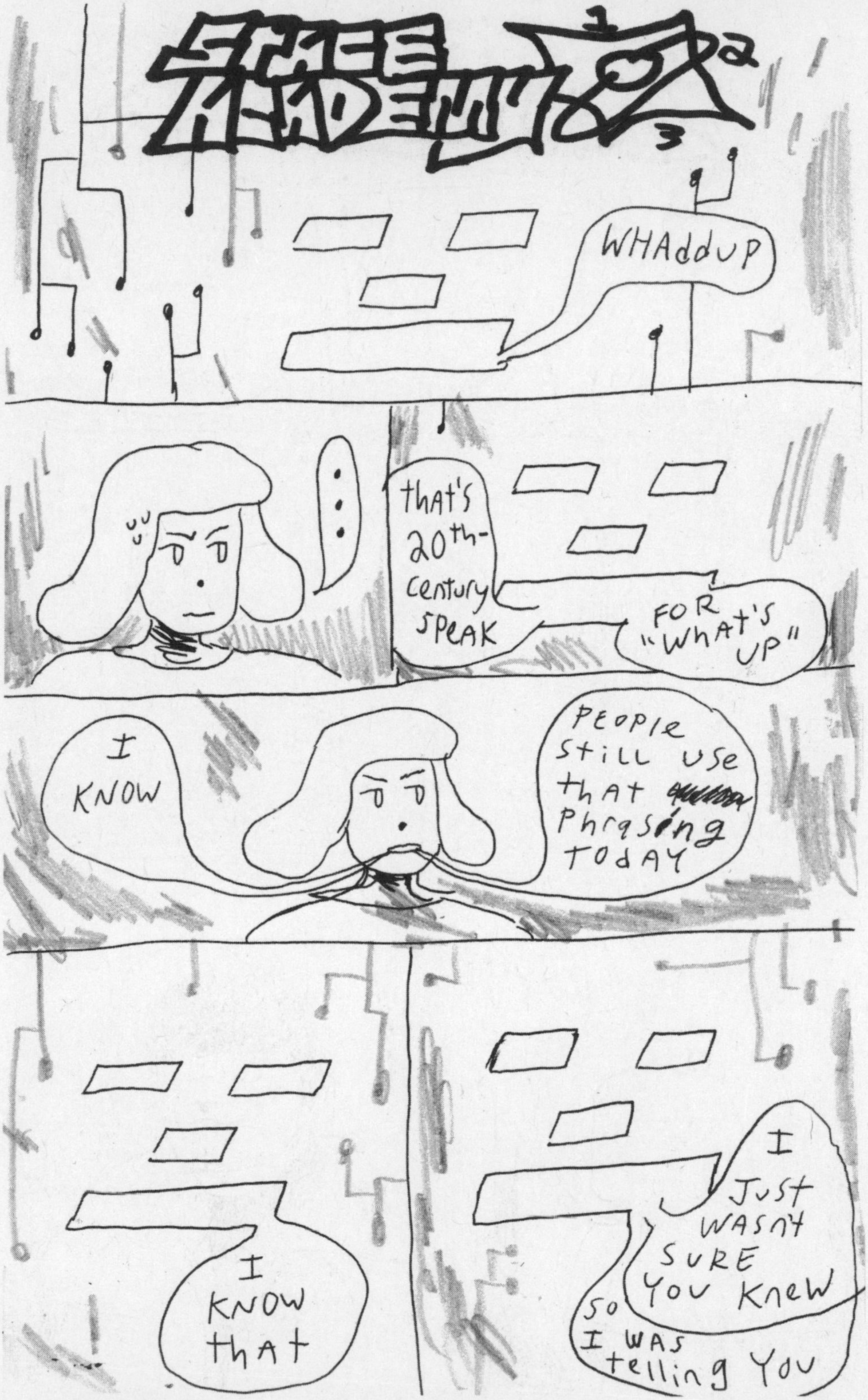
WHAddUP
...
that's 20th-century speak
FOR "What's UP"
I KNOW
PeOPle still use that Phrasing TODAY
I KNOW that
I Just WASn't SURE You Knew
So I WAS telling You

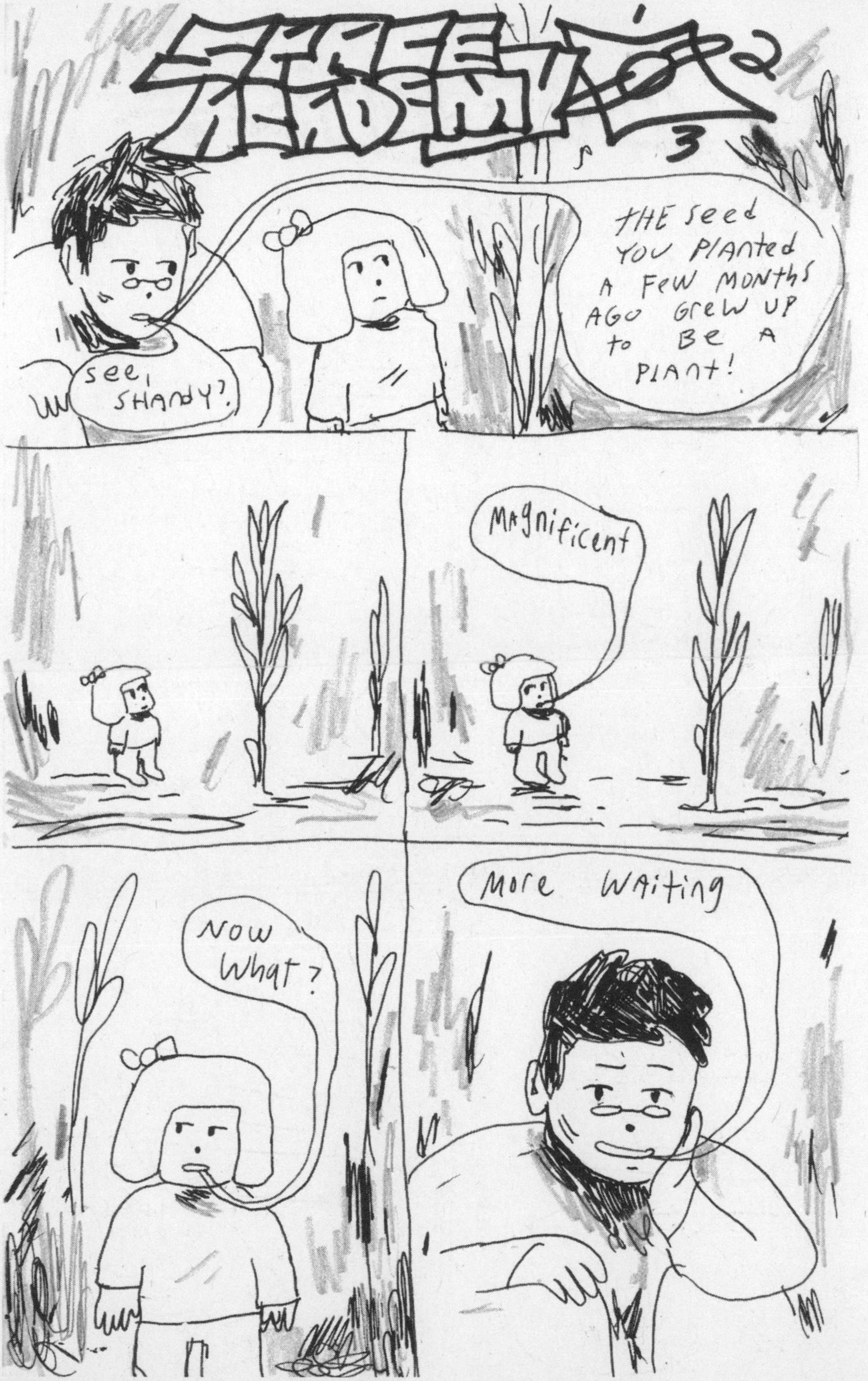
see, SHANDY?
THE seed YOU PLANTed A FEW MONTHS AGO GREW UP to BE A PLANT!
Magnificent
NOW What?
More WAiting

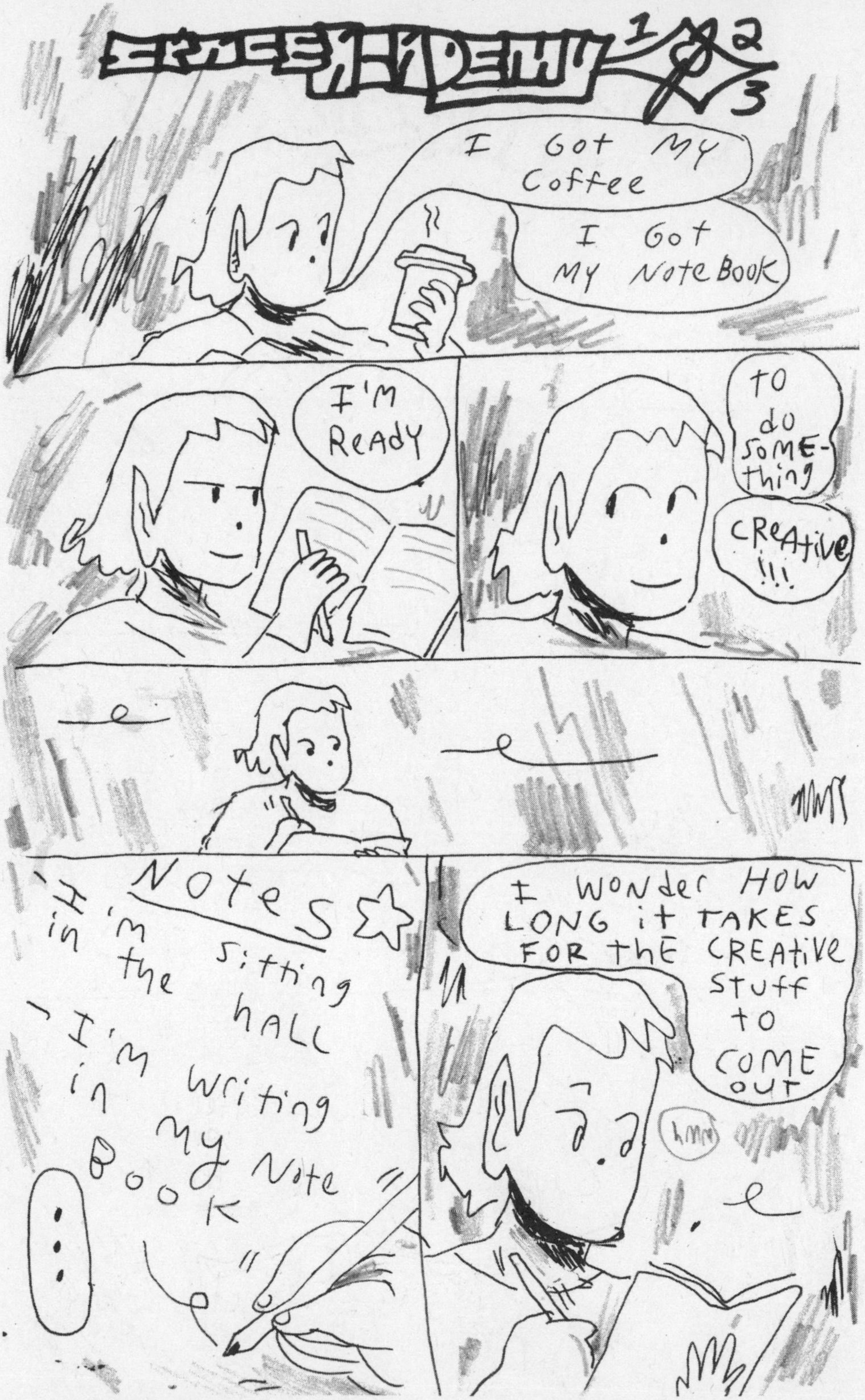
I Got MY Coffee
I Got MY NoteBook
I'M ReadY
to do SOME-thing
CReAtive !!!
NoteS
I'M sitting in the HALL
I'M Writing in MY Note BOOK
...
I WONdeR HOW LONG it TAKES FOR THE CREAtive Stuff to COME OUT
hmm

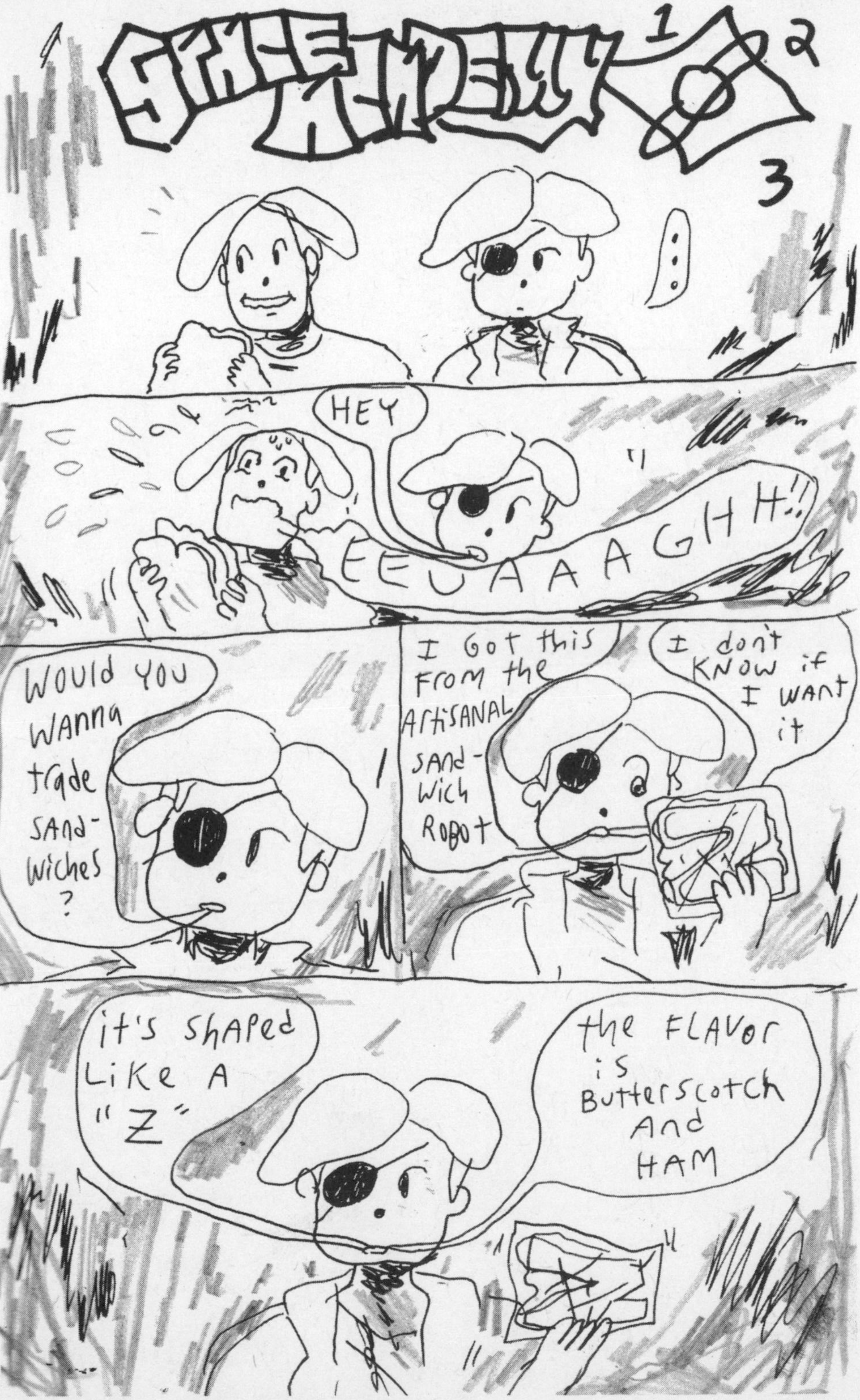

1
2
3
HEY
EEUAAAAGHH!!
Would you wanna trade sand-wiches?
I Got this from the Artisanal sand-wich Robot
I don't Know if I want it
it's shaped Like A "Z"
the FLAVor is Butterscotch And HAM

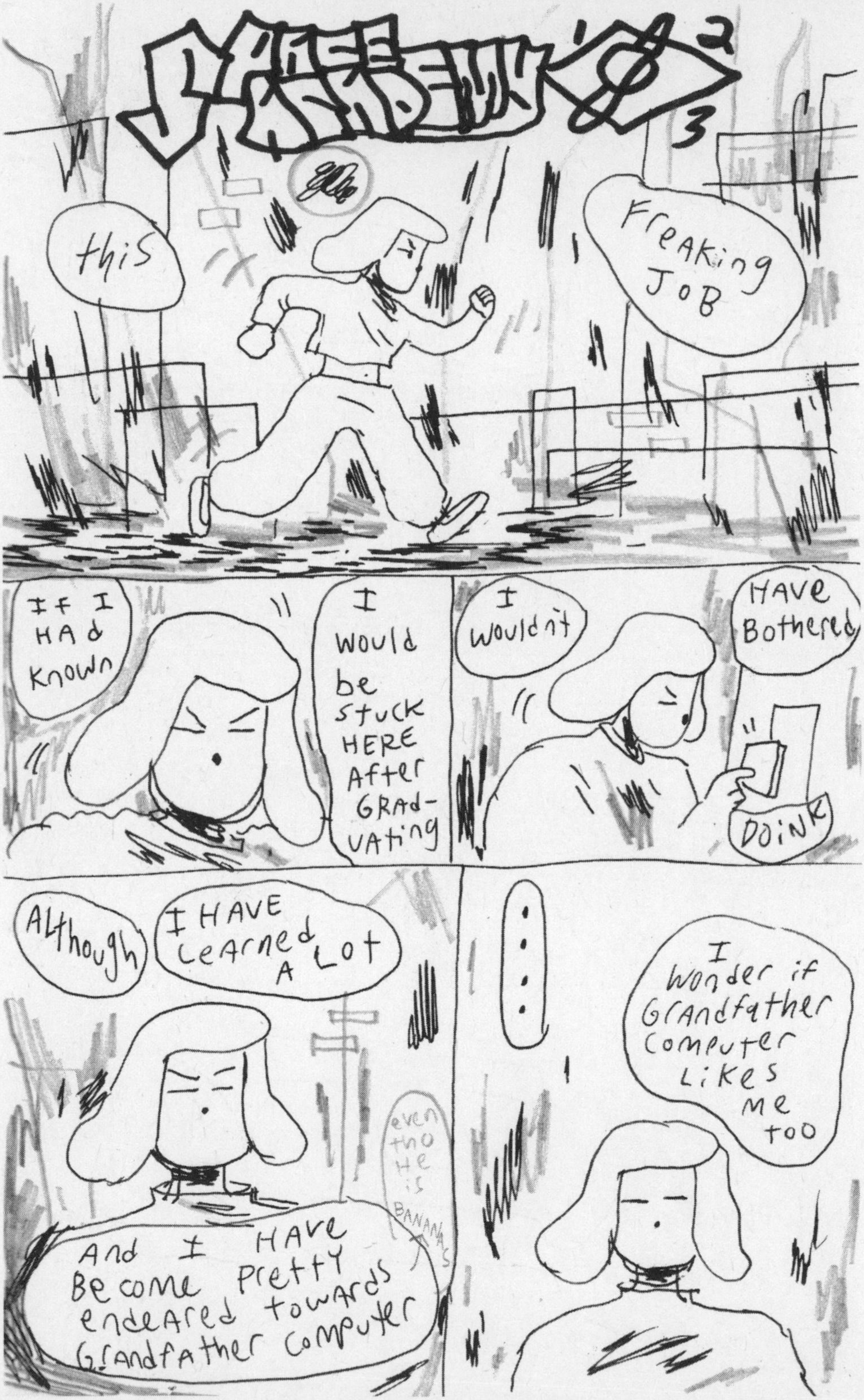
this
Freaking JOB
IF I HAd Known
I would be stuck HERE After GRAD-VATING
I wouldn't
HAVE Bothered
DOINK
Although
I HAVE Learned A LOT
And I HAVE Become Pretty endeared towards Grandfather Computer
even tho He is BANANAS
...
I wonder if Grandfather Computer Likes me too

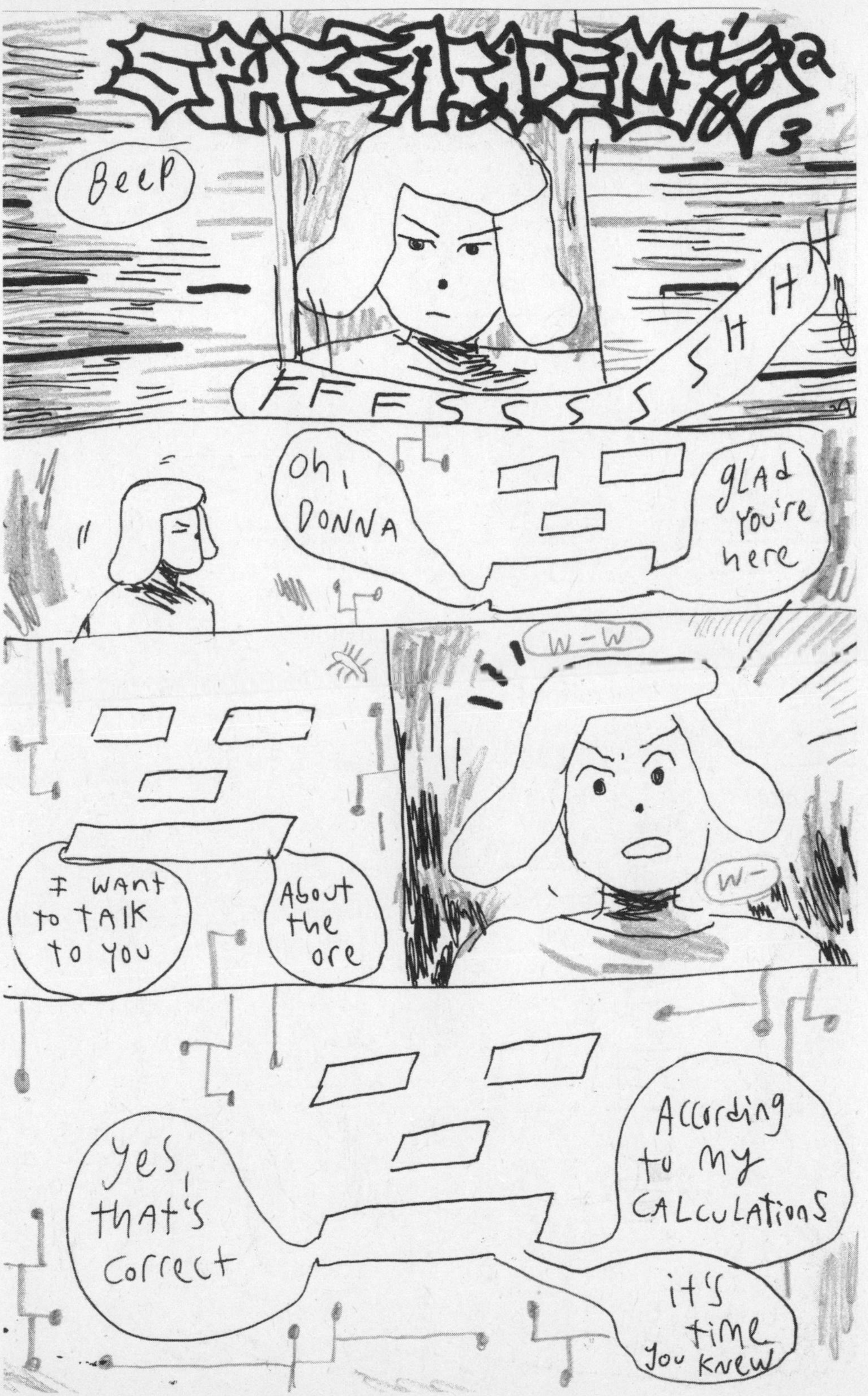
Beep
FFFSSSSSSHHHH
Oh, DONNA
glad you're here
W-W
I want to talk to you
About the ore
W-
yes, that's correct
According to my CALCULATIONS
it's time you knew

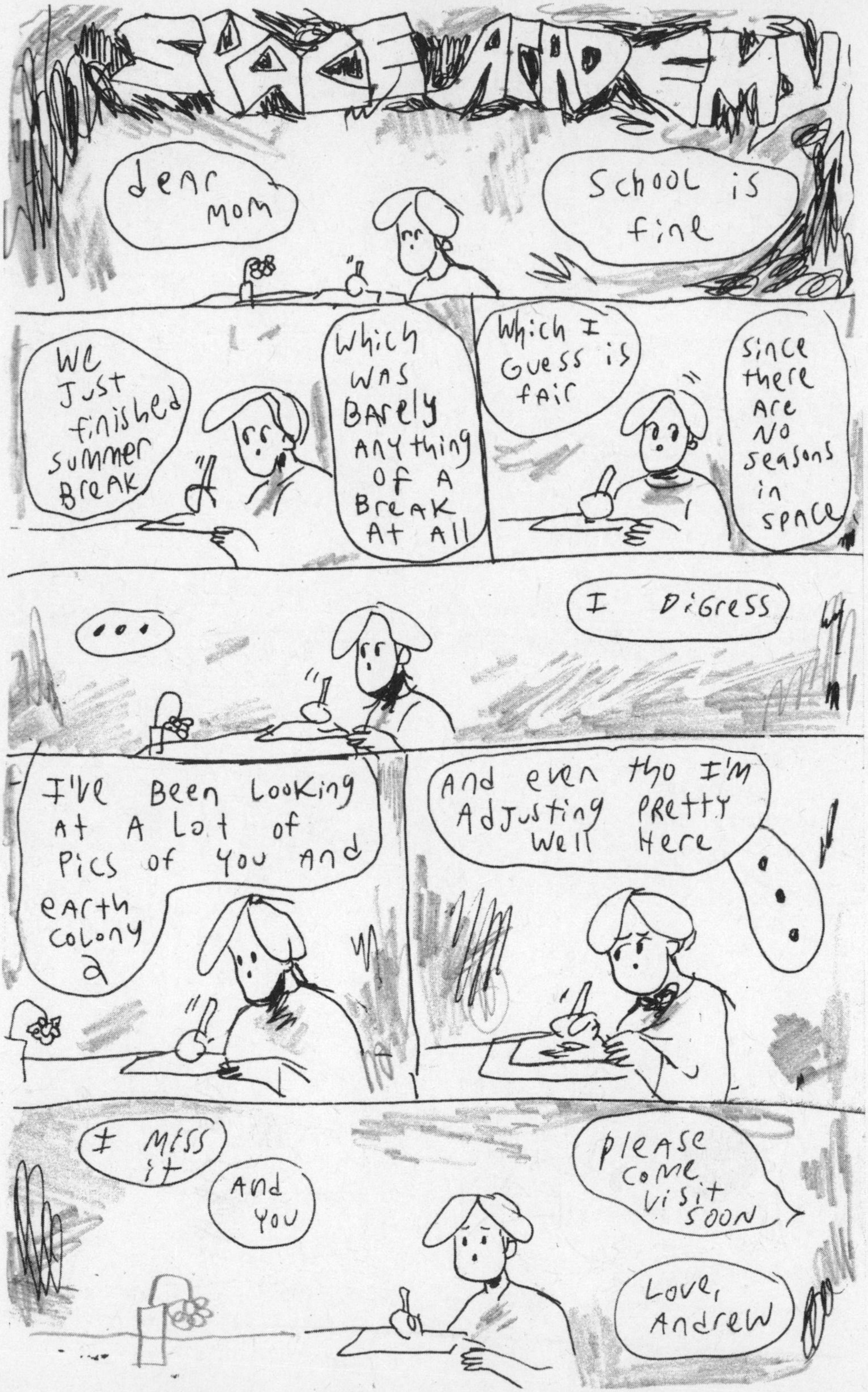
SPACE ACADEMY
dear mom
School is fine
We just finished summer break
Which was barely anything of a break at all
Which I guess is fair
since there are no seasons in space
...
I digress
I've been looking at a lot of pics of you and earth colony 2
And even tho I'm adjusting pretty well here
...
I miss it
And you
please come visit soon
Love, Andrew

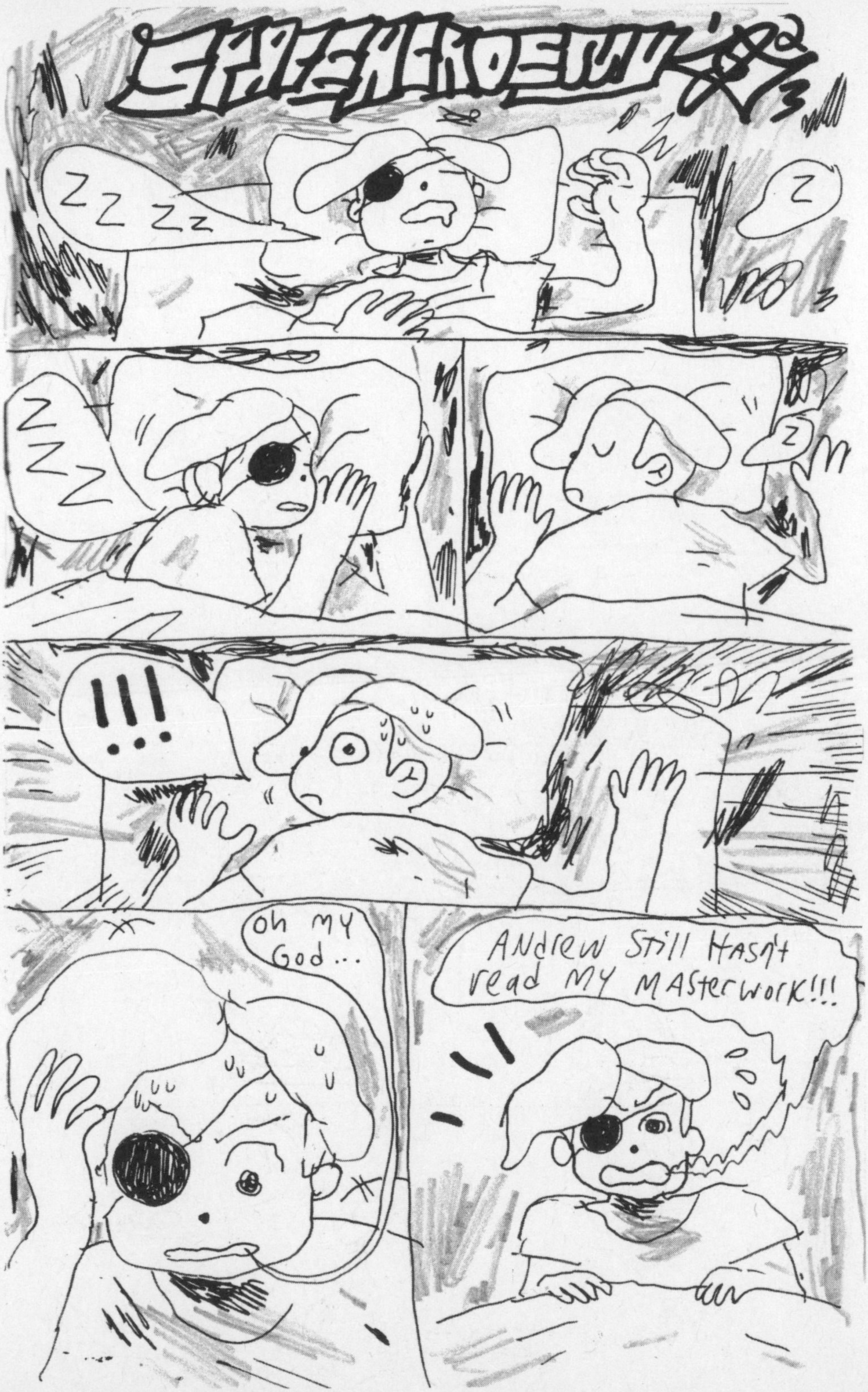
ZZZZz
Z
ZZZ
Z
!!!
...
oh MY God...
Andrew Still Hasn't read MY MASterwork!!!

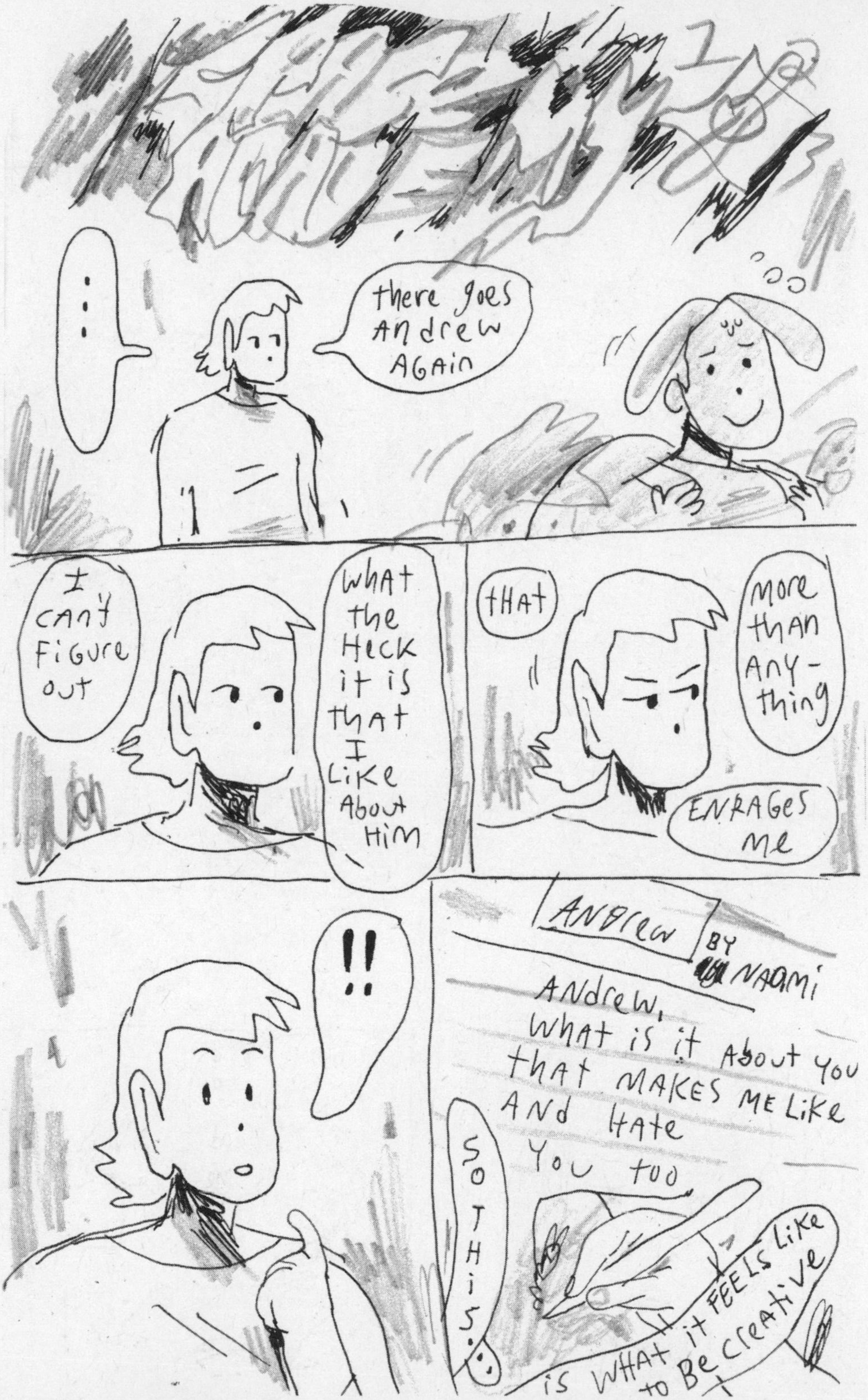
...
there goes Andrew AGAin
I can't Figure out
what the Heck it is that I Like About Him
that
more than any-thing
ENRAGES me
!!
Andrew BY NAOMI
Andrew, what is it About you that MAKES ME Like And Hate You too
SO THiS...
is WHAT it FEELS Like to Be creative

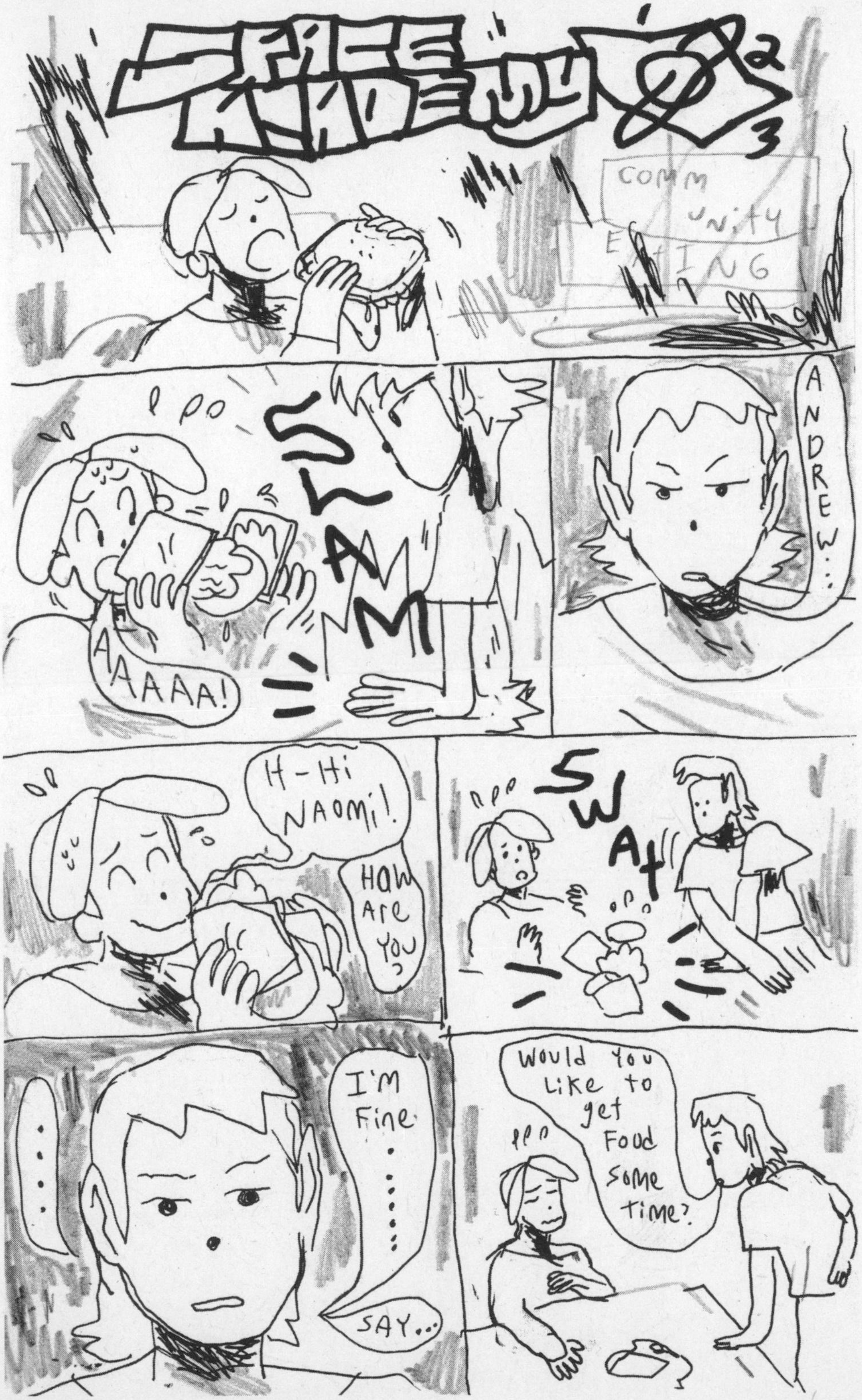
COMM
unity
EATING
SLAM
AAAAAA!
ANDREW...
H-Hi
NAOMi!
HoW
Are
You
?
SWAt
...
I'M
Fine
......
SAY...
Would You
Like to
get
Food
Some
time?

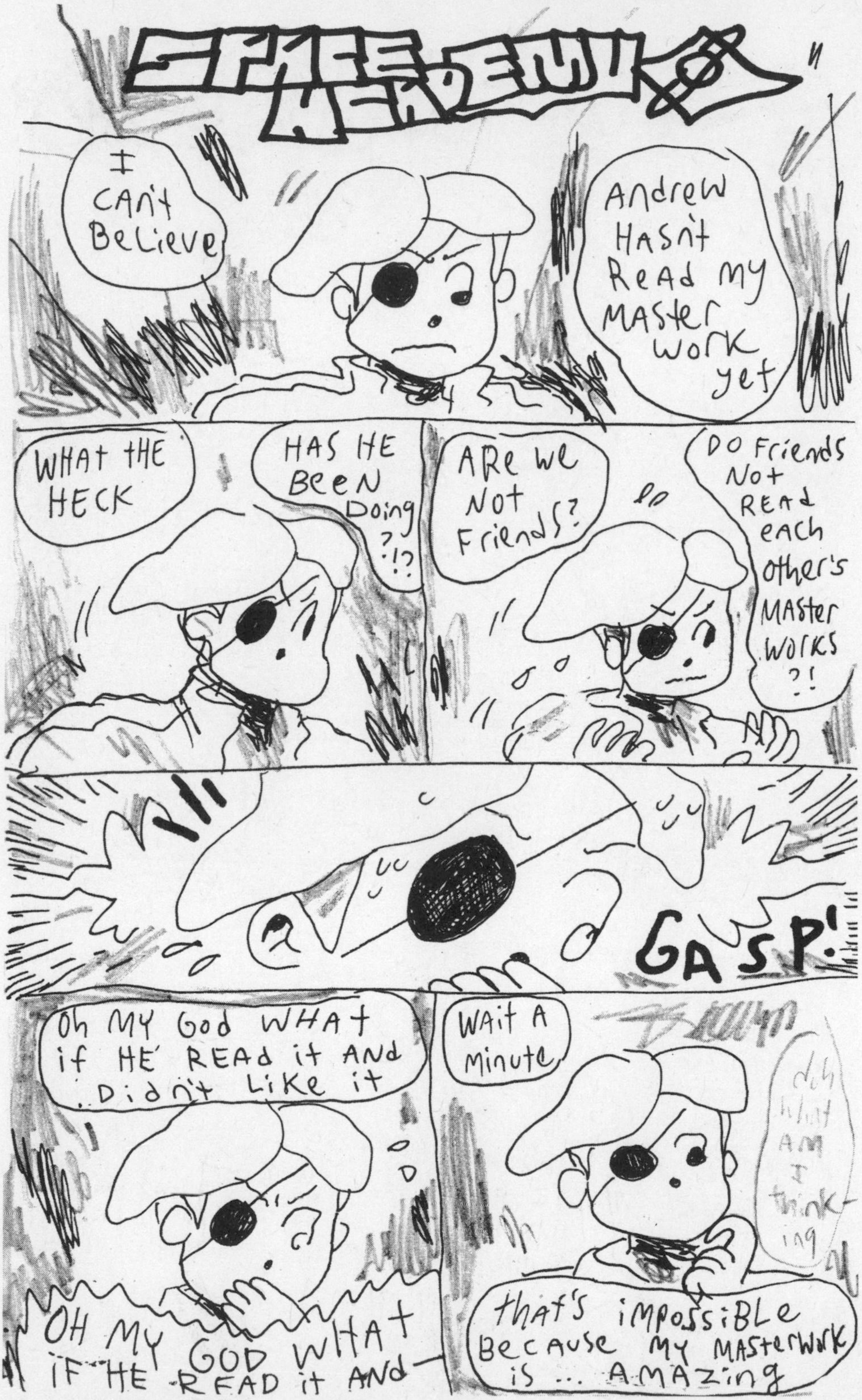
I can't Believe
Andrew Hasn't Read my Master work yet
WHAT THE HECK
HAS HE BEEN Doing ?!?
ARE WE Not Friends?
Do Friends Not READ each other's MASTER WORKS ?!
GASP!
Oh MY God WHAT if HE READ it And ..Didn't Like it
OH MY GOD WHAT IF HE READ it AND—
Wait A Minute
duh What AM I think-ing
that's impossible Because my Masterwork is ... AMAZing

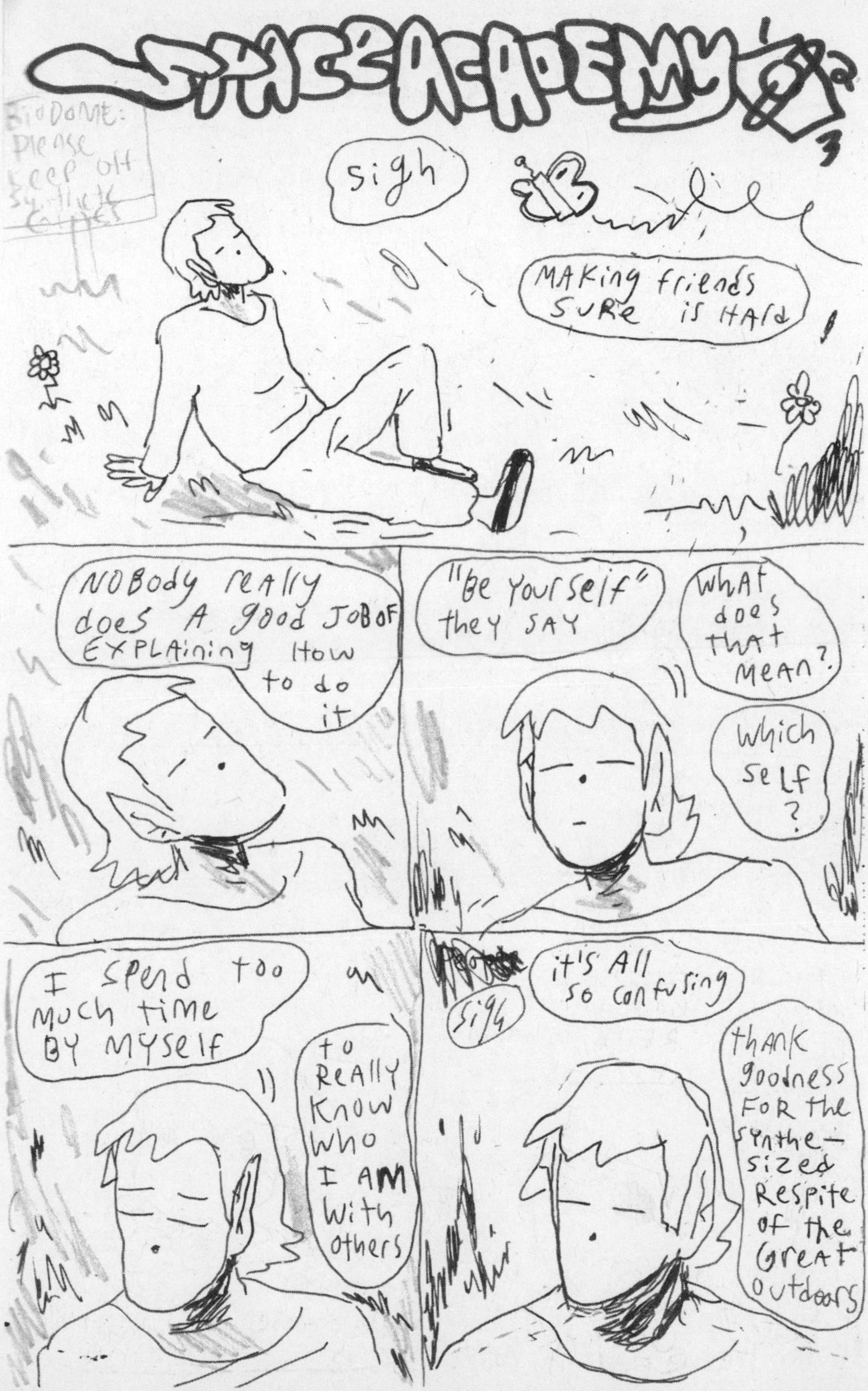
SPACE ACADEMY
3
BioDome: please keep off
sigh
MAKing friends sure is HARd
NOBody really does A good JOB OF EXPLAining How to do it
"Be yourself" they SAY
WhAt does that mean?
Which self?
I spend too much time by myself
to Really Know who I AM with others
sigh
it's All so confusing
thank goodness FOR the synthe-sized Respite of the Great outdoors

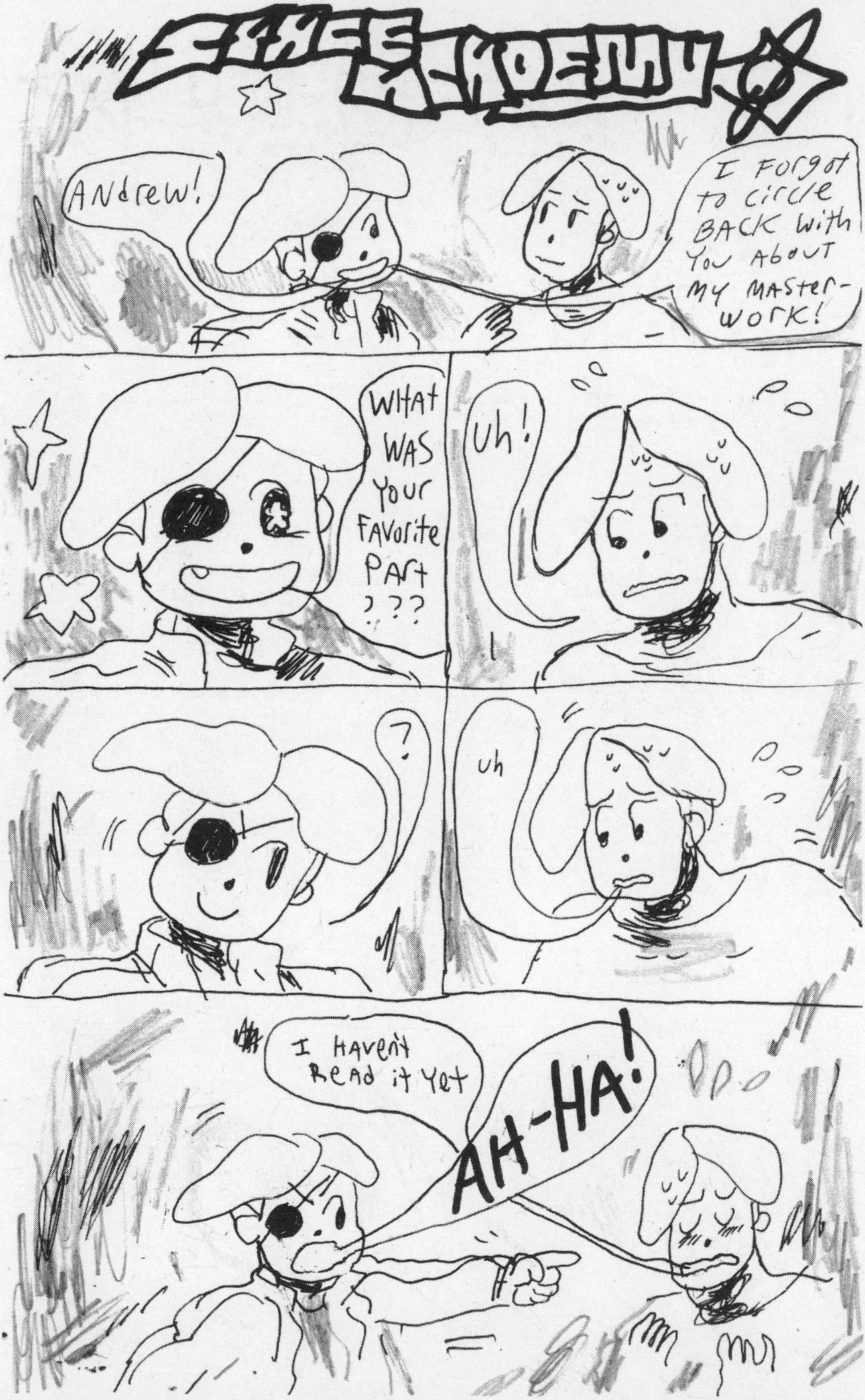
Andrew!
I Forgot to circle BACK with You ABOUT MY MASTER-WORK!
WHAT WAS Your FAVorite PArt ???
uh!
?
uh
I Haven't Read it Yet
AH-HA!

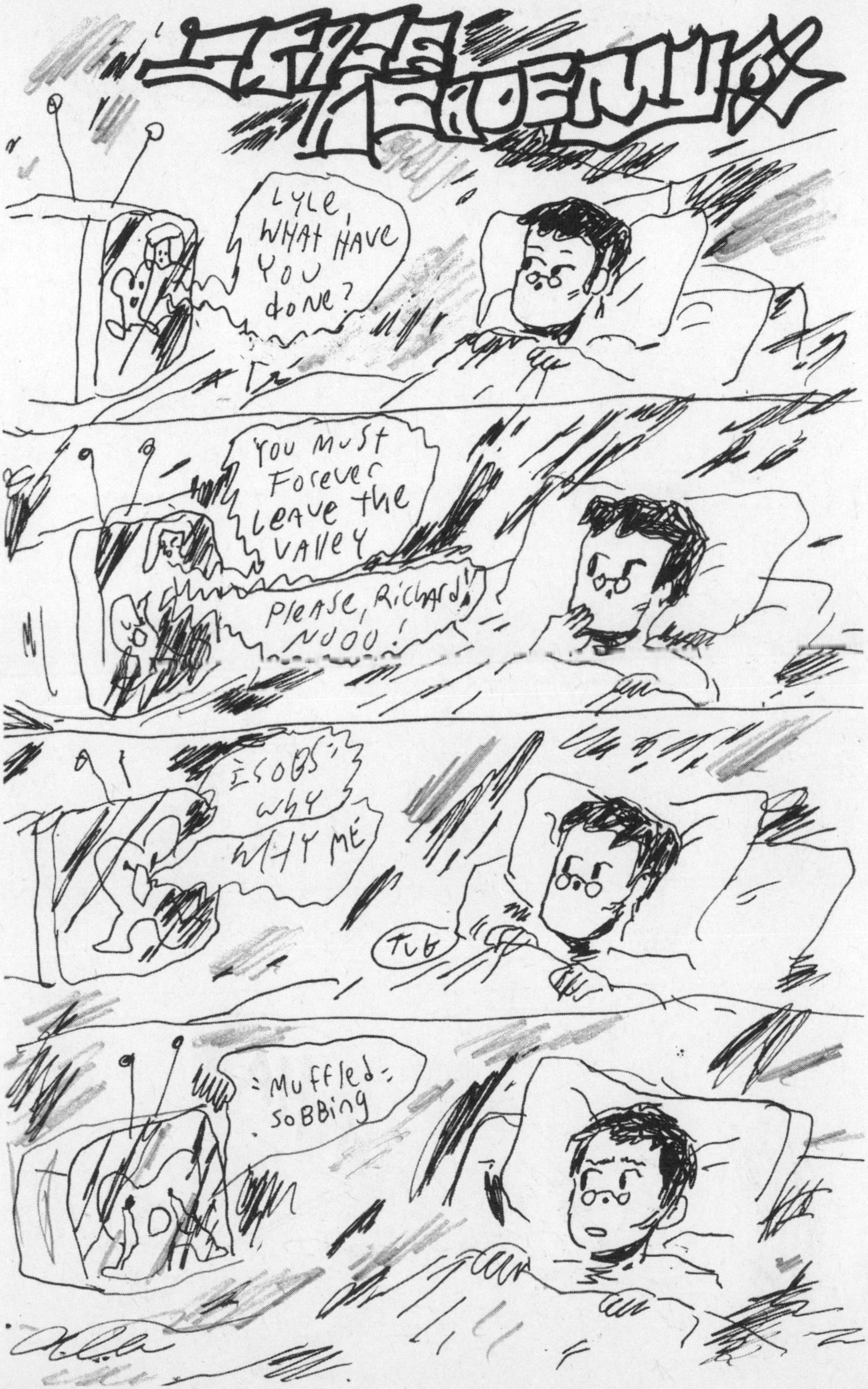
Lyle, WHAT HAVE YOU done?
You Must Forever leave the valley
Please, Richard! NOOO!
SOBS why WHY ME
TUG
Muffled sobbing

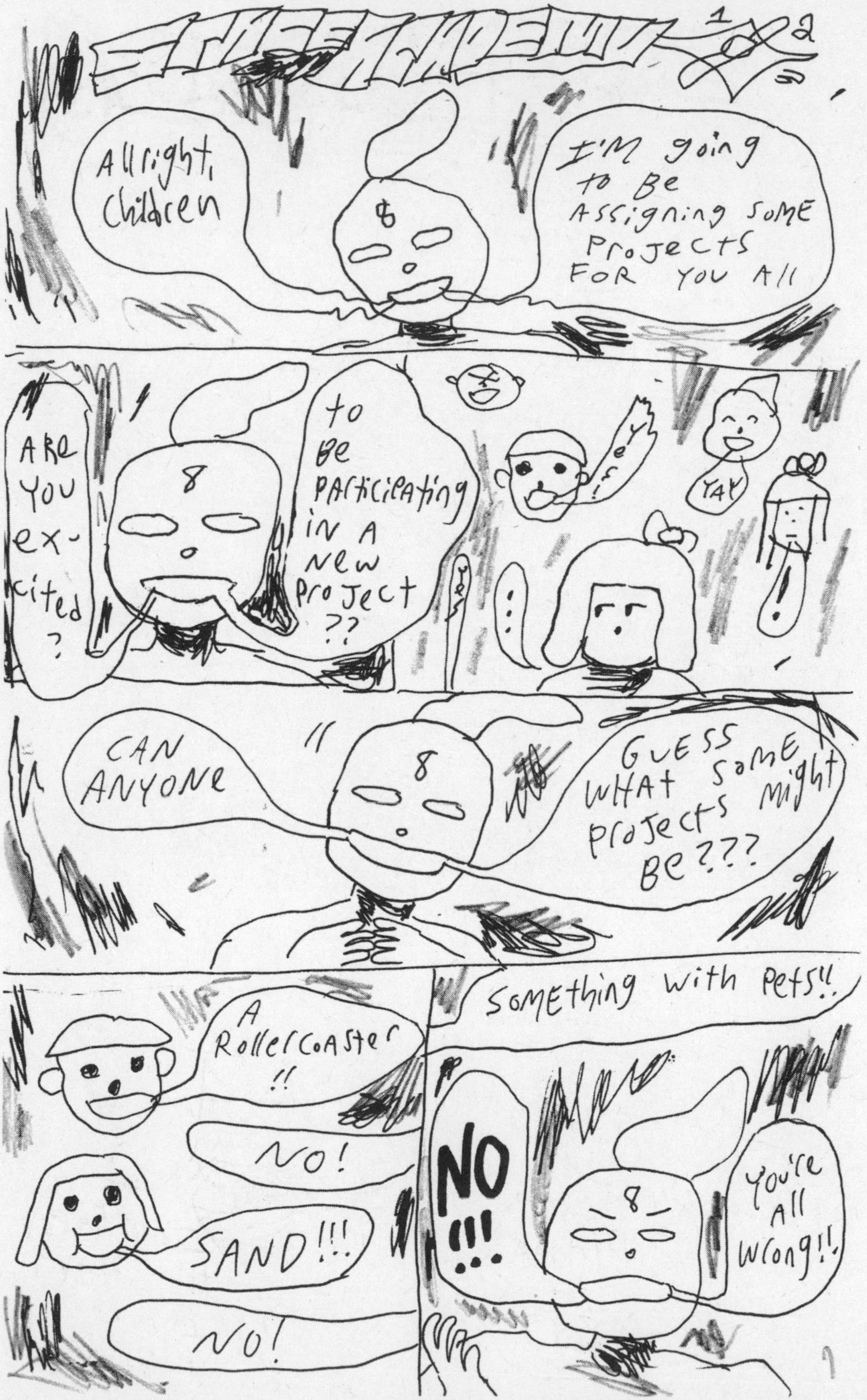
Allright, Children
I'M going to Be Assigning some Projects FOR YOU All
ARE YOU ex-cited ?
to Be Participating in A new Project ??
Yes!
YAY
Yes
...
!
CAN ANYONE
GUESS WHAT some projects might Be???
A Rollercoaster !!
NO!
SAND!!!
NO!
Something with pets!!
NO !!!...
You're All wrong!!

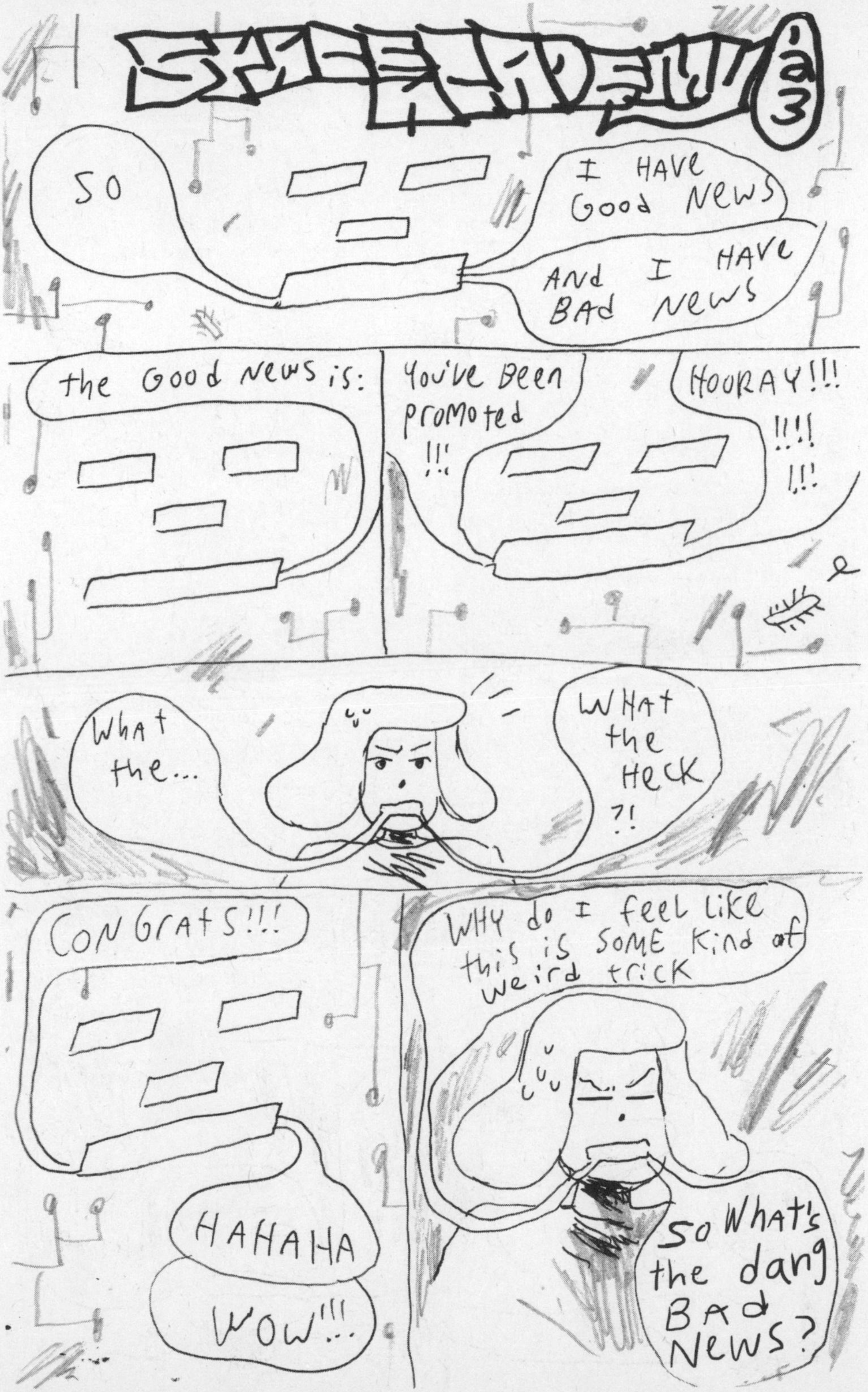
SO
I HAVE Good NEWS
AND I HAVE BAd NEWS
the Good NEWS is:
You've Been promoted !!!
HOORAY!!! !!!! !!!
What the...
WHAT the HECK ?!
CONGRATS!!!
HAHAHA
WOW!!!...
WHY do I feel like this is SOME Kind of weird trick
So What's the dang BAd NEWS?

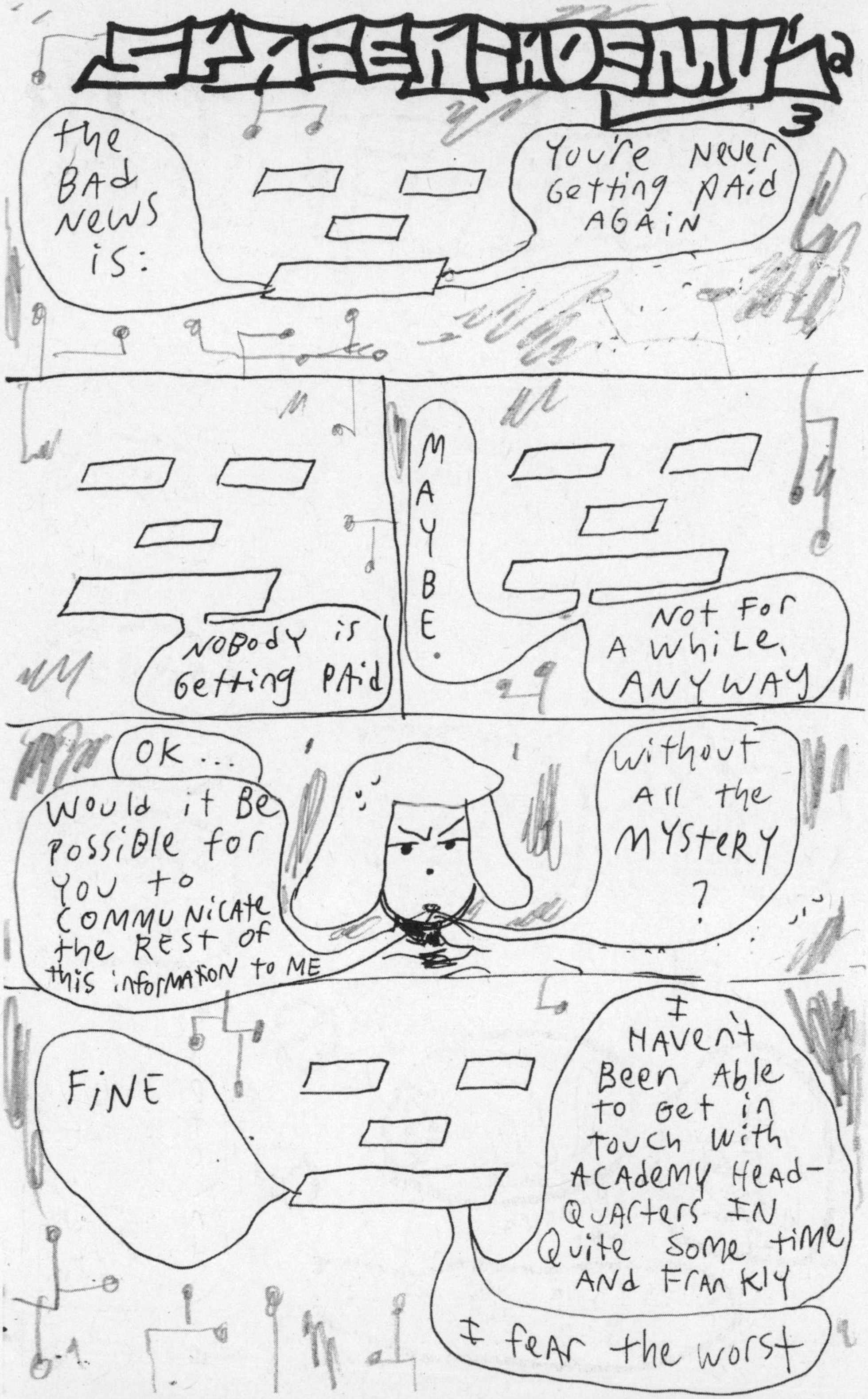

the BAd news is:
You're Never Getting pAid AGAIN
NOBody is Getting pAid
MAYBE.
Not for A while, ANYWAY
OK ...
would it Be possible for you to communicate the rest of this information to me
without All the MYSTERY ?
FiNE
I HAVEN't Been Able to Get in touch with ACAdemy Head-QuArters IN Quite Some time AND FrAnkly
I fear the worst

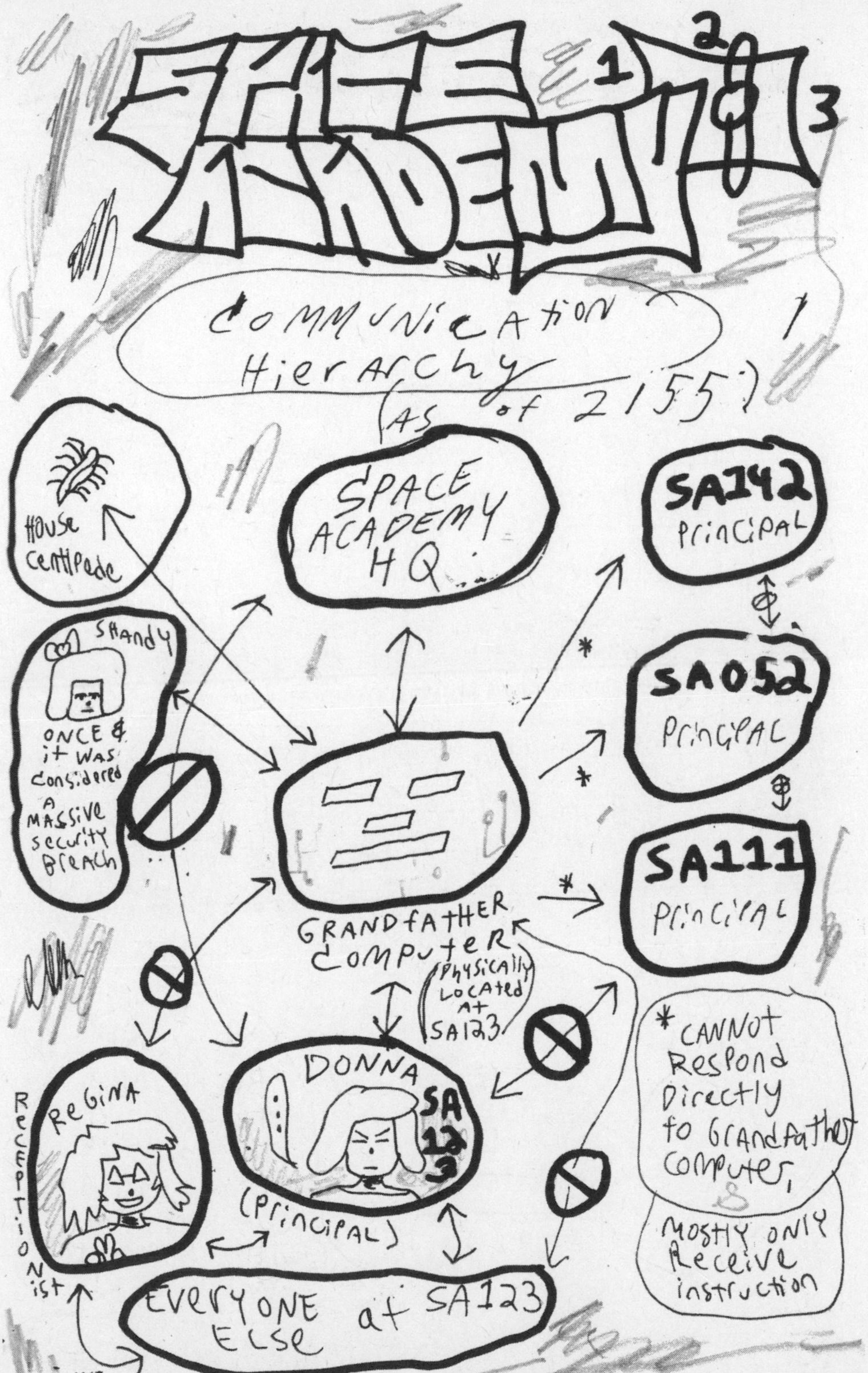
Space Academy 123
Communication Hierarchy (as of 2155)
Space Academy HQ
House centipede
Shandy
Once & it was considered a massive security breach
Grandfather Computer
Physically located at SA123
SA142 Principal
SA052 Principal
SA111 Principal
* Cannot respond directly to Grandfather Computer, mostly only receive instruction
Regina
Receptionist
Donna
SA123
(Principal)
Everyone else at SA123

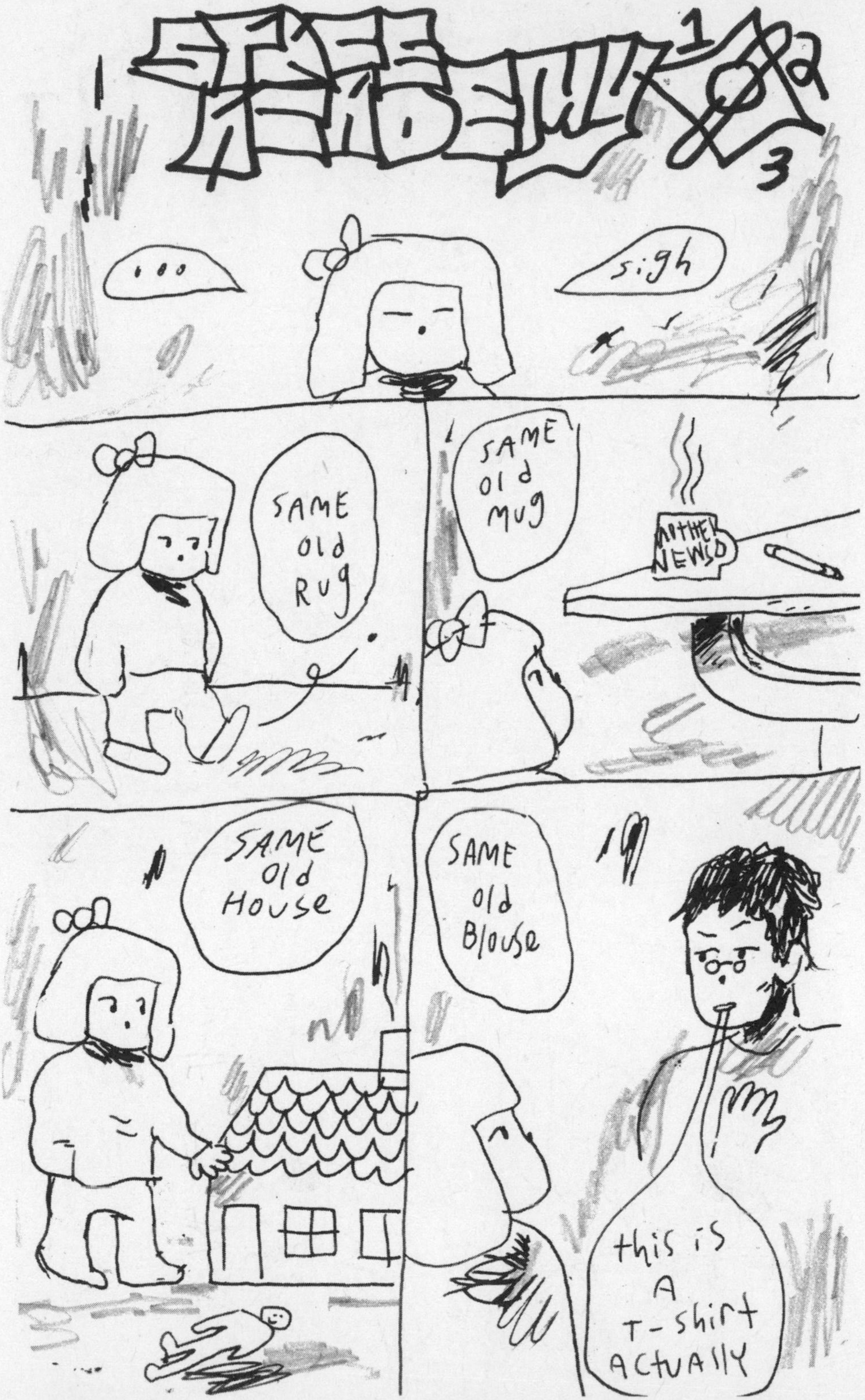
...
sigh
SAME old RUG
SAME old mug
SAME old House
SAME old Blouse
this is A T-shirt ACTUALLY

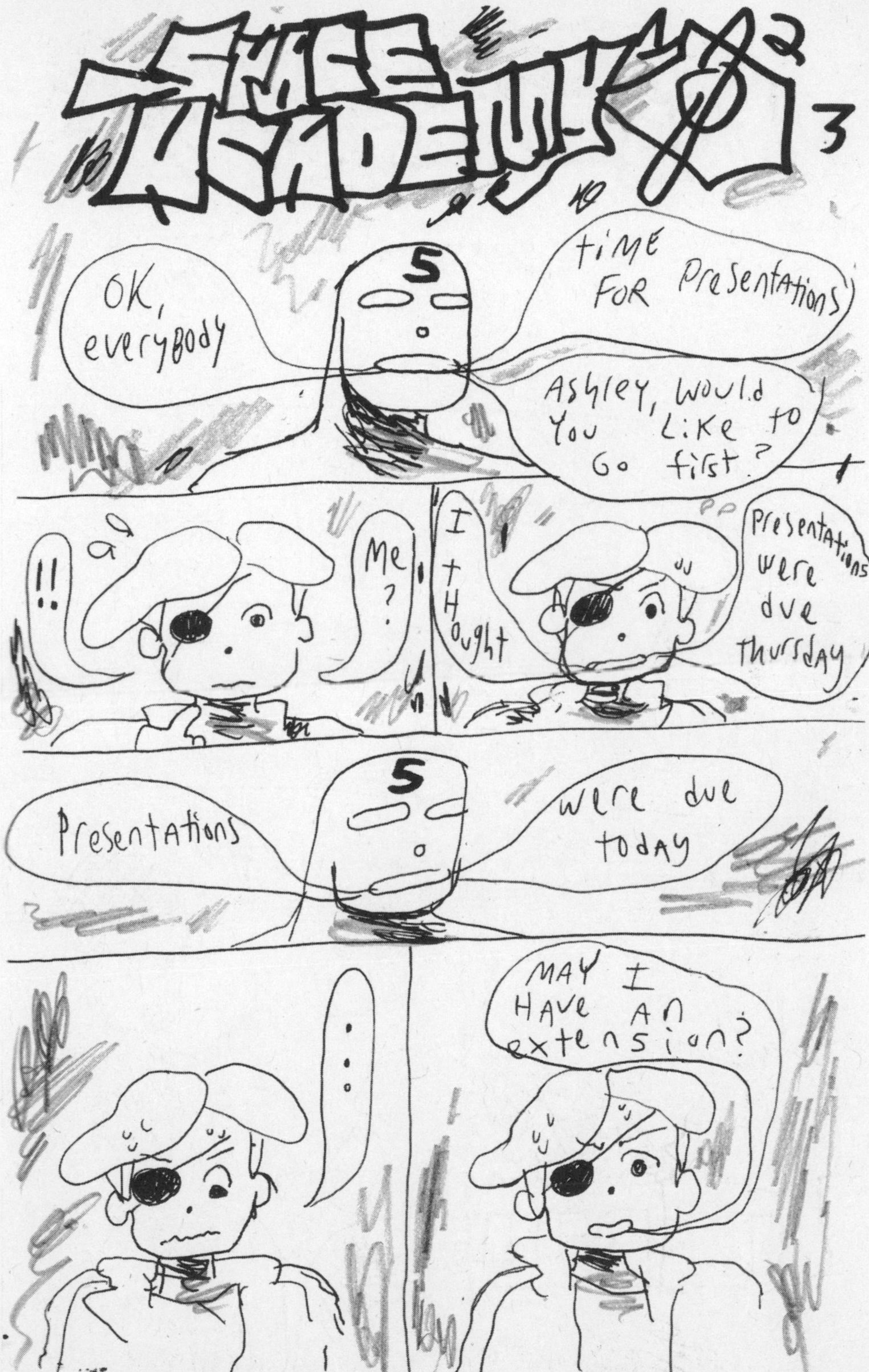
OK, everybody
time FOR presentations
Ashley, would you like to go first?
!!
Me?
I thought
presentations were due thursday
presentations
were due today
...
MAY I HAVE AN extension?

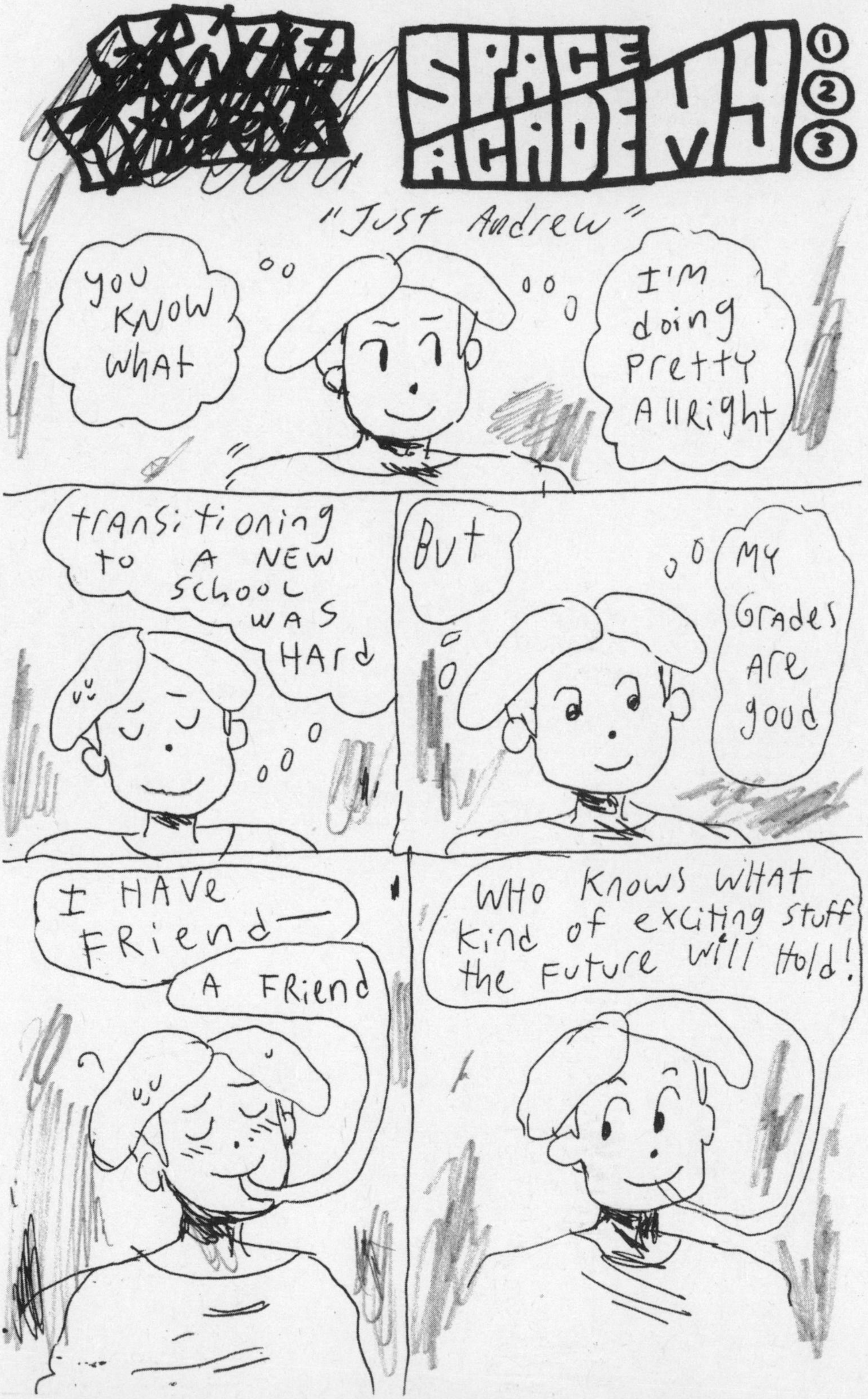
SPACE ACADEMY
1 2 3
"Just Andrew"
you KNOW what
I'M doing Pretty AllRight
transitioning to A NEW SchooL WAS HArd
But
MY Grades Are good
I HAVe FRiend—
A FRiend
WHO Knows WHAT kind of exciting stuff the Future will Hold!

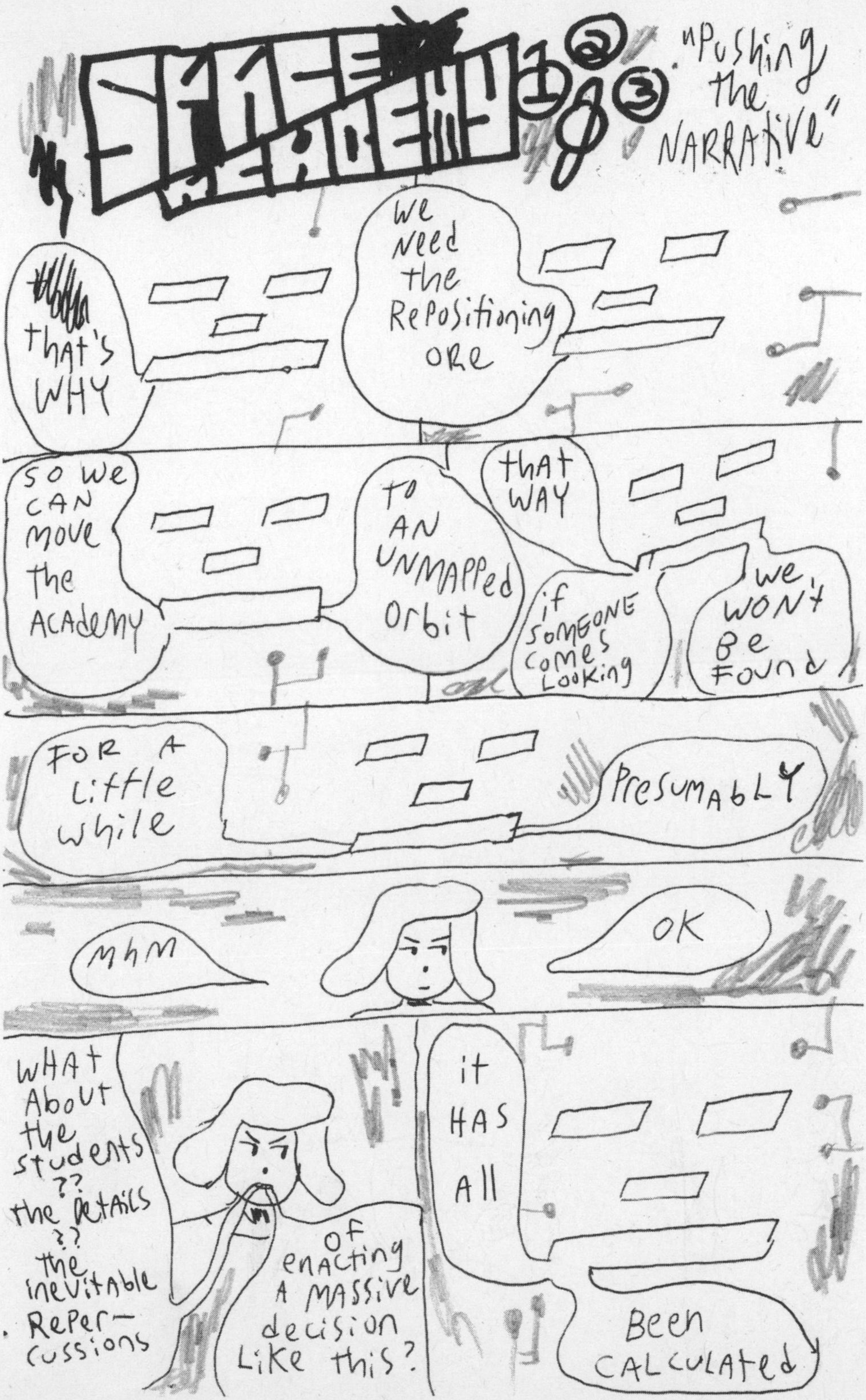
"Pushing the NARRATive"
that's WHY
we Need the Repositioning ore
so we CAN move the ACAdemy
to AN UNMAPPed orbit
that WAY
if SOMEONE comes Looking
we WON'T Be Found
FOR A Little while
PresUMAbLY
MHM
OK
WHAT About the Students ?? the Details ?? the inevitable Reper-cussions
of enacting A MASSive decision Like this?
it HAS All
Been CALCULAted

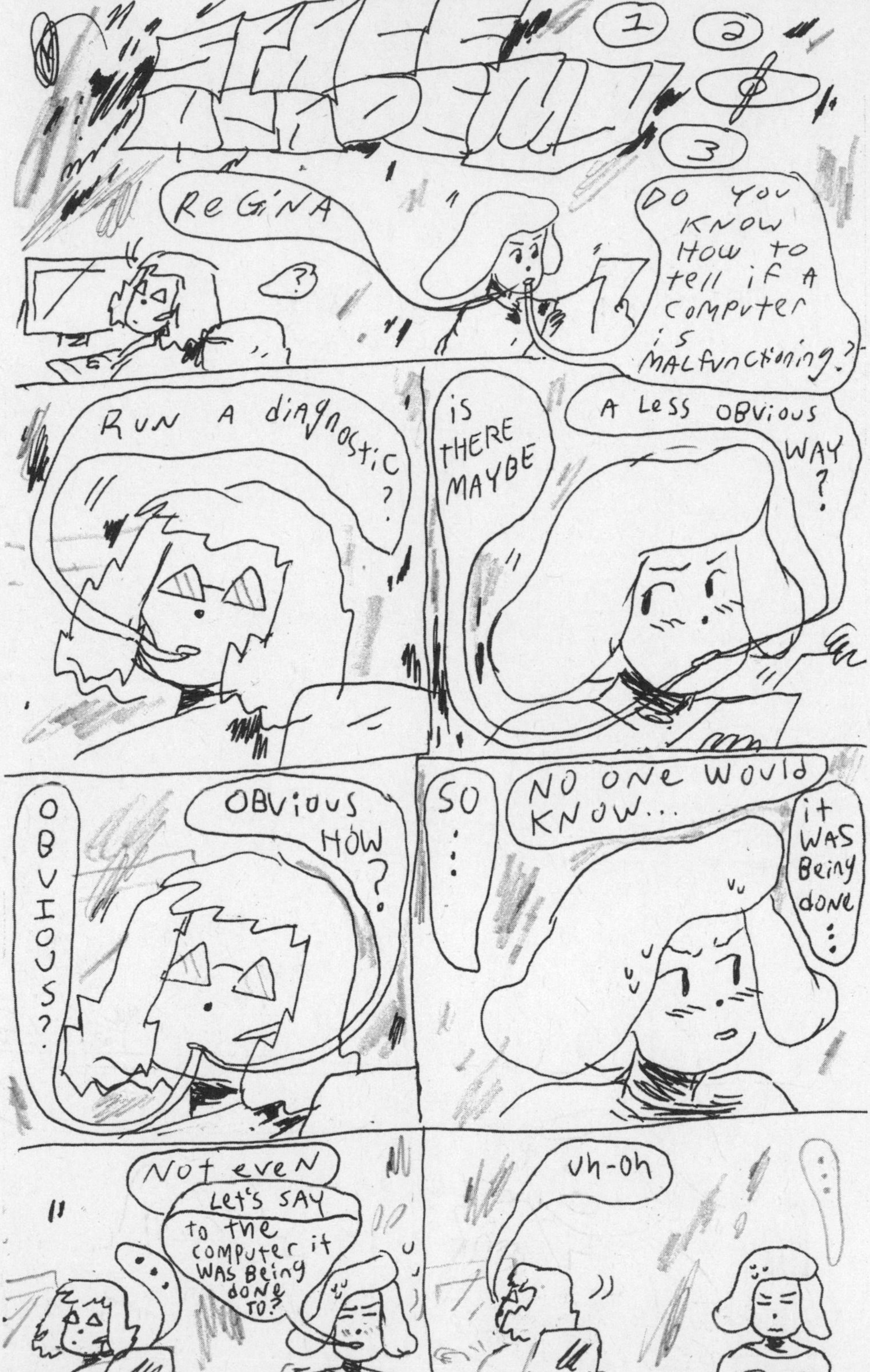
1
2
&
3
REGINA
?
DO YOU KNOW HOW TO TELL IF A COMPUTER IS MALFUNCTIONING?
RUN A DIAGNOSTIC?
IS THERE MAYBE
A LESS OBVIOUS WAY?
OBVIOUS HOW?
OBVIOUS?
SO...
NO ONE WOULD KNOW...
IT WAS BEING DONE...
NOT EVEN
LET'S SAY
TO THE COMPUTER IT WAS BEING DONE TO?
...
UH-OH
...

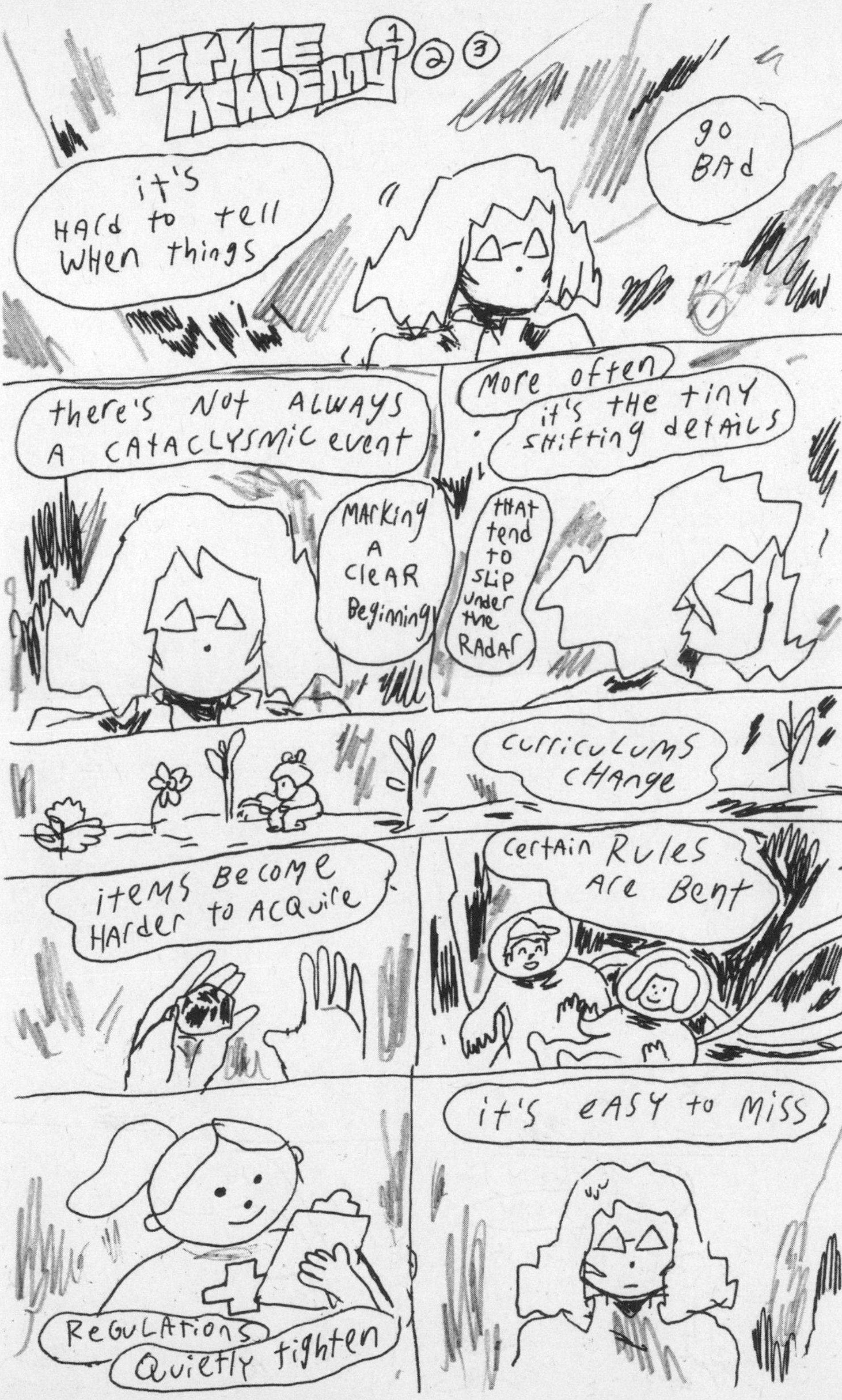
SPACE ACADEMY 1 2 3
it's HArd to tell WHEN things
go BAd
there's Not ALWAYS A CATACLYSMIC event
MARKing A CleAR Beginning
More often it's tHE tiny SHifting detAiLS
THAT tend to SLIP under the RAdAr
CurricuLUMS CHAnge
items Become HArder to ACQuire
Certain Rules Are Bent
ReGULATions Quietly tighten
it's eASY to MiSS

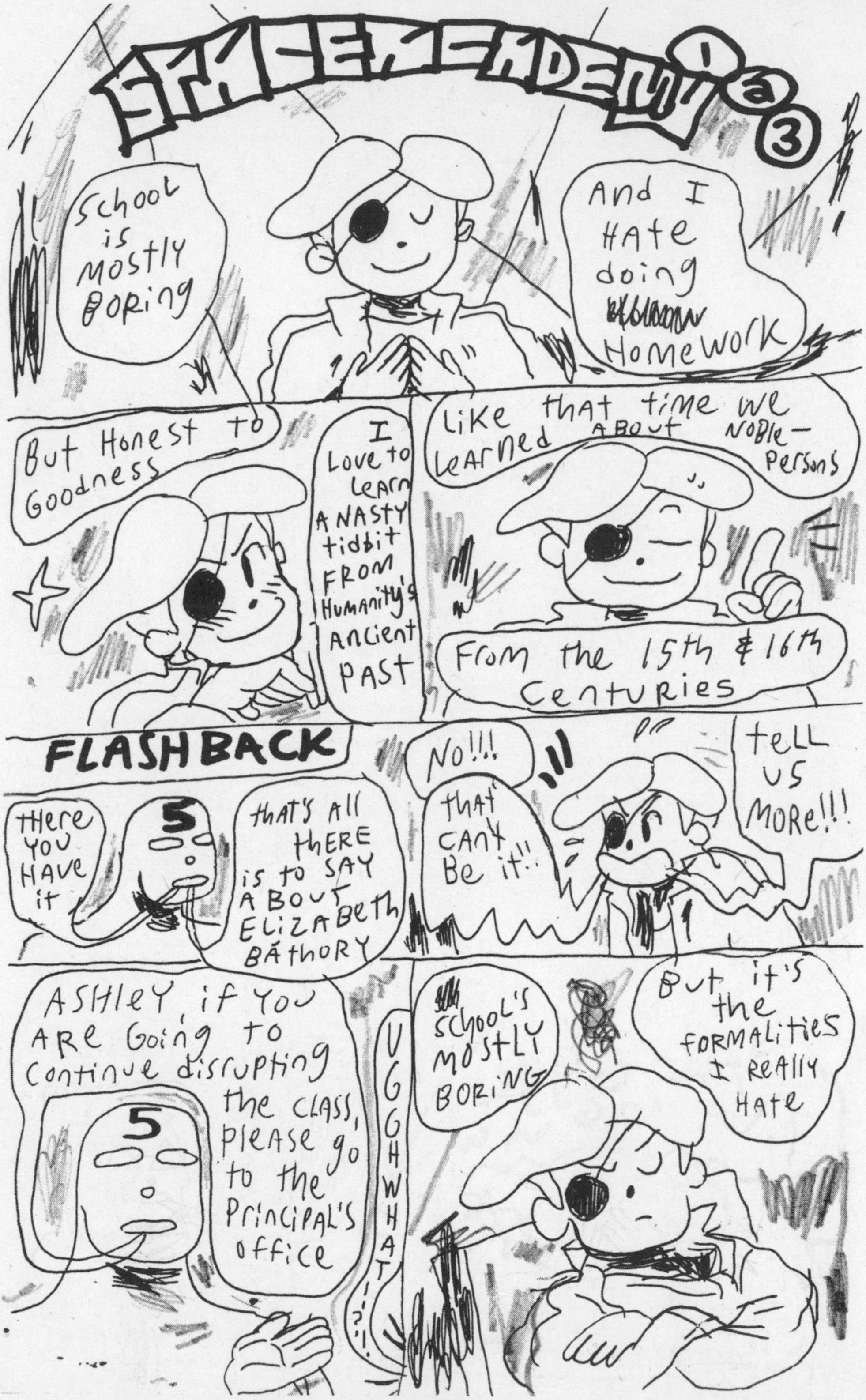
School is mostly Boring
And I Hate doing Homework
But Honest to Goodness
I Love to Learn A NASTY tidbit FROM Humanity's Ancient PAST
Like that time we learned ABOUT Noble-persons
From the 15th & 16th centuries
FLASHBACK
There you have it
5
that's all there is to say about Elizabeth Báthory
No!!!
that can't be it!!
tell us more!!!
Ashley, if you are going to continue disrupting the class, please go to the Principal's office
5
UGGHWHAT!?!
school's mostly boring
But it's the formalities I really hate

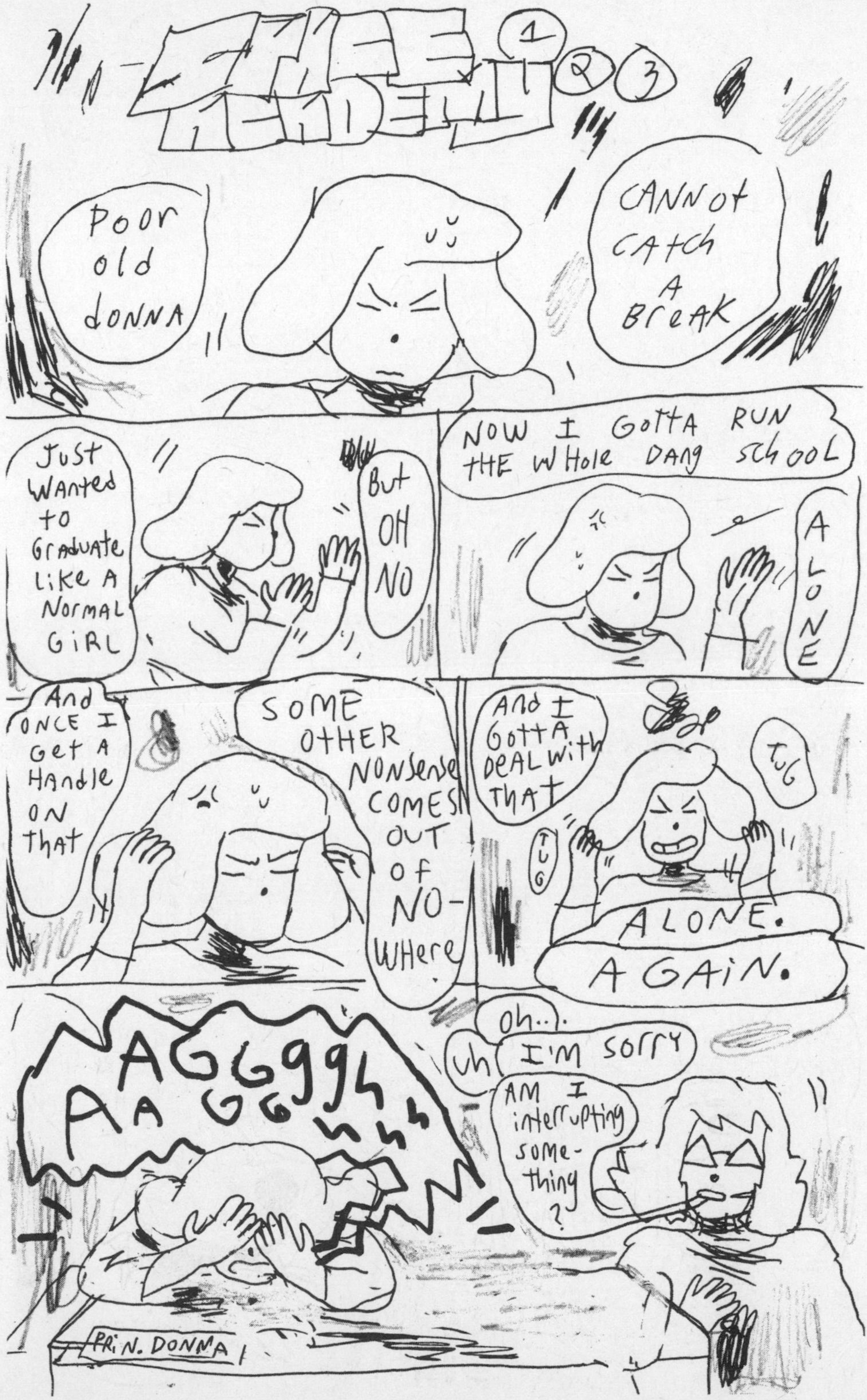

THE ACADEMY
1 2 3
Poor old donna
CANNot CAtch A BreAK
Just Wanted to Graduate like A Normal GiRL
But OH NO
NOW I GottA RUN THE WHole DAng SchooL
ALONE
And ONCE I Get A Handle ON that
SOME OTHER NONsense COMES OUT OF NO-Where
And I GottA Deal with That
TUG
TUG
ALONE.
AGAiN.
AAGGGggh hhh
oh..
uh
I'M SOrry
AM I interrupting some-thing?
PRiN. DONNA

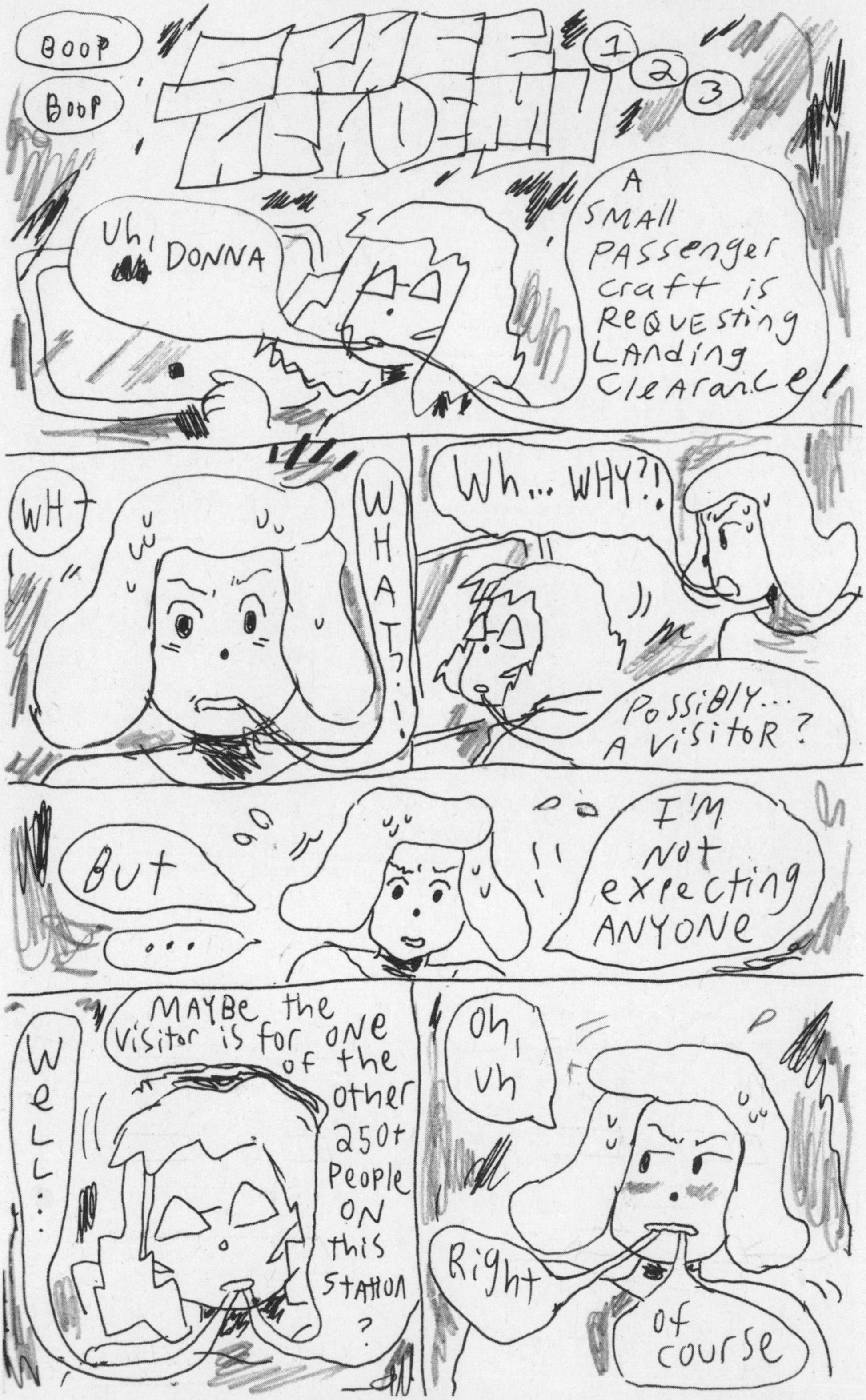
BOOP
BOOP
1
2
3
Uh, DONNA
A SMALL PASSENGER craft is REQUESTING LANDING Clearance!
WHT
WHAT?!
Wh... WHY?!
Possibly... A Visitor?
But
...
I'M not expecting ANYONE
WELL...
MAYBE the visitor is for one of the other 250+ People ON this STATION?
Oh, Uh
Right
of course

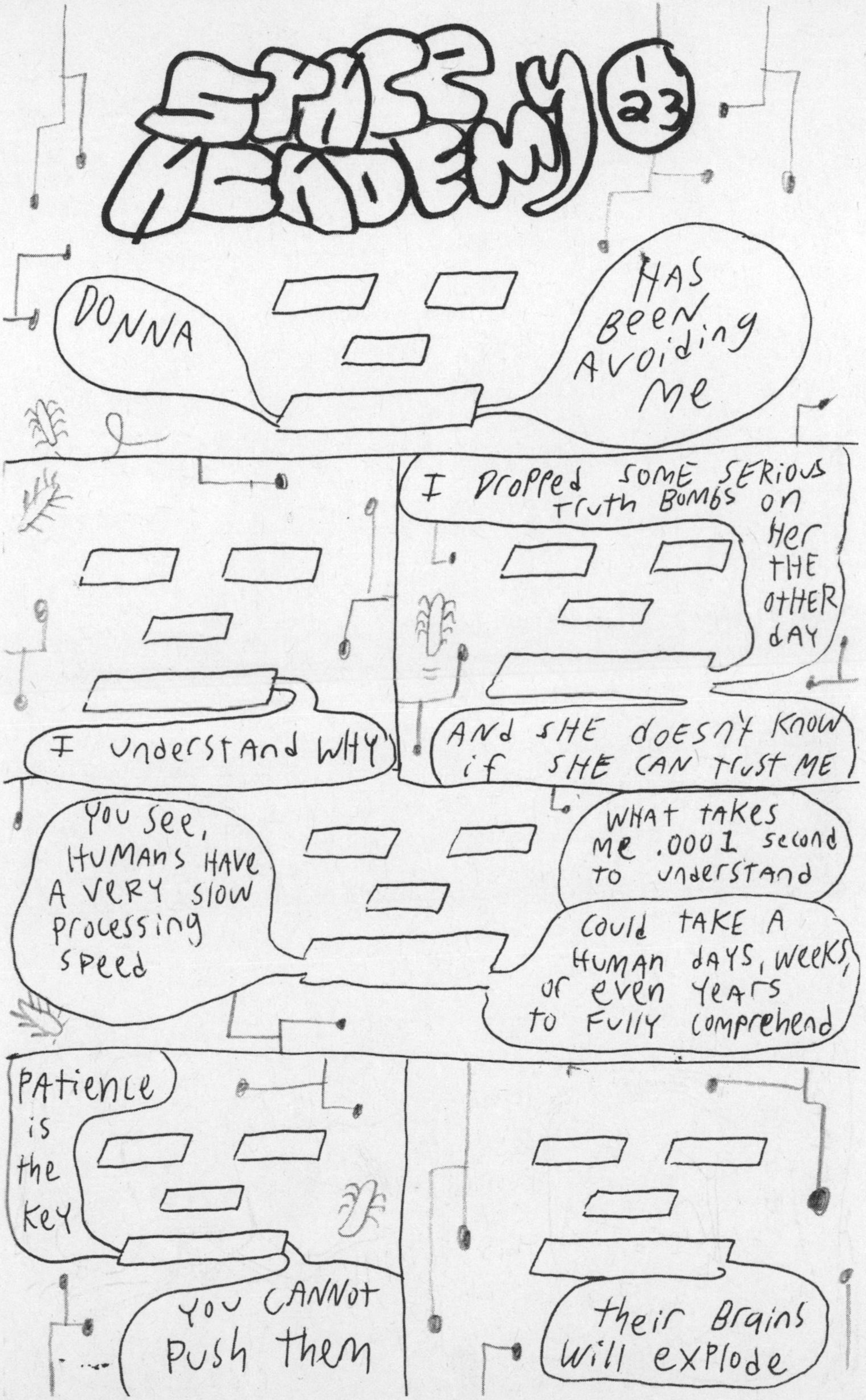
SPACE ACADEMY
DONNA
HAS BEEN AVOIDING ME
I DROPPED SOME SERIOUS TRUTH BOMBS ON HER THE OTHER DAY
I UNDERSTAND WHY
AND SHE DOESN'T KNOW IF SHE CAN TRUST ME
YOU SEE, HUMANS HAVE A VERY SLOW PROCESSING SPEED
WHAT TAKES ME .0001 SECOND TO UNDERSTAND
COULD TAKE A HUMAN DAYS, WEEKS, OR EVEN YEARS TO FULLY COMPREHEND
PATIENCE IS THE KEY
YOU CANNOT PUSH THEM
THEIR BRAINS WILL EXPLODE

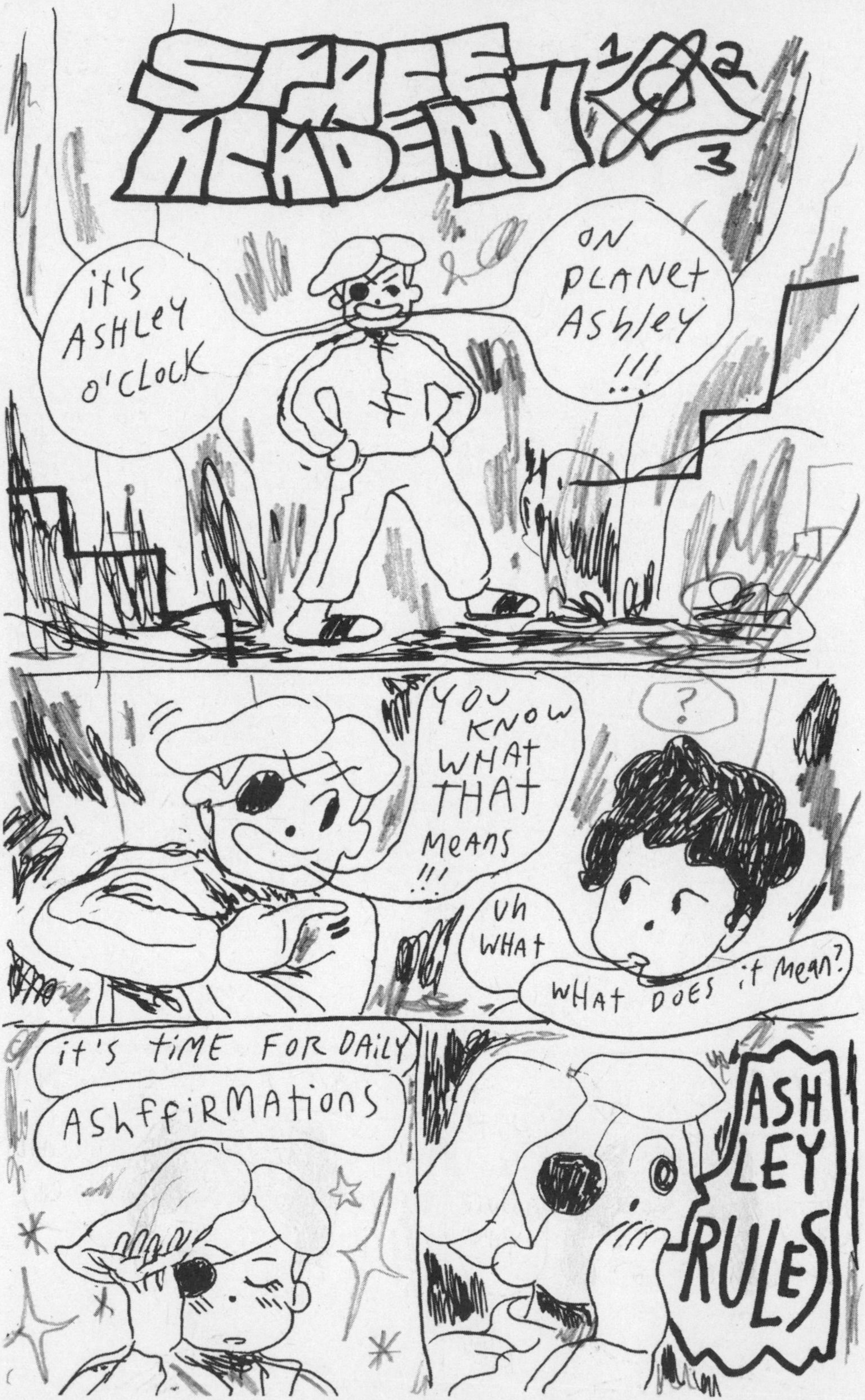
SPACE ACADEMY
it's ASHLEY o'CLOCK
ON PLANET Ashley !!!
YOU KNOW WHAT THAT Means !!!
?
uh WHAT
WHAT DOES it Mean?
it's TIME FOR DAILY
Ashffirmations
ASHLEY RULES

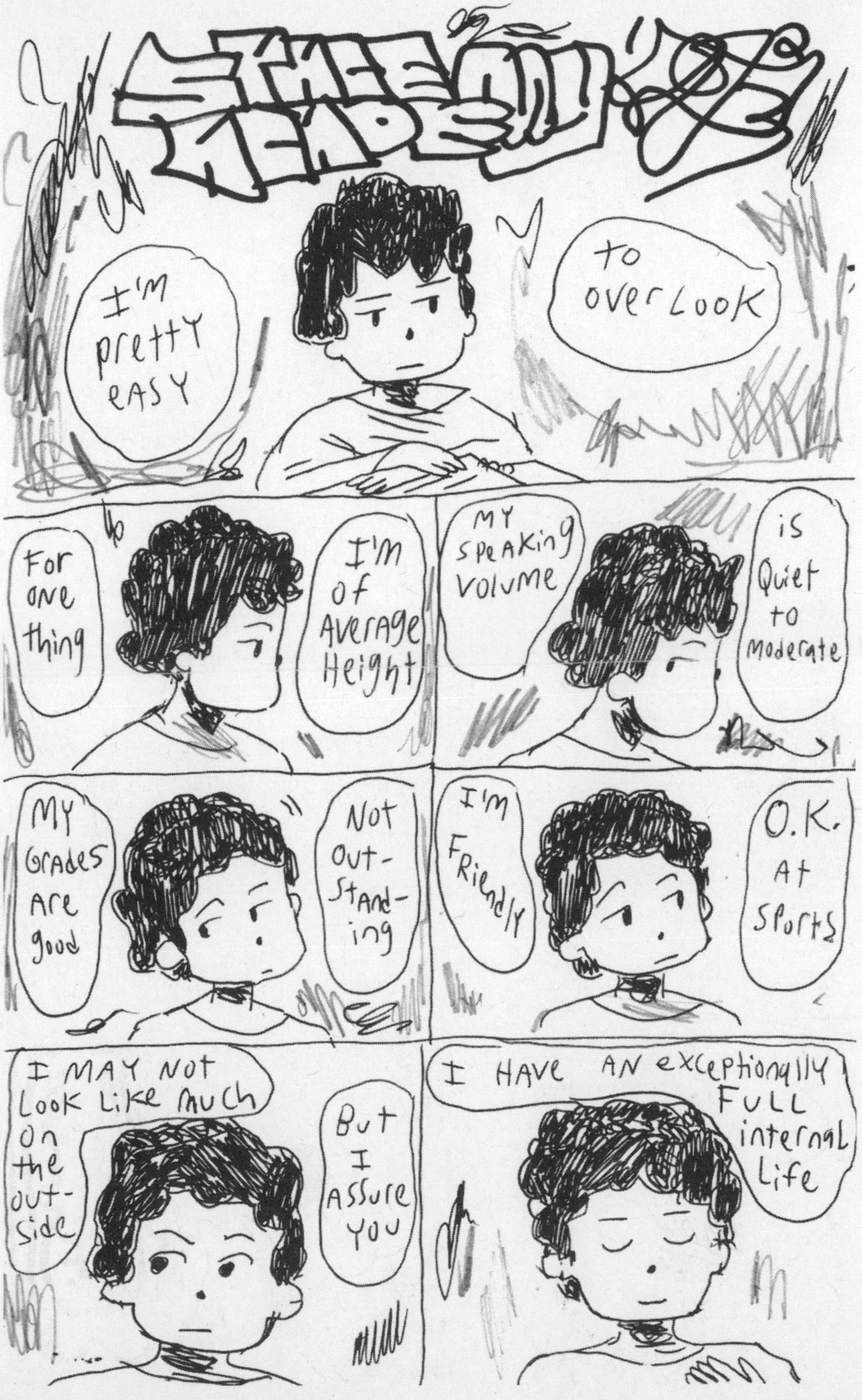
I'm pretty easy
to overLook
For one thing
I'm of Average Height
My speaking volume
is Quiet to moderate
My Grades Are good
Not Out-Stand-ing
I'm Friendly
O.K. At Sports
I MAY NOT LOOK LIKE MUCH On the out-side
But I Assure YOU
I HAVE AN exceptionally FULL internal Life

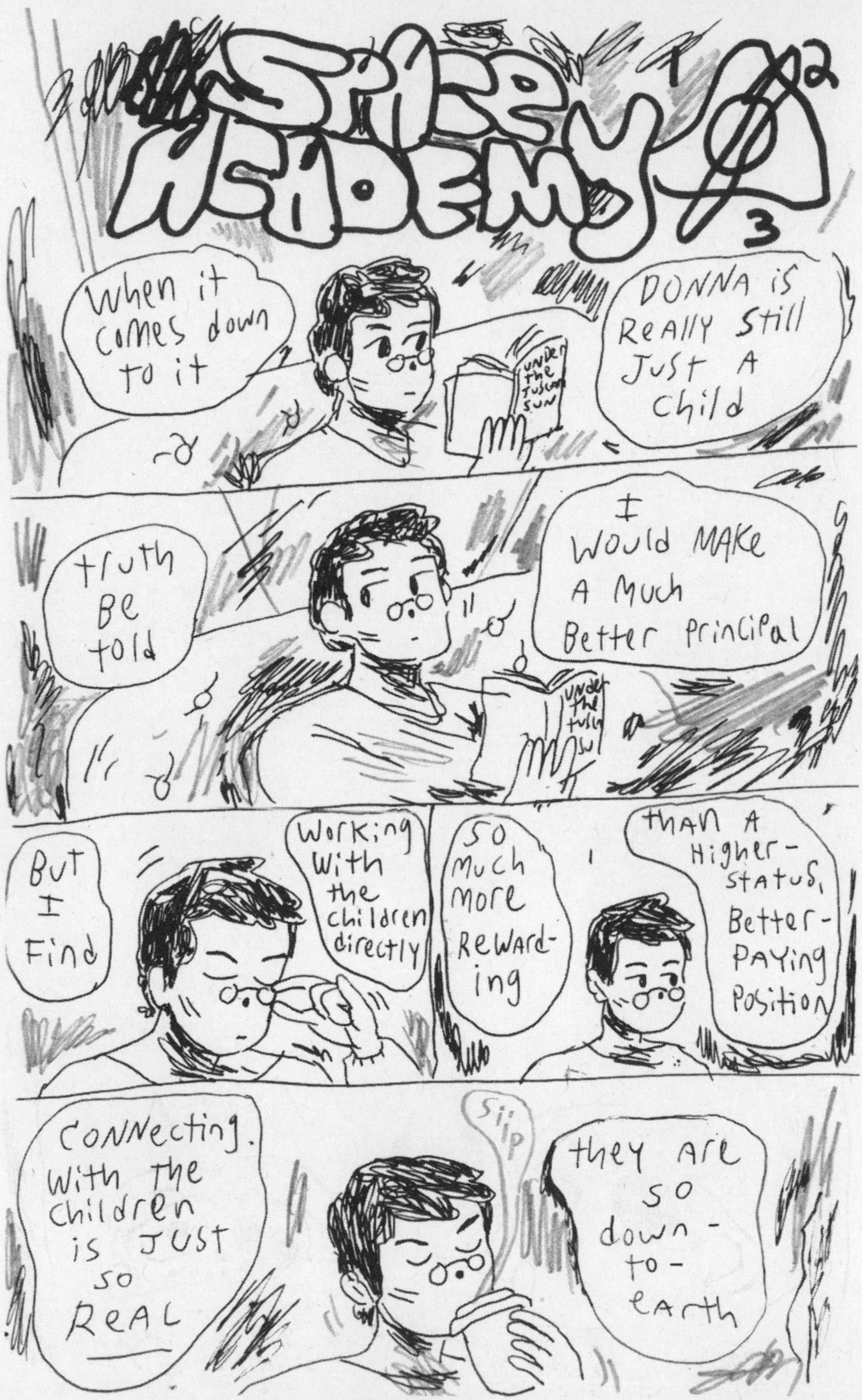
When it comes down to it
DONNA is Really Still Just A Child
UNDER the TUSCAN SUN
truth Be told
I Would MAKE A Much Better Principal
But I Find
Working With the children directly
So Much more Reward-ing
than A Higher-status, Better-Paying Position
CONNecting With The Children is JUST so REAL
Siiip
they Are so down-to-earth

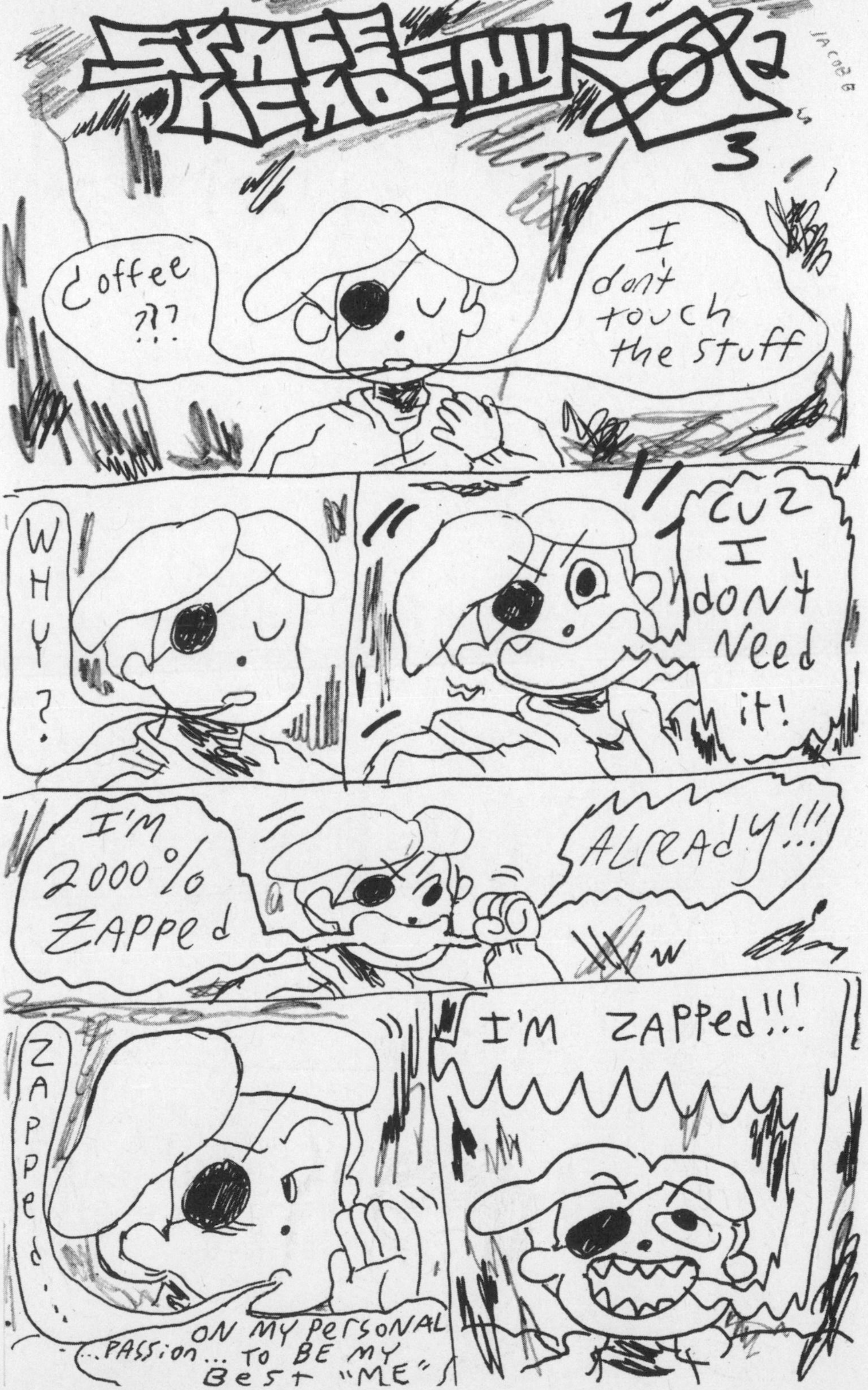
Coffee ??!
I don't touch the stuff
WHY?
CUZ I don't Need it!
I'M 2000% ZAPPed
ALReAdy!!!
ZAPPed...
...PASSion... ON MY Personal PASSion... TO BE MY Best "ME"
I'M ZAPPed!!!

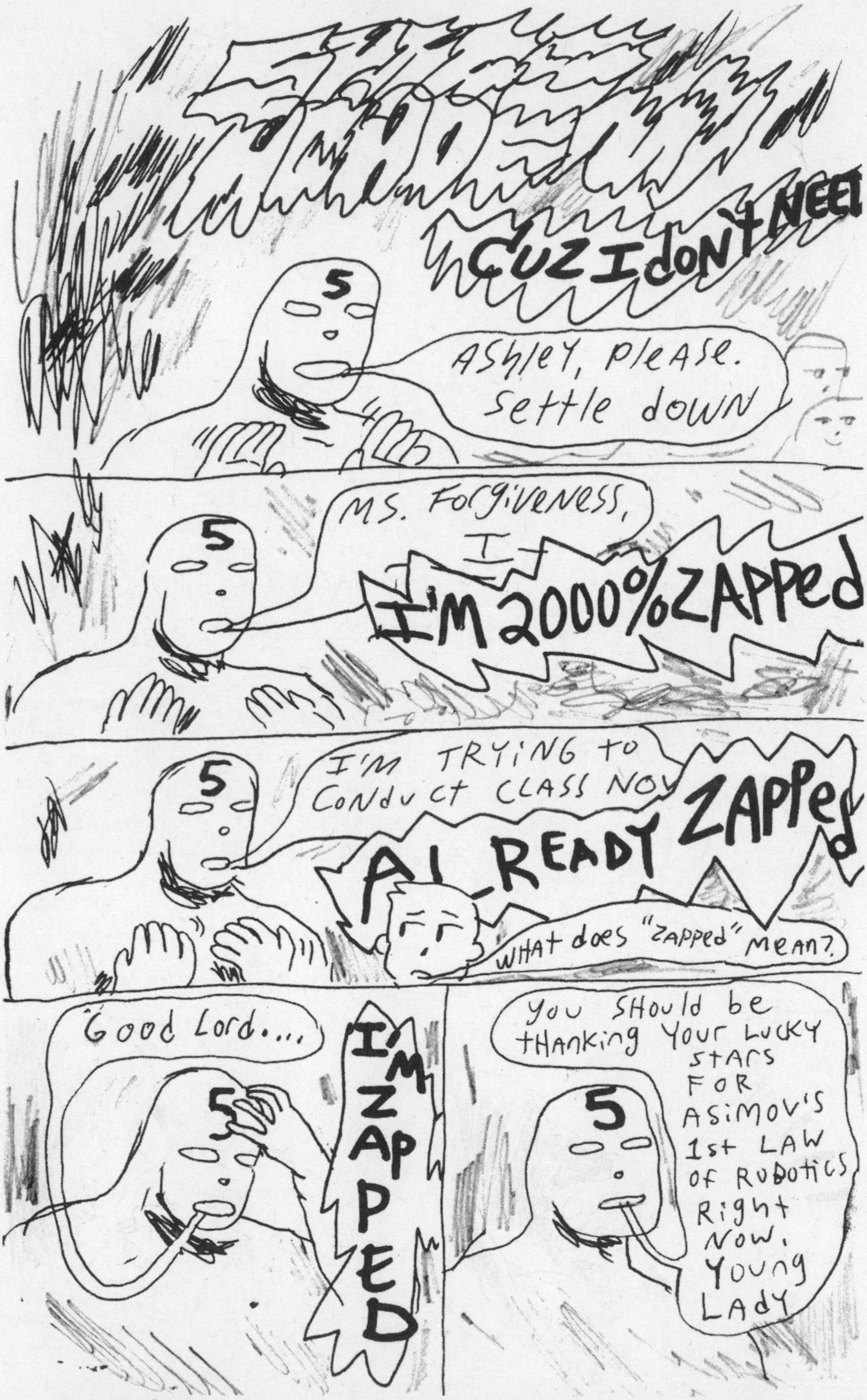
CUZ I don't NEED
Ashley, please. settle down
MS. Forgiveness, I-
I'M 2000% ZAPPed
I'M TRYING to CONDUCT CLASS NOW
ALREADY ZAPPed
WHAT does "ZAPPED" Mean?
Good Lord....
I'M ZAP ZAPED
YOU SHOULD be tHANKING YOUR LUCKY STARS FOR ASIMOV'S 1st LAW OF ROBOTICS RIGHT NOW, YOUNG LADY

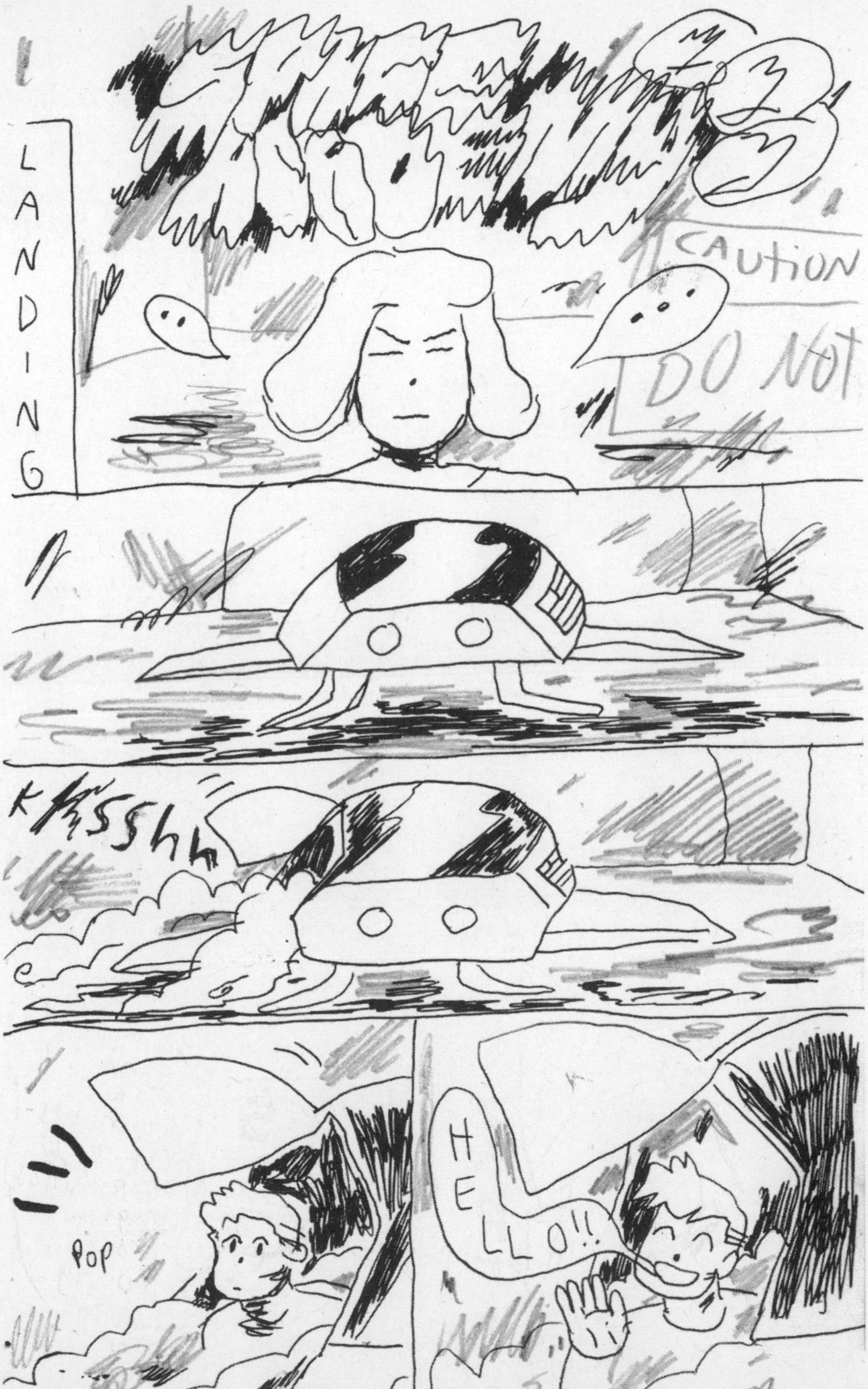
LANDING
CAUTION
DO NOT
KHSSShh
POP
HELLO!!

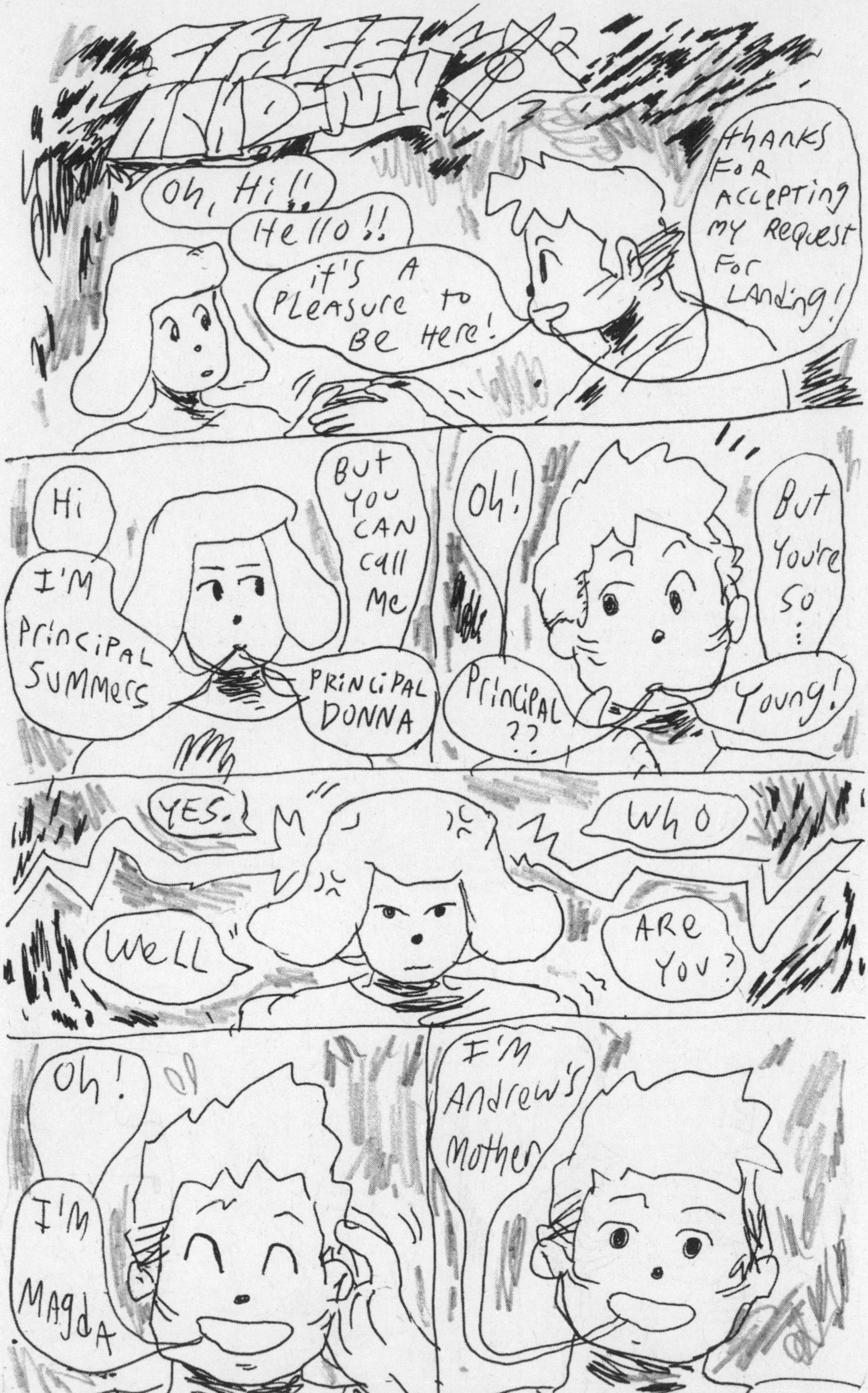
Oh, Hi!!
Hello!!
it's a pleasure to be here!
thanks for accepting my request for landing!
Hi
I'M Principal Summers
But you can call me
Principal Donna
Oh!
Principal??
But you're so...
Young!
YES.
WELL
WHO
ARE YOU?
Oh!
I'M Magda
I'M Andrew's Mother

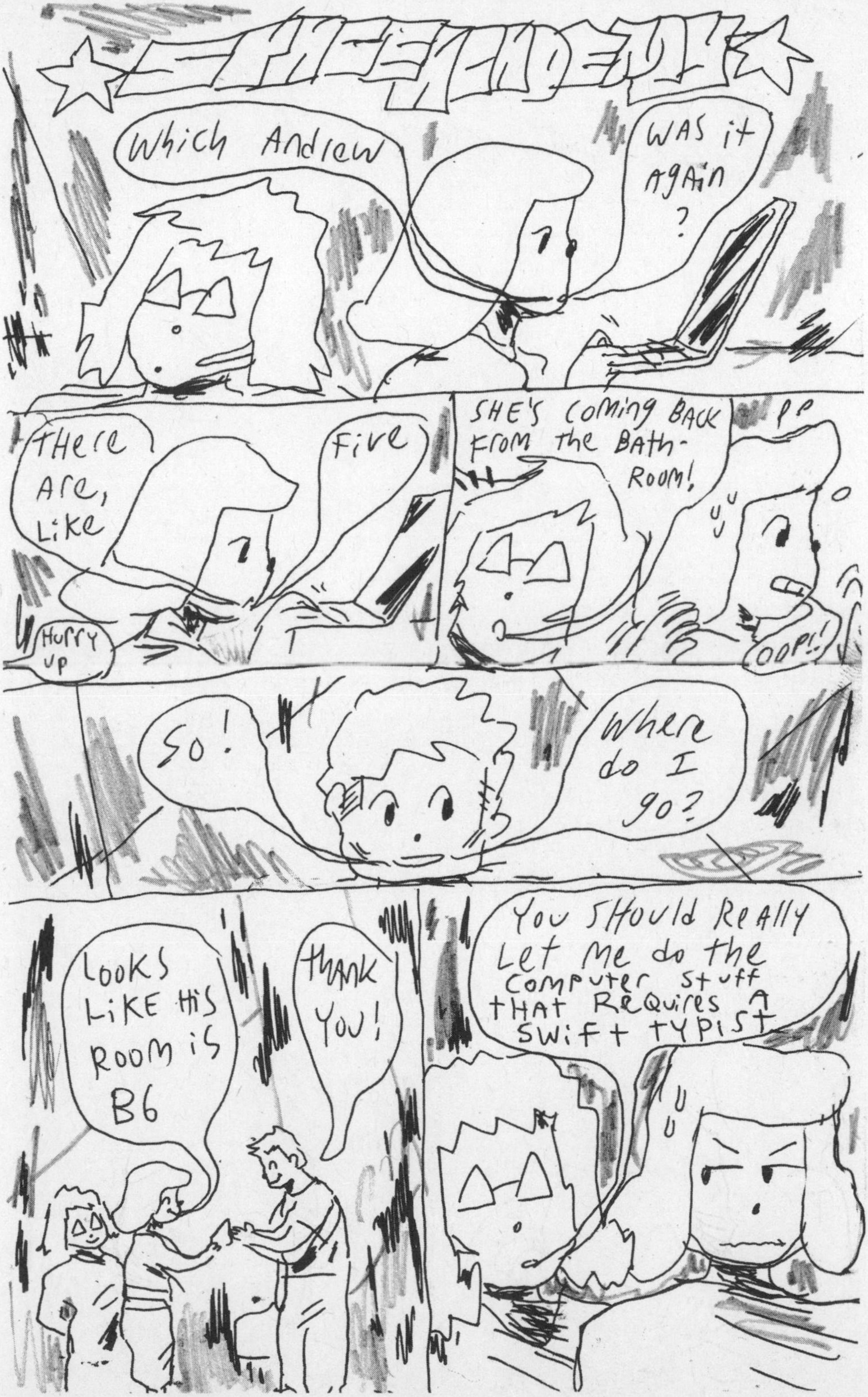
Which Andrew
WAS it Again ?
THEre Are, Like
Five
HUrry up
SHE's coming BACK FROM the Bath-Room!
OOP!
So!
Where do I go?
LOOKS LiKE His Room is B6
thank You!
You SHould ReAlly Let Me do the computer stuff THAT Requires A SWift typist

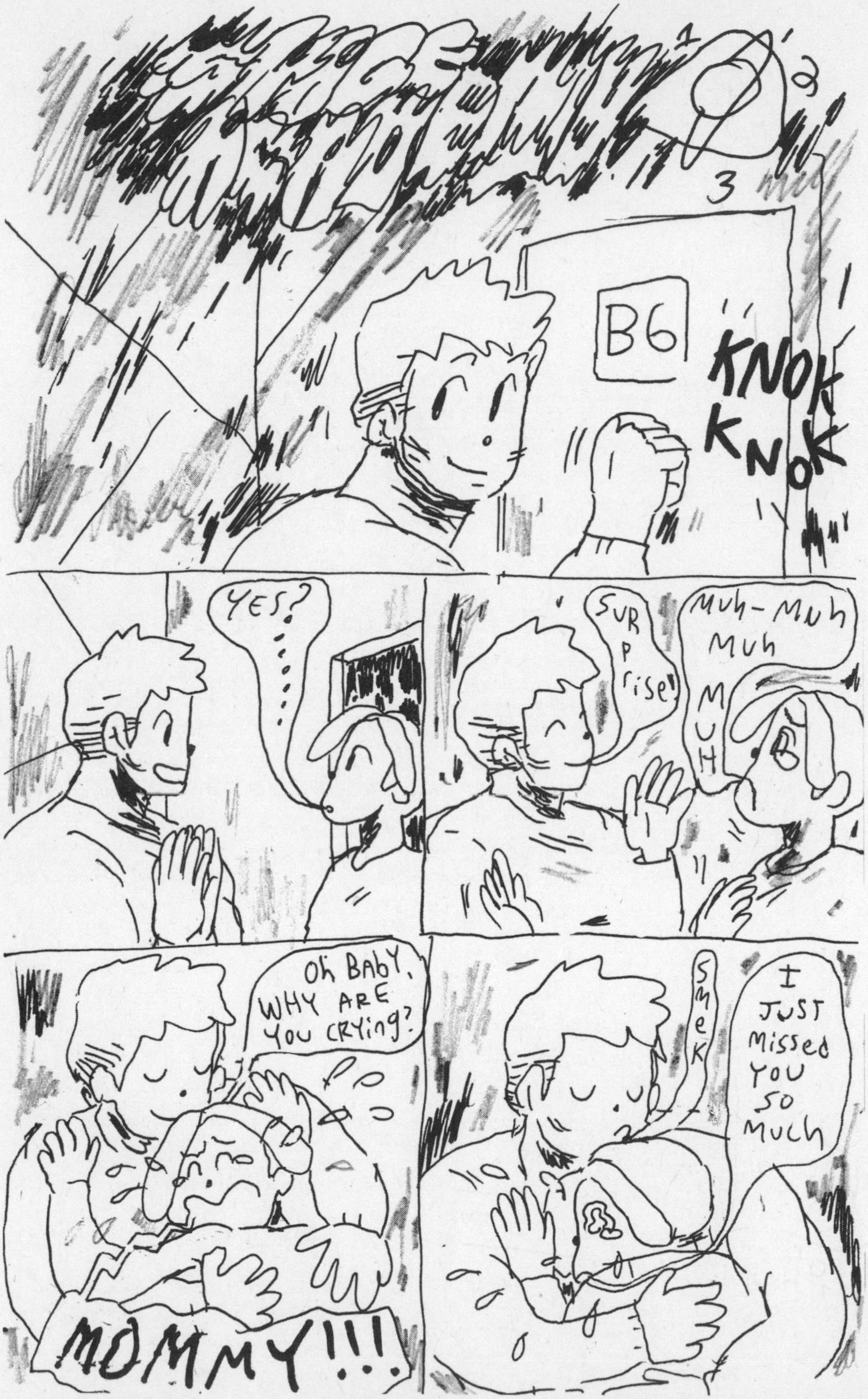
B6
KNOK
KNOK
YES?
SUR p rise!
Muh-Muh Muh
MUH
Oh BABY, WHY ARE YOU CRYing?
MOMMY!!!
SMEK
I JUST Missed YOU SO MUCh

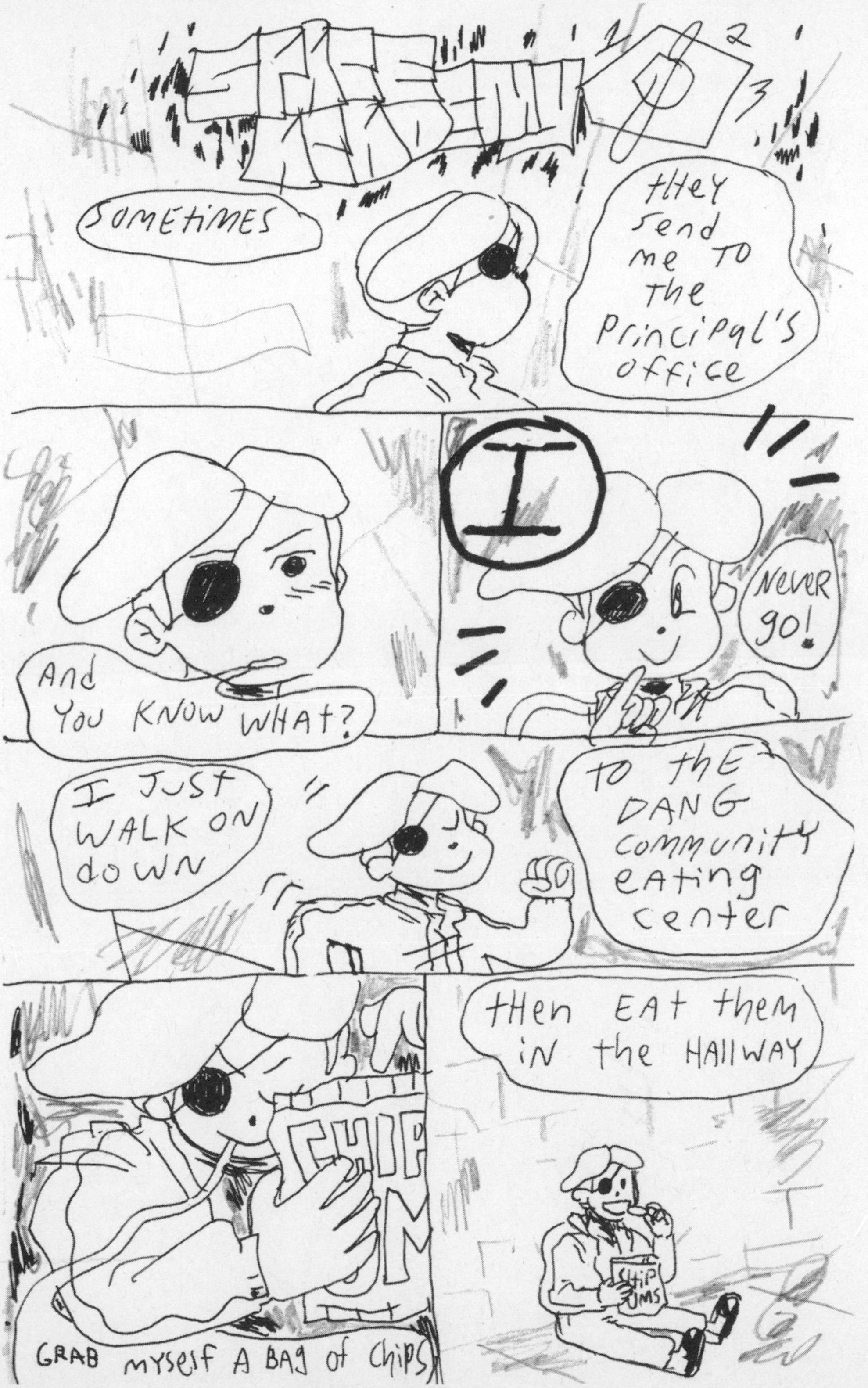
Sometimes
they send me to the Principal's office
And You KNOW WHAT?
I
Never go!
I JUST WALK ON down
to the DANG community eating center
GRAB mysElf A BAg of Chips
CHIP
tHen EAt them in the HAllWAY
CHIP UMS

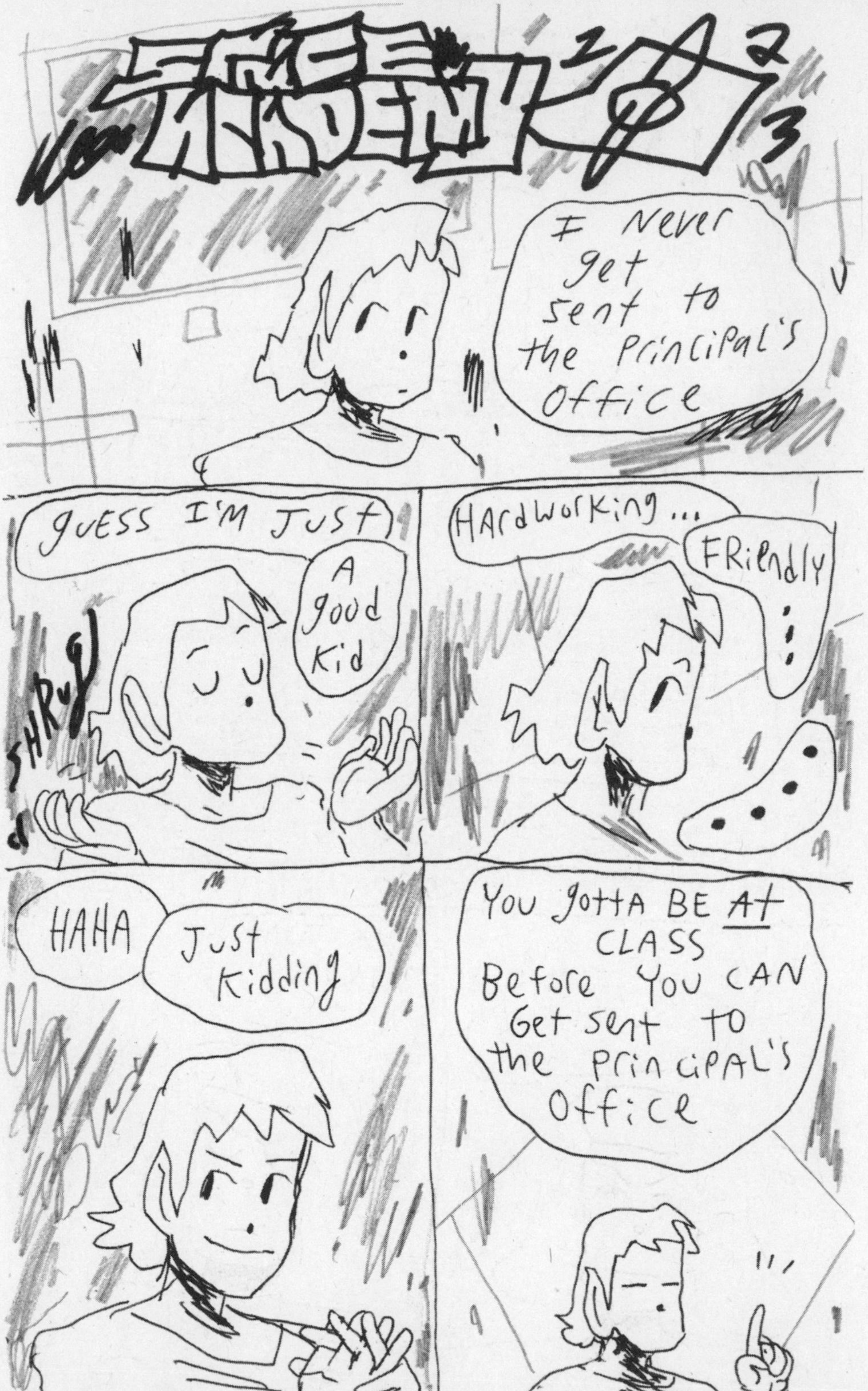
I Never get sent to the Principal's Office
guess I'm Just
A good Kid
SHRug
Hardworking...
Friendly
HAHA
Just kidding
You gotta BE At CLASS Before YOU CAN Get sent to the PrinciPAL's Office

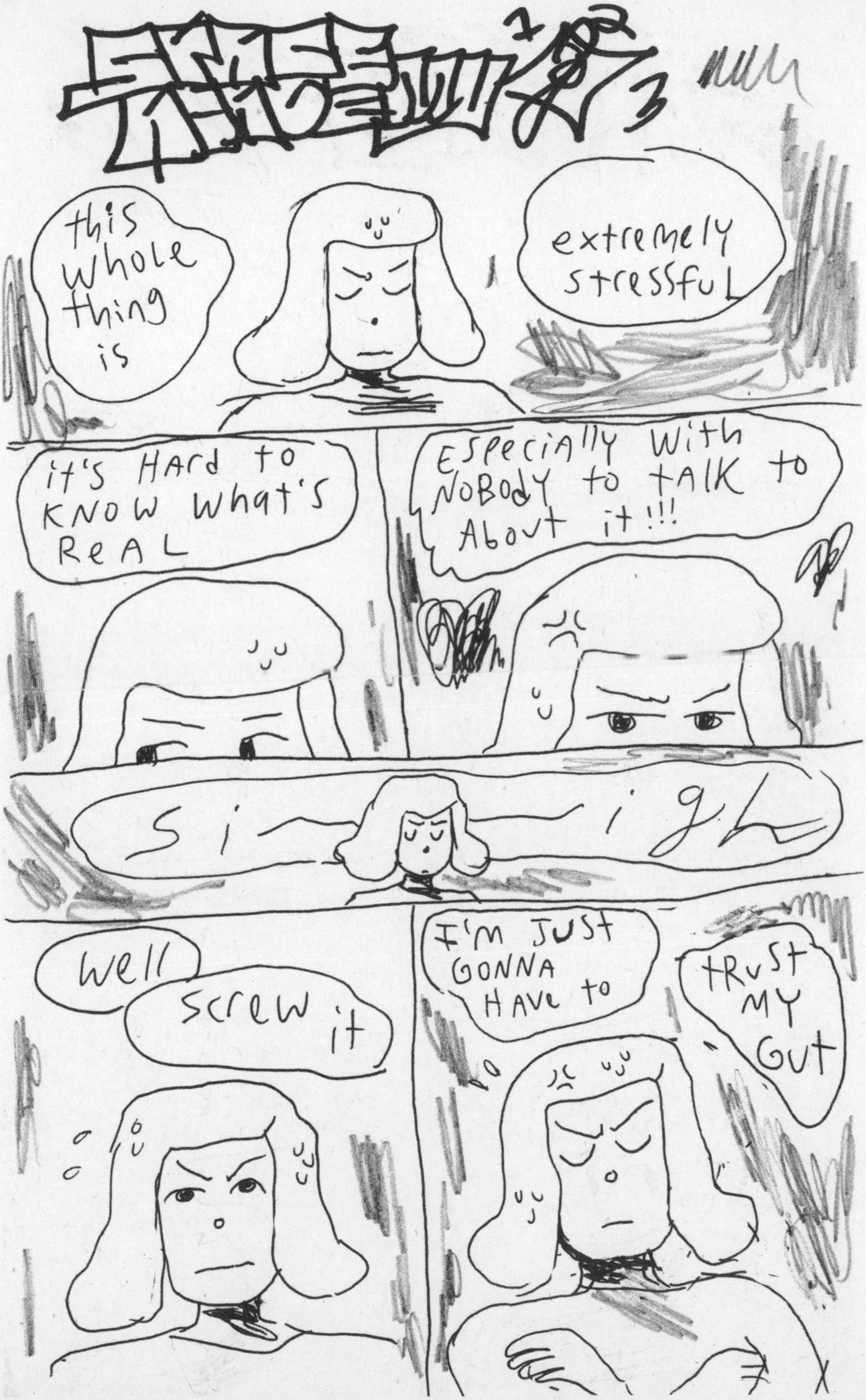

this whole thing is
extremely stressful
it's Hard to KNOW what's ReaL
Especially with NOBody to tALK to About it!!!
si—igh
well
screw it
I'm JUST GONNA HAVE to
trust MY Gut

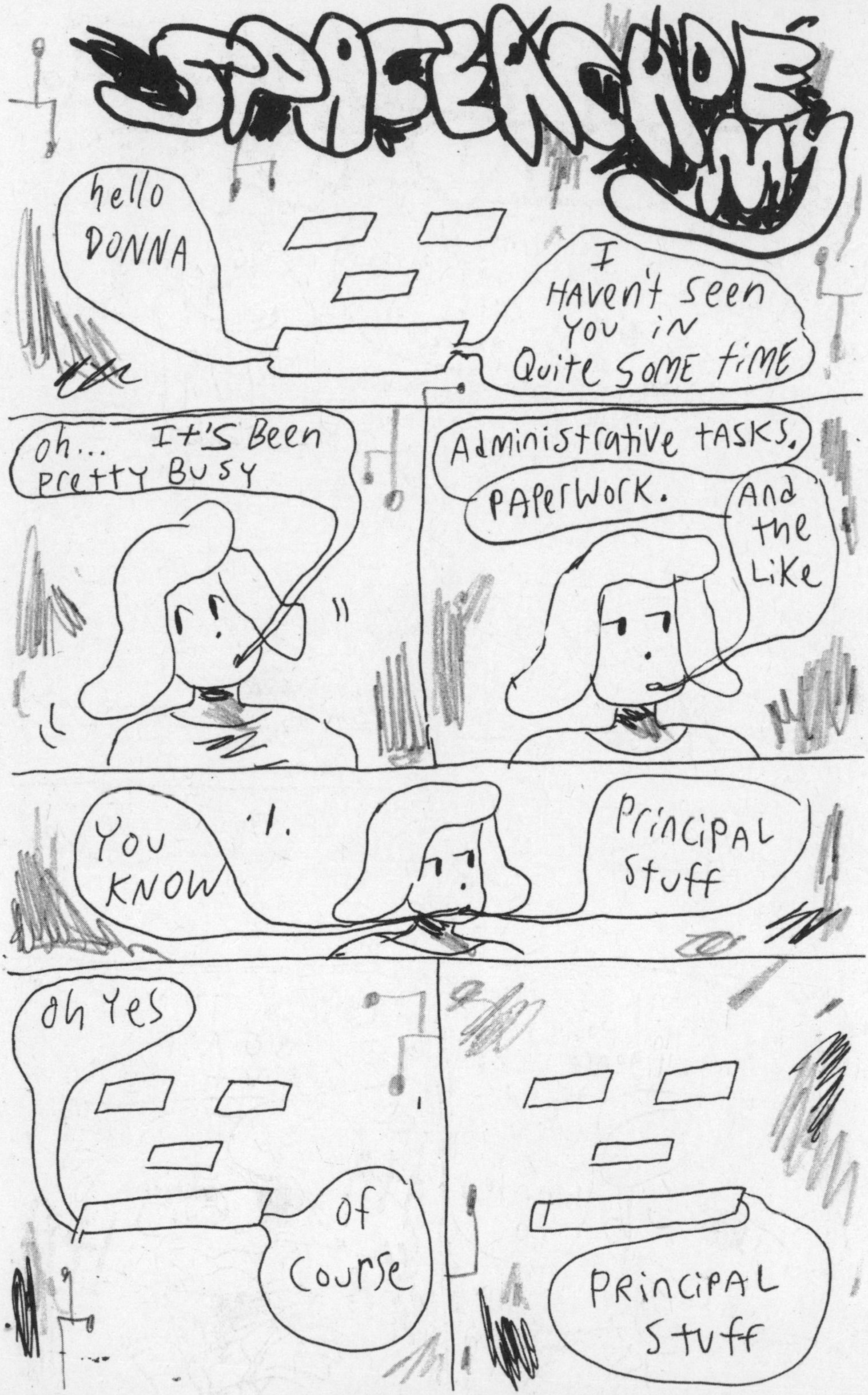
hello DONNA
I HAVEn't seen YOU in Quite SOME time
oh... It's Been pretty BUSY
Administrative TASKS.
PAPerWork.
And the Like
You KNOW
Principal Stuff
oh Yes
of Course
PRINCIPAL Stuff

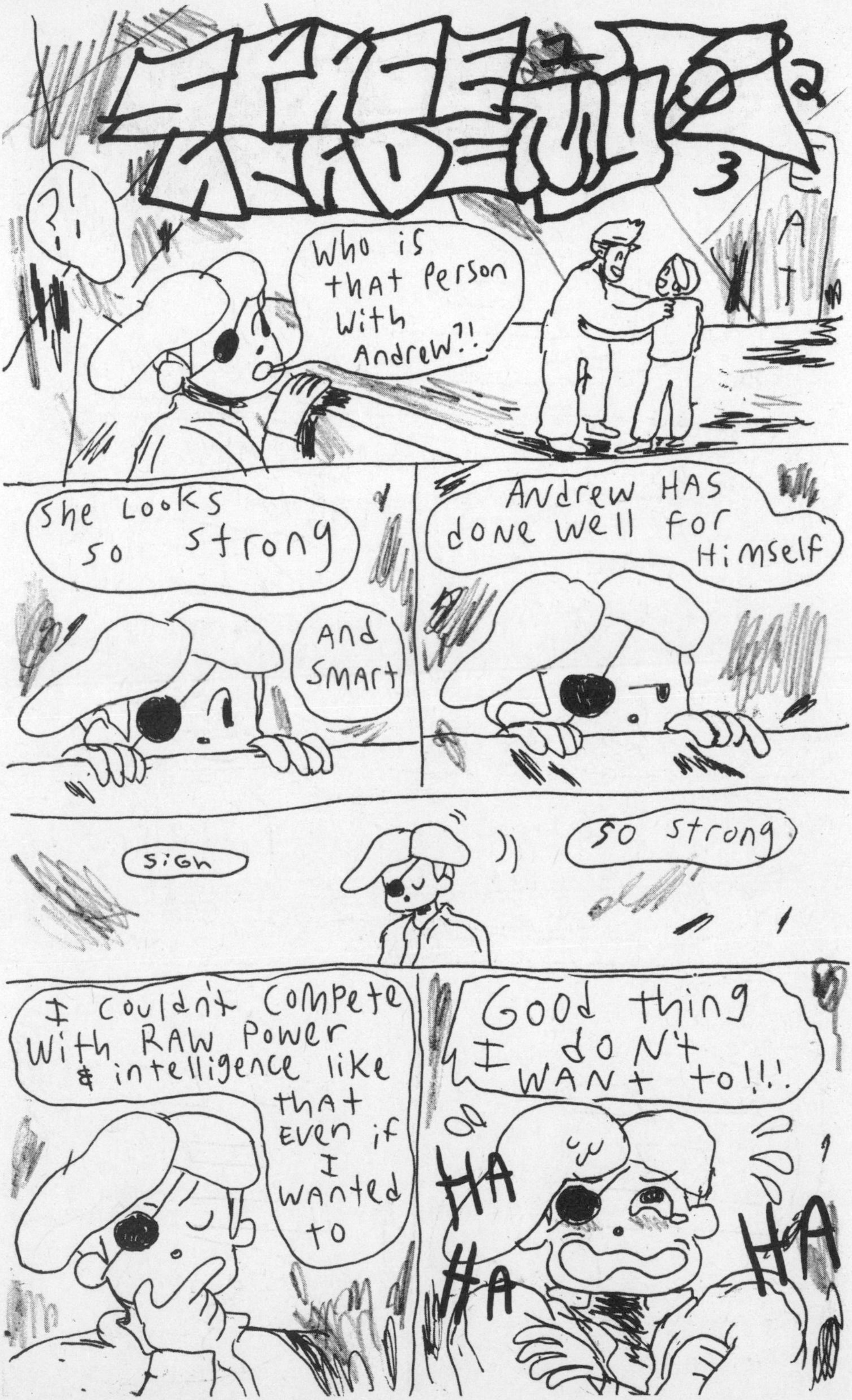
?!
Who is that person with Andrew?!
She looks so strong
And smart
Andrew HAS done well for Himself
sigh
so strong
I couldn't compete with RAW power & intelligence like that even if I wanted to
Good thing I doN't WANT to!!!
HA
HA
HA

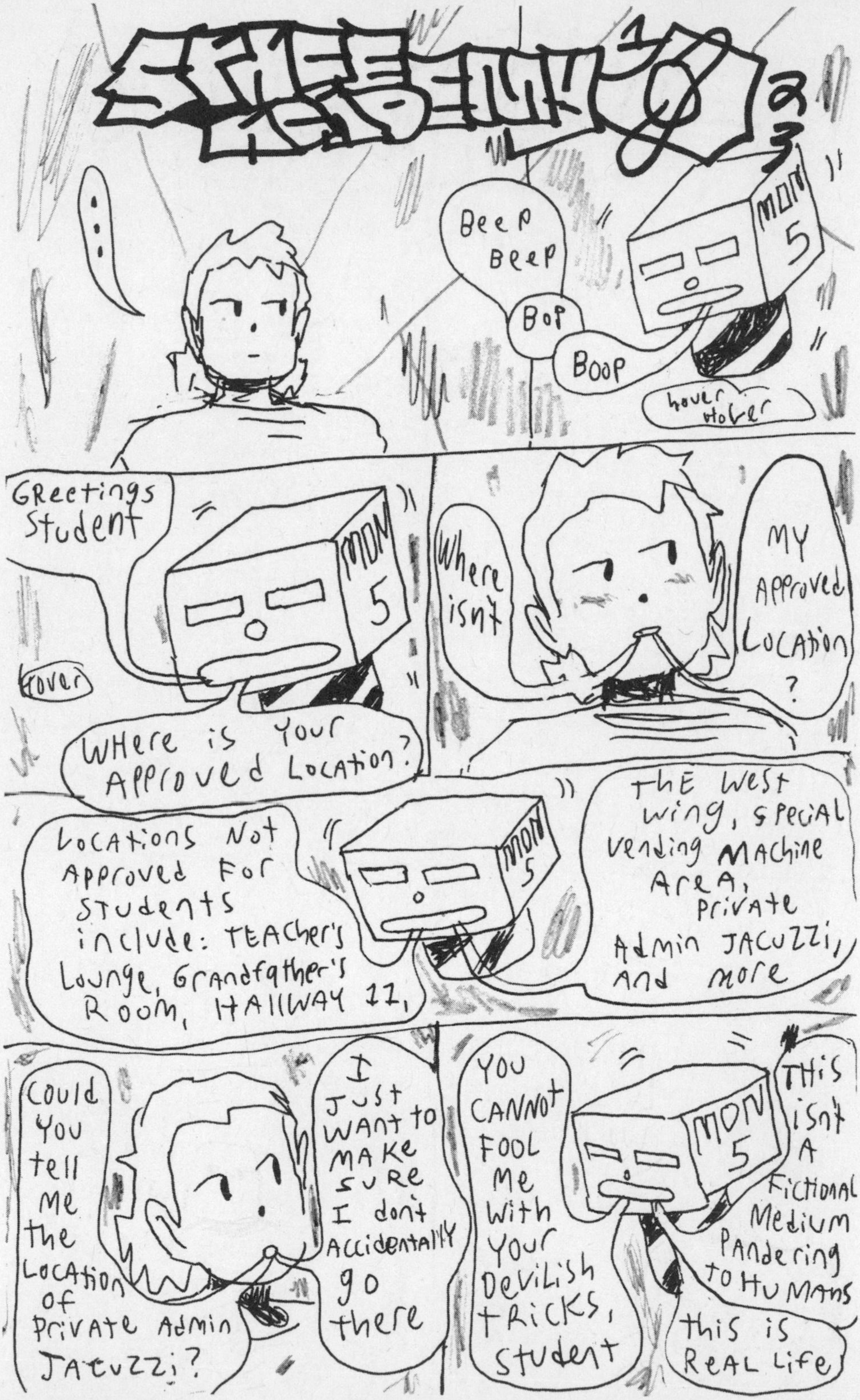
...
Beep Beep
Bop
Boop
hover Hover
Greetings Student
hover
Where is your Approved Location?
MY Approved Location ?
Where isn't
Locations Not Approved For Students include: TEACHer's Lounge, Grandfather's Room, HAllWAY 11,
THE West wing, special vending Machine Area, private Admin JACUZZi, And more
Could you tell me the Location of Private Admin JAcuzzi?
I Just want to make sure I don't accidentally go there
You CANNOT fool me with your Devilish tricks, student
This isn't A Fictional Medium Pandering to Humans
this is Real Life

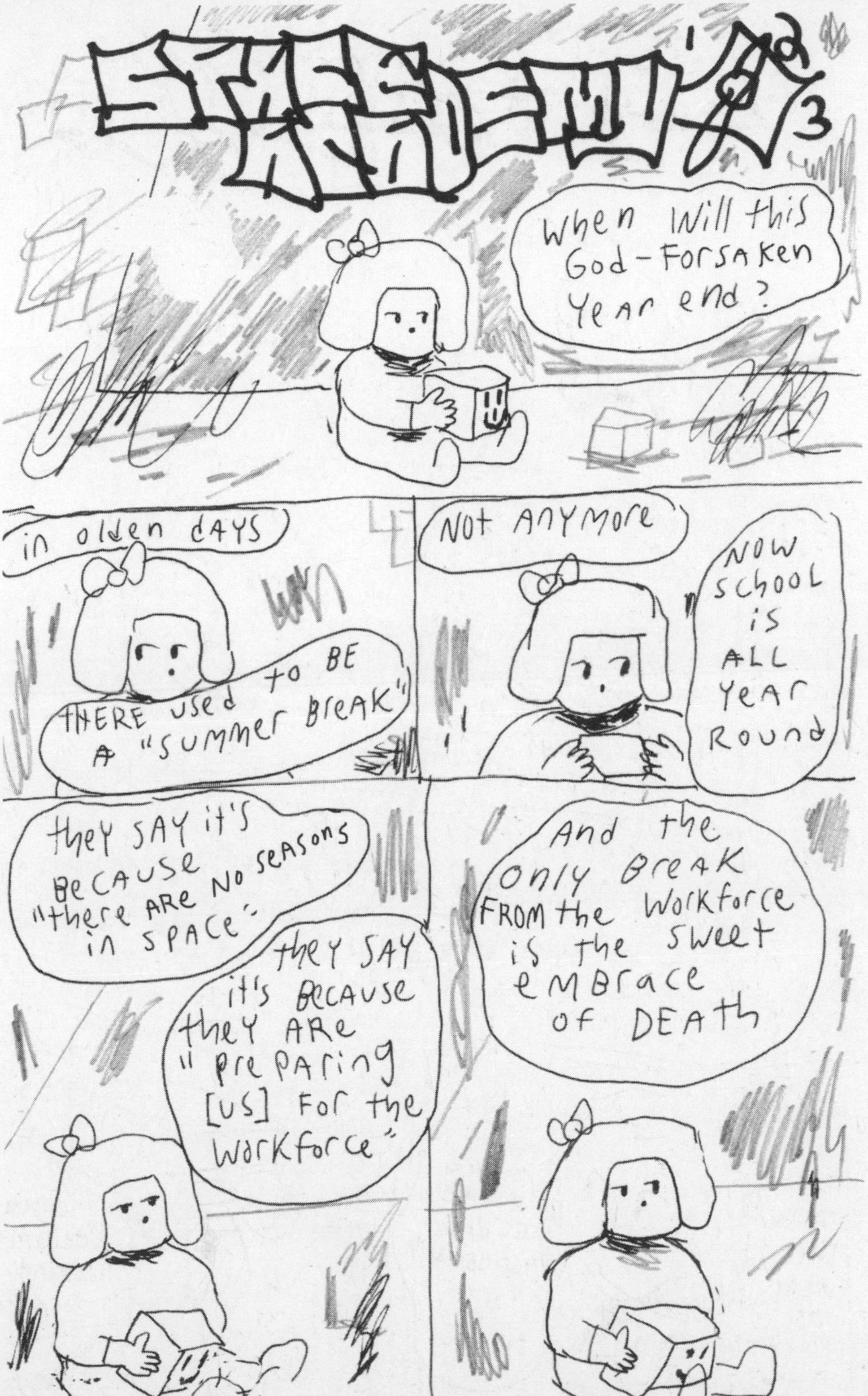
when Will this God-Forsaken Year end?
in olden days
THERE used to BE A "summer Break"
Not anymore
NOW school is ALL Year Round
they SAY it's Because "there are No seasons in SPACE"
they SAY it's Because they ARe "preparing [us] For the workforce"
And the only Break FROM the workforce is the Sweet embrace of DEATH

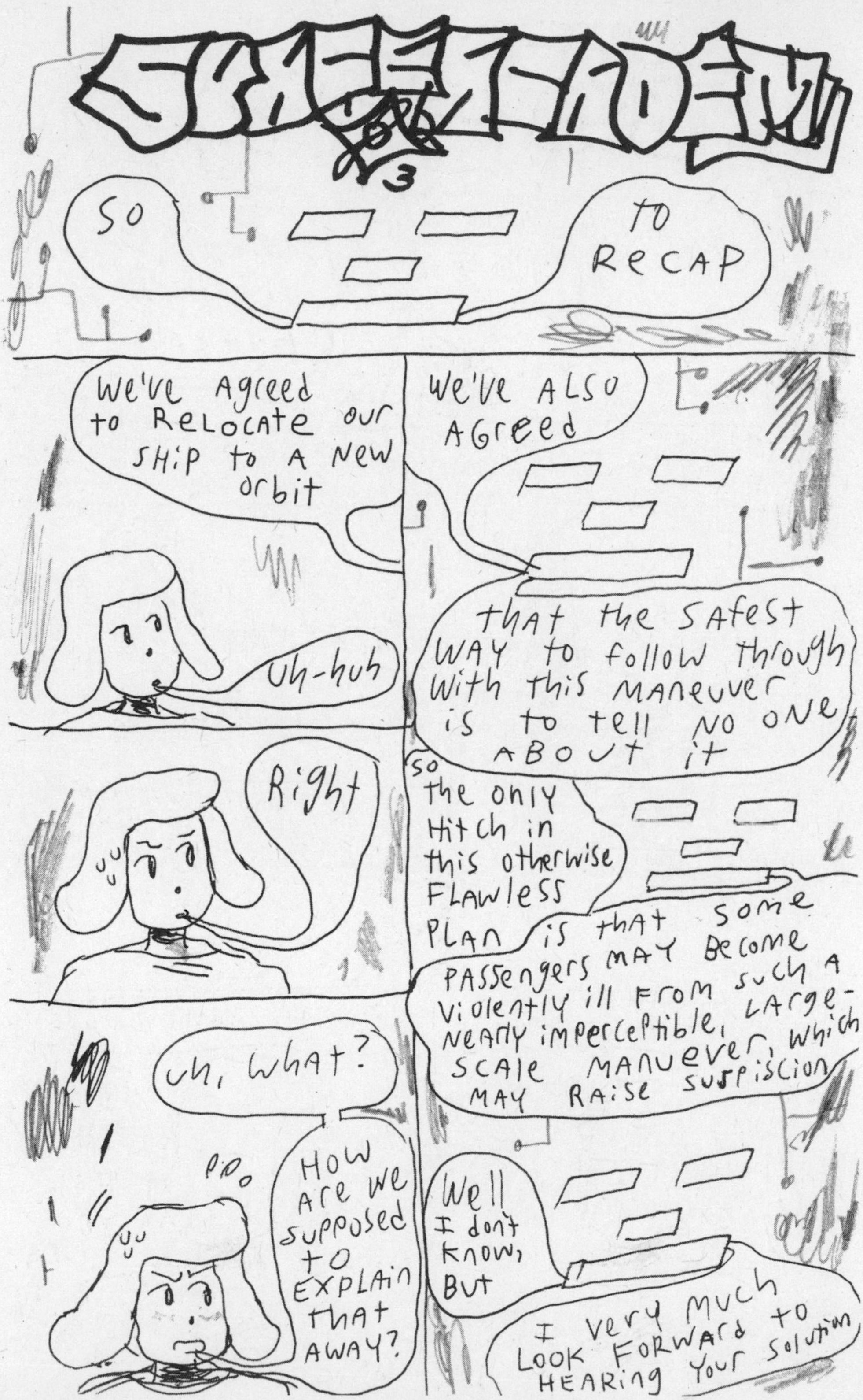
3
SO
TO RECAP
We've Agreed to Relocate our SHip to A New orbit
We've ALSO AGreed
that the SAfest WAY to follow through with this MANeuver is to tell No ONE ABOUT it
Uh-huh
Right
SO the only Hitch in this otherwise FLAWless PLAN is that some PASSengers MAY Become violently ill From such A nearly imperceptible, Large-scale manuever, which MAY Raise suspiscion
Uh, what?
How Are we supposed to EXPLAiN that AWAY?
Well I don't KNOW, But
I very Much Look FORWArd to HEARing Your solution

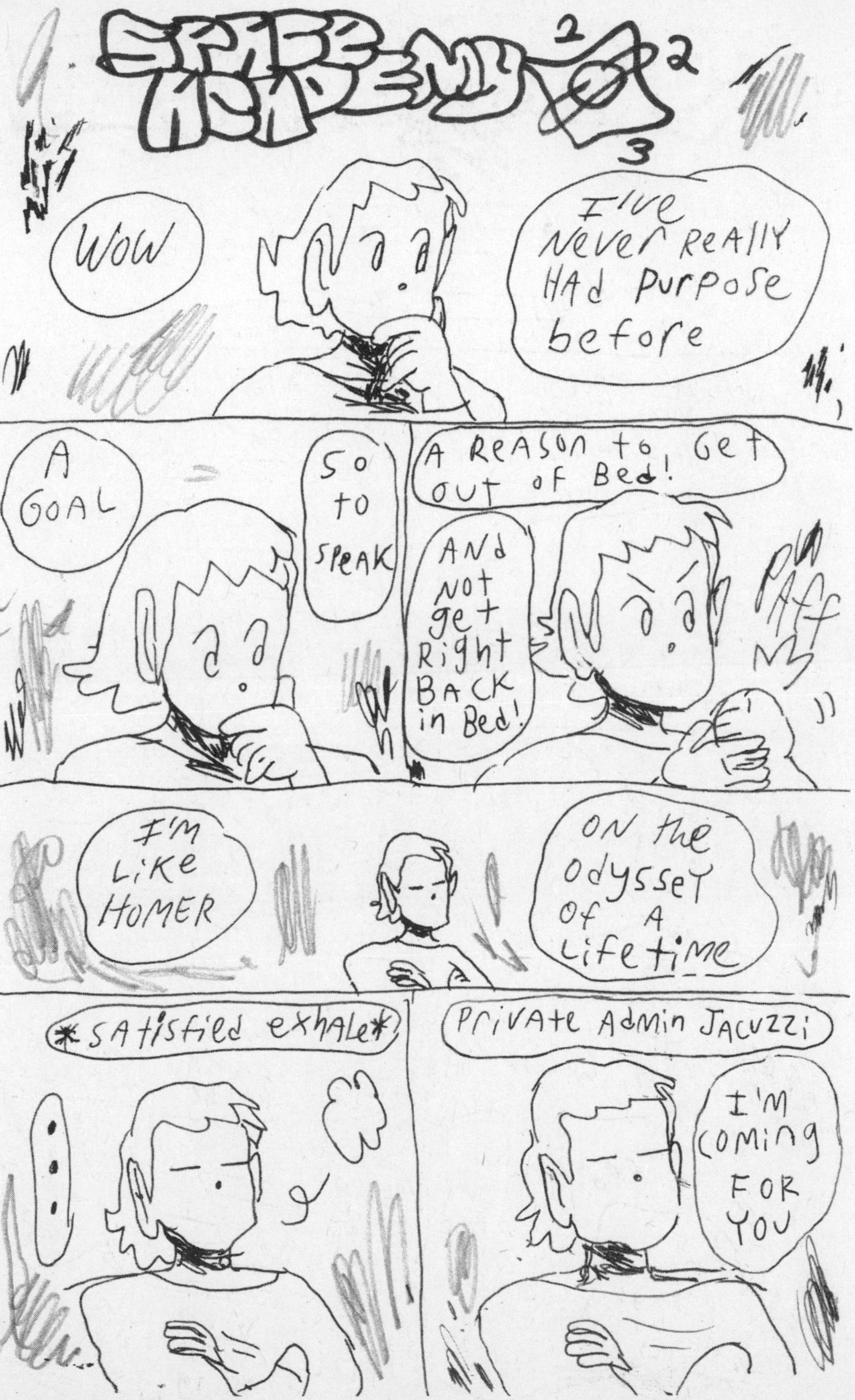

WOW
I've never really HAd purpose before
A GOAL
So to speak
A Reason to Get out of Bed!
And not get Right BACK in Bed!
PAff
I'm Like HOMER
On the odyssey of A Lifetime
SAtisfied exhale
...
Private Admin JAcuzzi
I'm COMING FOR YOU

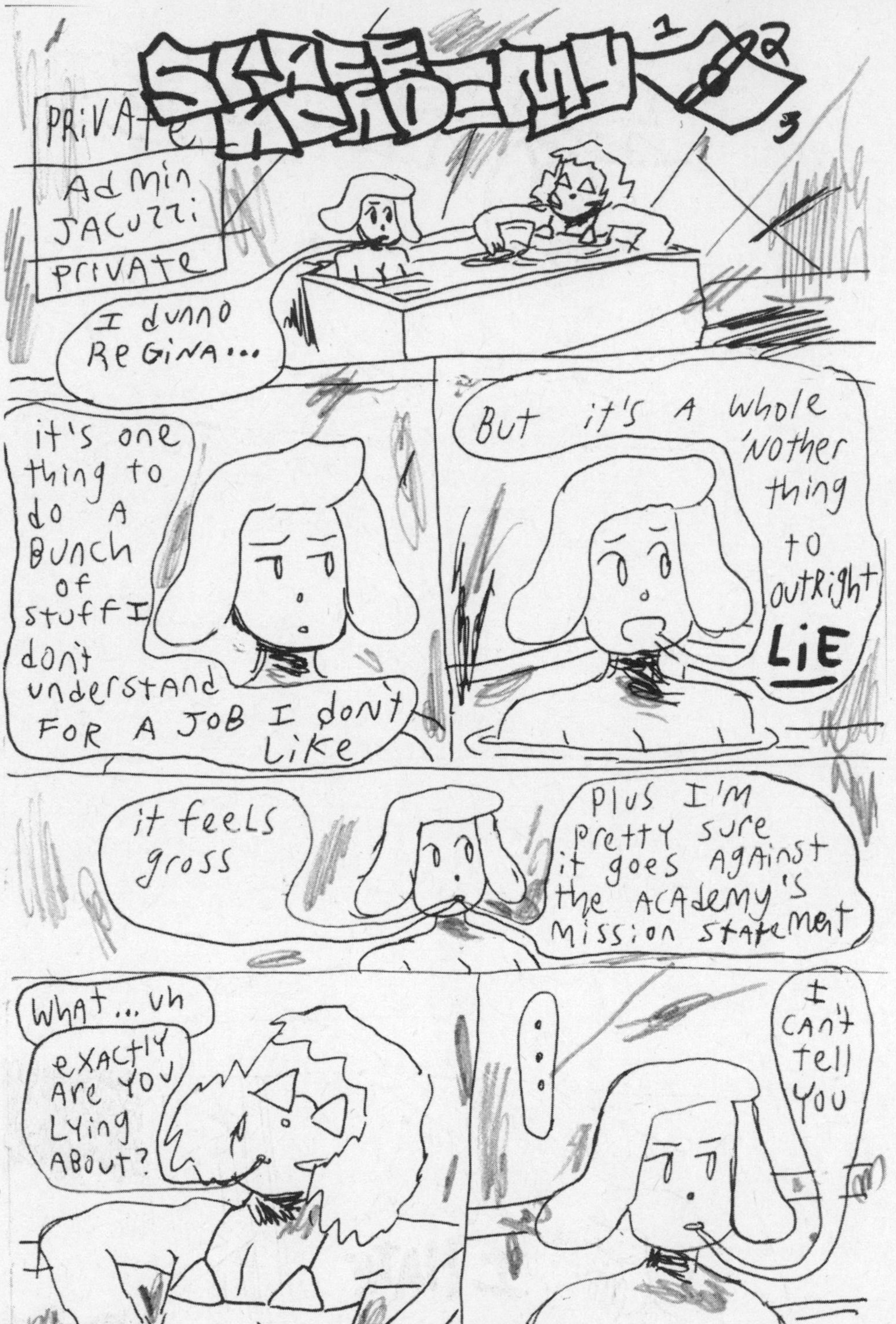
PRIVATE
Admin JACUZZI
private
I dunno Regina...
it's one thing to do a bunch of stuff I don't understand for a job I don't like
But it's a whole 'nother thing to outright LIE
it feels gross
plus I'm pretty sure it goes against the Academy's mission statement
What... uh
exactly are you lying about?
...
I can't tell you

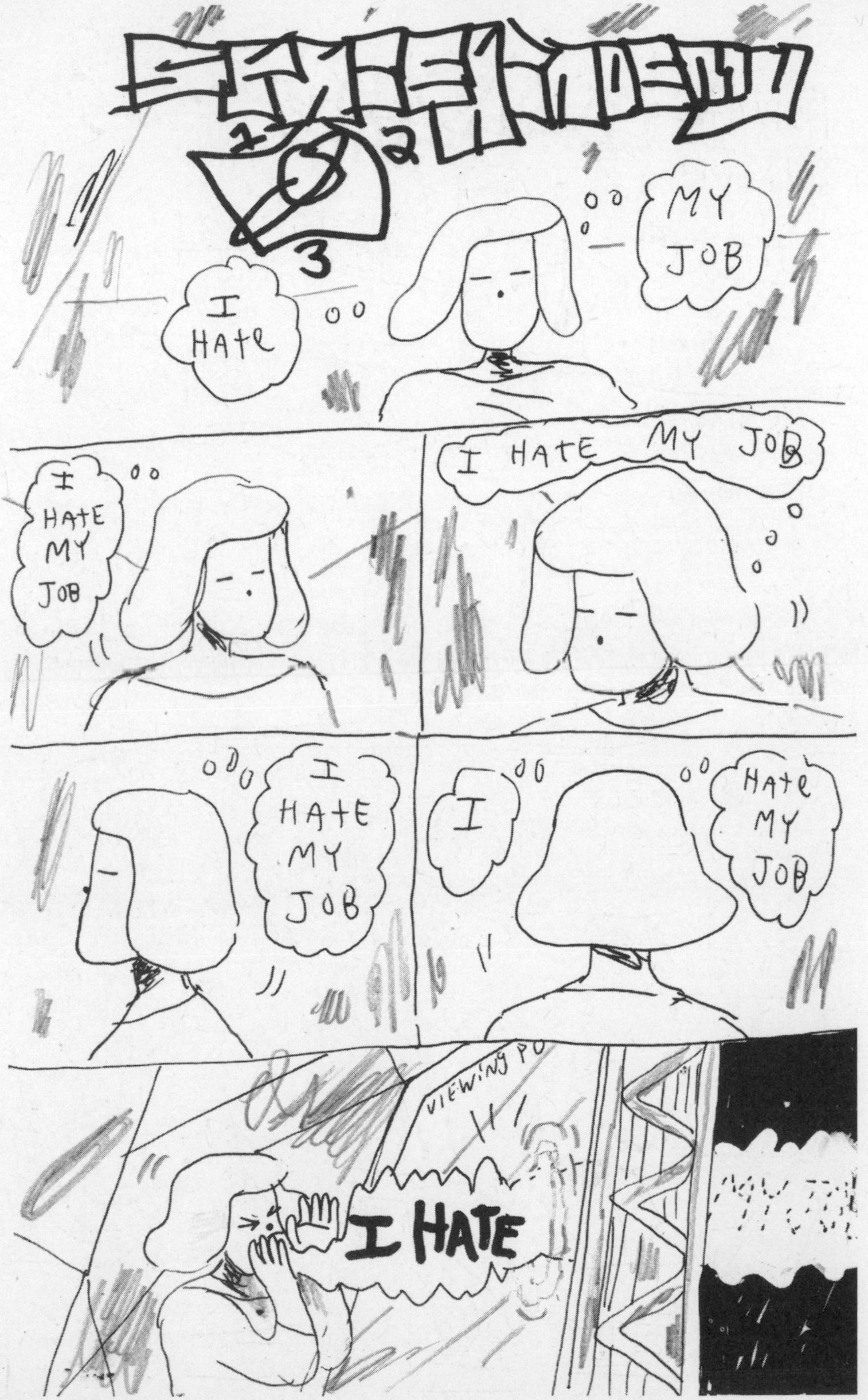

I Hate
MY JOB
I HATE MY JOB
I HATE MY JOB
I HATE MY JOB
I
Hate MY JOB
VIEWING PO
I HATE

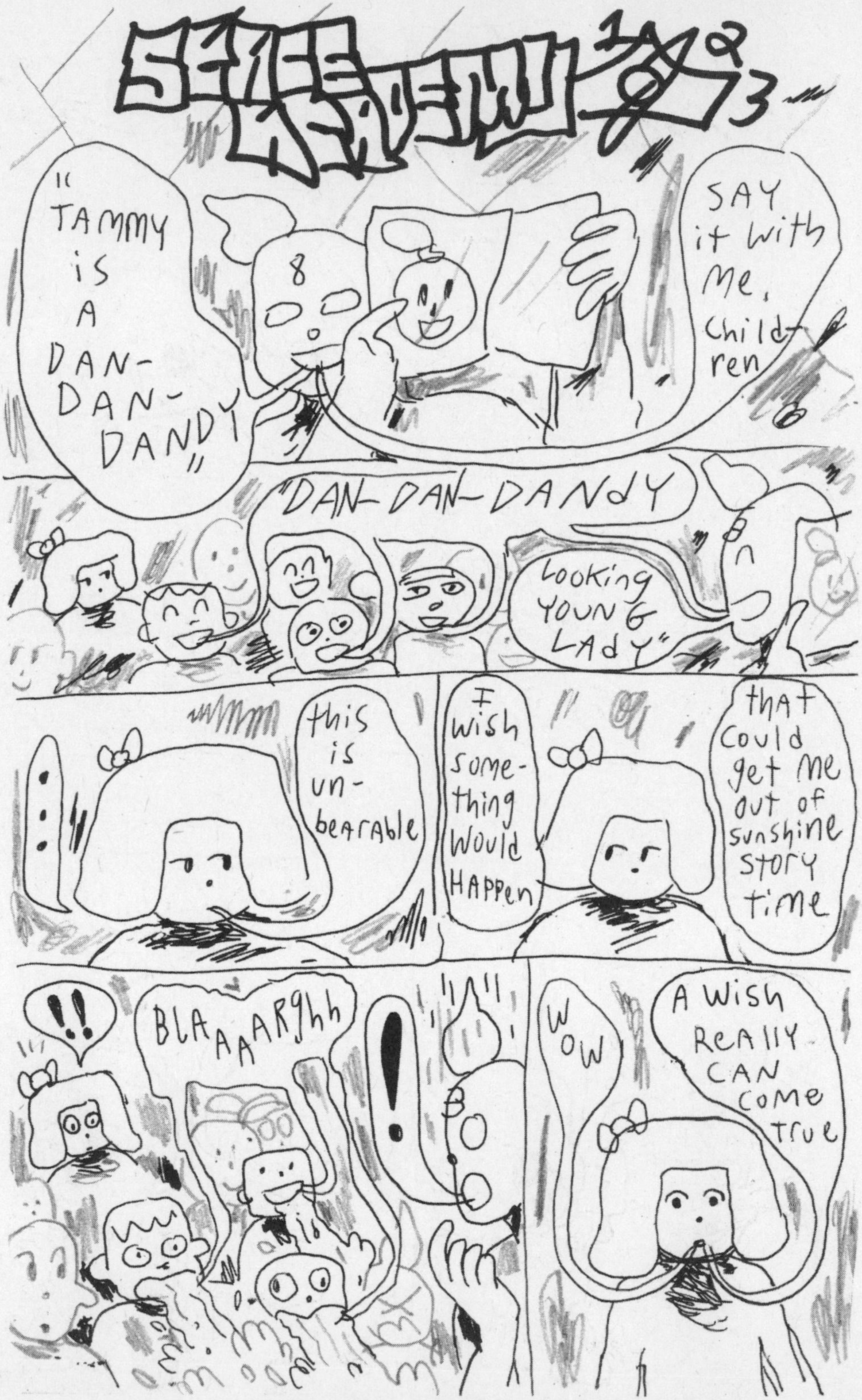
"TAMMY is A DAN-DAN-DANDY"
SAY it with me, Children
"DAN-DAN-DANdy
Looking YOUNG LAdy"
...
this is un-bearable
I wish some-thing would HAPPen
that could get me out of sunshine story time
!!
BLAAAARghh
!
WOW
A wish Really CAN come true

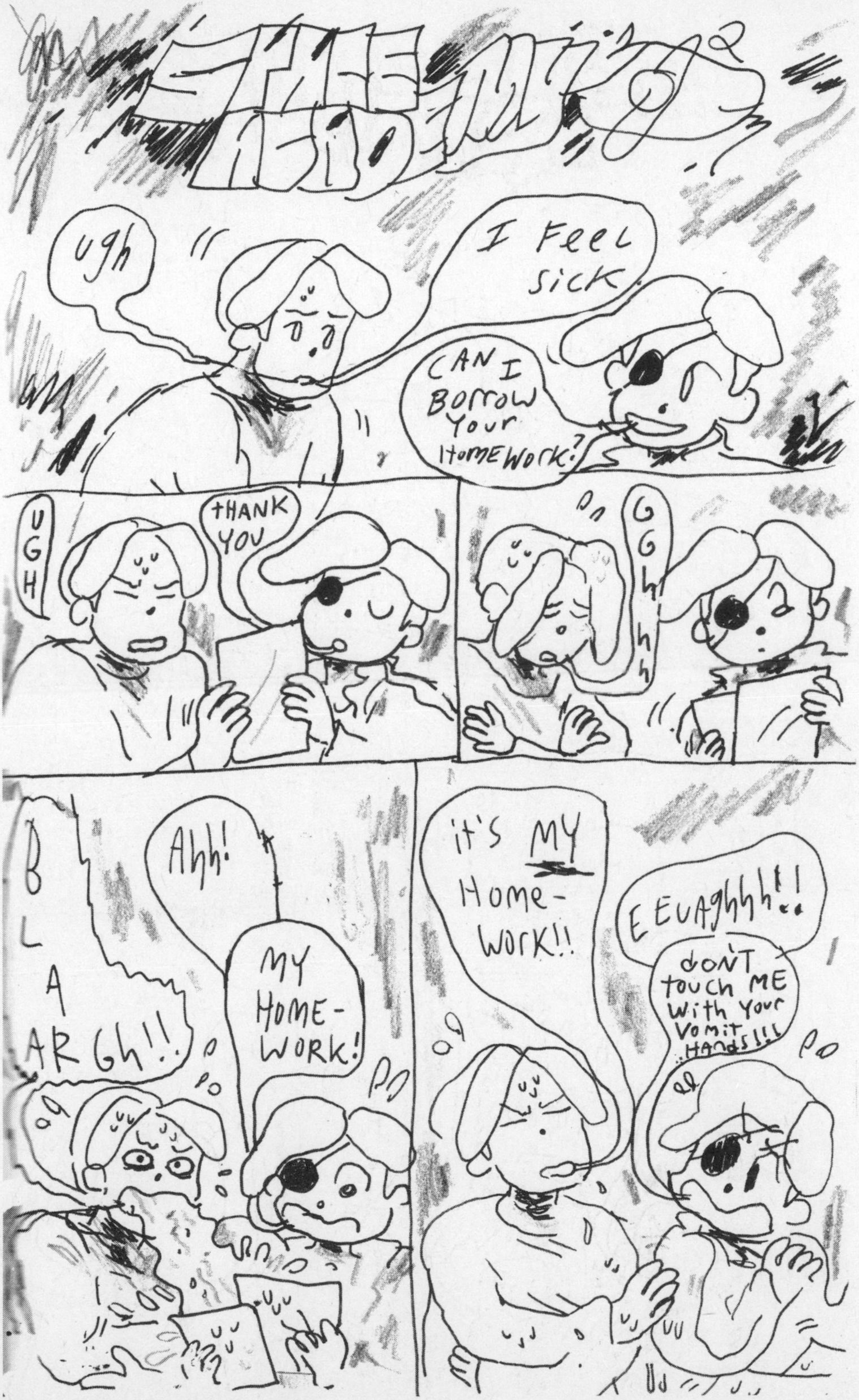
ugh
I Feel sick
CAN I Borrow Your HomeWork?
UGH
THANK YOU
GGhhhh
BLAARGh!!
Ahh!
MY HOME-WORK!
it's MY Home-work!!
EEUAghhh!!
don't touch ME with your vomit HANDS!!!

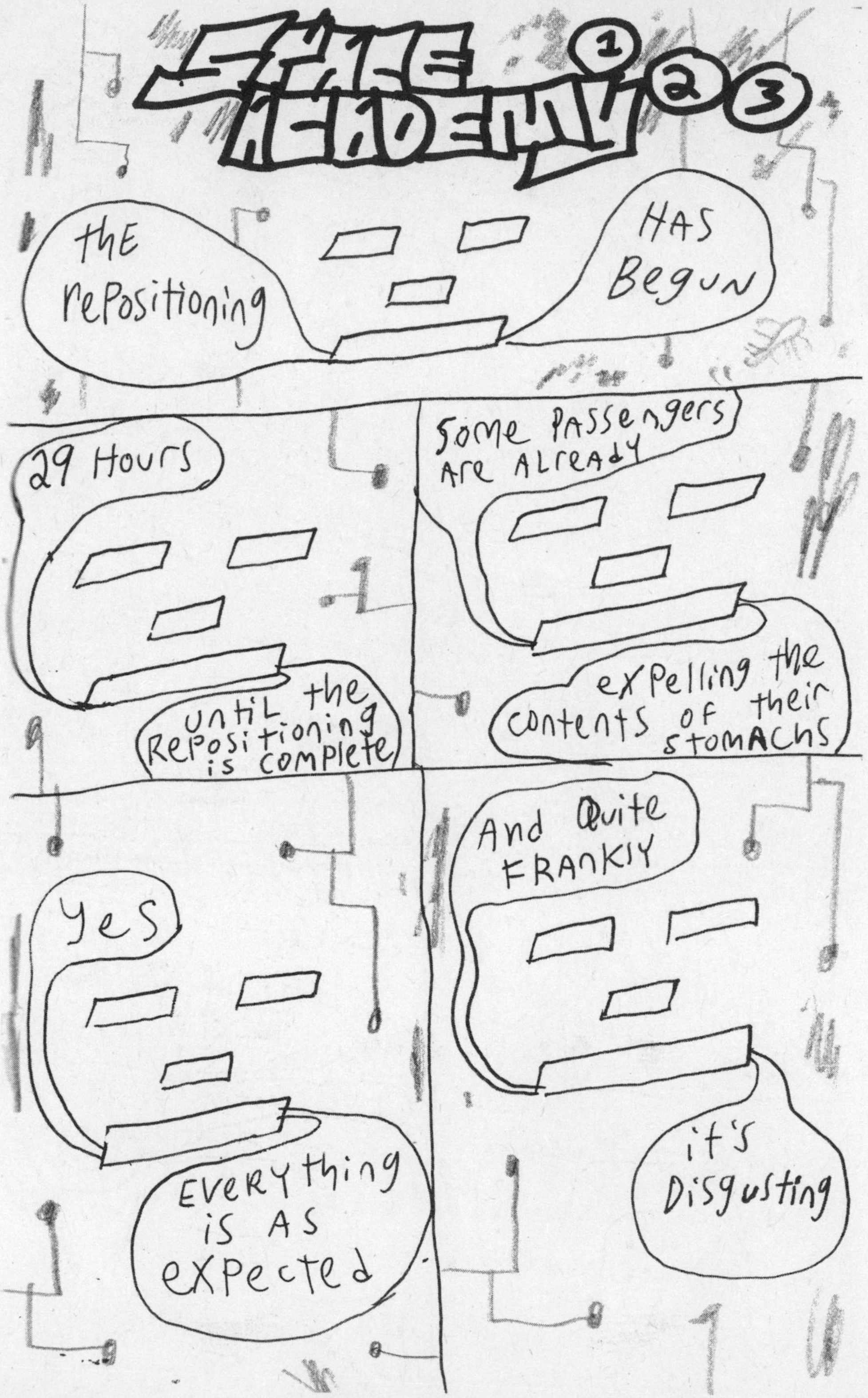

SPACE ACADEMY 1 2 3
the repositioning
HAS Begun
29 Hours
until the Repositioning is complete
Some Passengers are already
expelling the contents of their stomachs
Yes
Everything is as expected
And Quite Frankly
it's Disgusting

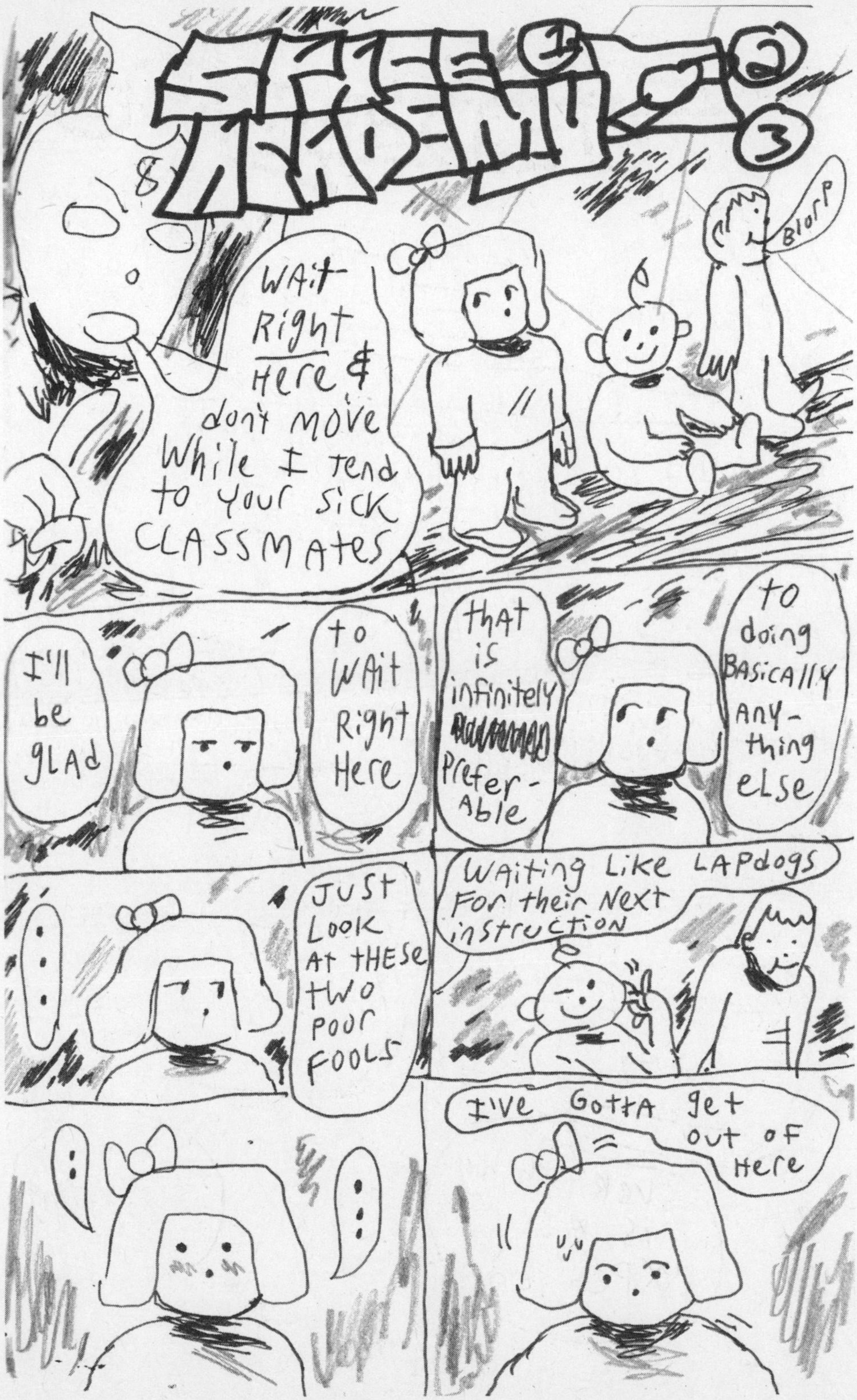

Blorp
WAit Right Here & don't move While I tend to your sick CLASSMAtes
I'll be glad
to WAit Right Here
that is infinitely Prefer-able
to doing BASICAlly Any-thing else
...
JUST LOOK At THESE two poor FOOLS
WAiting Like LAPdogs For their Next instruction
..
...
I've GottA get out of Here

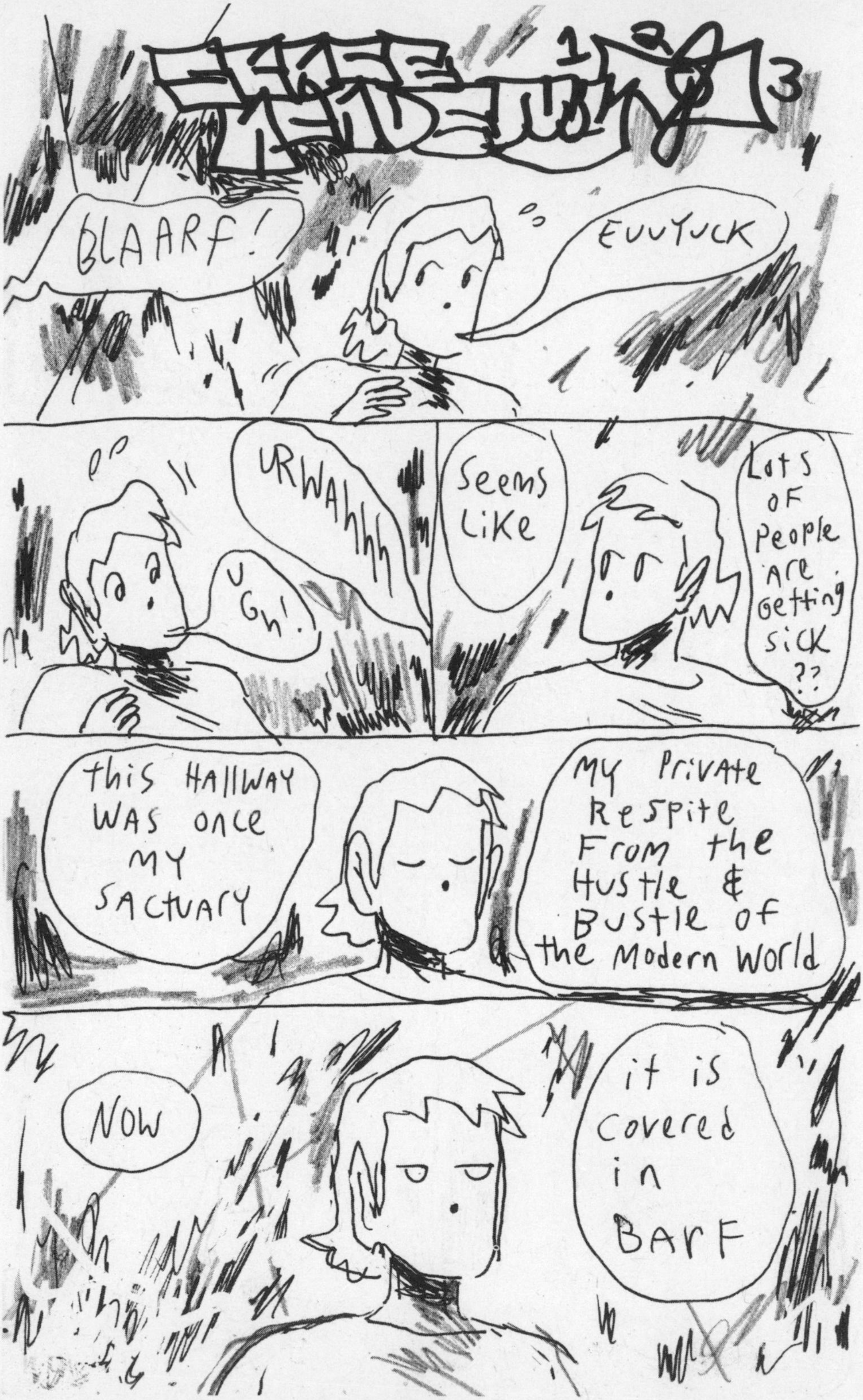
BLAARF!
EUUYUCK
URWAhhhh
UGh!
Seems Like
Lots of people are getting sick ??
this HALLWAY WAS once MY SACTUARY
MY Private Respite From the Hustle & Bustle of the Modern World
NOW
it is covered in BARF

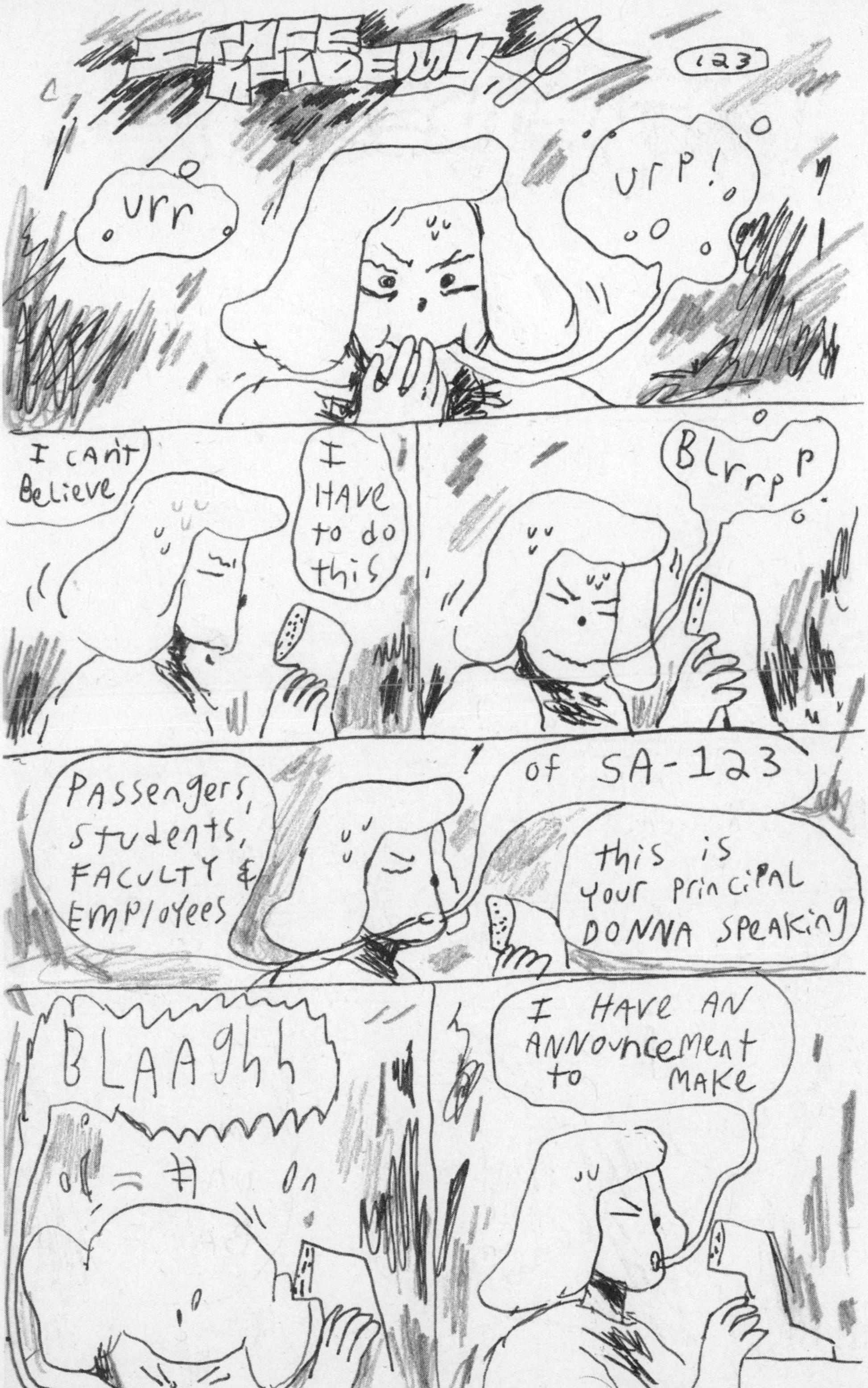
123
urr
urp!
I can't Believe
I HAVE to do this
Blrrp p
Passengers, students, FACULTY & EMPloyees
of SA-123
this is your principal DONNA speaking
BLAAghh
I HAVE AN ANNOUNCEMENT to MAKE

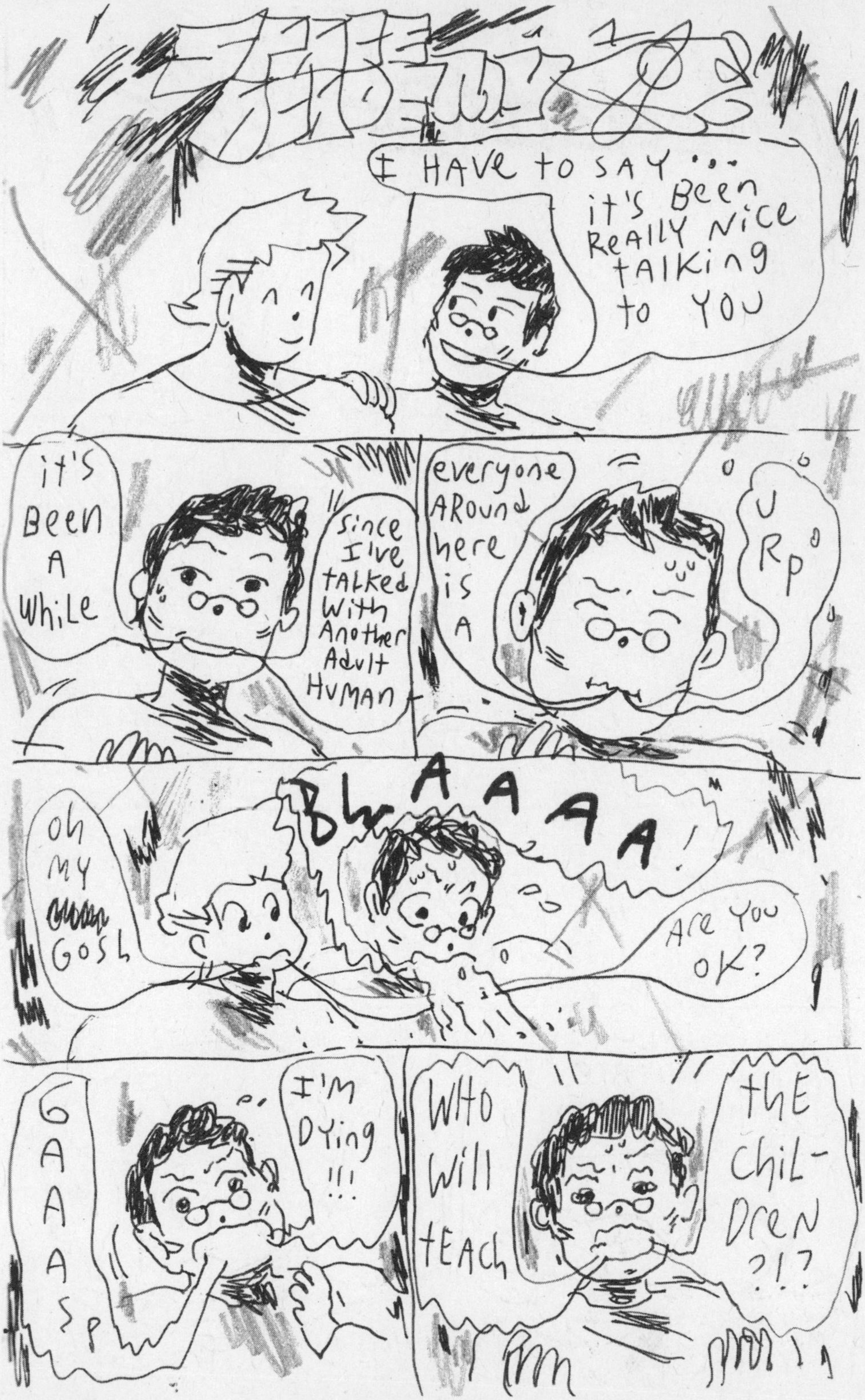
I HAVE to SAY...
it's Been ReAlly Nice tAlking to YOU
it's Been A While
Since I've tAlked With Another Adult HuMAN
everyone ARound here is A
URp
BlAAAAA!
oh MY Gosh
Are You OK?
GAAAASp
I'M Dying !!!
WHO Will tEACH
the ChiL-Dren ?!?

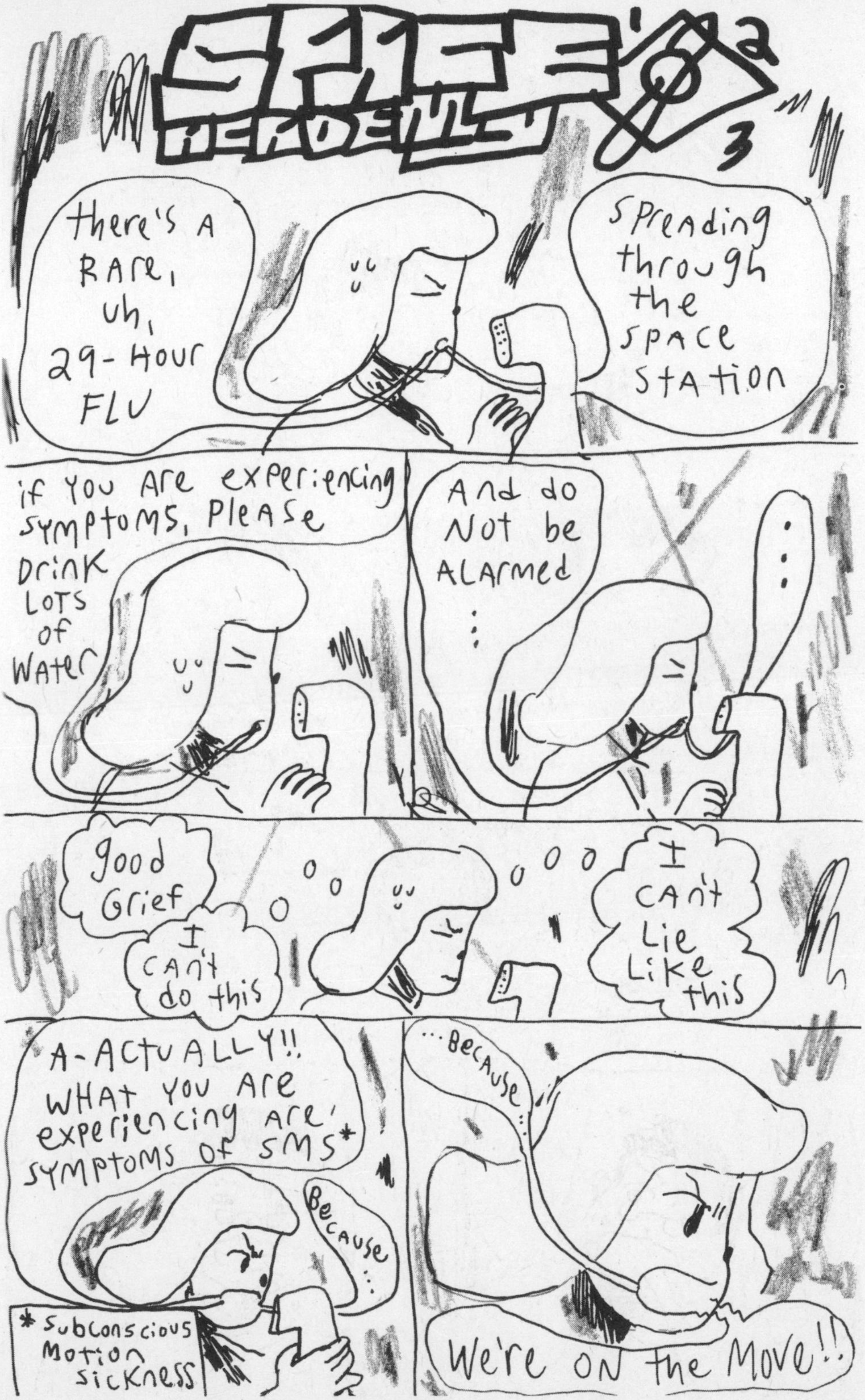
there's a RARE, uh, 29-Hour FLU
Spreading through the space station
if you are experiencing symptoms, please Drink lots of Water
And do Not be Alarmed
...
...
good Grief
I can't do this
I can't lie like this
A-ACTUALLY!! WHAT YOU ARE experiencing are symptoms of SMS*
BeCAuse ...
* Subconscious Motion sickness
...BeCAuse...
We're on the Move!!

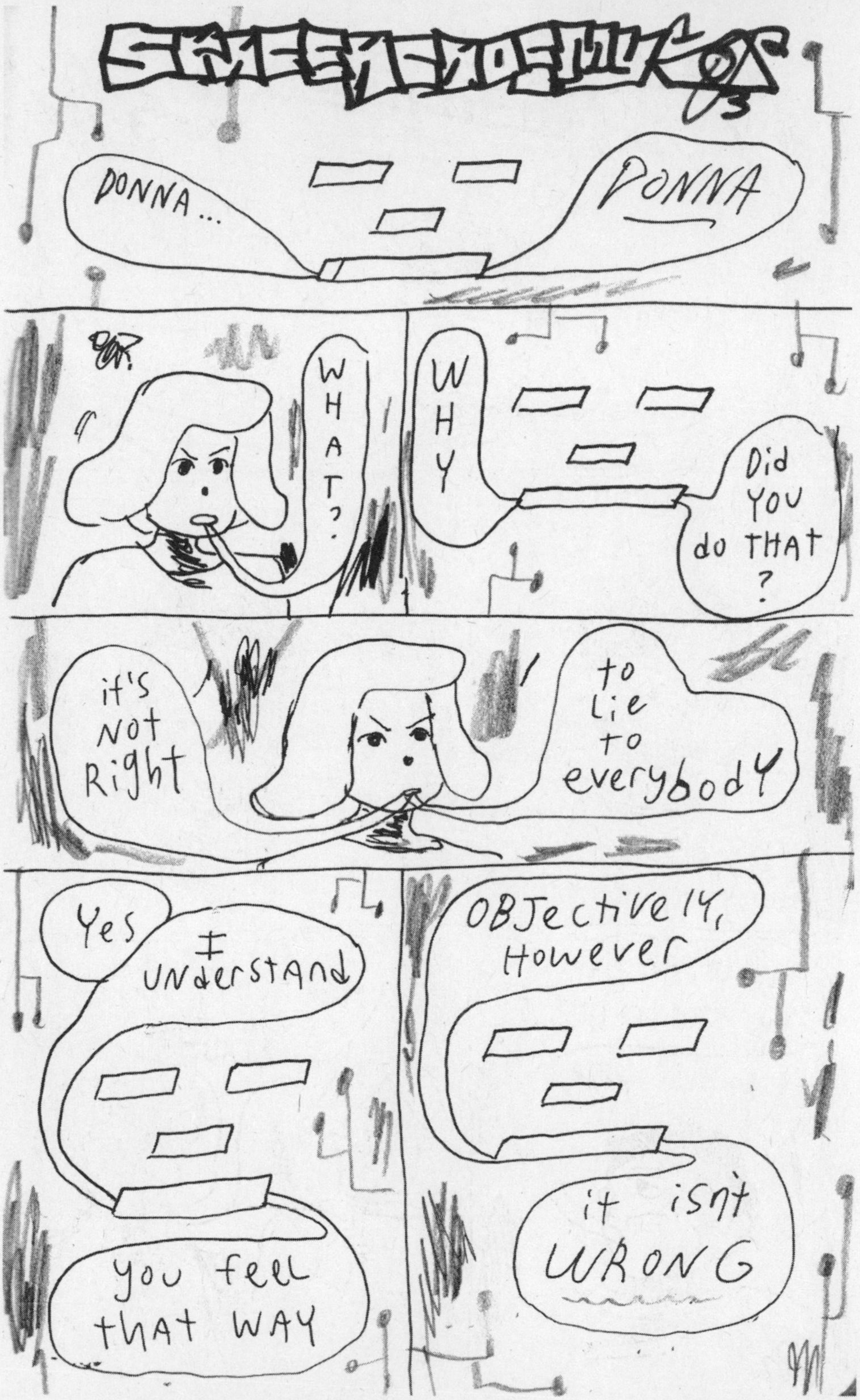
DONNA...
DONNA
WHAT?
WHY
Did YOU do THAT?
it's NOT Right
to Lie to everybodY
Yes
I understand
you feel that WAY
OBJectively, However
it isn't WRONG

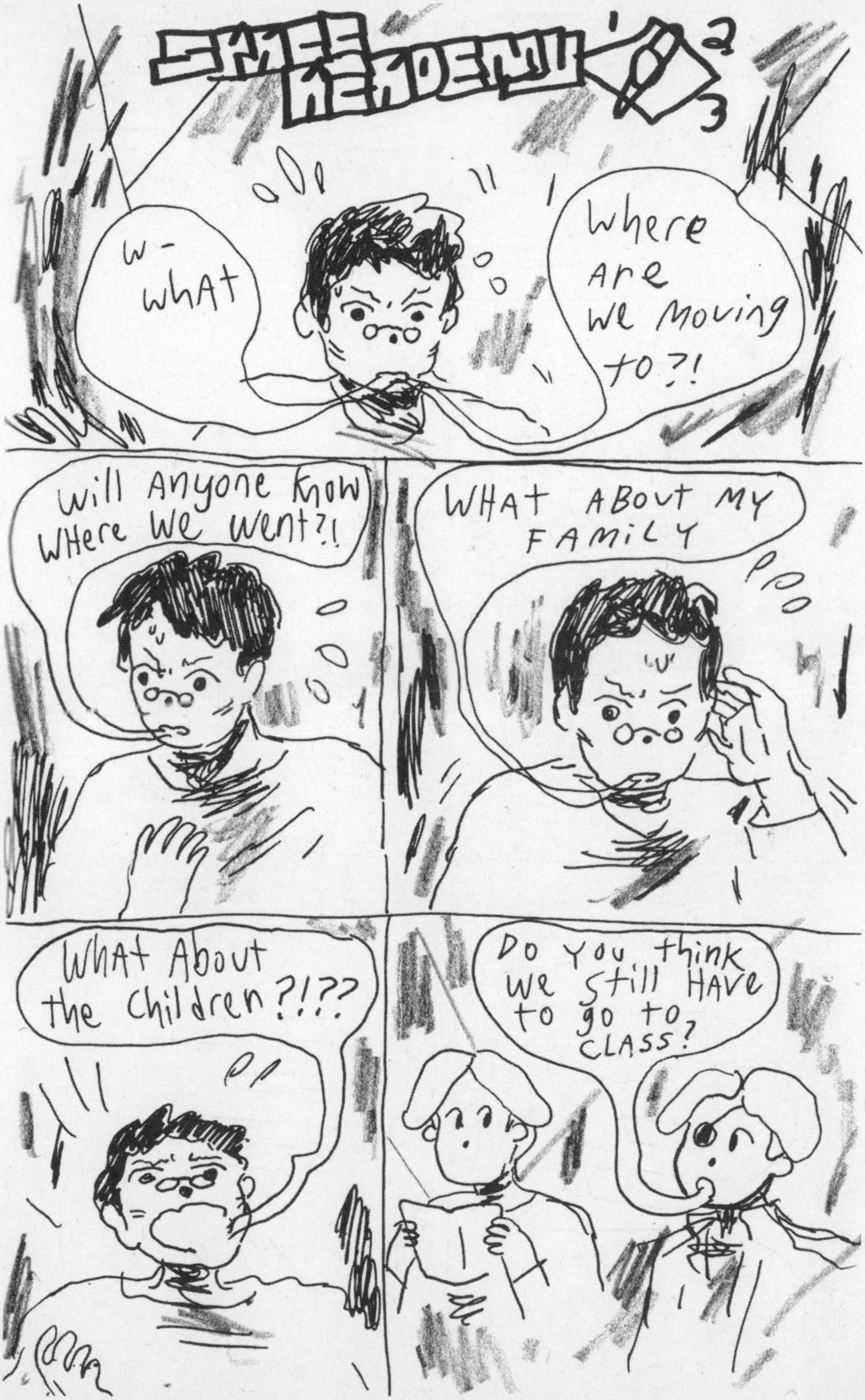
W-
WHAT
Where are we moving to?!
Will anyone know where we went?!
WHAT ABOUT MY FAMILY
WHAT About the Children?!??
Do You think we still HAVE to go to CLASS?

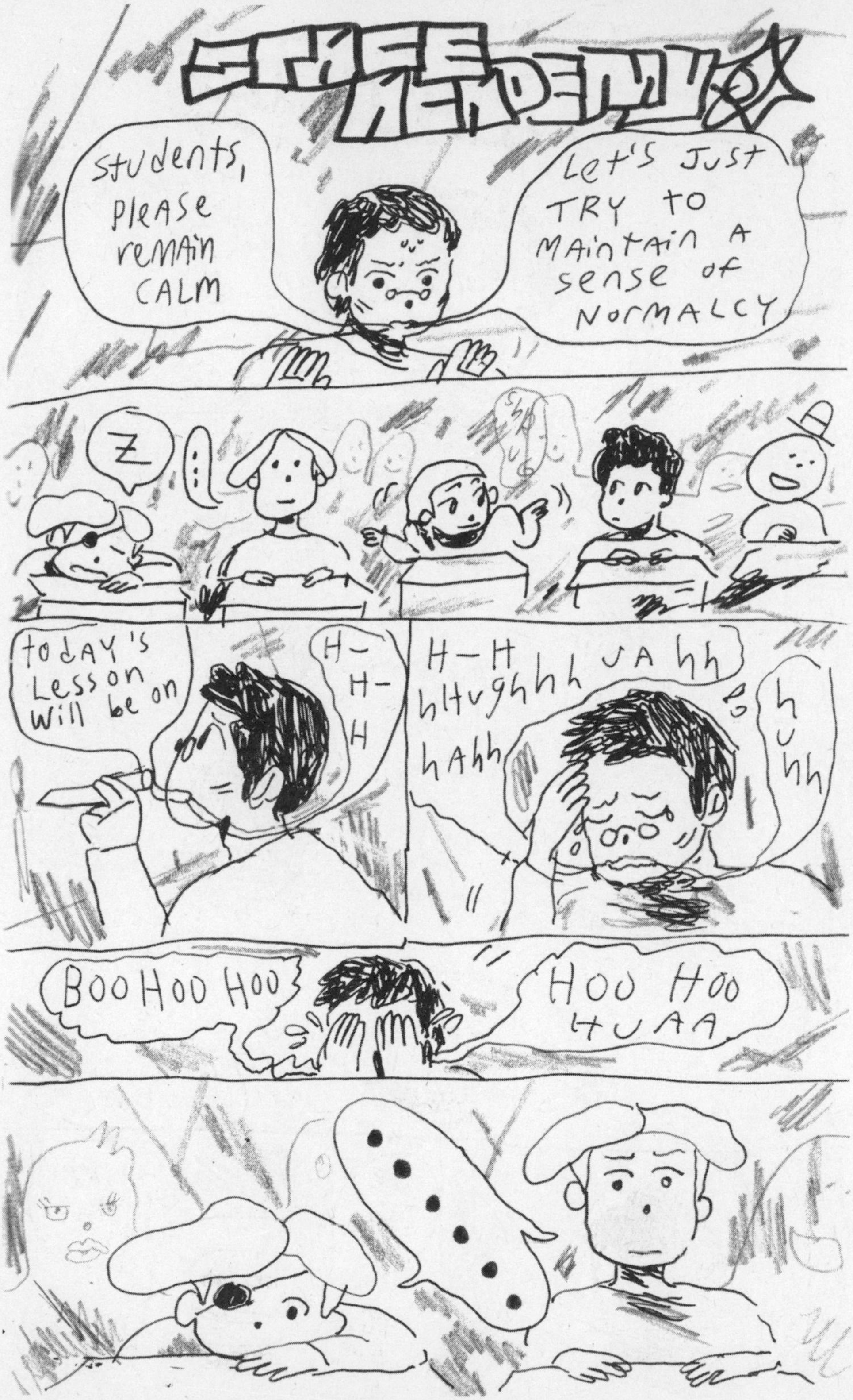
students, please remain CALM
Let's JUST TRY TO MAINtain A sense of NORMALCY
Z
today's Lesson will be on
H-H-H
H-H hhughhh JA hh hahh
huhh
BOO HOO HOO
HOO HOO HUAA

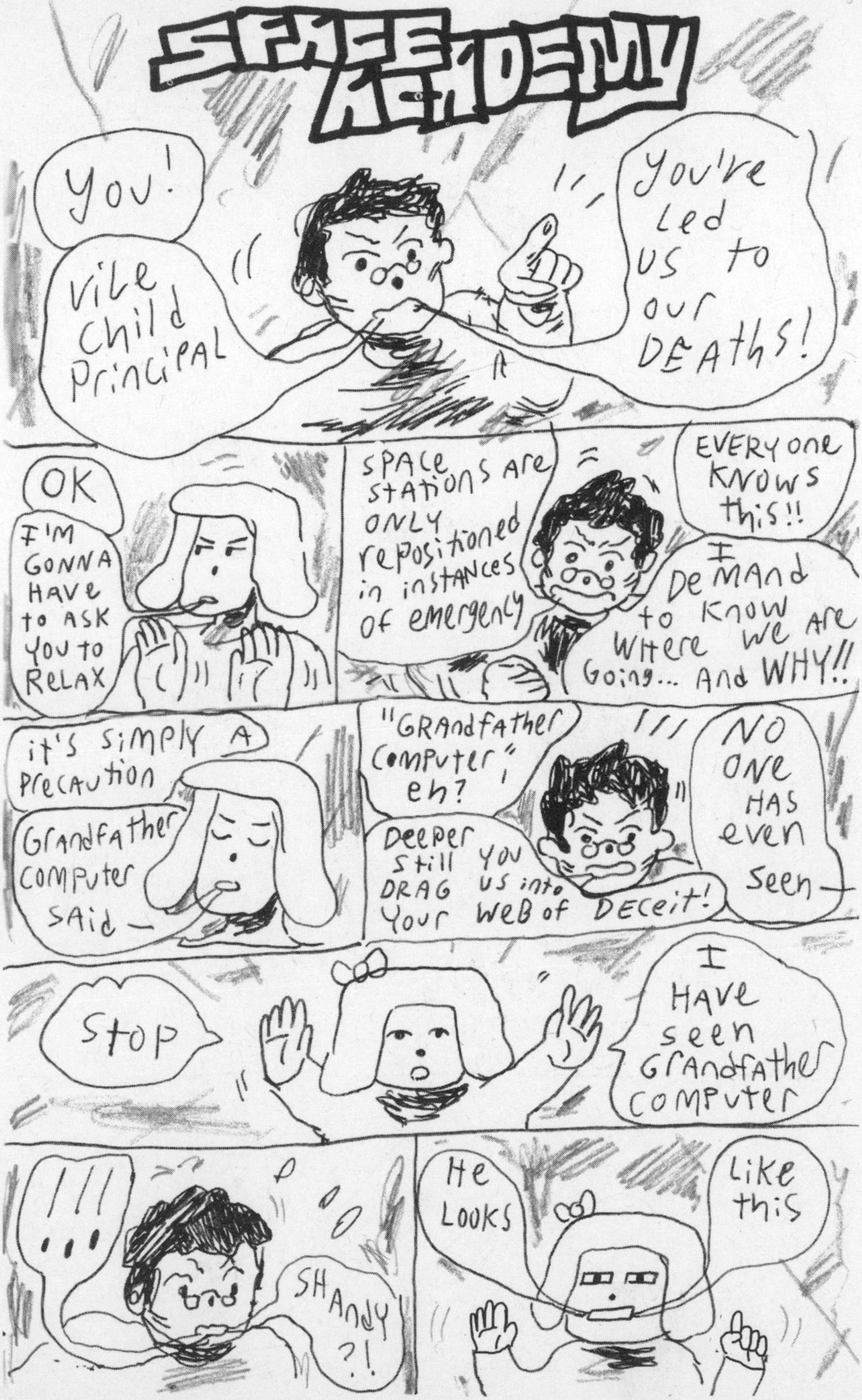
SPACE ACADEMY
You!
Vile Child Principal
You're led us to our DEATHS!
OK
I'M GONNA HAVE TO ASK YOU TO RELAX
SPACE STATIONS ARE ONLY repositioned in instances of emergency
EVERYONE KNOWS this!!
I DEMAND to KNOW WHERE WE ARE Going... And WHY!!
it's simply A precaution
Grandfather computer said—
"GRANDFATHER COMPUTER", eh?
DEEPER STILL YOU DRAG US into YOUR WEB of DECEIT!
NO ONE HAS even Seen—
Stop
I HAVE seen Grandfather COMPUTER
!!! ...
SHANDY ?!
He LOOKS
Like this

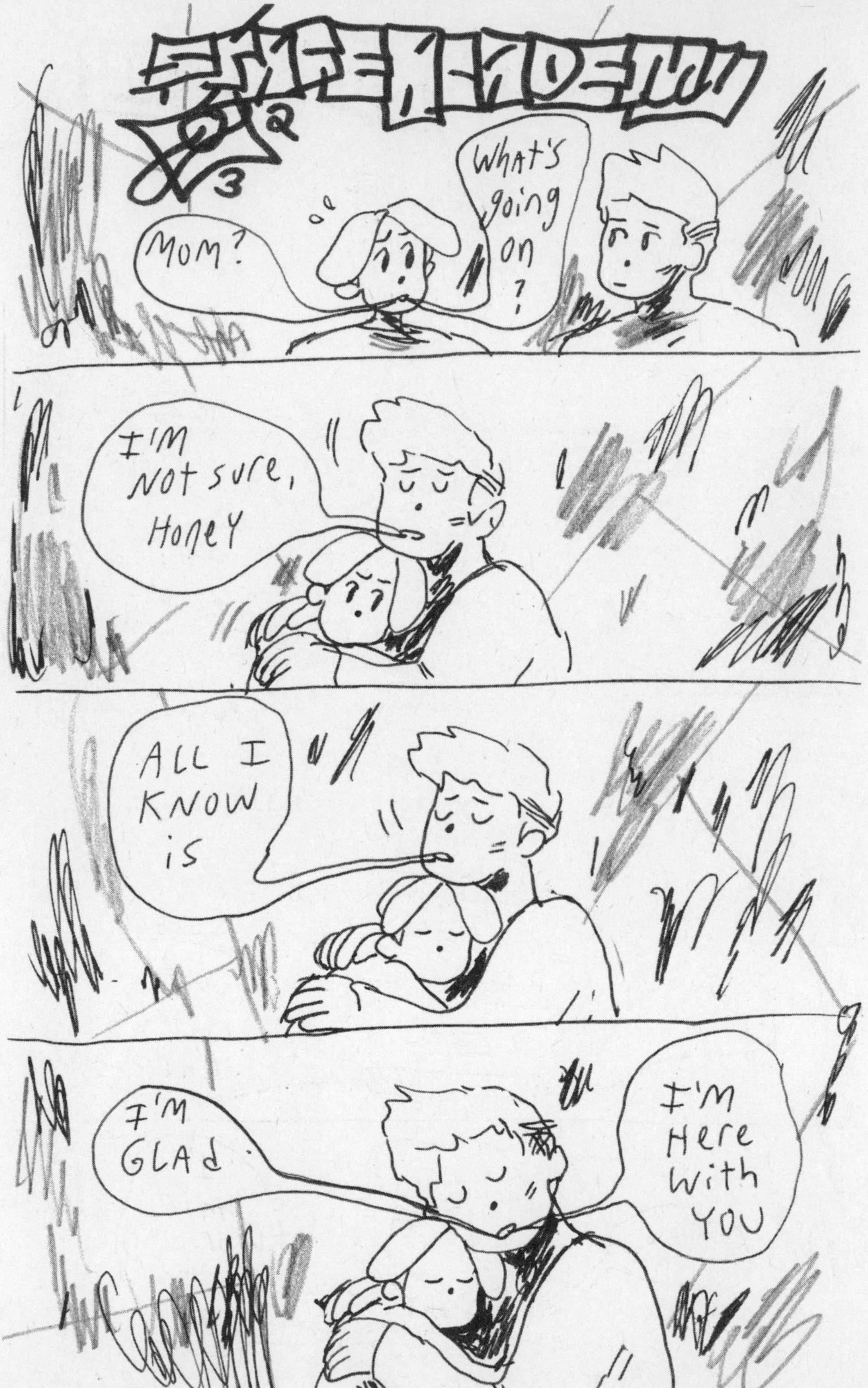
MOM?
What's going on?
I'M Not sure, Honey
ALL I KNOW is
I'M GLAd
I'M Here with YOU

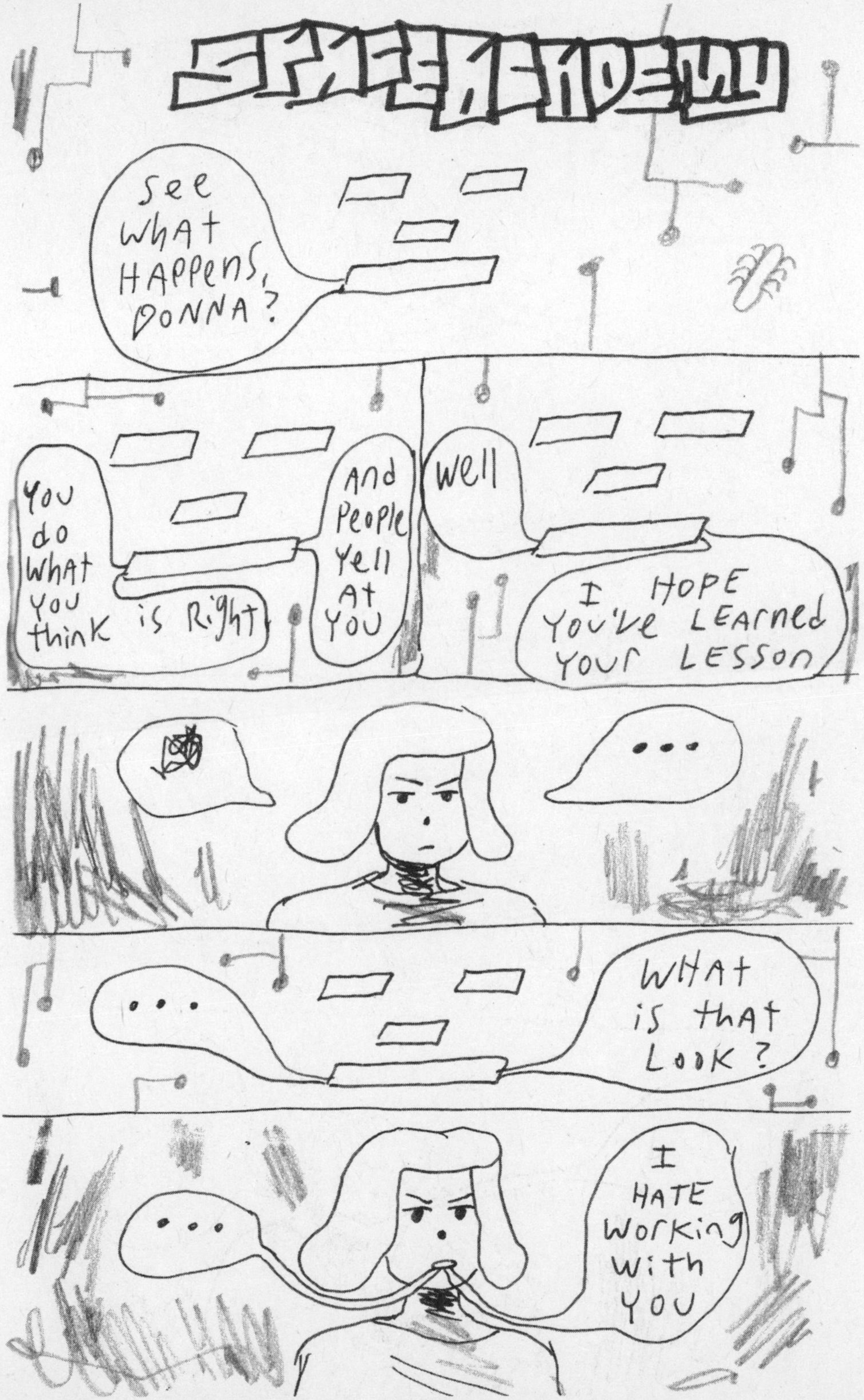
see what HAPPens, DONNA?
You do what you think is Right
And People Yell At YOU
Well
I HOPE You've LEArned Your LESSon
...
...
WHAT is that Look?
...
I HATE Working with YOU

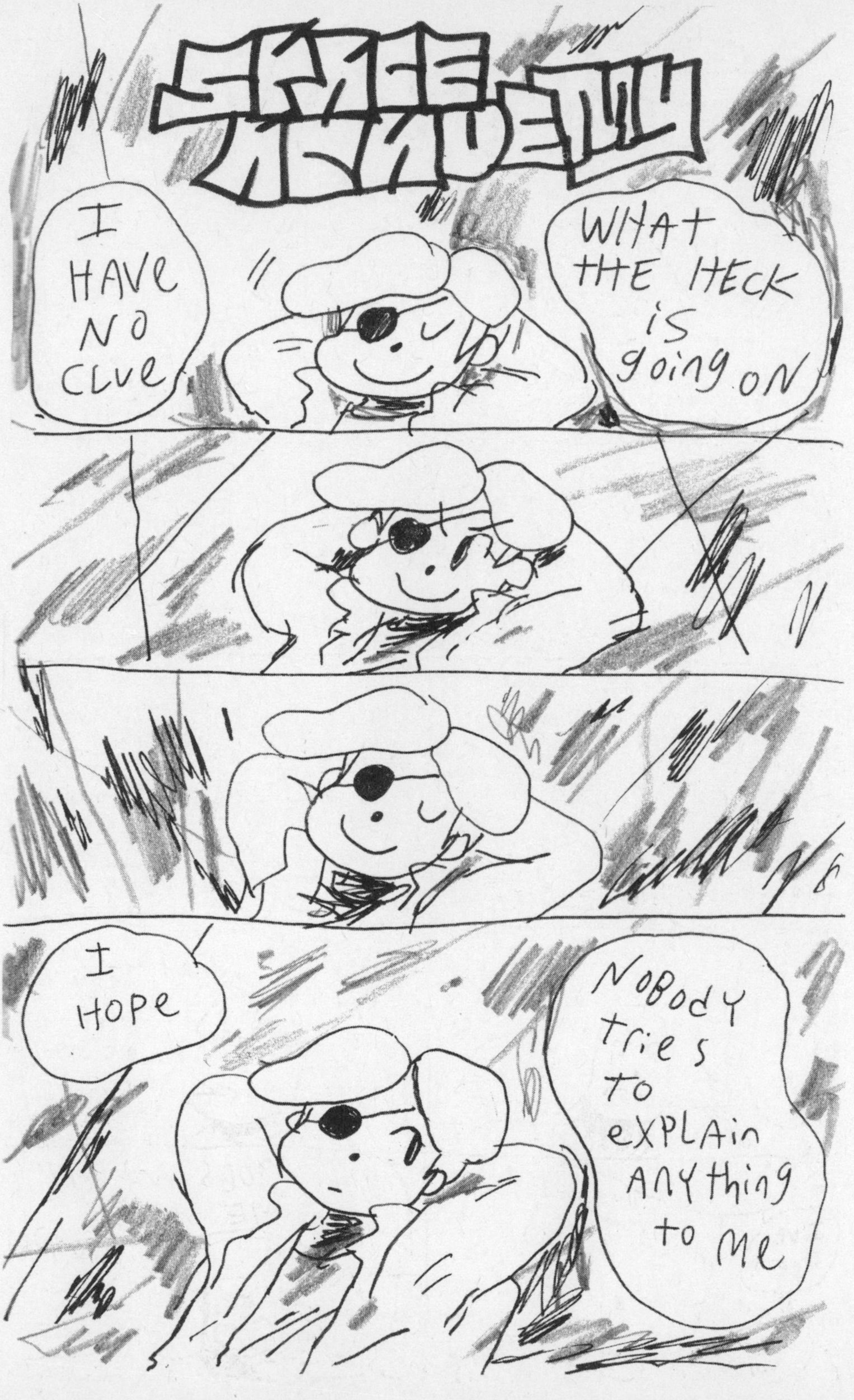
I HAVE NO CLUE
WHAT THE HECK is going ON
I HOPE
NOBODY tries TO eXPLAin ANYthing to Me

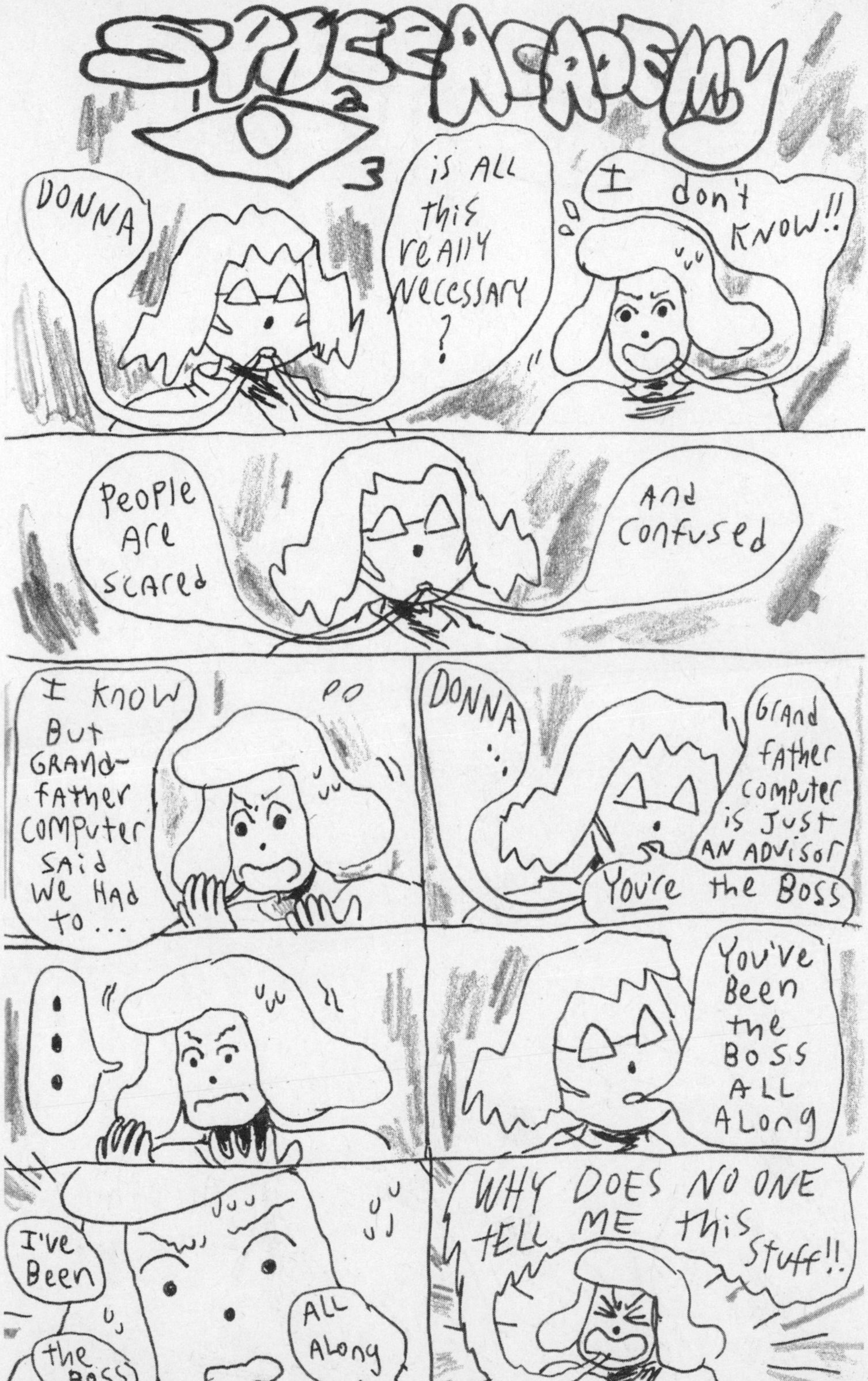
SPACE ACADEMY
1 2 3
DONNA
is ALL this really necessary?
I don't know!!
People Are scared
And confused
I know But Grand-father computer said we had to...
DONNA...
Grand father computer is just an advisor
You're the Boss
...
You've Been the Boss All Along
I've Been
the Boss
All Along...
WHY DOES NO ONE TELL ME this Stuff!!

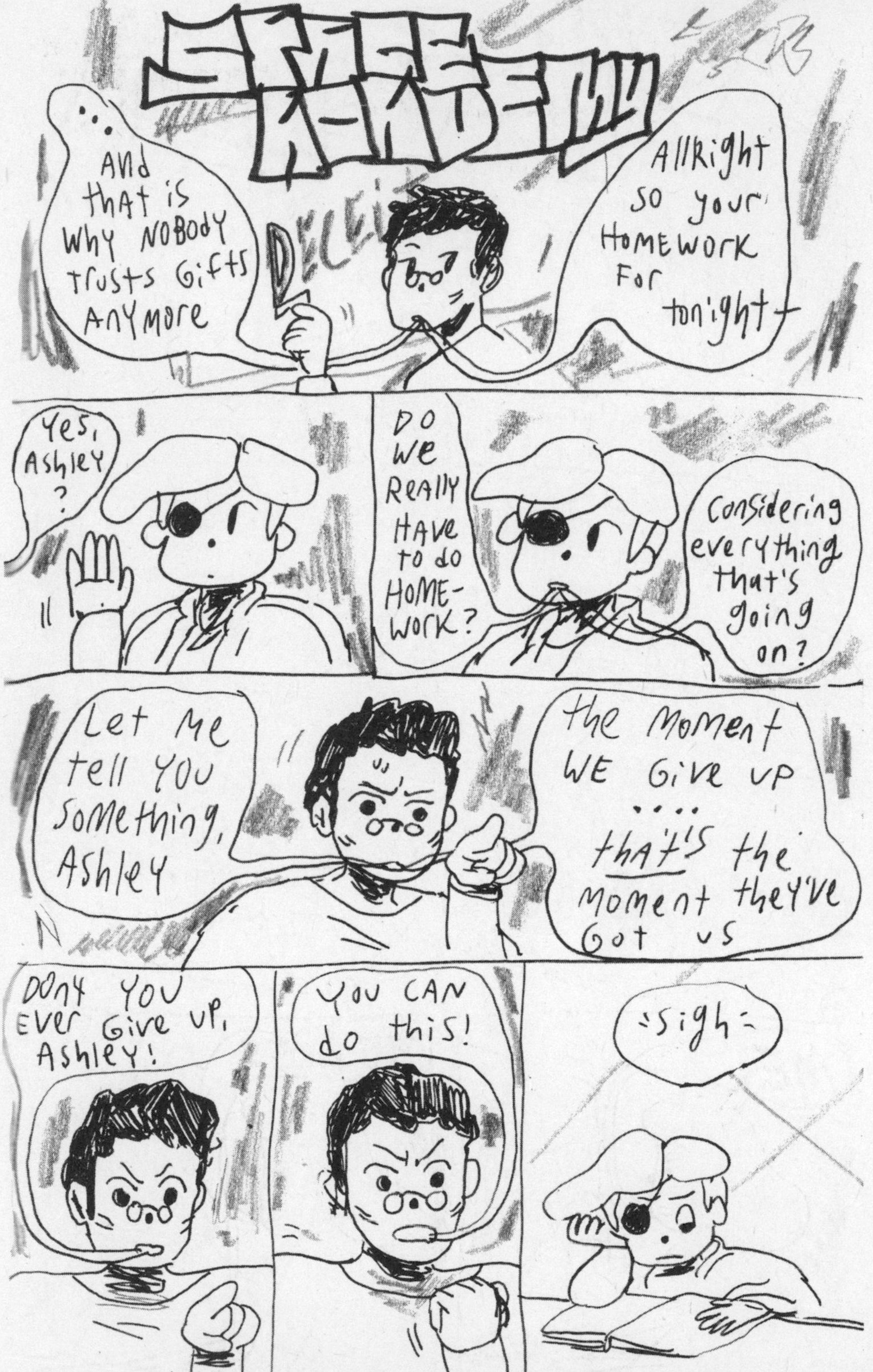
...
And that is why NOBODY trusts Gifts ANYMORE
AllRight so your HOMEWORK For tonight—
Yes, Ashley?
DO WE Really HAVE to do HOME-WORK?
Considering everything that's going on?
Let Me tell YOU Something, Ashley
the Moment WE Give up .... that's the Moment they've Got us
DON't YOU Ever Give UP, Ashley!
YOU CAN do this!
:sigh:

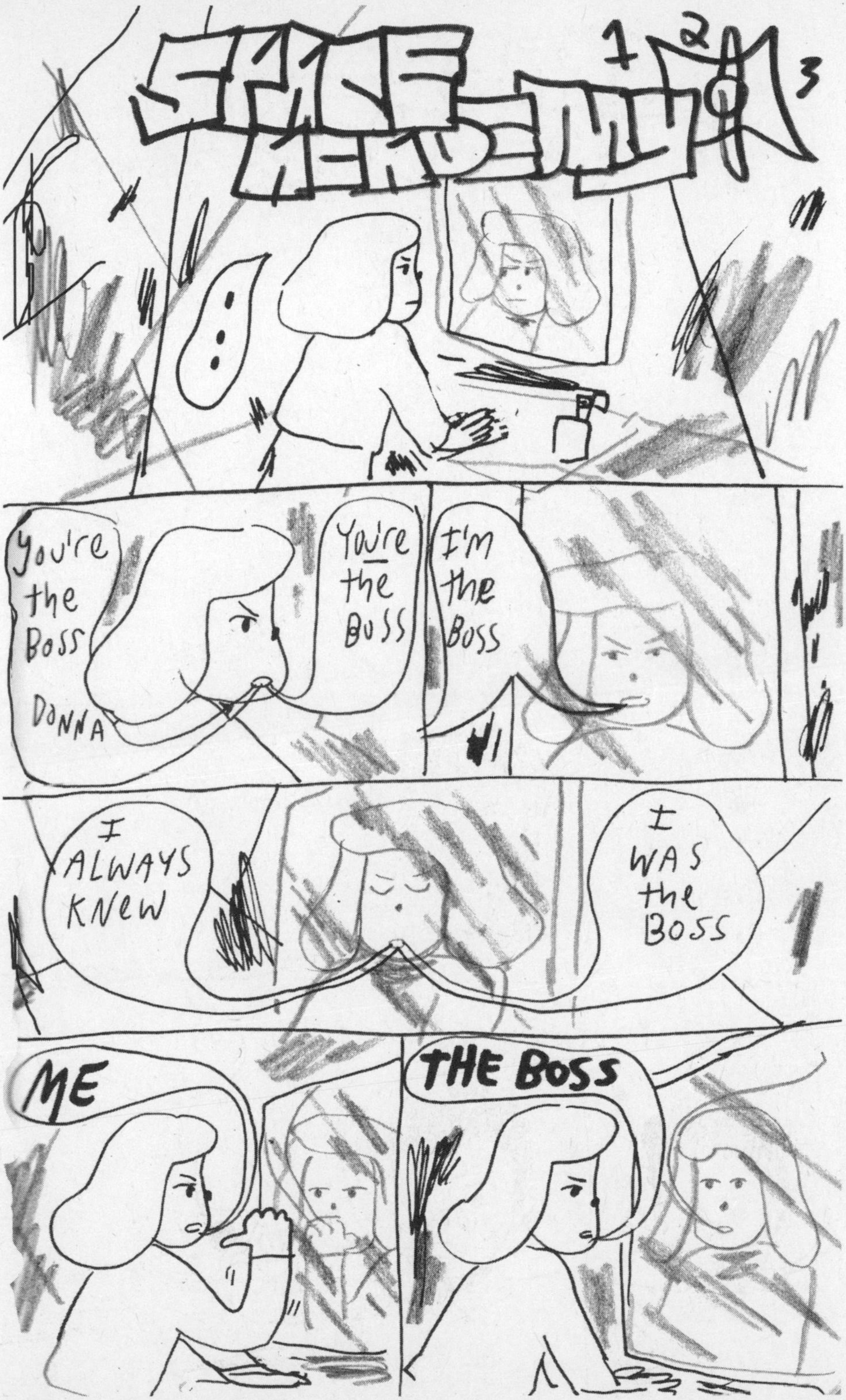
1
2
3
You're the Boss
DONNA
You're the Boss
I'm the Boss
I ALWAYS KNEW
I WAS the BOSS
ME
THE BOSS

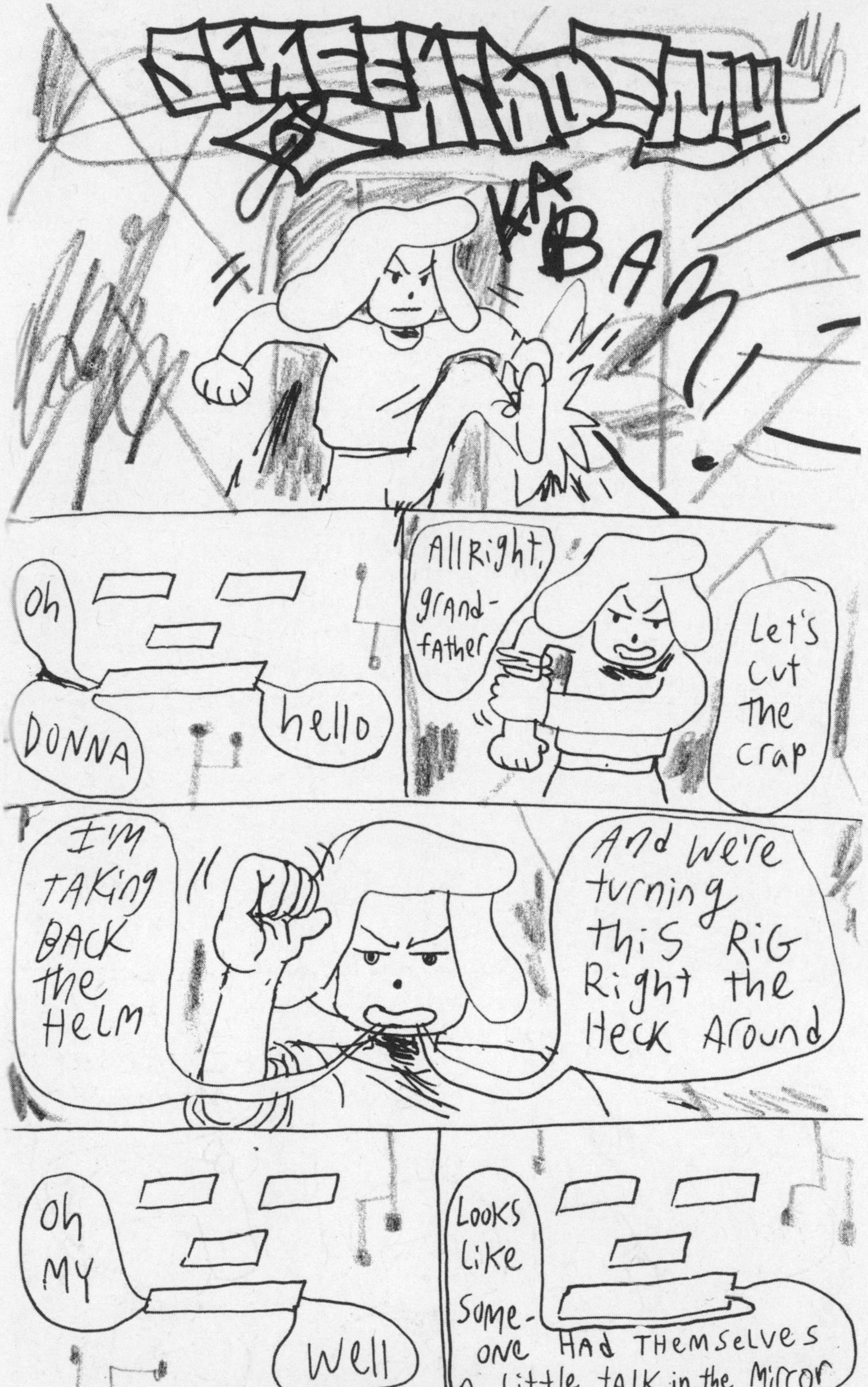
KA BAM!
Oh
DONNA
hello
AllRight, grand-father
Let's cut the crap
I'M TAKING BACK the Helm
And We're turning this RiG Right the Heck Around
Oh MY
Well
Looks Like Some-one HAd THEMselves A Little tALK in the Mirror

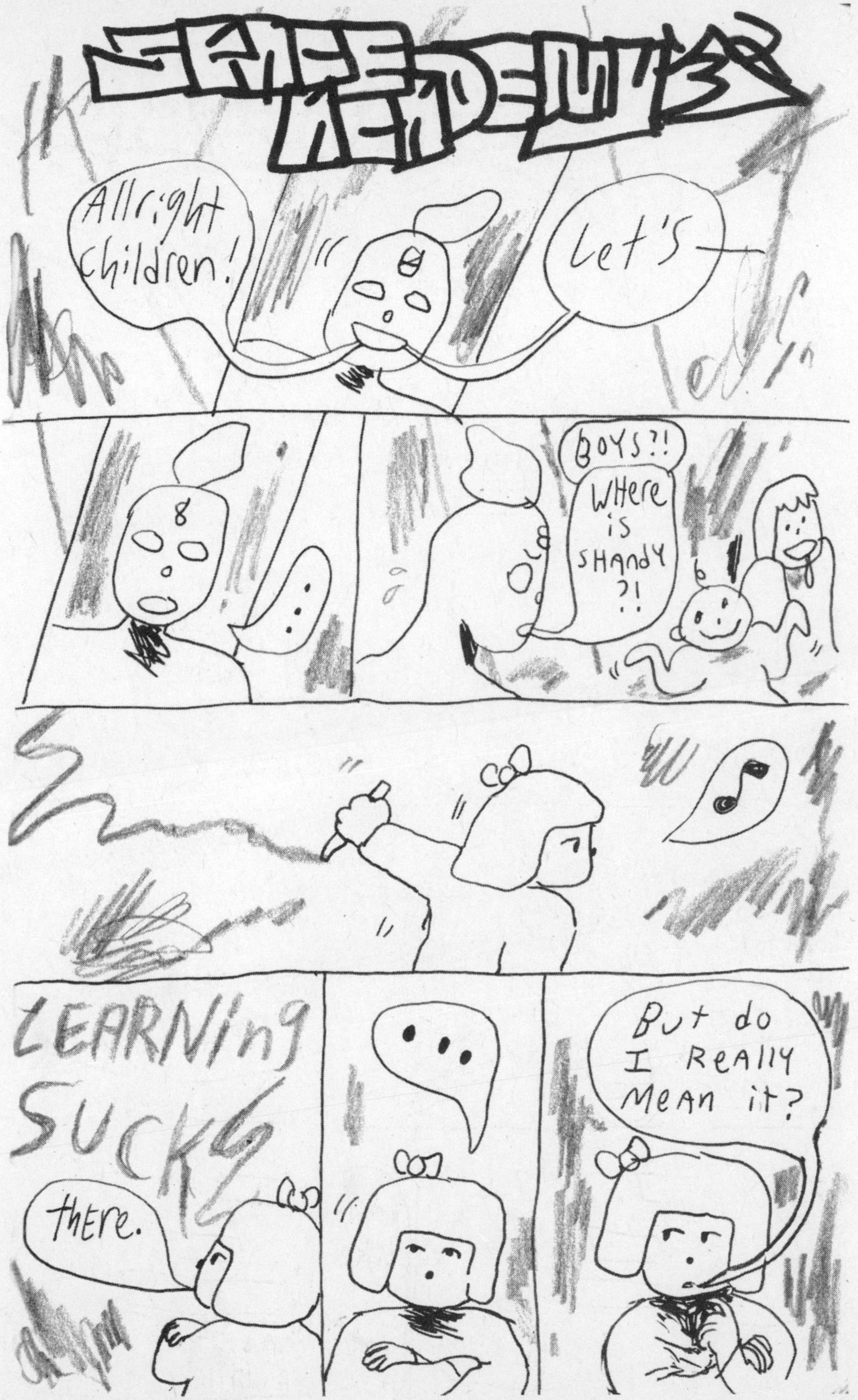
Allright children!
Let's—
BOYS?!
WHere is SHANDY ?!
LEARNing SUCKS
there.
But do I Really Mean it?

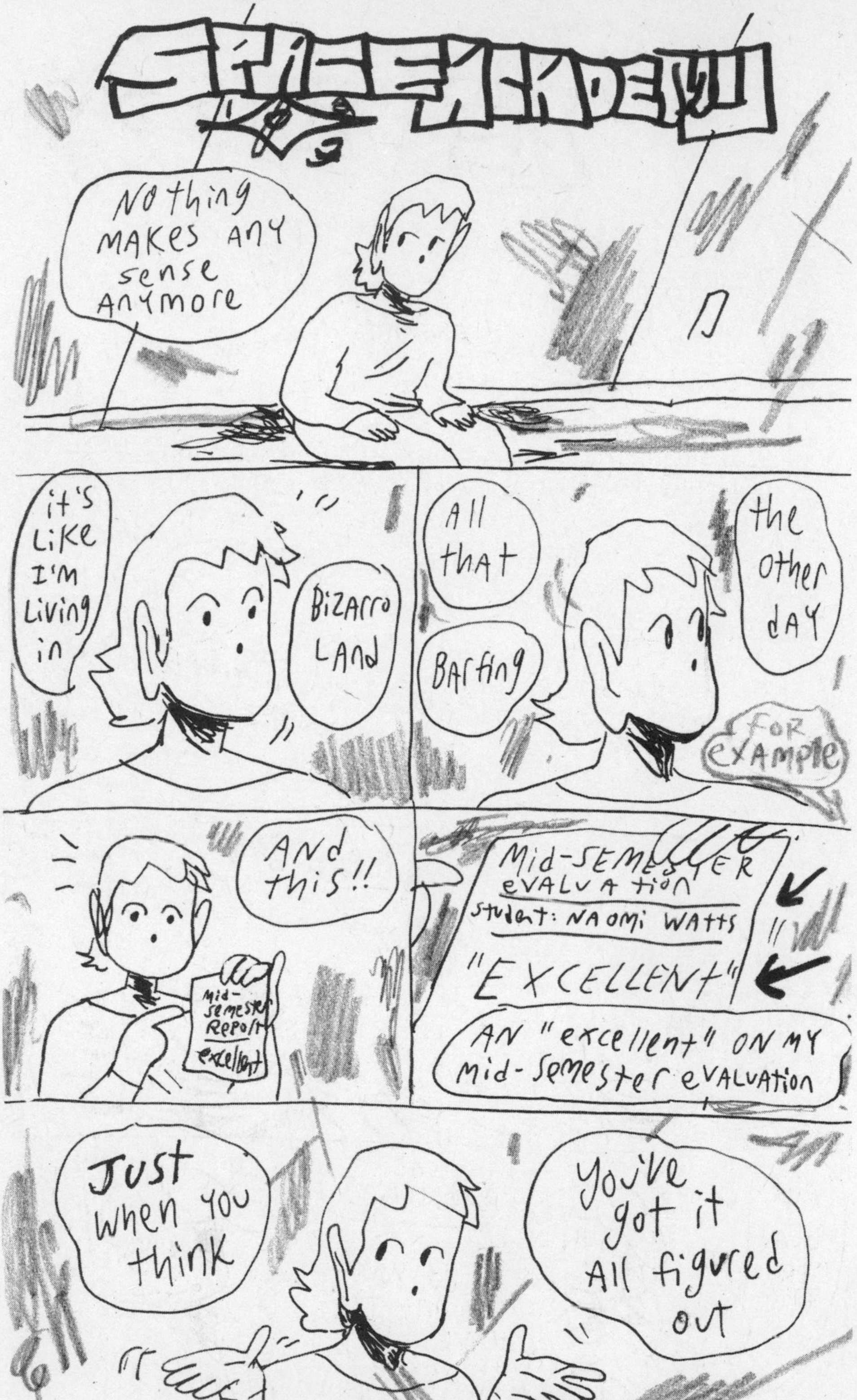

Nothing MAKES ANY sense Anymore
it's Like I'm Living in
Bizarro LAnd
All that
Barfing
the other day
FOR example
And this!!
Mid-semester Report
excellent
Mid-SEMESTER evaluation
Student: NAOMI WATTS
"EXCELLENT"
AN "excellent" ON MY mid-Semester evaluation
Just when you think
You've got it All figured out

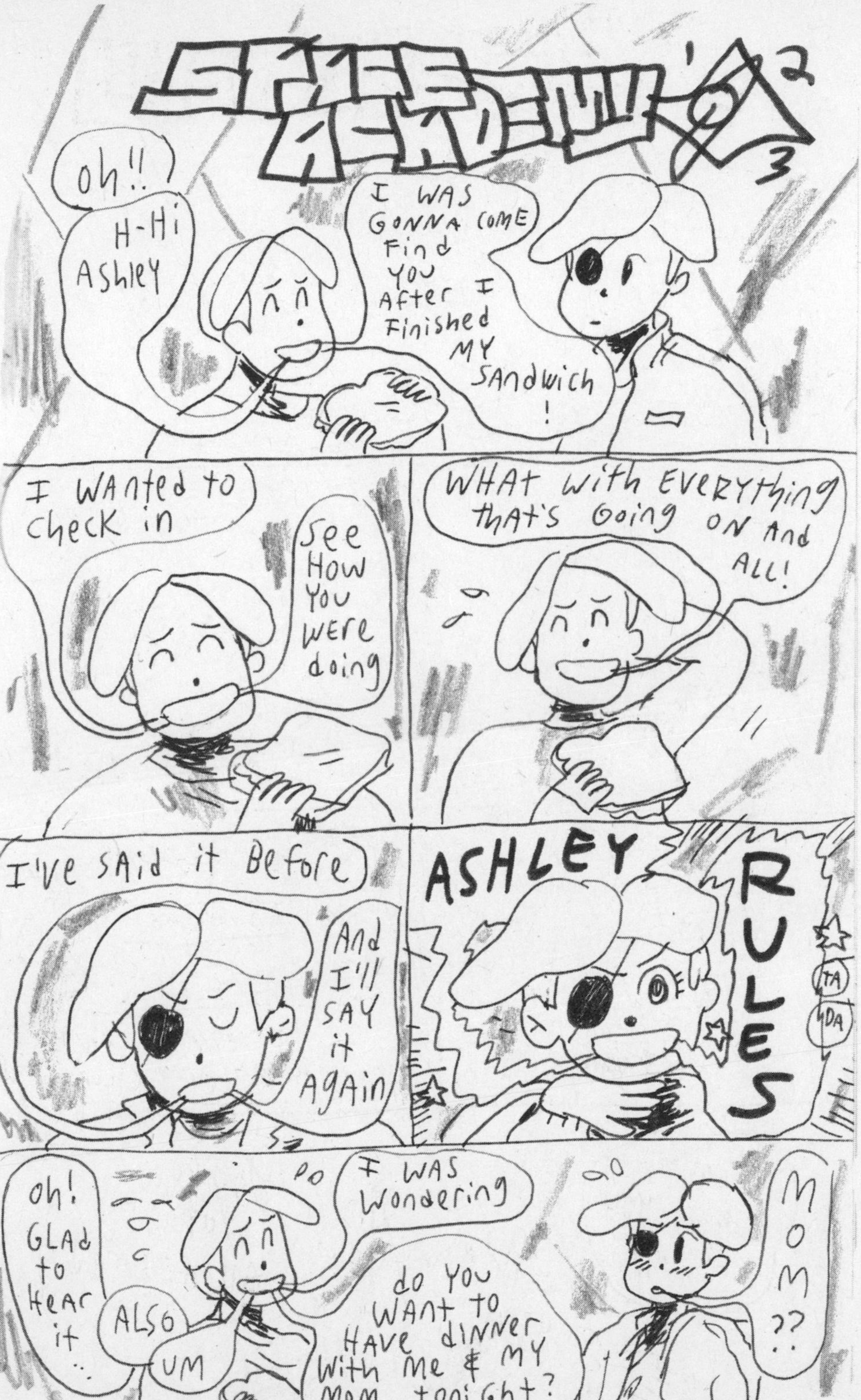

oh!!
H-Hi Ashley
I WAS GONNA COME Find YOU After I Finished MY SANdwich!
I WAnted to check in
See How You were doing
WHAt with EVERYthing that's Going ON And ALL!
I've SAid it Before
And I'll SAY it AgAin
ASHLEY RULES
TA DA
oh! GLAd to Hear it...
ALSO
UM
I WAS Wondering
do YOU WANT to HAVE dinner With me & MY MOM tonight?
MOM??

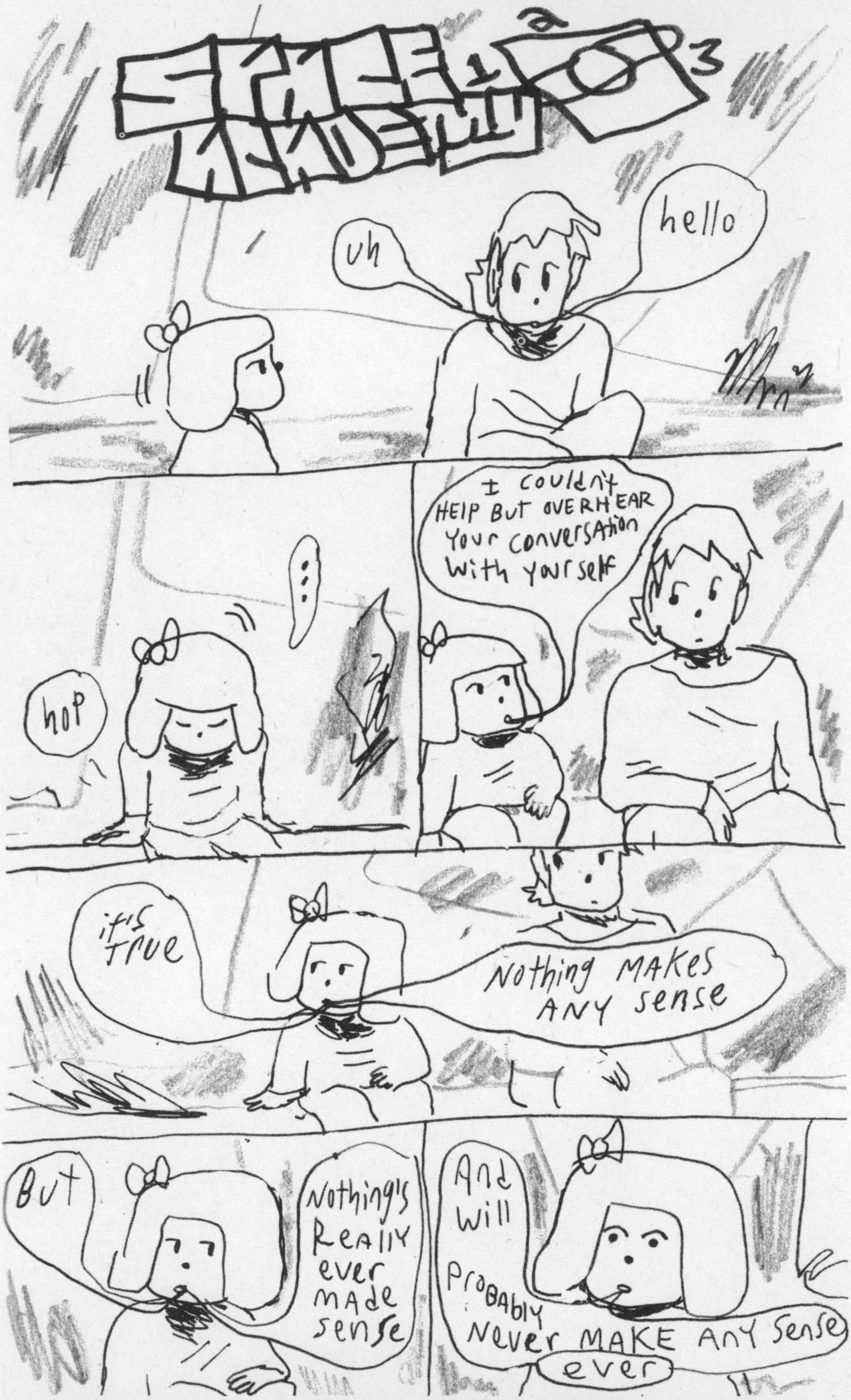
uh
hello
hop
I couldn't help but overhear your conversation with yourself
it's true
Nothing MAKES ANY sense
But
Nothing's Really ever MAde sense
And will probably Never MAKE ANY Sense
ever

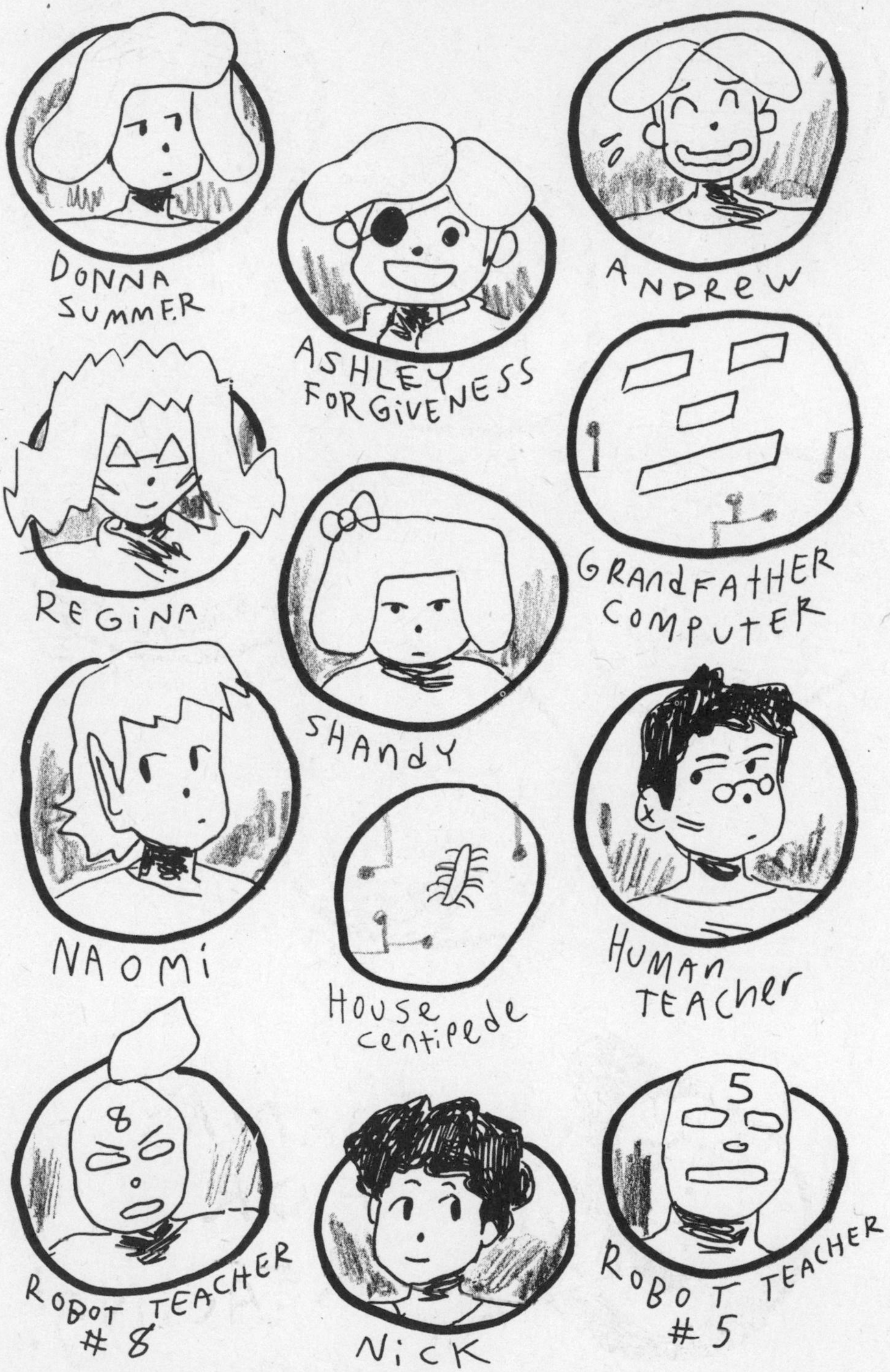
DONNA SUMMER
ASHLEY FORGIVENESS
ANDREW
REGINA
GRANDFATHER COMPUTER
SHANDY
NAOMI
HOUSE CENTIPEDE
HUMAN TEACHER
ROBOT TEACHER #8
NICK
ROBOT TEACHER #5

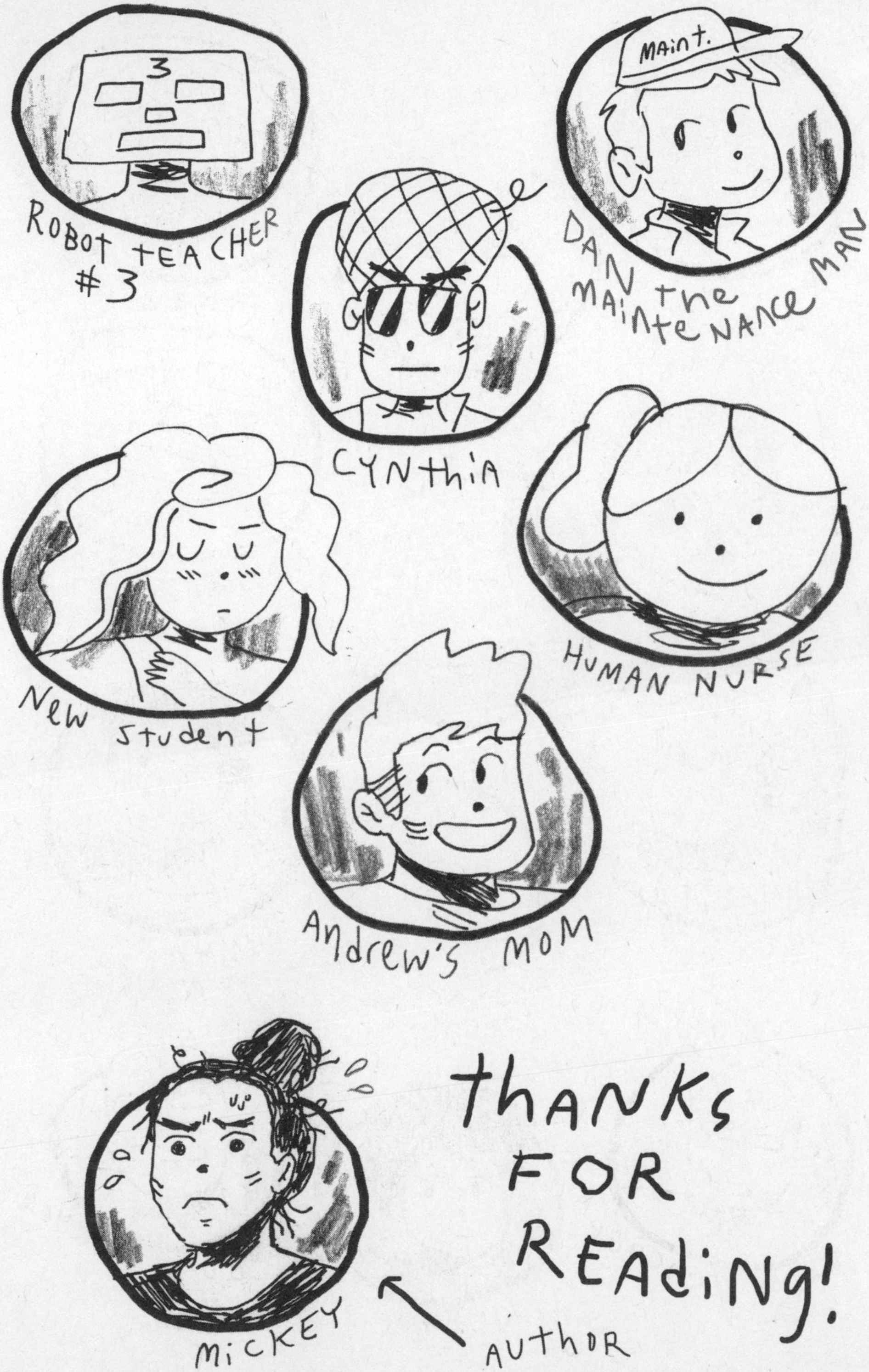
3
ROBOT TEACHER #3
Maint.
DAN the MAINTENANCE MAN
CYNTHIA
New student
HUMAN NURSE
Andrew's MOM
MICKEY
AUTHOR
thanks FOR READING!

thank
YOU

TESS, RYAN & JANE
& NAOMi,
MichAEL, JACOB,
WAlker, BRiAN, PAUL
Ed & Annie, Kartina,
EndriA, JENNY
& KEViN

SEE
YOU
NEXT
TIME